Daniel Harrison Jacques

Jacques' New Manual of the Garden, Farm and Barn-Yard

Embracing practical horticulture, agriculture, and cattle, horse and sheep husbandry.

Daniel Harrison Jacques

Jacques' New Manual of the Garden, Farm and Barn-Yard
Embracing practical horticulture, agriculture, and cattle, horse and sheep husbandry.

ISBN/EAN: 9783337377380

Printed in Europe, USA, Canada, Australia, Japan

Cover: Foto ©Lupo / pixelio.de

More available books at **www.hansebooks.com**

JACQUES' NEW MANUAL

OF THE

Garden, Farm and Barn-Yard,

EMBRACING

PRACTICAL HORTICULTURE, AGRICULTURE, AND
CATTLE, HORSE AND SHEEP HUSBANDRY.

WITH INSTRUCTIONS TO

CULTIVATE VEGETABLES, FRUIT, FLOWERS, ALL THE FIELD
CROPS, EXECUTE THE DETAILS OF FARM WORK, AND
BREED AND REAR THE VARIOUS SPECIES
OF DOMESTIC ANIMALS.

By D. H. JACQUES

AUTHOR OF "THE HOUSE," "HOW TO DO BUSINESS," ETC.

New and Revised Edition.

NEW YORK:
THE AMERICAN NEWS COMPANY,
39 AND 41 CHAMBERS STREET.

THE GARDEN:

A MANUAL

OF

Practical Horticulture;

OR, HOW TO CULTIVATE

VEGETABLES, FRUITS, AND FLOWERS.

EMBRACING

AN EXPOSITION OF THE NATURE AND ACTION OF SOILS AND MANURES AND THE STRUCTURE AND GROWTH OF PLANTS; DIRECTIONS FOR THE FORMING A GARDEN; DESCRIPTION OF IMPLEMENTS AND FIXTURES; INSTRUCTIONS FOR SOWING, TRANSPLANTING, BUDDING, GRAFTING, AND CULTIVATING VEGETABLES, FRUITS, AND FLOWERS;

WITH A CHAPTER ON

Ornamental Trees and Shrubs.

BY D. H. JACQUES,

AUTHOR OF "THE FARM," "THE HOUSE," "THE BARN-YARD," "HOW TO DO BUSINESS," "HOW TO BEHAVE," ETC.

Gardening was the primitive employment of the *first man*; and the *first of men*, among his descendants, have ever been attached to that occupation. Indeed, we can hardly form an idea of human felicity, in which a garden is not one of its most prominent characteristics.—T. G. FESSENDEN.

REVISED EDITION.

NEW YORK:
THE AMERICAN NEWS COMPANY,
39 AND 41 CHAMBERS STREET.

PREFACE.

THERE are many excellent works on Gardening in the English language; but there seemed to be room and a demand for another. No other work fills just the place that this is intended to fill—no other quite meets the popular want which we have aimed to satisfy in this.

We saw the need of a small, cheap work, embracing not only brief, simple, and easily understood directions for the cultivation of vegetables, fruits, and flowers, but also a succinct exposition of the theory of horticulture, as deduced from the nature of soils and manures, and the laws of vegetable life and growth; to give the reader something to fall back upon, whenever the practical instructions, which can not be adapted to every change of circumstances, shall fail to furnish a sufficient guide. How well we have succeeded in meeting this need we leave the reader to judge. We will only say, that our little book has been carefully prepared, and combines the results of experience, observation, and study. In preparing it, we have aimed simply at *usefulness*, and have made no effort for the attainment of any further originality than the end in view required. We are necessarily placed under heavy obligations to our predecessors in the walks of horticultural literature; but what we have derived from them has, in most cases, been re-written, and so modified, to adapt it to our purpose, that formal credit has, except in a few instances, been impracticable. Among the numerous works consulted, we take pleasure in acknowledging our indebtedness for valuable aid to each and all of the following :

⁰Loudon's Encyclopedia of Gardening.
⁰Mrs. Loudon's Gardening for Ladies
Delamer's Kitchen Garden.
    "   Flower Garden.
Neill's Gardener's Companion.
⁰Buist's Family Kitchen Gardener.
Fessenden's American Kitchen Gardener.
Every Lady Her Own Flower Gardener.
Barry's Fruit Garden.
⁰Downing's Fruits and Fruit-Trees.
⁰Jaques' Fruits and Fruit-Trees.
Tucker's Annual Register.
Farm and Garden Essays.
Thorburn's Descriptive Catalogues.
⁰White's Gardening for the South.
Horticulturist.
Country Gentleman.
⁰Southern Cultivator.
Allen's American Farm Book.
Boussingault's Economie Rurale.
Downing's Landscape Gardening.
⁰Lindley's Theory of Horticulture.
Gray's Botanical Text-Book.
⁰Darby's Botany of the Southern States.

To the works marked thus (⁰) we are under special obligations, either for matter derived from them, or for valuable facts or suggestions made more indirectly available.

Trusting that this little manual will be found worthy of a measure of the favor with which his previous humble attempts at usefulness has been received, the author now submits it to the judgment of the great Public.

CONTENTS.

INTRODUCTION.

The Garden of Eden—History of Gardening—Attractions—No Fruits like Our Own—Gardening favorable to Health—The Science of Horticulture—Object of this Work—How to Use it. .... Page 9-11

I.—STRUCTURE AND GROWTH OF PLANTS.

Germination—Conditions Essential to Germination—Time Required—The Process—The Root—How Roots Grow—Functions of the Root—Kinds of Roots—The Stem—Structure—Uses—Leaves—Structure and Functions—Flowers and their Structure—Fruit—Growth and Ripening—The Food of Plants—State in which it must be Taken up—Conditions Essential to Growth—Warmth, Moisture, Food, Air, Light............................... 13-29

II.—SOILS AND MANURES.

Classification of Soils—Heavy Soils—Light Soils—Loamy Soils—Calcareous Soils—Marley Soils—Vegetable Mold—Alluvial Soils—Subsoils—Improvement of Soils—Manures—Theory of Manures—Composts.............. 30-40

III.—FORMATION OF A GARDEN.

Situation—Exposure—Size and Shape—Laying Out—Fencing—Hedges—Preparation of the Soil—Draining—Trenching—Subsoil Plowing 41-45

IV.—IMPLEMENTS AND FIXTURES.

The Various Implements Required—Care of Implements—Fixtures—The Walled Pit—Hot Beds—Trellises—Rustic Structures.................. 46-50

V.—HORTICULTURAL PROCESSES.

Stirring the Soil—Applying Manures—Forcing—Sowing Seeds—Transplanting—Watering—Hoeing—Protection from Frost—Mulching—Destroying Insects—Saving Seeds—Rotation of Crops—Propagation—Suckers—Layers—Cuttings—Slips—Budding—Grafting—Pruning—Training....... 51-72

CONTENTS.

VI.—THE KITCHEN GARDEN.

Esculent Roots—The Legumes—The Cabbage Family—Spinaceous Plants—Asparaginous Plants—Esculent Bulbs—Salad Plants—The Cucumber Family—The Pumpkin Family—Miscellaneous—Sweet Herbs............ 78–110

VII.—THE FRUIT GARDEN.

The Apple—Origin—Varieties—Difficulty of Selecting—List of Summer Apples—Autumn Apples—Winter Apples—Crab Apples—Culture—Gathering and Preserving—The Pear—Lists of Pears—The Quince—Varieties—The Peach, with Lists of Varieties—The Nectarine—The Apricot—The Cherry—The Olive—The Orange—The Lemon—The Grape—The Currant—The Gooseberry—The Raspberry—The Blackberry—The Strawberry—The Fig—The Pomegranate—The Mulberry.................................. 111–142

VIII.—THE FLOWER GARDEN.

Uses of Flowers—A Word to the Ladies—How to become Healthy and Strong—Implements for Ladies' Use—Laying Out a Flower Garden—Arrangement of Plants—Climbing Plants—Shrubs and Trees—General Directions—Lists of Flowering Plants and Shrubs—Hardy Annuals—Hardy Biennials—Hardy Perennials—Tuberous Rooted Plants—Bulbous Rooted Plants—Flowering Shrubs—Climbers and Creepers 148–156

IX.—ORNAMENTAL TREES AND SHRUBS.

General Hints—Picturesqueness—Pruning—American Trees—Transplanting—Lists of Trees—Large Trees—Deciduous and Evergreen—Small Trees and Shrubs—Hedge Plants 157–161

APPENDIX.

The Bearing Year—Cause of Diminished Fertility—Removing Large Trees—New Varieties of the Potato—Luxuries of a Fruit Garden—Hyacinths in Glasses—Roses for Pot-Culture 162–164

INTRODUCTION.

It is written that God placed the first man in a garden to dress and to keep it; and that woman was there created as a help meet for him. That garden was the primitive paradise; and to this day, a tastefully planned, judiciously planted, and well-kept garden has, still lingering about it, many of the charms we are wont to attribute to the original Eden. To the true lover of rural life it seems, in the fullness of its summer beauty, to be indeed almost a Paradise Regained.

Gardens are frequently mentioned in ancient writings, both sacred and profane, but little is told us either of their productions or their cultivation.

At the close of the Roman commonwealth the catalogue of cultivated fruits had become considerable, and the principles of pruning and grafting were understood and practiced. With the decline of the empire, horticulture, in common with other useful arts, seems to have declined, and to have revived only when learning arose from the slumber of the dark ages. Since that time, it has kept pace with the general improvement of society. England, France, and Belgium have taken the lead in modern horticultural progress. The United States will not long remain behind.

It would be interesting to trace, at considerable length, the history of gardening, and show how, both as an art and as a science, it has been perfected, step by step, by means of study, observation, and experiment; but our limits will not permit this course, and we must refer the inquiring reader to "Loudon's Encyclopedia of Gardening," the most thorough and complete work on the subject in the English language. It is, however, too large and expensive to be generally accessible, except in public libraries.

Gardening, the earliest employment of man, is also the most attractive. It is Emerson, we think, who says, that after working in one's garden, nothing else seems worth doing. Here we seem to come into close communion with Nature, and to co-operate with her in adorning and enriching the earth. To plant one's seeds, to await hopefully their germination, to watch the daily development of the tender plant, to protect it from the encroachments of weeds and the attacks of insects, to loosen the soil around it, to care for it, watch over it, and rejoice in its growth and fruitage, and finally to enjoy the fruits of one's labors in the ripened harvest—what mere sensuous pleasure can be greater? The market affords no such pears, apples, peaches, or plums as grow on the trees we have with our own hands grafted and pruned. Our own squashes and melons are sweeter than any that our money could buy; and no potatoes, or cabbages, or turnips are like ours!

And health flows to us from the garden in two broad streams. One has its source in the invigorating out-door exercise it calls for and renders so delightful, and the other in the wholesome food which it furnishes to take the place of much less desirable aliments which would otherwise be supplied by the butcher and the grocer.

A taste for horticulture is almost universal in this country, and, as land is abundant and cheap, and the facilities for obtaining it great, very few outside of our cities and large towns are debarred from gratifying it, to a greater or less extent.

But a knowledge of the science of horticulture is far from being co-extensive with the practice of the art, and a truly satisfactory degree of success is only occasionally attained. A rich soil and a genial climate conspire to render the rudest and most empirical cultivation, under favorable circumstances, moderately productive. Plodding industry, however blindly applied, is looked upon with favor by all-loving Nature; but her richest gifts are reserved for united science and skill. In the cultivation of the earth, as in every other department of human effort, "knowledge is power."

To increase and extend a knowledge of the theory and practice of gardening is the object of the following pages, in which we have given due attention to both branches of the subject. The former is almost entirely ignored in most popular works on horticulture; they being nearly restricted to details of practice. These, though highly useful and even essential to the novice, are liable to lead him frequently astray, unless he is guided in their application by a knowledge of the principles on which they are founded.

The theoretical part of our work is necessarily brief, but will be found a useful auxiliary to the practical directions which follow. Carefully studied, thoroughly mastered, and constantly applied, it will be of more value to the reader than a heavy volume imperfectly understood and confusedly remembered. We would by no means, however, discourage those who have the leisure and disposition from pursuing the subject further.

NOTICE TO THE READER.

In making use of the practical directions given in this work, the reader should bear in mind that it was written in southern New York, and that where no other place or latitude is mentioned, in designating the time for planting seeds, etc., about 40° N., with a very slight elevation above the sea, is to be understood. Allowance must be made for situation north or south of this, and also for elevation of site, soil, aspect, exposure, and the general character of the season.

Our directions must also, of necessity, be subject to many modifications, in other respects, by soil, situation, and climate; but if the reader will study the general principles of horticulture, even in our brief and imperfect exposition of them, in the first part of this work, and exercise a little sound judgment, he will readily overcome the obstacles presented by local and temporary circumstances.

THE GARDEN.

I.

STRUCTURE AND GROWTH OF PLANTS.

With what increased satisfaction are the common processes of manuring or transplanting carried on, to say nothing of the more delicate operations of budding, grafting, and propagating by layers, etc., when we are acquainted with the structure of the plants we are endeavoring to control, nd comprehend the why and the wherefore of every step we pursue.—A. J. Downing.

I.—GERMINATION.

EVERY perfect and matured seed contains the germ of a new plant of the species to which it owes its own existence. If you separate the two lobes of a bean, or other seed of a similar character, you will discover, pressed between them at the undivided or stem end, or side, a minute kernel or bud. This, though a mere point, as it were, contains the rudiments of two or more undeveloped leaves, united by a solid or undivided portion, called, in the language of botany, the *radicle*, and constitutes an embryo plant, holding within itself all the elements of vegetable life. The commencement of the vital action which produces the development of this embryo is called *germination*.

The conditions essential to germination are the presence of *moisture, warmth,* and *oxygen gas.*

In the absence of moisture, no effect toward germination is produced by the presence of warmth and oxygen, or any other gas. Moisture and oxygen gas without warmth, are equally inefficacious; and so are moisture and warmth in the absence of the oxygen; for seeds will not germinate in a vacuum, nor in distilled or recently boiled water.

Moisture is necessary to soften and expand the various parts, to dissolve soluble matter, and to establish a sort of circulation. The embryo seems also to have the power of decomposing water; and it is probable that a portion of the oxygen required is obtained in this way. The rest must come from the air; for it is found that a communication with the atmosphere is absolutely essential to perfect germination. The effect of heat appears to be to set the vital principle in action, to expand the air in the numerous microscopic cavities of the seed, and to produce distension of all the organic parts. The degree of heat required varies with different species. The common chickweed will germinate at a temperature but little above the freezing-point, while the seeds of many tropical plants require a heat of from 90° to 110° (Fahrenheit) to call them into action. Wheat, rye, and barley will germinate at 44°. A degree of heat varying from 113° to 167° is capable of destroying the vitality of the various grains, beans, peas, etc. Direct light, so essential to subsequent vegetation, is unfavorable to germination.

The time required for germination is very different in different species of plants. Much also depends upon soil, climate, degree of

YOUNG RADISH, SHOWING SEED-LEAVES.

moisture, etc. Under favorable circumstances, wheat, rye, oats, and millet will germinate in one day; bean, turnip, radish, and mustard in three days; lettuce in four days; melon, cucumber, squash, and pumpkin in five days; barley in seven; cabbage in ten; parsley in fifteen; almond, peach, and peony in one year, and hawthorn in two years.

The time that seeds will retain their vitality also differs in different species, but in all cases depends partly upon the degree in which they are excluded from the action of moisture and light. Kidney-beans, peas, and carrot, parsnep, and rhubarb seeds are generally considered as losing their vitality at the end of one year, but will sometimes germinate after being kept much longer.

These facts have important bearings upon the subject of horticulture, and should be constantly borne in mind; and especially is it requisite that the essential conditions of germination be held in remembrance. A failure to germinate is doubtless often attributed to bad seeds, when the fault is entirely in the planting. It must be perfectly evident that if your seeds are insufficiently covered in a light, dry soil, they will lack the first essential of germination, and will be liable to wither and perish for want of moisture. This is why light soils should be pressed together and upon the seed in planting, either by means of a roller or otherwise. Seeds buried too deeply, or covered with a heavy, dense soil, pressed too closely upon them, fail to germinate for want of communication with the atmosphere. If there be not sufficient warmth in the soil at the time of planting, and it remain cold for a considerable time thereafter, the seeds just as surely perish. Remember the conditions of germination—moisture, warmth, and oxygen gas (or air containing oxygen).

Germination being established by the action of moisture and warmth, and maintained by the oxygen of the atmosphere, all parts of the embryo enlarge, and new parts are formed at the expense of a saccharine or sugary secretion, which the germinating seed possesses the power of forming. With the assistance of this substance, the root or radicle, at first a mere rounded cone, extends and pierces the earth in search of food, while the other extremity elongates in the opposite direction, bringing the *cotyledons*, or seed-leaves (except when these remain permanently in the ground, as in the pea, wheat, rye, etc.), and the rudimentary leaves and stem, to the surface of the soil. The process of germination is now completed—the plant is born.

II.—THE ROOT.

The root, the stem, and the leaves are called the fundamental organs of plants. Of them vegetables essentially consist; and the various organs known by other names are really but repetitions, under more or less modified forms, of these essential parts.

Germination, as we have seen, pushes the root downward into the earth, where, extending *by the addition of new matter to its point*, it soon enters upon the exercise of its function—*the absorption of the crude food of the plant from the soil*. This is carried up through the stem into the leaves, to be digested or assimilated, and returned to the stem and root, and used in the formation of new branches, leaves, and rootlets, as well as for increasing the length and size of those already formed. The more a plant grows, therefore, the more are the means of growth multiplied.

As the roots are extended by the addition of new matter to the extreme points, these points are exceedingly delicate and easily injured. *It is mainly through them, too, that absorption takes place.* It is readily seen, therefore, why the careless or unskillful removal of plants from the earth, for the purpose of transplanting, by destroying the delicate points of the roots, or *spongelets*, as they are called, always checks so greatly their growth, and often destroys their life.

Their peculiar mode of growth admirably adapt roots to pierce the earth and insinuate themselves into the minutest crevices. Thus they pass on from place to place in search of fresh pasturage, shifting their mouths, although their bodies remain stationary.

Roots seem to possess a principle akin to instinct, which guides them in their search for food; for they invariably extend themselves most rapidly and widely in the direction of the richest soil. If a strawberry plant be set in a sandy soil, deficient in nutritive matters, and rich earth placed on one side of it, the roots will immediately seek the fertile spot, although at first nowhere in contact with it. A decaying bone or a piece of rotten wood will in the same way be sought out by the roots of a plant requiring the nutritive elements it may contain; and such objects are often found completely covered by a network of minute rootlets.

The roots of plants have, to a certain extent, the power of selecting their food. In general, they absorb only those substances which are needed to develop and perfect their various parts. Thus, if a pea and a grain of wheat be planted side by side, and made to grow under the same circumstances, the wheat plant will absorb silex (in solution) from the earth, while the pea will absorb none. This power of selection, however, does not enable the roots of plants to reject, under all circumstances, any deleterious agents which may be brought in contact with them; and it is a curious circumstance that substances which are fatal to man are equally so to plants, and in nearly the same way.

In addition to their principal office, as feeding organs, the roots of plants are believed to be, to some extent, organs of excretion, throwing off any superfluous or deleterious matter which may have been imbibed either by themselves or by the leaves. They also possess the power of accumulating a store of sap, upon which the plant may draw in time of need. Striking examples of the last-named property are furnished by the turnip, the beet, the carrot, and other plants of the same class.

In general, roots do not produce buds, and are therefore incapable of multiplying the plant to which they belong; but to this rule there are many exceptions, some species having the power, under certain circumstances, of forming what are called *adventitious* buds. In such cases they may be employed for the purposes of propagation.

Roots are not inactive during the winter, as many suppose, except while actually frozen, but are perpetually extracting food from the earth, and storing it up for the next season's use. A long, mild winter is therefore favorable to the vegetation of the succeeding spring.

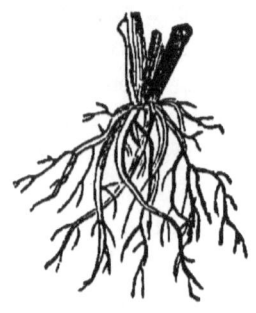
FIBROUS ROOT.

SPINDLE ROOT.

Roots are of various kinds. In reference to their duration, they are classed as *annual, biennial,* and *perennial.* An annual root lives but a single year. It is always *fibrous,* or composed of numerous branches or rootlets. Biennial roots are those of plants which do not blossom till the second year, at the end of which they perish. They are thickened or *fleshy,* and of various shapes—*conical,* as in the carrot; *spindle-shaped,* as in the radish; *tur-

TUBEROUS ROOT.

CREEPING ROOT.

nip-shaped, clustered, tuberous,* etc. Perennial roots are those which, like the roots of trees and woody plants, and some others, survive from year to year indefinitely.

A *tuber,* of which the potato is the best example, is not strictly a root, but a modification of the stem, running beneath the surface of the soil, and having buds (eyes) embedded in a cellular substance, consisting principally of starch.

Bulbs, whether formed in the earth, as is generally the case, or on the summit of the stem, as in the top or tree onion, are simply leaf-buds inclosed in scales or concentric layers.

III.—THE STEM.

As soon as the root enters upon the performance of its proper function, the stem begins to extend itself upward, and the primary leaf-bud, attracting to itself the food procured for it, and a part of the nutritive matter stored up in the seed-leaves, expands, and the two or more parts or leaves of which it is composed separate, and begin to manifest their distinctive features.

The stem is at first composed entirely of cellular tissue, possessing neither strength nor tenacity; but at the moment that the first rudiment of a leaf appears upon its growing point, the formation of woody matter commences. It consists of tough fibers of extreme fineness, which take their rise in the leaves, and thence pass downward through the cellular tissue and are incorporated with the latter, giving it the necessary strength and flexibility. In trees and shrubs these fibers combine intimately with each other, and form what is properly called wood; but in herbaceous and annual plants they constitute a lax fibrous matter. The woody matter thus plunged, as it were, into the cellular tissue, forms within the circumference of the stem a tubular partition, separating it into two parts— the bark and the pith. This gives us, in perennial stems, the three general divisions of pith, wood, and bark.

The *pith* consists entirely of cellular tissue, gorged at first with the nourishing juices of the plant, but afterward becoming empty and dry.

The *wood* consists of the proper woody fiber, interwoven with and bound together by thin plates or layers of cellular tissue, passing horizontally across it, and forming what are called the *silver grain* in maple, oak, etc. They represent the horizontal system of the wood—in botanical language, the *medullary rays*.

The *bark* consists originally of cellular tissue alone, but afterward the inner portion next the wood has the woody tissue formed in it, and becomes the *liber*, or fibrous inner bark.

Whenever a stem is wounded, it is the cellular or horizontal system which forms granulations that eventually coalesce into masses, within which the woody tissue is subsequently developed, and the communication between the two sides of an incision effected. In cuttings, the callus which forms at the end placed in the ground is the cellular or horizontal system preparing for the woody fibers, which are to pass downward in the form of roots.

The description we have given of the structure of a stem applies to all plants whose woody matter is augmented annually by *external* additions below the liber, and which are called *exogens*, or outside growers. All the trees and shrubs of the United States, except the few palms of our Southern confines, belong to this class. In the palms, which belong to the class of *endogens*, or inside growers, the woody matter is augmented annually by *internal* additions to their center, thus constantly pushing the woody

EXOGEN.

ENDOGEN.

growth of former years to their circumference. The stem of the asparagus exhibits a similar structure in an herb. In *endogens*, the cellular and fibrous systems are all mixed together, their mode of growth not requiring the same arrangement of parts as exists in the *exogens*.

Stems, during their growth, form on their surfaces minute vital points, each of which becomes, or may become, a leaf-bud, capable of forming another stem or branch like that on which it is found. These buds appear immediately above the point of union between the leaf and the stem, and are not, under ordinary circumstances, found anywhere else. They occasionally, however, appear on other parts, when they are called (as when found on the roots) *adventitious* buds. It is by means of the leaf-buds that a cutting is capable of producing a new individual like that from which it was taken. Leaf-buds are also capable, under fitting circumstances, of growing when separated from the parent branch. In some cases they are planted in the earth, when they put forth roots, and thereby sustain an independent existence. In others they are inserted below the bark of a kindred species, and, forming new wood, adhere to that on which they are placed.

The principal functions of the stem (aside from its continual multiplication of itself by means of buds) are the support of the leaves and the conveyance and distribution of the sap. In trees, the sap or crude food procured by the roots rises principally through the newer wood; but the assimilated sap returns from the leaves in the *newest* bark, or *liber*, whence it is horizontally diffused, through the *medullary rays*, into the sap-wood and other living parts. It is in the bark, therefore, and not in the wood, that we must look for the proper juices of a plant.

BUDS.

IV.—LEAVES.

A leaf, as defined by Dr. Lindley, is an appendage of the stem of a plant having one or more leaf-buds in its *axil*, or point of union with the stem. In some cases no leaf-buds are visible, but they are present, nevertheless, although latent, and may be developed by favorable conditions.

A complete leaf consists of the *lamina*, or blade, and the *petiole*, or leaf-stalk. In some leaves the *petiole* is wanting, the *lamina* resting immediately upon the stem, and in others there is no proper blade, the whole organ being cylindrical or stalk-like.

Considered in reference to their structure, it may be said

leaves are extensions of the green layer of the bark (which, where no proper leaves exist, fulfills their function) expanded into thin lamina and strengthened by woody fibers connected with the *liber*, or inner bark, and with the wood. These woody fibers form their frame-work, and afford, at the same time, by their microscopic ramifications, a complete and beautiful system of veins. The leaf, therefore, like the stem, consists of two distinct parts, the cellular and the woody. The cellular portion is not the structureless, pulpy mass which it appears to be to the naked eye, but presents a regular and beautiful arrangement of cells. The woody part forming the veins, and having, as we have seen, a double origin, is arranged in two layers; the upper, arising from the wood, and conveying the ascending sap to every part of the leaf, and the lower, connected with the *liber*, and establishing a communication with the bark, by means of which the assimilated juices pass downward. Encasing the whole of this wonderfully beautiful apparatus is the *epidermis*, or skin, pierced by numerous invisible *pores* or holes, called *stomates*, through which the plant breathes and perspires.

It would be interesting, in connection with the foregoing brief outline of the structure of the leaf, to give some account of the different forms of leaves, their various modifications, and their systematic and beautiful arrangement on the stem; but as the practical ends we have in view do not require us to pursue the subject further in this direction, we must forego it.

Leaves have been called the lungs of plants. They are something more than this, being not only organs of respiration, but of perspiration and digestion also. They are, at the same time, stomach, lungs, and skin. They receive the crude sap from the roots through the stem, and, by means of exposure to air and light, the decomposition of water and carbonic acid, and the throwing off of superfluous moisture, condense it and change it into organizable matter—the true food of plants. This elaborated sap is sent immediately downward, to serve for the nourishment of every part.

The nutrition of a plant depending upon its leaves, the former may be destroyed by simply destroying its foliage. In general, it does not immediately die, because it has the power of putting forth new leaves, which come into action and supply imperfectly the places of those removed; but if it be deprived of these essential organs during the entire season, its power of producing them ceases, and all functions are suspended.

V.—FLOWERS AND FRUIT.

A flower is that part of a plant which is formed for the purpose of reproducing its species by means of seeds. Fruit is the seed, or the seed and its *pericarp*, or covering. The *pericarp* includes whatever goes to make up the seed-vessel, whether it be a mere thin husk, a hard, bone-like shell, or a soft, fleshy pulp.

Anatomically considered, the parts of a flower are merely modified leaves, the whole forming a very short branch. What causes a plant to convert some of its leaf-buds into flowers, by fashioning the leaves into *calyx, corolla, stamens,* and *pistils*, while other buds become ordinary branches, it is not essential to our purpose to explain. It is pretty clear, however, that *their production depends upon the presence in the plant of a sufficient quantity of secreted matter, fit for their maintenance when produced.* If it happen, then, that, from any cause, there be not, at the usual time of flowering, any store of nutritive juices beyond what is required for the production of leaves and the growth of the stem, no flower-buds are put forth. This is illustrated in the failure of fruit-trees to bear at all the season next succeeding one in which an excessive crop has been produced.* Sometimes flowers are produced, but, the supply of nutriment proving insufficient, they drop off without producing fruit.

Lindley syllogistically says: "A flower being a kind of branch, as has been already shown, and the fruit being an ad-

---

* See Appendix, A.

vanced stage of the flower, it follows that a fruit is also a kind of branch." It has certainly the same organic connection with the plant as other branches, and, like them, requires to be supplied with food, without which it must perish.

So long as a fruit retains its original green, foliaceous character, it is capable of performing, partially at least, the functions of a leaf, decomposing carbonic acid, etc. A portion of the food required for its maturation may therefore be derived, by its own action, from the air; but the greater part must be prepared by the leaves from material furnished by the roots. This shows the necessity of the healthy and regular action of the leaves and roots in perfecting fruit, and the importance of fruit being placed near the leaves, so that it can readily attract the required nutriment from them. If you remove all the leaves from a branch containing fruit, you stop the growth of the latter almost as effectually as by separating it from the stem.

The juices furnished by the leaves undergo further alterations by the vital forces of the fruit itself, and this alteration varies according to the species. The fruit of the peach is sweet, but there is no perceptible sweetness in its leaves; and the fruit of the fig is sweet and nutritious, while the leaves of that plant are acrid and deleterious.

Among the principal immediate causes of the changes which occur in the secretions of fruits are heat and light. Fruits produced in warm seasons are always much sweeter than those which are matured in cold ones; and the products of hot climates abound in sugar, while in those of cold climates acidity prevails.

The ripening of fruit is hastened by dryness, and retarded by an excess of moisture.

Seeds are affected by all the circumstances which affect the fruit, which is created primarily for their nutrition and preservation. The fruit attracts organizable matter from the leaves, and the seeds attract it from the fruit. The better the fruit, therefore, the more perfect are the seeds.

All seeds will not equally produce vigorous plants; but the healthiness of the seedling will correspond with that of the seed from which it sprung. Where vigor is required, the plumpest and heaviest seeds should be selected.

A seed always produces a plant of the same species as that from which it was derived, but is not certain to reproduce any peculiarity that may have existed in its parent. For instance, the seed of a Green Gage plum will grow into a new individual of the plum species, but it is not certain, or even likely, to produce the variety known as the Green Gage. The variety must be propagated in some other way.

VI.—THE FOOD OF PLANTS.

The gardener should know precisely what substances plants require for their growth and the maturation of their fruit— that is, their natural food. This is ascertained by analysis. When we have learned of what plants are composed, we know what their food must necessarily contain.

The constituents of plants, as shown by analysis, are of two kinds, organic and inorganic. Only the organic constituents, however, are universally indispensable. These are oxygen, hydrogen, nitrogen, and carbon, which make up at least from eighty-eight to ninety-nine per cent. of every vegetable substance. The inorganic constituents, which are essential to the perfection of any but the lowest grade of plants, consist mainly of potash, soda, lime, magnesia, alumina, silex, sulphur, and phosphorus.

Now, where and how are the different kinds of food which plants require obtained? Mainly, no doubt, from the soil, and by means of the roots, which, we have seen, are the proper feeding organs. The air may, however (and evidently does, in some cases, as in the *epiphytes*, or air-plants), either directly or indirectly, supply all the organic elements.

But whether derived from the earth or from the air, *the plant's nourishment is wholly received either in the gaseous or the liquid form;* for the leaves can imbibe air or vapor only while the tissue of the rootlets is especially adapted to absorb liquids, and *is incapable of taking in solid matter, however minutely divided.* Let these facts be borne in mind while preparing your soils and manures.

The oxygen and hydrogen required by plants is probably derived principally from water.

The nitrogen is obtained mostly by the decomposition of ammonia (hartshorn), a compound of hydrogen and nitrogen, always produced when any animal and almost any vegetable substance decays. It is dissolved in water, absorbed by porous substances in the soil, and thus furnished to the roots of plants.

The source of the carbon, which forms much the larger portion of the bulk of plants, is still to be sought. Carbon itself is a solid, absolutely insoluble in water, and therefore not available. The chief, if not the only fluid composed of carbon, naturally presented to the plant, is that of carbonic acid gas, which consists of carbon united with oxygen. This gas makes up, on the average, one two-thousandth of the atmosphere, from which it may be directly absorbed by the leaves; but, being freely soluble in water, up to a certain point, it must be carried down by the rain and imbibed by the roots. The carbonic acid of the atmosphere is, therefore, the great source of carbon for vegetation. Carbonic acid is also produced in small quantities by the action of manures in the soil.

The carbonic acid absorbed is decomposed in the leaves by the action of solar light; the carbon being retained and the oxygen thrown off—beautifully reversing the process of animal respiration, and thus preserving the proper balance in the atmosphere.

The mineral matters which form the inorganic constituents of plants are all either soluble in water, or in the acids or alkalies mixed with it, and are therefore readily absorbed by the roots.

The following analysis of wheat will give the reader an idea of the principal mineral constituents of plants generally, as to the number of their elements; their proportion will **vary** greatly in different species. The wheat (the entire plant, including the seed) in 1,000 lbs. gave 11¾ lbs. of ashes, composed as follows:

Potash	2.25	Silica	4.00
Soda	2.40	Sulphuric acid	.50
Lime	.96	Phosphoric acid	.40
Magnesia	.90	Chlorine	.10
Alumina	.26	Iron, a trace.	

An analysis of perfected plants of the same species, although growing in very different soils, will give the same proportion; while different species, although growing in the same soil, will give very different proportions, showing that plants require definite quantities of the inorganic elements in order to perfect growth, and that in soil that does not yield these elements an imperfect growth only can be obtained.

These facts lie at the foundation of rotation of crops and manuring. When any given plant has exhausted the soil of the soluble elements requisite for its growth, another plant requiring different elements, or the same in different proportions, may grow luxuriantly and in perfection in the same soil. Generally the *grasses*, such as wheat, rye, oats, etc., require large quantities of silica; peas, clover, and tobacco, much lime; turnips, beets, and sweet potatoes, potash and soda. The stalk and fruit often require different elements in different proportions. Both of course must be supplied. These elements might exist in the soil, but not in a soluble condition, and of course yield no benefit to the plant.*

VII.—CONDITIONS ESSENTIAL TO GROWTH.

All the conditions essential to growth have already been either specially explained or incidentally mentioned; but it may be useful briefly to recapitulate:

1. *Warmth.*—Without this, as we have seen, the latent powers of vegetable life can not be called into action. It is

---

* See Appendix, B and also "The Farm," for more on this point.

not less essential to their continued activity. Although many plants will live at a temperature much below the freezing-point, yet no plant is able to *grow* unless the temperature is above 32°, for physical reasons which require no explanation. A temperature permanently much higher than a plant requires for its healthy growth over-excites, enfeebles, and finally destroys it.

2. *Moisture.*—Moisture is obviously essential, both because water itself in its pure state furnishes two of the essential elements which enter into the composition of all plants, and because it constitutes the medium through which the other substances required are conveyed into the roots. Excessive moisture, however, is destructive to most plants. It is a great point in horticulture to determine the degree of moisture most congenial to a given species, under given circumstances. As a general rule, *the plant should be most abundantly supplied with moisture when it begins to grow, and the quantity gradually diminished as it approaches maturity.* However, as one effect of excessive moisture is to keep the newly-formed parts of a plant tender and succulent, those the leaves or roots of which (as in the case of lettuce, radishes, etc.) are to be eaten uncooked, should be constantly supplied with moisture. Excess of moisture will also cause strawberries and other fruits to swell beyond their natural size; but their flavor is diminished in the same proportion.

3. *Food.*—A plant can no more live without food than a human being can. Deficiency of food dwarfs it, and prevents perfect development; and it must not be forgotten that *the presence in the soil of the nutritive elements is of no avail so long as they remain in an insoluble condition.* It is only in a gaseous or liquid form (allow us to repeat) that plants are capable of receiving their food.

4. *Air.*—Plants breathe (in their way), and must therefore have air. Much of their nourishment is derived either immediately or remotely from it.

5. *Light.*—It is by the aid of solar light alone that the leaves can properly perform their grand function—the assimilation of

the crude sap furnished them by the roots. It is only under the influence of light that they decompose the carbonic acid gas from which the large proportion of carbon they require is obtained. It is to light also that they owe their green color. In the dark this coloring matter is not formed, potatoes and other vegetables kept in cellars throwing out white stems and leaves. Some plants, however, require less light than others, and flourish in shady places. When we wish to blanch a plant, as in the case of celery, we exclude the light.*

---

* For a further elucidation of the various subjects discussed in the foregoing pages, see Lindley's "Theory of Horticulture," Gray's "Botanical Text-Book," Boussingault's "*Economie Rurale*," and Darby's "Botany of the Southern States," to all of which, and especially to the first-named, we have been indebted in the preparation of this chapter

II.

SOILS AND MANURES.

The soil should be good to the depth of two feet, and any necessary deepening beyond this, by manures or otherwise, should not be neglected.—Neill.

I.—CLASSIFICATION OF SOILS.

We are accustomed to recognize three primitive earths—silex (which includes sand and gravel), clay, and lime. These, together with decayed vegetable and animal matter, enter more or less into the composition of all soils. On the relative proportion of these ingredients and their texture, or degree of fineness or coarseness, depends mainly the character of each variety.

Soils may first be considered in two grand divisions—heavy and light, the former being characterized by a predominance of clay, and the latter by an excess of sand or gravel.

1. *Heavy Soils.*—The heavy or clayey soils are also known as wet and cold, from their strong affinity for water. In dry weather, however, they are liable to bake, or become hard and brick-like. They are difficult to work, and, till much modified by art and labor, generally unproductive.

2. *Light Soils.*—The light or sandy and gravelly soils are denominated dry and warm, because they permit the water to pass readily through them. They are subject to drouth, and have the further disadvantage of allowing a large proportion of the manure applied to them to pass through into the subsoil. They are easy to work, and crops can be brought to perfection much earlier on them than on clayey soils.

These grand classes of soils, running into each other by imperceptible gradations, and being variously modified, may be considered as embracing every variety found on the face of the globe.

3. *Loamy Soils.*—A mixture of from fifteen to sixty per cent. of sand with clay forms a loamy soil. If the sand do not exceed thirty per cent., it is called a clay loam; more than thirty per cent. constitutes it a sandy loam.

4. *Calcareous Soils.*—Calcareous soils are those in which lime, exceeding twenty per cent., becomes the distinguishing constituent. Calcareous soils may be either calcareous clays, calcareous sands, or calcareous loams, according to the proportions of sand or clay which may be present in them.

5. *Marly Soils.*—Soils containing lime, but in which the proportion does not exceed twenty per cent., are sometimes called marly.

6. *Vegetable Molds.*—When decayed vegetable matter exists in so great proportion as to give the predominant character to a soil, it receives the name of vegetable mold. Vegetable molds are of various kinds, and may be either clayey, sandy, or loamy, according to the predominant character of the earthy admixtures.

7. *Alluvial Soils.*—Alluvial soils are such as have been formed by the washings of streams. They are generally loamy, and very fertile.

Besides their principal component parts, every soil must contain, in greater or less quantities, all the elements which enter into the composition of vegetables. They may have certain substances which are not necessary to vegetable life, and such as are necessary may be in excess; yet to sustain a healthy, prolific vegetation, they must hold, and in a form fitted to its support, *silex, alumina, carbonate of lime, sulphate of lime, potash, soda, magnesia, sulphur, phosphorus, oxyd of iron, manganese, chlorine,* and probably *iodine*. These are called the inorganic or earthy parts of soils. In addition to these, fertile soils must contain *carbon, oxygen, nitrogen,* and *hydro-*

gen, which are called organic parts of soils, from their great preponderance in vegetables and animals.

For gardening purposes, a loamy soil, composed of nearly equal proportions of clay, sand, and lime, and enriched by deposits of decayed animal and vegetable matter, is perhaps the best; but a sandy loam similarly enriched is good. Very heavy and very light soils are objectionable; but the latter less so, since it may be much more easily improved.

Subsoils.—The productiveness of a soil depends to a considerable extent upon the subsoil or bed on which it rests, which may be either clayey, sandy, gravelly, or calcareous. A clayey subsoil is unfavorable, as it renders the soil wet and cold. Loose and leachy subsoils, consisting mainly of gravel or sand, are also undesirable, on account of the facility with which moisture and the soluble portions of manures escape into them. Calcareous subsoils are considered best.

II.—IMPROVEMENT OF SOILS.

As the original soil of one's garden can not always be a matter of choice, the garden being properly situated near the house, and the house depending for its location upon other circumstances besides the soil, it becomes important to know how to improve it if it happen to be of an undesirable character.

In order to set yourself about the work of improvement with a reasonable prospect of success, you should have a clear comprehension of the end to be attained. What, then, are the qualities desirable in a garden soil?

A garden soil should be loamy, rich in all the elements essential to the growth of plants, sufficiently light and friable to be easily cultivated, and to allow the roots to penetrate it in every direction, and at the same time sufficiently adhesive to retain moisture and the soluble portions of manures till they may be required by the growing plant.

Improvement of Clayey Soils.—If it be a clayey soil with which you have to do, you will probably, in the first place, find it too wet. The only effectual remedy for this defect is thorough underdraining. This not only draws off the surplus water, but opens the soil to the action of the atmosphere, which, in its passage through it, imparts its nutritive gases, and helps to warm and disintegrate it. Deep trenching will aid in the process of draining.*

Having thoroughly drained your plot, you should next give your attention to improving the texture of the soil in other ways. The natural remedy for their too dense and adhesive character seems to be sand; but to produce the desired effect large quantities are required—so large that the improvement in that way of large tracts of land is considered impracticable. In treating a small garden, however, the expense of the application may often be disregarded.

Lime is a valuable auxiliary in the improvement of clayey soils, forming, with their ingredients, chemical combinations, whereby their extreme tenacity is broken up, and adding, at the same time, an element of fertility, in which they may be deficient. Gypsum, or plaster of Paris, has the same effect in a still more powerful degree. Ashes, coarse vegetable manures, straw, corn-stalks, leaves, chips, etc., are also very useful, as they add new materials, and also help to separate the particles of the original soil.

In cold climates, clayey soils should be plowed or dug in the fall, the action of the frost and snow tending to break them up and destroy the adhesion of their particles. In the South, where there is little frost, and frequent and copious rains occur during the winter, this course is injurious rather than beneficial.

The frequent working of clayey soils with plow, harrow, spade, or hoe, if done when they are not too wet, will greatly improve them.

A persevering application of the various means we have indicated, will gradually bring the heaviest clay soil into the proper loamy consistency for horticultural purposes.

A loamy soil resting upon a clayey subsoil should in general

---

* For a chapter on Draining, see "The Farm."

be underdrained; but if the stratum of clay be shallow, trenching or subsoil plowing will answer a good purpose.

Improvement of Sandy Soils.—If your plot be sandy, its improvement, though equally necessary, is less difficult. The defects of sandy soils, as we have seen, are lack of adhesiveness, want of affinity for water, and a leachy character, which permits the escape of manures. Clay is the principal remedy indicated, and a few loads, well incorporated with the original soil, will have an astonishing effect in improving a sandy garden. The required tenacity is thus very readily imparted.

Lime is scarcely less valuable for application to sandy than to clayey soils; for while it separates the latter, it renders the former more adhesive. Gypsum, ashes, and clay marls are also exceedingly useful. To these applications should be added the frequent use of a heavy roller.

Where a sandy soil rests upon a clayey subsoil, as is not unfrequently the case, it may be greatly improved by trenching or deep plowing, by means of which a portion of the subsoil is thrown up and mixed with the surface soil.

Sandy soils, modified as we have indicated, being warm, quick, and easy of cultivation, are the best in the world for tap-rooted plants and bulbs, and for the production of early crops of almost every kind.

Gravelly soils resemble sandy soils in their characteristic defects, and require similar treatment; but they are less desirable, and require greater modifications to adapt them to gardening purposes.

The other soils named require similar treatment in proportion as they approach the clayey or sandy character.

Depth of Soil.—The soil of most gardens (except on the alluvial bottoms of the West) requires improvement in depth quite as much as in any other particular. In no part of your garden should you be satisfied with less than *two feet* of good, friable soil, easily permeable by the roots of plants. A still greater depth is desirable, especially in the fruit department. Few who have not had their attention specially drawn to the subject are aware how deeply the roots of some species of plants penetrate, when permitted by a proper state of the soil. The roots of a strawberry plant are said to have been traced *five feet* in a deep, rich soil.

Trenching and subsoil plowing are the processes by which the depth of soil is increased. The former is an expensive process, but, in gardening, a remunerative one; the latter is much cheaper, and, where it can be applied, serves a good purpose.

Trenching, or subsoil plowing, is positively essential where the summers are long and dry, as in portions of the Southern States. Mr. White, in his "Gardening for the South," says very truly that there is no point of greater importance than this. "Poor ground, deeply moved," he adds, "is better than rich land with shallow tillage; and when the ground has been once prepared in this way, it will feel the benefit forever after. Increasing the depth of the soil in this mode is, to all intents and purposes, increasing the size of your garden; for one fourth of an acre thus prepared will yield, in a dry season, as much as an acre will with shallow tillage, and the growth of plants in good seasons will be fully doubled."

Trenching should be performed in the fall, and any coarse manures you may wish to apply dug in at the time. For a description of the process of trenching, see Chapter III.

Color of Soils.—The color of a soil has an important relation to its capacity for heat and moisture, and consequently to its adaptedness for horticultural purposes. Dark-colored earths, all other things being equal, are the best.

Old Gardens.—Some old and small gardens are in a very bad state from excess of nutritive matters, or rather from the unavailable state in which these matters exist in the soil, which, instead of consisting of friable mold, presents only a black, shining substance, known to chemists as humic acid. This is the product of manures saturated with stagnant water, and is the result of excessive manuring, frequent watering, and lack of drainage. No condition can be more unfavorable to the growth of plants than this, and if they grow at all in such soil they will be gross, pungent, and unwholesome. The remedy is trenching, underdraining, and the application of lime, gypsum, ashes, etc.

Further means of improving soils will be treated of in the next section, under the head of Manures.

III.—MANURES.

If your soil be either wholly or partially deficient in any of the constituents of plants, these constituents must be supplied by adding to it substances which contain them. The substances thus added are called manures, which, in the broadest sense of the word, embrace everything which, being added to the soil, promotes directly or indirectly the growth of plants.

Manures directly assist the growth of plants either by entering into their composition, or by absorbing moisture and nutritive gases from the atmosphere, and holding them for their use. Indirectly, manures assist the growth of plants by destroying vermin or weeds, by decomposing the soil and rendering its elements available, by protecting vegetation from sudden changes of temperature, or by improving the texture of the soil. They are divided into two classes—organic and inorganic. The former embraces ordinary vegetable and animal substances, and the latter mineral substances.

Organic Manures.—The principal organic manures are the dung of animals, human excrements, urine, flesh, blood, fish, swamp-muck, sea-weed, and decayed leaves, hay, straw, and wood. Guano, though an animal product, contains so large a proportion of salts, and is so deficient in the characteristics of recent animal matter that it is generally classed with the inorganic manures.

Inorganic Manures.—The principal inorganic manures are ashes, lime, the marls, gypsum, bones, salt, charcoal, soot, and guano.

Theory of Manures.—The kind of manure which will prove most useful in a given instance must be determined by reference to several circumstances—the chemical composition and mechanical texture of the soil, the character of the climate or season, and the kind of crop to be produced. The manures most generally applicable are those composed of substances which directly enter into and are essential to the growth of plants.

The fertility of a forest is not only maintained but increased by the constant decay of its leaves, branches, and trunks, which returns to the earth not only the nutritive matter originally drawn from it, but also much that has been supplied by the atmosphere. This manure is just what the trees need—it keeps good the supply of the elements essential to their growth. So the parts of any plant decayed and rendered soluble are the best manure for its species. But the products of our gardens are mainly taken from them, and used as food. Every particle not thus made use of should be returned, mixed with other vegetable and animal matter, in the form of compost. For the rest, stable manures (of which the dung of the horse is the best) should be relied on as the grand staples.

All the ordinarily cultivated plants, as has already been stated, contain potash, soda, lime, magnesia, alumina, silica, iron, sulphur, phosphorus, chlorine, carbon, oxygen, nitrogen, and hydrogen. The four substances last named may, as we have seen, be derived either immediately or remotely from the air; but they are all essentials of a fertile soil, and, to perpetuate its fertility under cultivation, must be supplied in the form of manures.

Stable Manure.—Common stable manure contains potash, soda, lime, magnesia, alumina, silica, oxyd of iron, sulphur, phosphorus, chlorine, carbon, oxygen, nitrogen, and hydrogen. Lime exists both as a carbonate and as a phosphate, potash as a muriate and a sulphate, and soda as a carbonate. A comparison of this list of chemical substances with those enumerated in the preceding paragraph as the essentials of a fertile soil, will at once show the value of stable manure. Every part of it has been formed from vegetable substances, and it has only to be rendered friable and soluble to enter again into their composition. As plants can not, it will be remembered, absorb manures in a gross or solid form, the last point is an important one, and of universal application.

Night Soil.—Human excrements, composted with charcoal dust, leaves, turf, loam, etc., form a most powerful fertilizer. Quicklime should never be mixed with night-soil, for while it neutralizes the odor, it also expels its fertilizing qualities.

The Dung of Fowls.—The dung of fowls contains the essential qualities of guano, and is next to night-soil in value. It should be kept dry, or else mixed at once with a compost which will retain all the volatile and soluble matters which it contains.

Other Organic Manures.—Dead animals, blood, butchers' offal, fish, hair, bristles, hay, straw, leaves, sea-weed muck, rich turf, the refuse from the kitchen, and the slops from the chamber are all of great value as materials for a compost.

Ashes.—If any dried vegetable product be burned, the incombustible substance remaining behind is called the ash or ashes. This, though generally less than one tenth of its substance, is all that the plant *necessarily* derived from the soil. The substances expelled are carbon, oxygen, nitrogen, and hydrogen. They return to the air, from which they were either immediately or remotely derived. The ashes of vegetables, then, furnish just the inorganic elements required for their growth. Their value as a manure is evident, and it is astonishing that any person with a garden or a farm can allow a spoonful of them to be wasted. Leached ashes contain all the elements of the unleached, but are somewhat less valuable from having lost a portion of their potash and soda. Coal ashes, though inferior to wood ashes, are still very valuable as manure.

Lime.—We have already spoken of the value of lime in improving the texture of soils. It also condenses and retains the volatile gases brought in contact with it by the air and rains, and converts the insoluble matters of the soil into available food for plants, besides entering itself directly into the composition of nearly all vegetation.

The Marls.—Marls are composed of carbonate of lime mixed with clay, sand, loam, and frequently with phosphate and sulphate of lime and potash, and are valuable as manures in proportion to the lime and potash they contain.

Guano.—This substance is composed of the dung, food, and carcasses of sea-birds which have been accumulating for ages on some of the islands of the Pacific and Atlantic oceans. Of its value as a manure there can be no doubt. There is much fraud in its sale, however, and if great caution be not exercised, an adulterated article may be palmed off upon you. It must never, in a fresh state, come in direct contact with the seeds or roots of plants, as it is certain to destroy their vitality.

Other Inorganic Manures.—Common salt is valuable in small quantities for garden use. On account of its great affinity for water, it attracts the dews and atmospheric vapors, and is therefore a preventive of drouth. It is also useful in destroying worms, slugs, and larvæ. Old plaster, broken bricks, bones, charcoal, soot, and even broken glass, are useful as manures, and should be carefully saved and applied.

Having said so much of the various manures, we must repeat, in order to impress it upon the reader's mind, that our principal reliance should be upon stable manure (with which we would include that from the pig-sty) and the composts formed of home-made materials, according to directions we are about to give. The special manures most likely to be required by soils in general are lime, phosphate of lime, and potash.

Composts.—In or near the garden, and in some out-of-sight corner, there should be at all times a compost heap for receiving all kinds of rubbish that can have the least value as manure.

Make a shallow excavation of sufficient size, and a little lower at one end than at the other, forming with the earth thrown out a small embankment all around it. Into this throw green weeds, the sweepings of the yard, the refuse of vegetables, leaves, decayed vegetable matter of all kinds, woolen rags, old plaster, charcoal-dust, soot, soap-suds, brine, slops from the kitchen and chambers, etc. The heap should be dug over occasionally, adding a little ashes and lime. Animal manures should be composted in a separate heap, to which ashes and lime should not be added, as they would do harm by setting free the ammonia. In the latter case, charcoal-dust, plaster of Paris, and vegetable mold, leaves, turf, or swamp-muck should be used.

One who has never tried the experiment of carefully husbanding the elements of fertility which accumulate about a house, yard, and garden will be astonished at the annual amount and value of the compost which may, with very little trouble, be thus manufactured. Try it.*

---

* For a more complete exposition of the whole subject of Soils and Manures, see "The Farm."

III.

FORMATION OF A GARDEN.

Nothing conduces more to the successful completion of any piece of work than a good beginning.—A. Nonns.

I.—SITUATION.

AS it is desirable, if not absolutely necessary, that the garden should be placed near the house, the situation of which must be determined, in part, at least, by independent considerations, our range for the selection of a plot is generally quite limited. But it is well to know what kind of a situation is best, that we may exercise understandingly any liberty of choice that may be allowed us.

For early crops a southeastern exposure, with a slight inclination, is best, as it receives the full benefit of the morning sun. If sheltered on the north and northwest by higher grounds or by trees or high walls, so much the better. In warm climates, however, a northwestern exposure is better for many garden crops.

In selecting a situation for a garden, reference should also be had to soil. If this be originally good, the expense of making it so, artificially, will be saved, and only ordinary manuring required. Diversity of soils and exposures are also desirable combinations of advantages. Proximity to water is important, but very low grounds are, if possible, to be avoided.

II.—SIZE AND SHAPE.

The size of a garden will naturally depend mainly upon the wants, tastes, and means of its owner. An acre is not too much, but one half or even one fourth of an acre, well manured and skillfully cultivated, will furnish vegetables and fruits sufficient for the use of a small family. If you can consistently appropriate an acre or more for the purpose of a garden, do not be content with less. You will find a ready market for its surplus products, and at high prices, too, unless you happen to be situated at a great distance from any city or large town.

The form of a garden, like its situation and size, must depend upon circumstances. For convenience in laying out and cultivation, a square or a parallelogram is a good shape. If the form be a parallelogram, it is better that it should extend from east to west than from north to south.

III.—LAYING OUT.

The fruit and kitchen garden are to be looked upon from an economical rather than an esthetic point of view, and their internal arrangement should be simple, and, so far as circumstances will permit, regular and geometrical. In laying out a flower-garden or a lawn, however, no matter how small it may be, there is room for the exercise of taste and the creation of beauty; and we will reserve our directions on that point for the chapters devoted specially to those topics, confining ourselves here to the fruit and kitchen departments.

Whether within the same inclosure or not, the flower-garden will naturally be placed nearest the house. Passing through that, we enter the kitchen department, beyond which is the fruit-garden. It is better, however, in some cases to reverse the order of the last two, placing the fruit department next the flower-garden. In small gardens, too, these departments necessarily intermingle to some extent; but this should be avoided so far as is possible, as the trees are very detrimental to other crops—shading the ground, injuring tender plants by the drippings from their branches, and exhausting the soil by means of the heavy drafts made upon it by their roots. Dwarf pears may be admitted into the vegetable department with comparative impunity, provided the soil is sufficiently manured to withstand the double demand thus made upon it.

A large garden should have a walk through the center, extending the whole length, with a turning place at the extremity, and broad enough to admit a cart for bringing in the manure and conveying the heavier crops to the cellar or other place of storage. This walk may be crossed by another at right angles, and both should be bordered with currant or gooseberry bushes, or other shrubs. In small gardens these walks may be narrow and without borders, or may be omitted altogether. A border from four to twelve feet wide, and skirted by a walk three or four feet wide, should run entirely around the garden. The smaller compartments need not be separated by permanent walks, and their arrangement must be left to be decided by the circumstances of each case.

The only general direction that seems necessary in reference to laying out the fruit department is, that care should be taken to give the less hardy trees the most sheltered and warmest position, and to so dispose the various kinds that the larger trees shall not shade and dwarf the smaller. The fruit-garden should have its wall-borders for the cultivation of raspberries, blackberries, currants, gooseberries, etc. (unless these, as is generally the case in small gardens, are transferred to the borders of the kitchen department), and its trellises and arbors for grapevines.

IV.—FENCING.

A garden should be surrounded by a close fence, at least seven feet high, and picketed, to prevent the entrance of thieves. The height and closeness of the fence will increase the warmth of the air, break the force of high winds, which might injure tender plants and trees, and prevent, in a measure, the seeds of weeds from being driven into it by the wind. A close board fence, however, is an unsightly object, and a high close hedge, so soon as it can be grown, may advantageously take its place. The Osage Orange and, at the South, the Cherokee and single-white Macartney roses are suitable for this purpose.

V.—PREPARATION OF THE SOIL.

1. *Draining.*—If your soil require draining, this is the first thing to be attended to. If in digging a hole two feet deep, water be found to collect and stand in it, even during the wettest times, you may be sure that draining is required. "No one," J. J. Thomas says, "who has never given draining a full and fair trial can appreciate its importance. Very often the soil may be worked and planted from two to four weeks earlier in the spring—a most important advantage for early vegetables. Scarcely less is the benefit during the rest of the season in preventing hard-baked soil in times of drouth." Do not neglect this on account of the expense. No operation in gardening "pays" better. A quarter of an acre well underdrained will be more valuable than an acre of wet, cold, tenacious, undrained soil. Dig parallel ditches from twenty-five to thirty feet apart, and from three to four feet deep, forming a slightly inclined plane on the bottom, which may be from six inches to a foot wide. These ditches may be filled to a sufficient depth with rubble-stones or brush, and then covered with soil, if the arched tiles or tubes of burned clay, now mostly used, can not be procured. The average expense of the best underdraining is estimated at only from twelve to eighteen dollars an acre.

2. *Trenching.*—We have already (in Chapter II.) spoken of the necessity of depth of soil for horticultural purposes, and especially for the growth of trees, and of the means for deepening soils naturally too shallow, as nearly all are. Trenching is thus performed:

"At one end of the plot to be trenched, dig with the spade a trench three feet wide and at least two feet deep, throwing the earth out on the side opposite to the plot. Now open another trench of the same width, and put the surface spadeful of this into the bottom of the former trench, and the next spadeful upon that, until it is opened to the depth of the first one. When the plot is entirely trenched in this way, the last trench will remain open, and must be filled with the earth thrown out from the first one. If the subsoil be poor and gravelly, it is better to take off the first spadeful, and then loosen the bottom to the required depth without bringing it to the surface. If the soil require it, as it generally will, layers of manure may be added to those of earth alternately."

3. *Subsoil Plowing.*—The expense of trenching being great, where the plot to be prepared is large, subsoil plowing may be substituted, similar results in a somewhat inferior degree being obtained. In subsoiling, a common turning plow goes first, and the subsoil plow follows, loosening the earth to the required depth below the bottom of the ordinary furrow, but not turning it up.

The foregoing preparatory operations being thoroughly performed, we may consider the garden ready for the ordinary processes of cultivation. Of these we shall speak in another chapter.

IV.

IMPLEMENTS AND FIXTURES.

<small>Next to knowledge and skill are good tools.—*The Workman.*</small>

I.—IMPLEMENTS.

YOU should supply yourself with good implements of the various kinds essential to the proper performance of every necessary operation. To purchase those of an inferior quality because they can be procured at a somewhat lower price is false economy. Experience will prove them the more costly in the end. They soon get out of repair and become useless; besides, in their best estate, much less work can be accomplished with them, and that imperfectly.

The Spade.—It is convenient to have several spades of different sizes, but a No. 2 of Ames' cast steel will serve for most purposes. For the flower-garden, a lady needs a smaller and lighter one, manufactured especially for feminine use.

The Shovel.—A shovel is necessary for loading and spreading composts and for various other operations. The round-pointed ones are perhaps more generally useful in a garden than the square-bladed.

Hoes.—You need several hoes, of different sizes and shapes. The common square draw-hoes are most used. They are of various sizes. One of three or four and another of six or seven inches will be found most useful. To these it is desirable to add a pronged hoe, a thrust-hoe, and a triangular draw-hoe. The latter is useful for digging furrows for seeds.

Rakes.—The garden rake should be of the best wrought

iron, with teeth about two and a half inches long and one and a half inches apart. The handle should be from six to eight feet long. Drill-rakes, which are very useful, if not indispensable, are made of wood, with obtusely-pointed teeth, three or four in number, placed at a greater or less distance apart, for sowing different seeds. In using the drill-rake a line is stretched to guide it in making the first drill, and afterward the first tooth is kept in the drill last made, as a guide, and thus all the rows in a long bed can be made perfectly parallel. Several different sizes are required.

The Trowel.—The trowel is very useful for removing plants, with balls of earth for transplanting. It should be from five to nine inches long, exclusive of the handle.

The Dibber.—This is a short piece of round wood, obtusely pointed. A serviceable one may be made from an old spade or shovel handle.

The Reel and Line.—These are essential—at least the line, which may be used without the reel—where anything like straight rows and regularity are desired. The reel may be either of wood or of iron.

The Watering Pot.—One boiling four gallons is the best size. It should be made of double tin, and kept well painted.

Garden Shears.—These are of various sizes, and are used for clipping hedges and many other purposes. The seven and nine-inch size are very convenient. There is a smaller article made expressly for the ladies.

The Saw.—The pruning saw is from fourteen to eighteen inches long, and is made with fine teeth and a hooked handle, for hanging on the limb of a tree.

Knives.—A pruning knife of modern size and a budding knife will be essential in the fruit-garden.

Hand-Glasses.—Hand-glasses, either made of panes set in boxes, or bell-glasses, are necessary for protecting early plants of the tomato, egg-plant, etc.

Ladders.—A light, common ladder and a standing ladder will be found indispensable in the fruit department.

The Wheelbarrow.—The wheelbarrow is exceedingly useful in the smallest garden, and in a large one absolutely indispensable. It should be light, but strongly made.

Additional.—Several other implements are desirable, and in particular cases indispensable, among which are, *a crowbar, a pick, a manure fork, a forked spade, pruning shears, a garden roller, a lawn scythe, a hedge hook, vine scissors, a hand-cultivator, an orchardist's hook, a hand-syringe,* etc.

The plow, subsoil plow, and cultivator belong rather to the farm, and if you cultivate only a small garden, you will find it more economical to pay for the occasional use of these implements than to invest money in their purchase.

Preservation of Implements.—Having procured implements of a good quality, do not allow them to be destroyed for the lack of a little care on your part. An implement that in the hands of a careful and economical gardener will last and continue serviceable for ten years may be ruined in a single season by a negligent and wasteful one.

In or near the garden should be a tool-house or a room set apart for the purpose of storing the implements when not in use. Carefully clean your spades, hoes, and other implements of steel or iron, before returning them to their place. Implements of wood should be painted.

II.—FIXTURES, ETC.

The gardens and grounds of every rural residence of taste should have seats, arbors, and other structures of rustic work —that is, work made of the trunks and branches of trees, with their bark on and in their natural forms. They may be cheaply erected, and will add greatly to the out-of-door attractions. The tool-house we have recommended may be of this character, and be made ornamental as well as useful.*

Pits.—What is called a *sunk pit* is made by excavating the earth and forming walls of brick, stone, or boards. These are

---

* See "The House," for designs and descriptions.

sometimes covered with glass frames, and at other times with mats or boards. They are mostly used for the preservation of vegetables, such as celery, endive, lettuce, cauliflower, etc. The *walled pit* is partly sunk in the ground and partly above it. The walls are formed of brick or stone, finished with a wooden or stone coping, and covered with movable glazed sashes. Of this pit Buist says:

"There is no appendage to the garden of greater utility than this pit. It is two feet

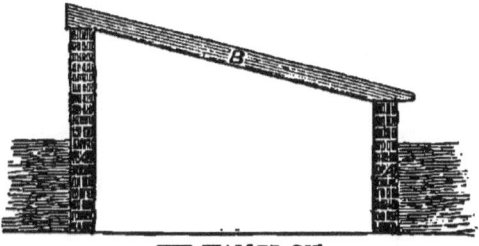

THE WALLED PIT.

under ground and one foot above it in front, and two feet above it at the back, and six or seven feet wide in the clear. It is an excellent winter apartment for plants when covered with sash and mats. Filled with very rich earth, it produces very fine cauliflowers, which will be in use from March to May. If filled with warm manure early in February, it will produce cucumbers that will be in use from April to July, or radishes and small salading in any quantity."

Hot Beds.—The common hot-bed frame is a bottomless box

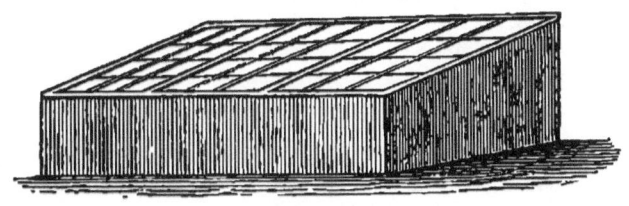

THE HOT-BED.

of wood, with a sloping top and covered with a sash. It may be of any length or breadth, but from four to six feet wide, and from six to ten feet long is a good size. The sashes are made without cross-bars, the glass overlapping like the shingles of a house. The glass should be proportionally much smaller than it is represented in our engraving—not larger than seven-by-nine at most. The lap of the panes should not be over half an inch. It should be bedded in soft putty, and the sash well painted. The sashes should be made to slide in grooves, so as to be conveniently moved whenever the bed may require to be opened, either wholly or partially, to the air.* The whole should be kept under cover when not in use. Directions for preparing hot-beds will be found in the next chapter, under the head of "Forcing."

Trellises.—Every garden should have one or more trellises for vines. They are of different kinds to adapt them to different situations and purposes. The posts should be made of some durable wood. Red cedar is the best. Under the head of the grape we shall describe the construction of the trellises required for its support. Designs for ornamental trellis-work may be found in "The House."

---

* Instead of the sashes for covering the frames, the following mode, called the German plan, may perhaps be adopted with advantage; but we have not tried it:

"Take white cotton cloth, of a close texture, stretch, and nail it on frames of any size you wish; take two ounces of lime-water, four ounces of linseed oil, one of white of eggs, two ounces of yellow of eggs; mix the lime and oil with very gentle heat, heat the eggs separately, and mix them with the former; spread this mixture with a paint-brush over the cotton, allowing each coat to dry before applying another, until they become water-proof. The following are the advantages this shade possesses over glass ones: 1. The cost being hardly one fourth. 2. Repairs are easily and cheaply made. 3. The light. They do not require watering; no matter how intense the heat of the sun, the plants are never struck down or burned, or checked in growth, neither do they grow up long, sick, and weakly, as they do under glass, and still there is abundance of light. 4. The heat arising entirely from below is more equable and temperate, which is a great object. The vapor rising from the manure and earth is condensed by the cool air passing over the surface of the shade, and stands in drops upon the inside, and therefore, the plants do not require as frequent watering. If the frames or stretchers are made large, they should be intersected by cross-bars about a foot square to support the cloth. These articles are just the thing for bringing forward melons, tomatoes, flower-seeds, etc. in season for transplanting."

V.

HORTICULTURAL PROCESSES.

Every operation in gardening depends for its complete and universal success upon a knowledge of the structure of plants, the nature of soils and manures, and the laws of vegetable life and growth.—M. Le Jardinier.

I.—STIRRING THE SOIL.

THE attentive reader of the foregoing chapters will not require to be told that a thorough stirring and pulverizing of the soil, as one of the first operations in gardening, is absolutely essential to any high degree of success in the steps which follow. His knowledge of the structure of roots and the nature of their food has prepared him to appreciate the importance of the mechanical division of soils. He knows that the ground must be readily permeable by the tender rootlets, pervious to moisture and air, and so broken up that the water, acids, and alkalies penetrating it may efficiently act upon its soluble parts.

Spading is the most effectual method of stirring the soil, but, where the plow can be advantageously used, will hardly "pay" in this country. In small gardens, and in portions of all gardens, spading is the only practicable operation. Whatever the means used, let the work be *thoroughly* done. Downing says: "If I had to preach a sermon on horticulture, I should take this for my text—'Stir the soil.'"

II.—APPLYING MANURES.

As the roots of plants usually penetrate every part of the soil of a garden, *manures, as a general rule, should be as thor-*

oughly mixed as possible with every part. Where the ground is to be plowed, they are generally spread upon the surface, and turned in by that process. In special cases, as will be seen further on, manuring in the hill or drill is advisable. Manures are also sometimes applied as top-dressings—that is, are spread upon the surface and not dug in. Vegetable and animal manures for common garden use should be thoroughly rotted and finely pulverized.

III.—FORCING.

Every garden should have one or more hot-beds for forwarding early tomatoes, cucumbers, cabbages, radishes, lettuce, etc. We have described the hot-bed frame in Chapter IV. The bed itself should be composed of stable manure and leaves, and must be not less than three feet deep. The manure should be first thrown in a heap to ferment, and worked over several times, adding water if it should become dry or musty. Sometimes the bed is made on the surface of the ground, and at others an excavation ten or twelve inches deep is made, in order to give the bed a less inconvenient elevation above the general surface. The manure and leaves should be spread evenly in layers, and pressed down. The bed should be at least six inches larger every way than the frame which is to cover it, and slope slightly toward the south. When neatly finished, put on the frame, close the sash, and keep all tight till the heat rises and steam appears on the glass. So soon as the heat rises, give the bed air at noon, or the warmest part of the day, but keep it carefully closed the rest of the time. In three or four days you may cover the surface with from four to six inches of fine, rich garden mold, and so soon as this is warmed through, the bed is ready for use. The seed may be sowed in drills, but, for facility of transplanting and to secure an unchecked growth, it is better to sow them in small pots, which are to be plunged in the mold. Sprinkle gently with water of the same temperature as the bed. When the plants appear they should have the air every day in which the weather will permit. Open the bed also to warm, gentle rains, but keep it carefully closed against cold or heavy storms. At night keep it well covered with matting or straw. Transplant as soon as danger from frost will permit.

In the South this forcing process may be commenced early in the winter, but at the North not till February or March, according to the latitude and the season.

IV.—SOWING SEEDS.

The first thing to be attended to in seed-sowing is the preparation of the bed by thoroughly pulverizing the soil; and the smaller the seeds the more finely should the earth be pulverized. The soil should be freshly stirred and moist, but not too wet. The depth at which seeds should be buried varies with species and with the state of the soil. The objects are to exclude the light and secure sufficient moisture for the purposes of germination. The latter object requires large seeds, other things being equal, to be covered more deeply than small ones. If seeds are covered too deeply, unnecessary impediments are thrown in the way of the ascending shoots; and germination may be prevented altogether by the exclusion of the air. Most garden seeds are sown in drills. The earth should be pressed upon them with more or less force, according to the nature of the soil, in order to secure the necessary degree of compactness to retain the moisture and to support the plant after germination. Specific directions, where they are required, will be given under the name of each plant.

V.—TRANSPLANTING.

In transplanting, the principal points to be attended to are—care in taking up, to avoid injuring the tender extremities of the roots, through which, as we have seen, the plant receives its nourishment; planting firmly, to give it a secure hold of the soil; shading, when necessary, to prevent the evaporation from its leaves being greater than the plant, in its enfeebled state, can support; and watering, that it may not lack moist ure. Moist weather should also, if possible, be chosen for performing the operation.

As a general rule, in transplanting, the collar of the root should not be buried. Cabbages, balsams, and some other annuals, which throw out roots above the collar, furnish exceptions; also pears on quince stocks, which must be set so as to bring the place where the scion is inserted below the surface of the soil.

The operation of transplanting herbaceous plants should always be performed with a trowel, removing a little ball of earth with the plant. A damp, cloudy day, an evening, or just before a shower, is a favorable time.

Tap-rooted plants are transplanted with great difficulty, and, if the operation be attempted, should be taken up with a considerable ball of earth.

In transplanting trees much depends upon the knowledge and skill exercised. Thousands of fine trees are lost every year through the ignorance and carelessness of transplanters.

In taking up a tree or shrub for transplanting, be careful to injure the roots as little as possible. But in all cases the roots will be maimed more or less. The feeding power of the tree is to the same extent decreased, and it will not be able to sustain the draft made upon it by the stem and leaves. These must be diminished correspondingly by heading back or shortening. In preparing a place for the reception of the tree, avoid, if possible, the sites of old trees. Dig a hole considerably larger than the clump of the tree's roots, and from fifteen to twenty inches deep, placing the sods, if in sward land, in one heap, the soil in another, and the subsoil in a third. The hole should be filled with a mixture of the soil, subsoil, and rich, black loam, or well-rotted compost manure, to the height where it is proper to place the tree. With the hand or spade, shape the soil for the roots into the form of a little cone, on which to set the hollow in the center of the clump of roots. If this is done some weeks, or even months, before setting the tree, it will be all the better.

If the ground be dry, or if the roots have been much exposed to the air since the tree was taken up, soak the roots and the lower part of the trunk in water twelve or twenty-four hours. Cut off all bruised and broken ends of roots smoothly with a knife, and shorten-in the longest, so that the clump of roots may have a somewhat circular form. In cutting a root, always enter the knife upon the under side, and bring it out, with a slope, to the upper side, so that the fibers which may shoot out from the edges of the cut shall strike downward into the ground, instead of upward, as they would were the cut made as it commonly is.

With good, rich soil fill up under, among, around, and above the roots, straightening them out with the fingers, and placing them in a fan-like and natural position, being very cautious not to leave any, even small, hollow places among them. If the root is one-sided, make the most you can of the weaker part. At this stage of the work, if you have patience, it is an excellent plan to make a circular dam around the edge of the hole, and keep it full of water for a half hour or more. In setting evergreens, this, by some, is deemed almost indispensable, unless the ground is quite moist. Next, put in a little more earth, pressing it around the tree with the foot. After this, throw on an inch or so of loose earth, and the work is done.

Another mode of filling up around the trees, called *mudding-in*, has proved very successful. Make the circular dam around the tree first, or as soon as it is needed, then let one person slowly sift the soil into the hole upon the roots, while another constantly pours in water, thus keeping the earth in a thin, muddy state.

Very large trees are most successfully transplanted by removing them with large balls of frozen earth in mid-winter, and placing them at once in a hole previously prepared to receive them.*

---

* See Appendix, C.

The fundamental principle to be generally observed in transplanting is to head back the top of the tree in proportion to the loss of root that it has sustained by being removed.

Some fruit-trees may be moved much more easily than others. Downing arranges them with reference to this point in the following order: Plums, quinces, apples, pears, peaches, nectarines, apricots, and, last and most difficult, cherries. It is an invariable rule, *that the larger the tree the less the chances of success.* In the northern parts of the United States small trees should always be set in the spring.

Medium-sized trees—say five to ten feet high—may be set equally well either in the autumn or spring. Trees of large size should be moved late in autumn, in the winter, or quite early in the spring.

The evergreen tribe are, however, best planted out just as their buds begin to swell in the spring; but they are sometimes successfully set in autumn, and also during the last of May and first of June. If their roots are exposed to dry, out of the ground, they are almost certain to die.

VI.—WATERING.

Watering, like every other operation in gardening, has its rules, founded on the general principles laid down in our first and second chapters. The most important points to be remembered are: 1. That on the nature of the plant, the stage of its growth, and the dryness or dampness of the atmosphere depends the quantity of water required; 2. That the soil should never be saturated with water, too much moisture proving injurious as well as too little; 3. That the water should not be applied at the base of the stem, as it is through the extremities of the rootlets mainly that it must be taken up, and these, except in tap-rooted plants, are at a greater or less distance from the original starting-point; 4. That in summer, the proper time for watering plants is evening, but that in colder weather it is better to water them at mid-day; 5. That rain water is better than well or spring water, and that when

HORTICULTURAL PROCESSES. 57

the latter is used it should be exposed to the air for some time before applying it; 6. That the water should never be colder than the plants to be watered.

VII.—HOEING.

The necessity for stirring the soil before planting has been already shown. As soon as the plants are well above ground it should be stirred again. In field culture, and to some extent in large gardens, this is done with the plow and cultivator. Where these can not go, the hoe must be faithfully applied. *The soil can not be stirred too often.*

One object in hoeing is the destruction of weeds. This should be thorough—the extermination should be complete. Spare not even the smallest. But keeping the weeds down is not the only good result attained by hoeing. The soil is thereby kept friable and porous, opened to the atmosphere and the fertilizing gases, and new, fresh, and cool surface is presented for the absorption of moisture. *Hoe deeply.* A mere scratching of the surface is not enough; and *do not fail to kill every weed.*

One year's seeding makes seven years' weeding.

VIII.—PROTECTION FROM FROST.

Straw and leaves laid several inches deep about their roots are very useful in protecting half-hardy plants during the winter. Garden-pots, empty boxes, barrels, hand-glasses, and cold frames should be brought into requisition in particular cases, for the protection of early plants from spring frosts, and later ones from those of the autumn. Common tumblers may be used for very small plants, but they must be raised whenever moisture accumulates.

Fruit-trees in blossom, or covered with young fruit just formed, may be protected by keeping up smoldering, smoking fires during the night in various parts of the garden, at the windward side. But little fire is required, the clouds of smoke effectually warding off the frost. The amount of fruit which might often be thus saved would repay a hundred-fold the labor and care bestowed in this way.

IX.—MULCHING.

Mulching is placing mulch or moist litter of various kinds upon the surface of the soil over the roots of trees, shrubs, and herbaceous plants. Its uses are the retention of moisture, the prevention of injury by frost, and the promotion of an equable temperature. Strawberries thinly mulched, the crown being uncovered, are rendered more productive and continue longer in bearing, especially in hot, dry climates. Newly planted fruit-trees are often greatly benefited by mulching.

X.—DESTROYING INSECTS.

The foes against which the gardener is forced to wage a perpetual war of extermination, though individually insignificant, are in the aggregate most formidable. We will try to give a few useful hints of a general character to aid the reader in this warfare.

Sowing a garden with salt, at the rate of six or eight bushels to the acre, will cause many insects to disappear. It should be done in the autumn. Digging the soil in the winter, and thus exposing it to the frost, will destroy many grubs, etc. Wide-mouthed bottles, partly filled with molasses and water, and hung up in a garden, make excellent traps for the moths, which are the parents of many destructive vermin. Mr. Downing mentions an acquaintance who thus caught and destroyed in a single season *three bushels of insects*, and preserved his garden almost free from them. A bright fire of resinous pine, tar, shavings, or any other combustible, kindled in the garden at night, on a platform erected for the purpose, will attract and destroy millions. Birds are among the best friends of the gardener, and should by no means be destroyed, although some of them may eat a few raspberries or cherries. Toads live almost entirely upon insects, and do no harm in a garden. Induce as many of them as possible to make it their home. Hens and chickens should have access whenever it can safely be permitted.

To drive insects away from plants various preparations are useful. A writer in the *Southern Cultivator* recommends the following:

"Put into a barrel of water a quarter of a pound of camphor, in pieces of the size of a hickory nut, and let it stand a day before using. Water your plants with this. The barrel may be refilled many times before the camphor will have all been dissolved. A cupful of strong lye put into the water will add to the strength of the mixture by causing the water to take up more camphor. Camphor is very offensive to most insects." Tobacco-water is another efficient remedy. Lime, charcoal-dust, ashes, soot, snuff, and sulphur sprinkled upon plants prove a defense against most destroyers. To expel the striped bug from cucumbers, squashes, etc., water the plants daily with a strong decoction of quassia, made by pouring four gallons of boiling water on four pounds of quassia, in a barrel, and, after twelve hours, filling the barrel with water. The intolerable squash or pumpkin bug may be thoroughly driven off by a decoction of double strength, containing a pound of glue to ten gallons, to make it adhere.

The most effectual and the cheapest remedy for the striped bug, however, consists in defending each hill of melons, cucumbers, squashes, etc., by a box about fifteen inches square, the sides being eight to ten inches high, covered with millinet or some similar thin material.

The following recipe for making a "barrier to insects" is given in the *Gardener's Chronicle*. It may be easily tried:

"Take of common resin 1½ lbs.; sweet oil, 1 lb.; place them in a pipkin over the fire until the resin is melted; stir the materials together, that they may be well blended; when cold the substance formed, which the discoverer calls 'rezoil,' will be of the consistency of molasses. To use the rezoil it should be spread with a brush upon shreds or any fitting material, and wrapped round the stem of the plant; if any support is used, that should be brushed over also. No insect can possibly, or will attempt to cross this barrier; the rezoil never dries, but always remains sticky and clammy—its action as a trap is therefore obvious."

But, however numerous and effective the other remedies, "eternal vigilance" can not be dispensed with in dealing with the pests of the garden.

XI.—SAVING SEEDS.

Choose the best plants for seed—the most *true to their kind* and the most perfectly developed; allow the seeds to become perfectly ripe before gathering them; gather when dry, and especially take care that they are perfectly dry when put up; store them in paper bags carefully labeled, and keep them in a dry, cool place. Great care is necessary in raising seeds to preserve the sorts unmixed, as varieties of the same species or similar species are almost sure to mix if planted near each other. If you raise more than one kind of corn, or pumpkin, or cucumber, or melon in the same garden, you can not be sure of pure seed. The squashes and pumpkins may mix, or the melons with either, the pollen of one being conveyed by the wind, or sometimes by bees or other insects, to the pistil of the other.

XII.—ROTATION OF CROPS.

Why rotation of crops is beneficial has been already shown, and if the reader has forgotten, let him turn back to the first chapter. The following is a good rotation for a given portion of a garden:

    First year, cabbages.
    Second " onions.
    Third " carrots, beets, or parsneps.
    Fourth " potatoes or turnips.
    Fifth " celery, spinach, or lettuce.

Celery is excellent to precede asparagus, onions, cauliflowers, or turnips; old asparagus beds are good for carrots, potatoes, etc.; strawberry and raspberry beds do well for the cabbage tribe, and the cabbage tribe may be followed by the tap-rooted plants—carrots, beets, etc.

A large portion of every garden, even at the North, should be made to produce two crops each season. All the space occupied by early peas, beans, and potatoes can be made available for turnips and cabbages. Turnips (English or Dutch) may also be sown broadcast among the corn and later potatoes after the last hoeing.

XIII.—PROPAGATION.

There are, properly speaking, but two modes of propagating plants—by seeds and by division. By the first the species is perpetuated, and new varieties raised. The second mode multiplies specimens of the individual itself, with all its peculiarities, which may be and generally are lost in the seed.

There are several distinct modes of propagating plants by division, all, however, depending for their success upon *the presence of leaf-buds*, each of which, as we have seen, being capable, under favorable circumstances, of forming a distinct and independent individual.

1. *Suckers.*—Some plants, such as the rose, the raspberry, the lilac, etc., throw up suckers or sprouts from their roots. These spring from what have been described as adventitious buds. We have only to divide these from their parent and transplant them in a suitable soil to secure their independent growth. Offsets and runners are of a similar nature to the suckers of the woody plants. The former are young bulbs which form by the side of the old one, and merely require breaking off and planting. The latter are shoots springing from the collar or crown of a plant, and throwing out roots at their joints. These have only to be separated from the parent plant to become independent individuals. The strawberry is the most noted example of this mode of propagation.

2. *Layers.*—The tendency manifested by many plants to throw out roots from their joints early suggested to gardeners

the idea of making layers. A twig growing out of a tree, at a point not far from the ground, is bent down, and the middle portion of it buried just under the surface of the soil, and fastened there by means of a hooked peg, or by a stone or turf placed above it. Success is rendered more certain by checking the downward flow of the sap. This may be accomplished by cutting a slice off the under side of the part of the twig that is placed under ground, or, more perfectly, by entering the knife on the under side at this point, and splitting the twig upward about one or two inches, fastening the split open with a little wedge or pebble. The sap accumulating at this point induces the throwing out of roots, and the conversion of the shoot into a new plant. Trees or shrubs purposely headed down for raising layers are called *stools*. A single quince-bush, thus made into a *stool*, and its twigs layered, is capable of producing many finely-rooted plants in a single season. Of some kinds of layers nearly every bud will form roots of its own.

3. *Cuttings.*—Cuttings are shoots removed from the parent tree or plant without roots. The branches nearest the ground are considered best for cuttings, as the tendency to throw out roots is greater in them than in those more elevated. They should be cut off just below a joint. Some species, however, as the willow, the currant, etc., will throw out roots from any part of the stem, and generally succeed with even the most careless planting. The best time to take off cuttings is in November, but in a cold climate they are more likely to succeed if kept in damp mold in a cellar, and not planted till spring. In planting, bury them to the second joint, leaving one or two joints above the surface of the soil. Press the earth compactly about the lower end. Cuttings of delicate plants are generally *struck* (rooted) in pots, and sometimes it is necessary to cover them with a bell-glass, to prevent too rapid evaporation.

4. *Slips.*—Slips are cuttings made from the root or collar of a plant, or branches stripped off, with a small portion of the root or stem attached. They are treated like other cuttings. Many kinds of fruit-trees may be readily propagated by slips.

5. *Budding.*—Budding consists in introducing the bud of one tree or shrub, with a portion of the bark and wood adhering to it, below the bark of another tree or shrub. The operation is thus performed: With a sharp budding-knife, upon a smooth place on the side of the stock, cut a longitudinal slit an inch or more long. Across the top of this cut a transverse slit from a quarter to half an inch long, so that both slits, taken together, shall resemble the letter T. Next, cut from your stick of buds a thin slice of bark, with a little wood in the central portion of it, entering the knife about half or three-fourths of an inch below, and bringing it out about as far above a bud. This slice of bark and wood, taken together, is called a *bud*, the part of the bud which grows into a twig being technically called its *eye*.

With the ivory haft of your budding-knife, or, if you have not such a knife, with any little wedge of wood or ivory, raise up the corners of the slit in the stock. Taking hold of the bud by its foot-stalk, enter it, and gently push it down to the bottom of the incision. The eye of the bud will now be from one fourth to three fourths of an inch from the transverse part of the slit. The part of the bud, if any, projecting above this transverse slit, should be cut off, by passing the knife through it, into the transverse slit again, so that the upper end of the bud and this transverse part of the slit shall make a good joint together. Bind the bud firmly with shreds of bass-matting, so as to cover every part of it except the eye. Woolen yarn or corn husks will answer when no matting is at hand. The stock (trunk or branch) should be from an eighth of an inch to not more than an inch in diameter.

To prepare a *stick of buds* for budding, take a scion of the present season's growth, and cut off the portions of each end of it containing buds that are imperfectly developed. Next, cut off the leaves at a point about in the middle of their stems or *footstalks*. The

STICK OF BUDS.

buds which are to be used lie in the angle on the upper side of these stems.

Budding is generally performed in the summer or early part of autumn. It is essential to success—1st. *That the bark of the stock should part freely from the wood*, and 2d. *That the bud which is to be inserted should be well ripened*, otherwise it will not have vital energy sufficient to establish itself in its new location. Whenever these conditions can be secured, budding may be successfully performed. The buds put in early, however, especially in the South, make a considerable growth the same season. Buds should be inserted on the north side of the stock, if practicable. The operation is one of some nicety, and to be successful must be performed *rapidly, and with fresh, healthy buds, smooth cuts, and cleanly rising bark*. A few days after budding, the stock should be cut off within ten or twelve inches of the bud, and when this has grown three or four inches, the stock may be cut off again near the budded shoot. All sprouts, or "robbers," as they are called, that appear on the stock must be carefully removed.

TREATMENT OF THE BUD.

Care should also be taken not to allow branches from the main shoot of the bud to grow, and to secure an upright position of it, a ligature of the matting may be passed around the sprout and the upper end of the old stock.

In spring budding, some gardeners recommend to make the incisions in the form of an inverted ⊥, but we see no good reason for this inversion, and believe that the other mode is equally successful.

Annular budding is applied with success to trees of hard wood and thick bark, or those which, like the walnut, have buds so large as to render the common mode of budding difficult and uncertain. A ring of bark is taken from the stock, and one of equal size, containing a bud, from the scion. If the stock be larger than the scion, an entire ring will not be taken off, but only what may be filled by the ring of bark from the scion. If the ring of bark from the scion be too large for the stock, it will be reduced so as to just inclose the stock. When thus fitted, tie with matting, and cover the wound with clay or grafting-wax, and the work is done.

6. *Grafting.*—In grafting, a shoot with two or more buds on it, instead of a single bud, is transferred from one tree or shrub to another. The operation, in all its forms, consists essentially in bringing in contact portions of growing shoots, so that the *liber* or inner bark of the two may unite and grow together. The same general principles apply to it as to budding.

The shoot to be transferred is called a *scion*. The best time to cut scions is from the middle of January to the last of February, although they *may* be taken from the trees at any time from late autumn until spring. In order to keep them until they may be used, nothing more is necessary than to thrust their lower ends into the ground, in a shady place—say close on the north side of the trunk of the tree from which they were cut; or a better way is to set them half their length deep in a box of fine soil in a cellar.

In cutting scions, take from the extremity of the limb of a tree that part of it which grew the preceding season, and keep the shoot or twig entire till wanted for use.

Scions are united to their stocks in several ways. Whatever may be the mode of operating, however, the principle is always the same—namely, *the sap-vessels of the graft and the stock must be so adapted to each other that the sap can flow uninterruptedly from the one to the other.*

Cleft grafting is the mode in most common use. Stocks from half an inch to two inches in diameter are usually worked over in this way. The whole top of a large tree may thus be headed back and grafted, so as to become even more valuable than one that was grafted in the nursery.

CLEFT GRAFTING

The operation is performed as follows: Saw off the stock

crosswise, then pare the end smoothly with a knife. Next, split it down about two inches with a thin, sharp knife, driven with a hammer. A narrow wedge is now driven into the middle of the cleft, so as to keep the top of it open about a quarter of an inch. Cut the scion (which should not contain more than three or four buds) at the lower end, in the form of a wedge, about one and a half inches long, contriving to have a bud or eye at the top of the part so formed, to insure greater success. The scion is next to be inserted on one side of the stock, and fitted nicely into the cleft, so that the inner bark of the outer side of the scion shall exactly meet that of the stock. On large stocks two scions are thus inserted, one on each side.

The scions being adjusted, carefully withdraw the wedge which stands erect between the scions. Make a ball of wax, and lay it on the head of the stock, between the scions, and press it down, and spread it so as to cover the head, and lap over three fourths of an inch all around upon the bark, and rub it down smoothly, being careful to make an air and water-joint around the scions and over the end of the stock. Where the wax passes over the corner of the stock, it should be quite thick, to prevent it from cracking. Then cover the cleft on each side quite below its lower extremity, and the work is done. The next spring cut off nicely the poorest scion in each stock, as one is usually quite sufficient.

For small seedling stocks, or small sprouts on larger trees, less than half an inch in diameter, it is well to adopt the *whip* or *splice* method.

Cut the stock with a sharp knife, obliquely upward, without bruising or starting the bark, and the scion downward, with a corresponding angle, to make the two parts fit nicely, care being taken that the inner bark of the stock and scion exactly meet. Then lay the parts together, and bind them snugly with a strand of matting or bass-bark, and cover the splice with grafting-wax or clay, to shield it from the air and water.

Allied to splice grafting is what is called *saddle grafting*. On stocks of half an inch or more in diameter and scions of the same size, this mode is sometimes employed with excellent success. In this process, cut the stock with a drawing-knife upward, forming a wedge; then split with a fine saw the scion, and with a knife pare away each side to a point, so as to fit the stock; place the parts together, and bind them firmly with matting or bark, and cover the whole with clay or grafting-wax. At the end of two months the union will generally be sufficiently perfect to allow the removal of the covering and the ligature, which, if left on too long, will injure the growth.

In-arch grafting is used when others will scarcely succeed. The two trees must stand close to each other. A twig of each, without being cut from its tree, must be pared with a long, corresponding slanting cut, and the two raw edges must be fitted nicely, and bound firmly together, and the joint covered with the composition. When the union has taken place, the trees are so separated as to leave the scion on the tree where it is wanted.

A mode called root grafting is practiced extensively in nurseries. The two-year seedling stocks are headed down to within an inch or so of the collar or crown; they are then split, and the scion inserted, as in common cleft grafting. The scion is held in its place by a piece of matting bound round the stock. The stocks to be used for this purpose are generally taken up in the fall, grafted in the winter at the fireside, and packed away in the cellar till spring, when they are properly planted; the point of insertion of the graft being covered with the soil. No wax or clay is necessary. Scions may also be grafted on small roots by common splice grafting. The point of union should be covered with soil to the depth of two inches.

Grafting may be performed at almost any season of the year with scions properly kept; but by far the best time is from the middle of February, in mild weather, all along until the middle of May at the North, and till the end of March at the South—stone-fruits first, and other fruits somewhat later.

Neither grafting nor budding can be successful, unless between different varieties of the same species, as the apple upon a seedling apple-tree stock; or between nearly allied species of the same genus, as between the apple and the pear, which unions are comparatively imperfect and short-lived; or, thirdly, between nearly allied genera, as between the cherry and the plum, which maintain a feeble existence for a limited period, and then die. All unions, therefore, between widely different genera and species, are utterly impossible, as the graft can not live upon the sap supplied by the stock, any more than a lion can be fed upon grass.

To produce dwarf trees, Apple is grafted upon Paradise (or Doucin) stocks; the Pear upon the Quince, Thorn, or Mountain Ash; the Peach upon the Plum; the Plum upon Mirabelle Plum seedlings; the Cherry upon the Cerasus Mahaleb, and, in general, any tree upon any other kindred tree of slower or smaller growth.

The stock and the graft (scion or bud) exert influences upon each other mutually. The stock often affects the size and flavor of the fruit borne by the graft. Of a graft or stock, either may communicate its own diseases and infirmities to the other. It is pretty well established, also, that stocks bearing early fruits have an influence in accelerating the ripening of the fruits which may be made to grow upon them by grafting.

Grafting Wax.—To make grafting wax of an excellent quality, take four parts of resin, two of beeswax, and one of tallow; melt the whole together, pour the composition into cold water, and work it over thoroughly, pulling it as you would molasses candy. The hardness of the wax may be increased or lessened by applying more or less tallow. In cold weather keep the composition in warm water, and in warm weather in cold water, to secure the proper consistency for use. In using it, the hands should be slightly greased.

XIV.—PRUNING.

The principal objects sought to be attained by pruning are to promote the growth, improve the form, and increase the fruitfulness of trees. No operation in horticulture requires the exercise of more knowledge, judgment, and skill, in order to the attainment of complete success; but in general no operation is more carelessly, ignorantly, and bunglingly performed, or more frequently neglected.

Pruning to promote the growth of a tree proceeds upon the principle that the sap which would have been appropriated to the support of the branches, or parts of the top, taken off, will go to increase the vigor of the parts which remain. This is true within certain limits, but the process must not be carried too far. *Sufficient top must be left to supply leaves for the elaboration of the sap.*

Young trees, two or three years from the seed, or one year from the graft, are not infrequently headed down to two or three buds, on purpose to strengthen their growth. A single bud is then trained vertically, and the rest pruned away in the course of the summer. In such cases, the growth of the top being attended with a corresponding increase of fibrous roots, the tree at once becomes vigorous and healthy.

Peach trees, in our climate, are highly benefited by thus shortening-in annually, in the spring, one half, or thereabouts, of their entire growth of the previous summer, all over the heads of the trees.

Dwarf pears on quince also require a similar heading-in, annually each spring, so long as they continue to make a growth of scions.

Pruning to improve the form is applied mostly to ornamental trees, to which almost any desirable shape may be given by this means. If one part of a tree should outgrow another part, the former may be shortened-in in winter, and the shoots pinched off the next summer, till the sap is thrown in the right direction into the weaker branches, and the balance restored. When you desire the new shoots of a branch to take an upright direction, prune to an inside bud; while, if you wish an open, spreading top, prune to an outside bud, etc. Do not trim the stems or trunks of your trees (whether ornamental or fruit-trees) to bare poles, but allow the branches to form near the ground, as they naturally will in open ground. Your ornamental trees will thus be more beautiful, and your fruit-trees more likely to bear well.

Everything that is favorable to rapid and vigorous growth is unfavorable to immediate fruitfulness, hence pruning to induce fruitfulness is performed after vegetation has commenced. This checks the growth of the wood, impedes the circulation of the sap, and promotes the formation of fruit. Top pruning or shortening-in is the most common form of pruning to induce fruitfulness. Pruning the roots has a similar effect. The operation of root pruning is thus performed:

At a few feet from the trunk of the tree, varying the distance according to its size, dig a circular ditch around it, eighteen or twenty inches deep, cutting off all the lateral roots smoothly, close to the circular mass of earth in which the tree stands, removing the outer pieces of roots from the surrounding ground, as much as can be done conveniently. Fill up the trench with good, rich soil, and the tree will, in this country, generally be brought into a permanent fruit-bearing state. Repeating the operation annually, apples, pears, and other fruit-trees may be rendered productive dwarfs—even so as to be planted only six or eight feet apart. And, if at the same time we apply the *shortening-in* process above described, they may be kept in a beautiful pyramidal form, and rendered very profitable. This work may be done in autumn, in winter, or early in the spring.

Pruning ought to be performed with sharp tools. When the saw is used, the ends of the limbs should afterward be carefully pared with a knife. They should then be covered with some composition to protect them from the weather. Downing's *Gum-Shellac* is admirably adapted to this purpose. This preparation is made by dissolving a quantity of the gum in alcohol, so that the composition shall be of the consistency of thin molasses. The liquid should be kept in a wide-mouthed bottle, the cork of which should have a wire (running through it into the bottle), with a sponge attached to the end of it.

When the object of pruning is to promote the growth or improve the form of a tree, the operation is generally performed in the winter or early in the spring. Some, however, recommend pruning in May or June.

XV.—TRAINING.

In England, where fruit-trees generally are trained on walls and trellises, this process requires much time and labor on the part of the gardener. In this country it is hardly applied at all, except to vines and pear-trees, and to the latter only occasionally. The principal object of training is to produce from a certain number of branches a larger quantity of fruit than would grow on them if left in their natural state. This is effected by spreading and bending the branches so as to form numerous depositions of the returning sap, aided, where the tree is trained against a wall, by the shelter and reflected heat which the latter affords.

Directions for training the grapevine will be given under its proper head.

A new mode of training fruit-trees, practiced in the north of Russia, is well deserving of trial in the colder parts of New England, especially for cultivating the peach. A tree, one year from the graft, is headed down to two healthy, strong woodbuds. These are trained horizontally, about ten or twelve inches from the ground, to a south wall—perhaps the north side of a wall might do quite as well, in our more changeable climate. These *arms* are suffered to throw up vertical shoots, which become covered with fruit-spurs. These vertical shoots are kept shortened-in, to a length of not more than about one or two feet; and these, with the two horizontal arms from which they spring, and the short trunk of about ten to fourteen inches in length, constitute all there is of the tree above ground. The whole tree may be covered, through the winter, with two feet or more of soil heaped over it, with a deep bank of snow, or with straw, evergreen boughs, or the like.

Peaches, we are convinced, can be raised in this way where they fail entirely under ordinary treatment. It has hardly been fairly tried, however, in this country.*

---

* In preparing the condensed directions for transplanting, budding, grafting, pruning, training, etc., contained in this chapter, we have been deeply indebted to the valuable little manual of George Jaques, entitled "A Practical Treatise on the Management of Fruit-Trees," which we cordially recommend. See also **Barry's** "Fruit Garden" on these points.

VI.

THE KITCHEN GARDEN.

I consider the kitchen garden of very considerable importance, as pot-herbs, salads, and roots of various kinds are useful in housekeeping. Having a plenty of them at hand, a family will not be so likely to run into the error which is too common in this country, of eating flesh in too great a proportion for health.—Dr. Deane.

I.—ESCULENT ROOTS.

1. THE POTATO—*Solanum Tuberosum*.

THE potato, called by the French *la pomme de terre*, and by the Germans bie Kartoffel, is a native of the elevated equatorial regions of South America, and is still to be found in a wild state in the neighborhood of Quito and other places. It appears to have been introduced into North America and cultivated by the Virginia colonists as early as 1584. A few years later it was carried to England by Sir Walter Raleigh.

The varieties of the potato are numberless; and, while old sorts are constantly disappearing, new ones are every year coming into notice and taking their places. The duration of a variety is believed by Knight and others to be limited to fourteen years. Very few sorts continue to be cultivated even that length of time. New varieties are readily produced by planting the seed found in the balls. The operation is a simple one, and should more frequently be undertaken. There is no doubt but that varieties will yet be obtained in this way far superior to any yet known. We give in the Appendix full directions for producing and proving new sorts.

To give a list of the best varieties of the potato, were it practicable, would be useless. The best sorts of this year may be put in the second or third rank next year; besides, those to which the preference is given in New York may be considered inferior in Pennsylvania, and worthless in Georgia. Select for planting those varieties which experience has decided to be best adapted to your soil and climate, and to combine the various qualities required for table use.

In a cold, moist climate the potato thrives best in a light but rich loam. In a dry, hot climate a heavy loam is preferable, except for the earliest crop. Vegetable manure is best for the potato. Ashes and, where the soil needs it, lime, may be added with advantage, but, in garden culture, animal manures should, so far as possible, be avoided, as their use tends to make the tubers moist and waxy. The manure should be well rotted, and thoroughly mixed with the soil. Where you can not get sufficient manure of the right kind to properly enrich the whole soil, you may scatter it into the drill or hill to the thickness of three or four inches.

In garden culture, plant in drills made with the plow or the hoe, from eighteen to twenty-four inches apart (some varieties requiring more room than others), placing the sets about nine or ten inches apart in the drills. Cover to the depth of from four to six inches, according to the texture and condition of the soil—a heavy, moist soil requiring less depth of covering than a light and dry one.

In reference to the sets or seed, many and contradictory opinions prevail. Some contend that the largest-sized potatoes alone should be used for planting; others prefer a medium size; while many use those which are too small for the table. Some plant them whole, while others divide them, making from two to eight sets from each. Even scooped-out eyes have had their advocates. We have no room in this little work to advance arguments or adduce evidence, and must be content to give our opinion (as indicated by the mode pursued in our own garden), which, however, we believe to be based on sound theory and supported by general experience. *We choose for planting medium sized, fully matured, and every way sound and perfect tubers*—such as we would select for the table—and, if we have plenty of seed, plant them *whole*. If there be a deficiency of seed, or the price be very high, we divide them longitudinally, making two sets of each potato, and plant them with the eyes upward. They should be cut a week before planting; and it is a good plan to roll them in ground plaster of Paris or old slaked lime. Something may be gained in earliness by cutting the potato transversely in the middle, and planting only the seed end, which should be set upright in the ground.

In garden culture, potatoes should generally be hoed at least three times, to keep the weeds down, earthing them up a little each time; but if the ground be little infested with weeds. twice will do. The first hoeing should be given soon after the shoots appear above the surface of the ground. If they should be partially covered with earth by the operation, no harm will be done. Potatoes should never be hoed after the blossoms appear. Pinching off the flower-buds will considerably increase the crop of tubers.

Potatoes should not be harvested till the tops are mostly dead. They should be exposed to the sun only long enough to dry them for storage. Store in a dry cellar (when there is danger from frost), and cover them with sand or straw. When sprouts begin to grow, as they will toward spring, carefully rub them off. Their growth will greatly injure the quality of the tuber for table use. Those intended for seed should be frequently turned over to prevent premature growth.

Of the *potato rot*, as it is called, little can be profitably said. Its cause and remedy are yet to be made known. As preventives, a dry soil, the use of lime and ashes, the absence of fresh stable manure, early planting, and new, healthy varieties are recommended. For arresting the disease, cutting off the tops on the first appearance of the blight is sometimes effectual.

Potatoes for an early crop are planted in this country from the first of January to the first of May, according to the climate and season. In the latitude of New York they may in ordinary seasons and in favorable situations be put into the ground from the tenth to the twentieth of March.

For raising *Irish* potatoes (as they are invariably called there) at the South, the plan published by Mr. Peabody of the *Soil of the South* is undoubtedly a good one. We have tried the same mode with fair success at the North, using here, however, less straw. Mr. Peabody's directions are substantially as follows:

"As soon after Christmas as possible, plow or spade up the plot of ground designed for the potato patch, and lay it off in furrows two feet apart, and eight or ten inches deep. Fill these furrows with decomposed straw or leaves. Divide each potato once, and place the sets, cut side downward, upon the straw; now level the ridge made by the furrow, covering seed, straw, and all, and then scatter straw evenly over all to the depth of eighteen inches or two feet. No further culture is required. In the dryest seasons the yield will be greater than when planted in the ordinary way. Many have failed in this mode of culture because they have not applied half straw enough."

2. THE SWEET POTATO—*Convolvulus Batatas.*

This best of all esculent roots belongs to the *convolvulaceæ* or bind-weed family. It is a native of the East Indies, but grows in perfection in our Southern States. It is raised in large quantities in Delaware and New Jersey, and even farther north, but the quality of the tubers is inferior to that of those produced at the South.

A dry, loamy soil, inclining to sand, is best for the sweet potato. It should be well manured. The special manures indicated by an analysis of the root are potash and the phosphates.

Where the season is sufficiently long to mature it, the sweet potato may be propagated by cutting the seed into slips, and planting them where they are to grow; but at the North the sprouts must always be started in a hot-bed. Place the potatoes in the bed early in April, covering them three or four inches deep. They will throw up sprouts in three or four weeks. When these are about four inches above the surface, they may be separated from the parent tuber and planted out in hills, leaving the latter to put out other shoots for future plantings. The hills or beds should be about four feet apart, and raised from six inches to a foot above the common level of the ground. Some make continuous ridges four feet apart, and plant the sprouts on the top, about a foot asunder. They must be kept free from weeds till the vines cover the ground. They are fit for gathering when the vines are dead. They are very difficult to preserve through the winter. A careful seclusion from air and light, the absence of frost, and absolute dryness are essential to their preservation. The best way to cook them is by baking.

3. THE TURNIP—*Brassica Repa.*

The French call the turnip *le navet*, and the Germans ber Stecrübe. It has been in cultivation at least two hundred and fifty years. There are many varieties. For early crops the Purple-Top Strap-Leaved, Snow-Ball, and the Early Yellow Dutch are to be preferred. For later sowing we would name Robertson's Golden Stone, Stone Globe, Golden Ball, Sweet German, the Purple-Top Swede, Skirving's Improved Swede, the White French, River's Swede, and Ashcroft's Swede. Skirving's Improved is, perhaps, the best of the Swedes.

Turnips thrive best in a rich, sandy loam. Bone-dust, lime, ashes, and plaster of Paris are good special manures. Sow in drills about two feet apart. Thin out the plants gradually to six or eight inches apart. They may be readily transplanted if desired. Stir the soil well, and keep the weeds in subjection. English turnips do well sown broadcast. Sow the early sorts from February to May, according to climate and season. Other sowings may be made in July and August for winter use. In the latitude of Georgia they may be sowed as late as October. Harvesting should be deferred till the approach of cold weather—or at the South they may remain in the ground all winter.

4. THE BEET—*Beta Vulgaris.*

The beet (Fr. *Beterave*) is a native of the south of Europe. It takes its name from the form of its seed-vessel, which resembles the Greek letter *beta* (β). The best varieties are Extra Early Turnip or Bassano, the Early Turnip, the Long Blood, and the London Blood.

A light soil, well enriched with manure and well broken up, snits the beet. It will grow in almost any soil. Sow in drills a foot apart and about an inch deep. Drop the seeds three inches apart, cover smoothly, and press the earth firmly upon them. Radishes may be sown in the same bed, as they will be removed before the beets are ready for thinning. Keep the ground well stirred and free from weeds, and thin the beets to about six inches apart. Sow the early sorts in March, or the first of April, in the latitude of New York. The later varieties may be sowed in May or June.

In gathering your beets, cut off the leaves an inch or two above the collar, and be careful not to break or bruise the root. To preserve them through the winter, store in a dry cellar. They keep best packed in sand.

5. THE CARROT—*Daucus Carota.*

The carrot (Fr. *Carotte*) is supposed to have been introduced into Europe from the island of Crete. The Early Horn is the most forward in ripening, and fully equal in color and flavor to any other sort. It may be sown from the middle of April to the middle of July in the latitude of New York, and in the South from January to April inclusive. The Long Orange grows very long and large, but is not equal in flavor to the Early Horn. The Altringham is a bright-red variety, of an excellent flavor, and keeps well for winter use. It is not quite so hardy as the other sorts.

The carrot succeeds best in a light, rich soil. It must be deeply dug and well broken up, or the roots will grow forked and crooked. Choose a warm spot and a calm day for sowing. Sow in drills half an inch deep, and for the Early Horn nine inches apart. For the other varieties twelve inches apart is better. Radishes may be sowed in the same bed. Stir the ground frequently and deeply, and thin out to from three to six inches apart. The latter is the proper distance when the plants are to be left to grow to the full size. The directions for preparing and preserving them for winter use are the same as for beets.

6. THE PARSNEP—*Partinaca Sativa.*

This very palatable and exceedingly nutritious root is a native of Sardinia, and in its wild state is said to be poisonous. In French it is called *le panais.* The best variety is the Sugar or Hollow Crown. Soil and culture the same as for the carrot and beet. Bone-dust and ashes are the special manures most likely to be required. Late in the fall take up as many as you need for winter use. The rest may remain in the ground, as frost seems to improve their flavor. In the South, lift them as wanted during the winter.

7. SALSIFY—*Tragopogon Porrifolium.*

The Salsify, or Oyster Plant, is a native of England, and is less known in this country than it deserves to be. Sow and cultivate the same as the parsnep. A portion of the crop may remain in the ground all winter. Prepared and cooked according to the following directions, it will be found to resemble the oyster in flavor:

Scrape the roots slightly, soak them in water for an hour, and then boil till quite tender. Now let them drain for a short time; meanwhile make a thick batter with white of eggs beaten up with a little flour. Grate the roots tolerably fine, press them into flattened balls of the size of an oyster, dip them in the batter, roll them into grated crackers, and fry them in a pan till brown. Another way is to parboil, cut in slices, and fry either with or without the batter. Try it.

8. JERUSALEM ARTICHOKE—*Helianthus Tuberosus.*

This plant is a species of sunflower, and is occasionally cultivated for its tuberous roots. It may be planted like the potato, and will grow anywhere.

II.—THE LEGUMES.
THE PEA—*Pisum Sativum.*

This universally cultivated plant originated in the south of Europe. The catalogues of the seedsmen embrace twenty or more varieties, and new sorts are constantly appearing. Of the early peas, the earliest at present known is Dillisotone's Early, and next, perhaps, and better known, is Early Dan O'Rourke. Hovey's Extra Early and Landreth's Extra Early, improved American varieties of great merit, are nearly if not quite as early as the Dan O'Rourke. Champion of Paris, Champion of England and Advancer, all excellent sorts, are a little later. Tom Thumb is an early variety remarkable for its extreme dwarfness, seldom rising over twelve inches in height.

Blue Imperial, King of the Marrows, and the Ne Plus Ultra are among the best to succeed the early crops. To follow the last-named, for late crops, British Queen or Mammoth; Carter's Victoria, Competitor, Knight's Tall Green Marrow and Champion of Scotland may be recommended.

It is well enough to give the new varieties yearly introduced a fair trial, as sorts superior to any now named may be originated; but the claims set up for new kinds by interested propagators are often unfounded and preposterous.

For the early sorts a light, warm, dry, and moderately rich soil is to be preferred. If manure be used, it should be well rotted; but it is better to take ground which has been made sufficiently rich by a previous year's manuring. The later and taller varieties require a heavier soil.

You may plant your early peas at almost any time when the ground is not actually frozen, covering with mulch if necessary. In the latitude of New York they may generally be planted before the twentieth of March—sometimes on the first—and require no protection. In the South, any time from January to March will do. Plant in double drills, from six to nine inches apart, according to the variety. The rows should be three feet apart for the smaller sorts, and from four to six for the larger. Cover the early kinds one inch deep, and the late an inch and a half. The sticks should be from two and a half to three feet for the early sorts. The British Queen reaches the height of five or six feet, and Knight's Tall Marrow is a still loftier grower. When the plants are about two inches high, stir the ground well, and earth them up a little. Repeat this operation several times before setting the sticks or brush, which should be done when the peas are from six to eight inches high. If the season be dry, watering will much increase the crop. Topping off the points of the vines soon after the first blossoms appear will hasten the growth of the fruit. The smaller kinds of early peas may be planted about half an inch apart in the drills, and the later and larger sorts from a third of an inch to an inch. It is well to soak them twenty-four hours before planting.

To forward an early crop, plant in lines from east to west, and stick a row of cedar, spruce-fir, or other evergreen branches along the north side, sloping so as to bend over the plants at one foot or eighteen inches from the ground. These protect them from cold rains and at the same time leave them open to the full influence of the sun. Behind this temporary hedge there should be a close board fence, a brick or stone wall, or a high close hedge.

Beans, cabbage, lettuce, radish, or celery may be planted between the rows of peas, especially of the earlier sorts.

Peas which are to be ripened or dried should not be sowed before the tenth of June, as all earlier crops will be infected with bugs.

2. THE BUSH-BEAN—*Phaseolus Vulgaris.*

The bean is believed to be a native of India, whence it was brought to England near the close of the sixteenth century. In one form or another it is universally esteemed. Of the common Bush, Snap, or Kidney bean there are many varieties. Among the best are the Early Mohawk (a very hardy sort), Early Six Weeks, Early Valentine, Early Dun Colored, Early Pink Eye, Early White Marrow, Late Valentine, and the Royal Kidney. The tender pods of all these sorts are eaten as string-beans; but they are also excellent taken from the pods after they are nearly or quite grown, and boiled and prepared in the same way that Lima beans usually are. For this mode of cooking we prefer the Pink Eye and the Early White Marrow.

Beans will thrive in almost any soil; but for an early crop it should be light and dry. If the ground be too wet, they are liable to rot. Bone-dust, ashes, and super-phosphate of lime are very useful as manures. The bean is destroyed by a slight frost, and can therefore seldom be planted, in this climate, till the middle of April, or even later. Plant once in two weeks till the last of August, to keep up a succession for the table. Plant in drills from eighteen inches to two feet asunder, dropping the beans two inches apart, and covering them about an inch deep. Give them frequent and deep hoeings, drawing a little earth to the stems.

The Small White bean, so extensively used in New England for baking, may be planted in any vacant spots in the garden in June or July, and will require no care except to keep the weeds down.

3. THE COMMON POLE BEAN—*Phaseolus Multiflorus.*

Of the common running or pole bean (*le haricot à rames* of the French), the best varieties are the Dutch Case Knife, London Horticultural, White Cranberry, and Scarlet Runner. Plant in hills from the first to the middle of May, and give them poles when they begin to put forth runners; or, better, set the poles first, and plant the beans around them. Or they may be planted in drills along a border, or on each side of a walk, and trained on a slight trellis of laths and lines, and thus be made ornamenta. as well as useful.

THE KITCHEN GARDEN.   83

4. THE LIMA BEAN—*Phaseolus Limensis.*

Of the *Phaseolus Limensis* there are three varieties cultivated in the United States—the Green Lima, the White Lima, and the Carolina Sewee. The White Lima is to be preferred. It requires a strong, rich soil, and should not be planted till settled, warm weather, as the seed is very liable to rot in the ground if the weather be cool.

Beans of all kinds can easily be preserved for winter use, with very little loss of flavor. You have only to pick them in the same state as when for immediate use, and dry them thoroughly in the sun. You may have green beans all the year with very little trouble.

5. THE PEA-NUT—*Arachis Hypogea.*

This plant, known also as the pindar ground pea and ground nut, is a *legume* bearing its seed under ground. It is cultivated extensively in some of the Southern States as a field crop, but a few hills may find place in the Southern garden. Make the hills two and a half or three feet apart, and drop three or four of the shelled seeds in each. Cover them two inches deep. Thin the plants to two in a hill, and keep the ground free from weeds.

III.—THE CABBAGE FAMILY.

1. THE COMMON CABBAGE—*Brassica Oleracea.*

The cabbage (Fr. *chou pomme*) is one of the most ancient of garden vegetables. It is mentioned by Pliny as being much esteemed in his times. It was a favorite with the Romans, who probably introduced it into England. Its varieties are almost numberless. Of the common cabbage, the following are the most desirable: Early York (very early, and of a delicate flavor), Atkins' Matchless (small but tender and delicately flavored,) Large York, Early Drumhead, Winningstadt (intermediate in season), Bergen Drumhead, Large Drumhead, Marblehead Mammoth, Champion of America, Mason, and Stone-Mason (late). The Bergen Drumhead, Marblehead Mammoth and Stone-Mason grow to a very large size, and are favorites with market-gardeners. The large Red Dutch is one of the latest of cabbages. It is chiefly used for pickling. The Utrecht Red is a smaller red cabbage of fine quality.

The cabbage will grow in any soil sufficiently enriched and properly prepared. It must be plowed or dug deeply, and well pulverized. Common salt, ashes, plaster of Paris, and bone-dust may be used with advantage, as the plant abounds in sulphur, phosphorus, soda, and potash. Animal manures may also be freely used.

For producing early spring cabbages, various plans are pursued. The best mode for general adoption is the following: About the tenth of September, for southern New York (a little earlier for New England, and a little later for the South), sow seeds of the Early York, Nonpareil, or Vanack in a seed-bed of rich, light soil. If the weather be dry, sprinkle the bed with water a few times, to promote germination. When large enough to transplant, set them quite thickly in a cold frame or walled pit, for protection during the winter. The frame or pit may be covered with boards, adding straw, if necessary, when the frost is severe. Give the plants air whenever the weather will permit. Carefully exclude the rain, as too much moisture will injure them. Early in the spring transplant into the compartment of the garden designed for them. Where the winters are not too severe, they may be brought forward a week or two earlier by planting them out in the fall in good, rich soil, previously prepared by throwing it up into high ridges, running east and west, and about two feet apart. On the south sides of these ridges set out the plants one foot apart. They will then be shielded from the north winds, and receive all the benefit of the sun. When the weather becomes severe, cover with straw, laying it across the ridges. This may be removed whenever mild weather returns. Early cabbages may also be obtained by starting the plants in a hot-bed, sowing in February or March.

In transplanting cabbages, especially the early ones, the **growth of which it is important not to check, take them up** with a trowel, removing considerable earth with them, in order not to disturb their roots.

For summer, autumn, and winter use, sow Early Dutch and Drumhead in April and May. Transplant into rows two feet apart, and eighteen inches apart in the row. Give the plants a copious watering the evening previous to taking up, and water again after setting out. The whole secret of their after-culture lies in *frequent and deep hoeing*. Hoe while the dew is on, if practicable. Never strip off the lower leaves.

To preserve cabbages in perfection through the winter, the following is the best mode with which we are acquainted: As late in the fall as the weather will permit, dig trenches eighteen or twenty inches apart, parallel to each other, and of any convenient length. Now dig out your cabbages with a spade, and transplant them into these trenches as close together as they will stand, covering root and stem to the lower leaf. Around this bed raise a kind of frame with old posts, rails, or boards and earth, making it a little higher at one side than the other, and high enough at the lower side to prevent its roof or covering from coming in contact with the cabbages. Across this frame place poles, lath, or narrow boards, and cover the whole thickly with straw, bean haulm, corn-stalks, or any material of that sort. In this way you may have cabbages up to April, of as fine a flavor as when transplanted into the trenches. A few may be transplanted into a similar trench in the cellar, where, of course, they will require no covering.

2. SAVOY CABBAGE—*Brassica Oleracea Sabauda.*

This member of the great cabbage family takes its name from Savoy. It differs from the common cabbage in the wrinkled character of its leaves. There are only two varieties worthy of culture—the Curled and the Drumhead. The former is to be preferred for family use. It is superior in delicacy to the common cabbage. Cultivation the same as the winter varieties of the latter.

Brussels Sprouts (*chou de Bruxelles*) is considered a subvariety of the Savoy. It is a celebrated vegetable in Europe, but is not often seen in American gardens. Sow in April, and transplant in June into rows eighteen inches apart. Cultivate like cabbages. The stem grows to the height of two feet or more, and is crowned with numerous little heads of from one to two inches in diameter. After they have been frosted (which is necessary to their perfection), they may be gathered. To prepare them for the table, soak an hour in cold water; boil about twenty minutes; drain; season to the taste; stew gently in a sauce of cream or floured butter, stirring them constantly. They are sometimes served with tomato sauce. They may also be cooked simply as cabbages, and eaten with meat.

3. BORECOLE—*Brassica Oleracea Fimbriata.*

This plant, also called German Greens (Fr. *chou vert*) and Scotch Kale, is one of the most delicate and valuable of the cabbage tribe. It has large, wrinkled leaves, forming an open head or stool. It is perfectly hardy, frost only improving it. It remains green and eatable all winter, requiring only a slight protection in the Northern States, and none at all at the South. For winter and spring greens it is unequaled. Sow and cultivate the same as the cabbage. No garden should be without it.

4. THE CAULIFLOWER—*Brassica Oleracea Botrytis.*

The cauliflower is a kind of cabbage, with long, pale green leaves, surrounding a mass or head of white flower-buds. The French very appropriately call it *le chou-fleur*. It was introduced into England from the island of Cyprus. There are only two true varieties—the Early and the Late.

The cauliflower requires a very rich soil and careful culture. For the early spring or summer crop, sow the seed from the first to the twentieth of September, in a properly prepared seed-bed. When the plants are two inches high, transplant them into a bed of very rich, light soil, three inches apart each way, so that they may grow firm and stocky for removal to their final place of growth. This should be a bed of the richest light earth, two feet deep, and one third of it well-decomposed manure, surrounded by a frame or wall, and covered with glass or shutters. An open exposure, sheltered from the northwest, is essential. The bed should be prepared about the first of October, to give it time to settle. Into this bed remove your plants about the middle of October (or earlier in a very cold climate), setting them eighteen inches apart. Take them up carefully with a trowel, and in planting press down the soil pretty firmly upon the roots, giving it a gentle watering at the same time. No further watering will be required till spring. Protect the plants carefully against frost, covering the sash or shutters with matting or straw if necessary; but do not neglect to give them the air every mild, clear day. They must not be left open to the rain, as too much moisture will cause them to "damp off," as it is called, at the neck. When the weather becomes warmer in spring, copious waterings may be given. Soap-suds and other liquid manures are applied with advantage. Early lettuce may be sowed in the same bed between the rows of cauliflowers.

When a cauliflower has attained its full size, which will be indicated by the opening of the border, cut off the head with several inches of the stem, and most of the leaves, these being taken off, however, before cooking.

For the autumn crop sow in April, transplant into rich soil, two feet apart. Hoe frequently and deeply, and if the season be dry, water copiously. They must not suffer from drouth. You may know when they need water by the drooping of the leaves. The hills about the plant should form a hollow basin to retain the moisture.

The cauliflower is a wholesome and nutritious vegetable, and should be more generally cultivated. To cook, soak an hour in cold water with a handful of salt in it; then boil till tender in milk and water, taking care to skim the surface, so that not the least foulness may fall on the flower. It may be served up with sauce, gravy, or melted butter.

5. BROCCOLI—*Brassica Oleracea Botrytis Cymosa.*

This plant is similar to the cauliflower, from which it is supposed to have originated. It differs from the latter in its undulating leaves, its larger size, and its color. It is also a hardier plant, but not so delicate in flavor. Grange's Early White and the Purple Cape are the best varieties. White recommends the latter for the South. Sow in April or May, and treat in the same manner as the late cauliflower. They will commence heading in October. To have them during the winter, in a northern climate, they must be pitted in a cellar or shed. South of Virginia they need little, if any, protection.

The turnip cabbage (kohl rabi), *Brassica napo brassica,* and the turnip-rooted cabbage, *Brassica caulo rapa,* may be added to our list, although they are little cultivated. The former, of which the *Char Navet de Laporie,* from France, is the best, requires the same cultivation as the cabbage, and the latter should be treated like the Swede turnip. The Green Stemmed and the Purple Stemmed are recommended.

IV.—SPINACEOUS PLANTS.

1. SPINACH—*Spinacea Oleracea.*

This vegetable—*l'epinard* of the French—is a native of Spain, and is extensively cultivated on the continent of Europe. It is excellent for greens, and should receive more attention than has yet been accorded to it in this country. There are three varieties—the Prickly-Seeded, the Round-Seeded, and the Flanders. The first is best for sowing in the fall for winter crops, in a cold climate; but for spring sowing, and for a mild climate, the second is to be preferred. The Flanders is little known in this country, but is said to be superior to either of the other sorts.

Spinach requires a rich soil. Sow in drills a quarter of an inch deep and nine inches apart. For winter and early spring crops, sow about the last of August, and again about the middle of September. For summer use, sow from the first of

April to the twenty-fifth of May. Select an open situation. If the soil be light and dry, it must be trodden down or rolled with a roller on sowing. Thin out the plants to nine inches apart. Hoe frequently and thoroughly. The winter crop will require the protection of a thin layer of straw during the severe weather.

2. New Zealand Spinach—*Tetragonia Expansa*.

This is an annual plant from New Zealand. It furnishes a good substitute for spinach during the summer, when the latter fails, but, as it requires to be forwarded in a frame or hot-bed, is hardly worth the trouble it costs in a northern climate.

Garden Orache (*atriplex hortensis*) and Garden Patience (*rumex patienta*) are sometimes used in the place of spinach, but are only worthy of a mere mention here.

V.—ASPARAGINOUS PLANTS.

1. Asparagus—*Asparagus Officinalis*.

The asparagus plant is a native of the sea-coasts of Great Britain. The varieties may be reduced to two—the Green Top and the Purple Top.

Asparagus is propagated only by seed, but in forming a new bed it is the most economical plan to procure plants two or three years old from some nurseryman or gardener. If you purpose to raise your own plants, sow early in the spring, in a seed-bed formed of rich, sandy loam, in drills an inch and a half deep, and eighteen inches from row to row, pressing the earth firmly upon the seed. Keep the bed free from weeds by frequent hoeing. About the first of the following November spread stable litter or something of the sort over the ground, to keep the young plants from the frost.

For the permanent bed, a rich, sandy loam is best. Select, if possible, an open situation and a warm southern exposure. Trench or spade deeply, digging in a plenty of manure, as the soil can hardly be made too rich or too deep. Over a plot forty feet long and twenty feet wide (which will be large enough for a moderate family), sow from fifty to a hundred pounds of salt, incorporating it with the soil to the depth of four or five inches. The ground having been well pulverized and leveled, lay it off into beds about four feet wide, with alleys two feet wide between them. Drive a stake at each corner. This work should all be done toward the end of March. Now cut a small trench or furrow six inches deep, lengthwise of the bed, and about nine inches from the edge. Take up the plants very carefully from the seed rows, and set them in this trench or furrow, nine inches apart, with the crown of the root two inches below the surface, and cover them at once. Proceed in the same manner with the whole, making the rows twelve or fourteen inches apart. A damp day should be chosen for the operation, which must be carefully and skillfully performed. Keep the weeds down during the summer, and on the approach of severe weather cover the beds to the depth of three or four inches with rotten manure. The first two years the plants are permitted to run up to stalks, that strong crowns may be formed at their base for a future crop. The winter dressing of manure must be continued while the bed lasts, the tops being cut off and removed each fall. In the spring, so soon as the frost will permit, loosen the surface of the beds with a manure fork, introducing it three or four inches into the soil, and turning it up, being careful not to injure the crown of the roots. A full crop may be expected the fourth year after planting, or at the South a year earlier. Cut when about four or five inches above the surface. The shoot should be cut off slantingly about three inches below the surface, using a long, sharp-pointed knife. The cutting should never extend beyond the middle of June.

With good culture, an asparagus bed will continue productive for fifteen years, but too many shoots must not be cut from it, nor the cutting prolonged beyond the time we have named.

2. Sea Kale—*Cramba Maratima.*

This plant is closely related to the cabbage, and is called by the French *le chou marin.* It is easily cultivated, and we recommend our readers to try it.

Sea Kale flourishes best in a sandy soil, well enriched with decomposed vegetable manure and a top-dressing of salt. Sow the seed in March or April, watering the bed freely if the weather be dry. Thin out the plants gradually to two or three inches apart, keeping the bed free from weeds by frequent hoeing. In November cover the crowns of the plants with a few inches of earth. In the spring, prepare beds as for asparagus, and remove your plants in a similar manner, setting them about two feet apart, and covering the crown of the root about two inches deep. Water occasionally, if the season be dry, and hoe frequently. Allow no plants to go to seed. Early in November give the bed two inches of well-rotted manure, forking it over lightly at the same time. Now cover the crowns of the plants with three or four inches of light soil, or with pure sand if you can readily procure it. The bed being thus finished, cover the crowns of the plants with large pots or boxes, sinking them one or two inches in the ground, and carefully stopping any holes in them. Then procure a quantity of leaves from the woods, mix them with about the same quantity of warm stable manure, and cover the ground and boxes to the depth of twenty inches. In severe weather throw over this some dry litter or boards. The materials will come to a heat in two or three weeks; and in three or four weeks more it will be time to examine a pot or two, and when the plants are found to have sprouts from six to eight inches long, they may be cut for use. Remove a portion of the earth, and cut close to the crown, and then replace the box or pot, and the other materials, and other shoots will soon appear. The plants will continue in a vigorous state of growth for two months, giving you a supply for the table nearly the whole winter; and having your bed once formed, the forcing process just described may be repeated every year for fourteen or fifteen years. In the spring remove the covering gradually, digging in a few inches of the decayed material to strengthen the plant for a future crop.

To have sea kale without forcing, cover the plants early in the spring with eight or ten inches of sand, or fine, light soil. They will produce strong shoots, which, on clearing the ground around them, will be found to be of a clear white color; or they may be blanched by covering them deeply with oat-straw. They are useless unless well blanched. The shoots are cooked in the same way as asparagus.

VI.—ESCULENT BULBS.

1. THE ONION—*Allium Cepa.*

The onion is supposed to be a native of Asia. Its culture is of "inscrutable antiquity." The most useful varieties are the following: Red Dutch, Portugal, Strasburg, and Silver Skinned. The first two varieties named are very hardy and keep well, but are of too strong a flavor to suit a delicate taste; the last two are mild-flavored, but are not good keepers. The Silver Skinned is much used for pickling. For winter use we should choose the Strasburg.

The onion requires a light and friable, but rich and somewhat moist soil. The manure used should be well decomposed. It need not be deeply mixed with the soil, as the roots of the plant do not extend far below the surface. The whole must be thoroughly pulverized. The onion may be sowed so soon as the ground is in a condition to be worked in the spring. Sow in drills half an inch deep and nine or ten inches apart. After sowing, press the soil down firmly with a board. Keep the bed free from weeds, and stir the soil frequently, but not deeply. The onion should not be earthed up at all. It is better that the bulb should be formed entirely above the surface. They should be thinned out to two inches apart. This we consider the best mode of culture for the main crop.

For an early crop, sow the seed thickly in drills early in April; and when the bulbs have grown to the size of peas, lift them, and put away in an airy loft, to keep till the next spring, when set them in shallow drills, covering very lightly, if at all. They will be ripe in June or July. Soap-suds will not be wasted on the onion bed. Soot and ashes are also good for top-dressings.

To preserve the winter crop, pull in a dry day, put them under a shed or similar shelter to dry, and store in a loft where they can have plenty of air.

Onions may be sparingly eaten as a salad, but in the raw state are rather difficult of digestion. They are most wholesome boiled. Boil twenty minutes in water, with a little salt; then pour off the water entirely, and put in equal parts of hot water and milk, or skimmed milk alone, and boil twenty minutes more. They may be fried or roasted, but are more difficult of digestion in those modes of cooking.

2. THE TOP OR TREE ONION—*Allium Proliferum.*

This is a very hardy species, producing little bulbs at the top of its seed-stem. It is easily cultivated, comes early to maturity, and never fails to produce a crop. Plant the little bulbs very early in the spring, cultivating the plants in the same way as the other species. They will be ready for use in May or June. If large bulbs are required, the seed-stem must be broken off. Those not thus treated will produce seed for the next year. The top bulbs are considered excellent for pickling.

3. POTATO ONION—*Allium Tuberosum.*

This is supposed to be the kind of onion that was worshiped by the Egyptians. It is said never to produce either flowers or seed. It is propagated by offsets from the bulbs which should be planted in March, in drills eighteen inches apart. Set them three inches below the surface, and six inches apart. Keep the ground well stirred, but do not earth up the plants. They may be lifted by the top as they ripen, which will be shown by the drooping and withering of the leaves. In this climate they generally ripen in August. They are milder in flavor than those raised from the seed, but the bulbs are not so large.

4. THE SHALLOT—*Allium Ascalonicum.*

This plant—*l'eschalote* of the French—was introduced into

Europe from the town of Ascalon, in Syria. It is little used in this country, except by the French, but is to be preferred to the onion for some of the purposes of cookery. It is propagated by offsets, which may be planted in the spring, like the sets of the onion. Store in the same way as other onions.

5. The Leek—*Allium Porrum*.

The leek (Fr. *porreau*) is cultivated in France to an almost incredible extent, as it forms an absolutely essential ingredient of the soup on which the great body of the nation lives. The London Flag and the Musselburgh are improved varieties of the common leek.

The soil for the leek must be rich, deep, and well worked. The manure used must be well decomposed. Sow the seed thinly, in drills six inches apart and half an inch deep. Thin out the plants to an inch apart. When about eight inches high, transplant them into a bed previously prepared for them. Shorten the roots to about an inch from the plant, and cut off two inches or more from the extremity of the leaves. Dibble them in drills eight inches apart, and so deeply as the plant will admit, without covering the young leaves pushing from its center. Choose moist or cloudy weather for the operation; or, if dry, give the plants a copious watering. Hoe frequently, drawing the earth about the plants as they grow. They will be fit for use in October. The whole plant is much used in soups and stews, but the most delicate part is the blanched stems.

6. The Garlic—*Allium Sativum*.

The garlic is much used in southern Europe in sauces and salads; but its unpleasant odor will, we suspect, debar it from American tables almost entirely. The bulb is divisible into numerous parts called "cloves," by means of which it is propagated. Plant in the spring, in drills two inches deep and six inches apart. When the bulbs are grown, take them up, clean them, and hang up in bundles. A very slight flavor of garlic is not unpleasant in soups and stews.

7. THE CHIVE—*Allium Schœnoprasum.*

This little alliaceous plant is sometimes used as a spring salad, or a seasoning for soups. It is easily propagated by dividing the bulbs or roots either in autumn or spring, and planting them in any bed or border. It will grow anywhere, but prefers a moist, rich soil. It is generally spoken of in the plural as chives or cives.

VII.—SALAD PLANTS.

1. LETTUCE—*Lactuca Sativa.*

The lettuce is appropriately placed at the head of the list of modern salad plants. There are two grand varieties of the lettuce—the Cabbage and the Cos or Upright—and numerous sub-varieties of each. The best of the cabbage sorts are the Early White Spring, White Gotte, Early Simpson, Summer Cabbage, Green Curled, Green Winter Cabbage, White Silesian, Ice Cabbage, India, Versailles and Victoria. The last will make good heads most of the summer. Of the Cos or Upright sorts the best are the White and the Green Paris.

A deep, rich, sandy loam suits the lettuce plant. Salt and ashes are useful as special manures. Sow as early as the season will permit, and repeat at different times during the spring and summer. For forcing in a hot-bed, the Early Cabbage should be chosen. For a winter crop, the Brown Dutch may be treated as we have recommended for Early York and Nonpareil cabbages. In the South it will need no protection.

The Cos lettuce must be sowed in September, protected during the winter, and transplanted out in the spring; or sowed in a hot-bed in February. The Cos varieties are improved by tying up the leaves several days before cutting, to blanch them.

Lettuce may be had through the winter, by sowing in October in a walled pit or frame, and protecting from frost by means of sash and straw mats, giving it air in warm, clear days. The earth should be within eight inches of the glass. Let the plants stand eight or ten inches apart. Water occasionally, and pick off all decayed leaves. It is a good precaution to surround the frame or pit with leaves or straw. Lettuce requires frequent and deep hoeings.

2. CRESS—*Lepidum Sativum.*

Of the garden cress there are two varieties—the Curled or Pepper-Grass and the Broad-Leafed. The former is generally preferred. It forms an excellent salad, and is easily cultivated. To have it early, sow in a hot-bed in February. In the open ground it may be sowed about the last of March. The soil should be light and warm for the first sowing. Sow in shallow drills, covering the seed very lightly. To have it during the season, sow every fortnight. It should grow rapidly, and be used when quite young and crisp.

Water-cress is found in brooks, in various parts of the United States, but is seldom cultivated. It also is excellent for a salad.

3. MUSTARD—*Sinapis Alba.*

This salad plant is cultivated in the same manner as cress. Cut the leaves for use while they are crisp and tender. Wash them carefully in water to free them from the sand that is liable to adhere to them. To have a constant supply, make frequent sowings. Table mustard is made from the seeds of *Sinapis nigra.*

4. ENDIVE—*Cichorium Endiva.*

This plant is a native of China and Japan, and is much cultivated in Europe. The variety generally used for salads is the Green Curled. The Broad-Leaved or Batavian is used for cooking, in stews and soups.

A light, rich soil is desirable for the endive. An open exposure should also be chosen. The best time to sow for an early crop is about the first of July in this climate. If sowed earlier, it is apt to run quickly to seed. In New England, however, it may be sowed by the middle of June. In the South, White says, sow in August and September. Sow in drills about four inches deep, and about a foot apart, and scatter sufficient earth upon the seeds to cover them, leaving the drills to be filled up in the process of future cultivation. Water once or twice, if the weather be dry. When about two inches high, thin out the plants to ten inches apart; and when nearly full grown, the leaves may be gathered up in a close, rounded form, and tied with a shred of matting or other soft string, drawing up a little earth to the stems at the same time. Choose a dry day for this operation, and tie up only a few plants at a time, or in proportion as they may be wanted for use. They may also be blanched by covering them with pots or boxes. It will take about ten days in warm weather, and about twenty in cold weather, for the leaves to blanch for use.

For late crops, sow about the end of July. To have endive in perfection during the winter, it must be moved into frames or walled pits about the first of November, taking up considerable earth with the roots. Give air and light in mild weather, but protect from heavy rains and severe frosts.

5. CELERY—*Apium Graveolens*.

Celery is a native of Great Britain, and in its wild state is a coarse, rank weed. Cultivation has made it one of the pleasantest-flavored of all salad plants. There are several varieties. The Red Solid is the hardiest, and is therefore generally preferred in the colder portions of our country; but the White Solid is crisper and more delicately flavored. Cole's Superb Red, Laing's Improved Mammoth Red, Seymour's Superb White, Boston Market and Turkey or Prussian are the kinds to be preferred

The soil best suited to the celery plant is a moist, rich vegetable mold, to which salt, ashes, and lime may be advantageously added, as special manures. The animal manures used must be thoroughly decomposed. The cultivation of celery embraces three distinct operations:

1. *Forwarding the Plants.*—Sow in a hot-bed from the first to the middle of March, or in a warm border in the open ground, at several different times, from the first of April to the tenth of May. The seed-beds should be of light and finely-pu.verized soil. Rake in the seeds lightly and regularly, and

in dry weather water moderately, both before and after germination. Liquid manures are very beneficial. Thin out the plants to half an inch apart.

2. *Stocking or Hardening.*—When the plants are two or three inches high, prick them out, at successive times, into intermediate beds, three or four inches asunder, watering if the weather be dry, and protecting from frost with boards or mats, if necessary. This intermediate bed should be made very rich with well-rotted manure. The plants that remain in the seed-bed should be shortened by cutting off their tops occasionally, to make them grow more stout, and watered frequently. Of the transplanted ones, those intended for late celery should also be cut off nearly to the crown several times, which will retard them and make them grow stout. When the plants are from six to twelve inches high, they must be transplanted into trenches previously prepared for them.

3. *Trench Culture.*—It is well to trench the compartment of the garden intended for the permanent culture of celery, as this process turns the richest soil to the bottom where it will be most needed for the nurture of the plant. In ground thus prepared, or at least deeply spaded or plowed, mark out the trenches a foot wide, and from three to three and a half feet apart; dig out each trench lengthwise, ten or twelve inches in width, and a light spit deep, that is, six or eight inches. Lay the earth dug out equally on each side of the trench; put at least four inches of very rotten dung into the trench, then pare the sides, and dig the dung and parings with several inches of the loose mold at the bottom. A pint of salt to every fifty feet of trench, thoroughly mingled with the soil, is recommended by some, and must, we think, prove beneficial. Trim the tops and roots of the plants, and then set them in single rows along the middle of each trench, allowing four or five inches distance from plant to plant. When this work is finished, give the plants water in plenty, and occasionally water them from time to time, if the weather be dry, and likewise let them be shaded, till they strike root and begin to grow.

Their after-culture consists in stirring the soil in the trench frequently with a small hoe, and watering copiously in dry weather. About the middle of August or the first of September, you may begin to earth up your plants for blanching. Tie the leaves together, or hold them tight with one hand, while you draw the earth, which must have been finely pulverized with the spade, around the stems, being careful not to cover the heart or center of the plant. You may now repeat this operation once in ten days, till the plants are fit for use; but this earthing-up must never be done when the plants are in the least wet. About the first of October earth up firmly and evenly, and with a decided slope from the base, nearly to the tops of the leaves. To take up the crop, it is best to begin at one end of a row, and dig clean down to the roots, which then loosen with a spade, and they may be drawn up entire, without breaking the stalks.

To preserve this plant during the winter, on the approach of frost take up a part of the crop, and lay it under sand for winter use. That left in the beds may be covered with litter, to be removed in mild weather. In planting, the white and red sorts may conveniently be mixed in the same trench, so that only one trench need be opened to obtain both.

6. THE RADISH—*Raphanus Sativus.*

The radish (Fr. *rave*, Ger. ritig) is a native of China. Of the numerous varieties, the Scarlet Short Top is the earliest and best. The Early Salmon, Red Turnip-Rooted, White Turnip-Rooted, White Summer, and Yellow Summer are all desirable sorts. For supplying the table in winter, the Black Spanish should be chosen.

Any deep, rich soil, well broken up, will do for the radish, but for early crops it is desirable to have it light, dry, and warm. Sow as early as the weather will permit, and for a continued supply repeat your sowings about once in two weeks through the season. The Black Spanish may be stored in the cellar, and will keep till spring.

7. Horse Radish—*Cochlearia Armoracia.*

The horse-radish grows best in a rich, moist soil, contiguous to water, but may be cultivated in almost any situation. It is propagated by sets from the root, which may be dropped into holes made with a dibble fifteen inches deep, in soil previously trenched or deeply spaded. Fill up the holes with fine earth. The plants should stand about ten inches apart. It may be planted either in spring or in November. In taking up the roots for use, you may leave a small portion at the bottom to serve as a new set. In the fall, lift enough for winter use, and leave the rest in the ground. It is an excellent condiment. The root is scraped into shreds, or grated fine, and eaten with vinegar.

8. Corn Salad—*Fedia Olitoria.*

This plant, sometimes called lamb's lettuce, is a native of Europe. It is in use to some extent as a spring salad. Sow from the tenth to the twentieth of September, in shallow drills six inches apart, and cover lightly, pressing the soil with a roller or a board. Keep it clear of weeds, and in November cover with straw, and pick the leaves as wanted. If the winter prove mild, it may be in use the whole season.

VIII.—THE CUCUMBER FAMILY

1. The Cucumber—*Cucumis Sativus.*

The cucumber is found wild in almost all warm countries, and is cultivated all over the world. The best varieties for forcing, or for an early crop in the open air, are the Russian and the Early Frame. London Long Green, Long Green Turkey, White Spined and Underwood's Short Prickley are good for the main crop. The White Spined is one of the best for table use, and Underwood's Short Prickly for pickling. The Gherkin, a French variety, is also much prized for the latter purpose.

A light loam is best for the cucumber, but it will grow in almost any soil, and is very easily cultivated. Make excavations for your hills a foot in diameter and fifteen inches deep, at the distance of six feet apart each way. Fill these holes with a rich mixture of well decayed manure and light soil, adding, if convenient, a little ashes, bone-dust, and common salt. Raise the hills a little above the level of the ground, by covering the manure mixture with loam, and make them slightly concave on the top. Plant about the first of May, or so soon as the season will admit, putting eight or ten seeds in a hill. When the plants have made rough leaves, thin them out to three in a hill. Nipping off the points of the vines to make them branch out will hasten their fruiting. Stir the ground frequently, and keep it free from weeds.

By forcing in hot-beds, cucumbers may be had in March or April; but few except professional gardeners care to undertake the somewhat delicate operation. They may be much forwarded, however, with little trouble, by the use of small boxes covered with glass, or by the following method:

Make a hole, and put into it a little hot dung; let the hole be under a warm fence. Put six inches deep of fine rich earth on the dung. Sow a parcel of seeds in this earth, and cover at night with a bit of carpet or sail-cloth, having first fixed some hoops over this little bed. Before the plants show the *rough* leaf, plant two into a little flower-pot, and fill as many pots in this way as you please. Have a larger bed ready to put the pots into, and covered with earth, so that the pots may be plunged in the earth up to their tops. Cover this bed like the last. When the plants have got two rough leaves out, they will begin to make a *shoot* in the middle. Pinch that short off. Let them stand in this bed till your cucumbers *sown in the natural ground come up;* then make some little holes in good, rich land, and, taking a pot at a time, turn out the *ball,* and fix it in the hole. These plants will bear a *month sooner* than those sown in the natural ground.

The second week in July is sufficiently early to plant for the fall and pickling crop, in the Northern States. In the South, the late planted crops are apt to be destroyed by the melon-worm.

Cucumber plants being climbers by means of their tendrils, some branchy sticks being placed to any advancing runners, they will ascend, and produce fruit at a distance from the ground, of a clean growth, free from spots, and well flavored.

2. The Melon—*Cucumis Melo*.

The melon is a tropical plant. Our finest varieties are supposed to have come from Persia and Affghanistan. In the south of Europe it is much used as an article of food by the lower classes. This use may be made of it with advantage by all classes in every country where it can be produced. Its varieties are numerous and constantly increasing. The common mush-melon, formerly so extensively cultivated, has generally given way to newer and better sorts, among which the Green Citron, Monroe's Green Flesh, Nutmeg, Christina (very early), White Japan, Prescott Cantaloup, (a French variety, Orange Cantaloup, Pine Apple and Skillman's Fine Netted are much esteemed. [For the water-melon which belongs to a different genus of the same natural order, see the next section.]

The melon should have the same soil and culture as the cucumber (except that it requires less moisture), and may be forced in a hot-bed, or forwarded by means of the glass-covered boxes in the same way. Never allow more than three plants to grow in a hill. Three will produce more fruit than six. As the fruit appears and attains the size of a walnut, place under each a piece of tile, slate, or glass to protect it from the dampness of the earth, and assist it in ripening by reflecting the rays of the sun.

IX.—THE PUMPKIN FAMILY.

1. The Pumpkin—*Cucurbita Pepo*.

The pumpkin is a native of India and the Levant. Numerous varieties are cultivated, some of which, originated by means of crossings with the squash, can hardly be distinguished from that vegetable. The Cashaw and Large Cheese are the best that we have tested. The Valparaiso is said to be a good variety, and the Honolulu, from the Sandwich Islands, and the *Citronelle de Touraine*, from France, are new varieties which we would recommend for trial.

The pumpkin will grow anywhere, and with almost any treatment. The culture indicated is the same as that for the melon or the cucumber. It should never be planted in a garden, if one has other ground in which it can be cultivated, as it will be sure to mix with and contaminate the squashes, melons, and cucumbers. New England farmers often raise a large crop by planting it with their field corn.

2. The Squash—*Cucurbita Melo pepo*.

This plant forms the connecting link between the pumpkin and the melon. It originated in the Levant. The best summer varieties are the Early Bush Scalloped, and the early Bush Crooknecked. Of fall and winter sorts the Boston Marrow is the best that has had a fair trial in various soils and climates. It is difficult now, however, to obtain it pure. The Hubbard, Custard, Green Striped Bergen, Egg-shaped, Turban, Honolulu, Mammoth and Yokohama are more recent and esteemed varieties; the Hubbard in particular being deservedly popular.

The soil and cultivation required are the same as for pumpkins, melons, and cucumbers.

3. Vegetable Marrow—*Cucurbita Succada*.

This is a species of gourd. It is cooked like the egg-plant when young; when half grown is used as squash; and when matured is used for pies. Cultivated the same as the squash.

4. The Water Melon—*Cucurbita Citrullus*.

The water-melon belongs to the same natural family or order as the musk-melon or cantaloup, but to a different genus or subdivision. It is a native of the tropics. The best varieties are the Black Spanish, the White Spanish, the Orange, the Mountain Sweet, the Carolina, the Texas, the Sugar White, the Syrian, and the Lawson. The Texas, the Sugar White (sometimes called Ice Cream), and the Syrian are all new varieties—new to us, at least. We have tested only the Texas, which is a superior sort.

The best soil for the water-melon is a light, sandy loam. Animal manures, well decomposed, bone-dust, and super-phosphate of lime should be used in moderate quantities. Cultivate the same as mush-melons or cucumbers. If grown near any other melon, squash, pumpkin, or cucumber, you can not be sure of pure seeds; and the same remarks will apply to the other members of the pumpkin and cucumber families.

X.—MISCELLANEOUS OBJECTS OF CULTIVATION.

1. INDIAN CORN—*Zea Mays*.

Every garden should have a few rows of Indian corn. The best garden sorts are the Extra Early and Eight-Rowed Sweet. New varieties, however, are constantly being produced.

To produce a good crop, Indian corn requires a good soil, and there need be no fear of giving it too much manure. A handful of ashes in each hill will benefit the crop. Plant in hills three feet apart, dropping five or six seeds in a hill, but thinning out to three or four at the first hoeing. If sufficient manure have not been mixed with the soil on plowing or digging, put a small shovelful in each hill. Plant so soon as the season will permit, and make successive plantings till August, if you desire a continuous supply. Hoe frequently, making broad, flat hills in earthing up the plants. Never plant more than one kind of corn in the same garden at one time, as it will mix and deteriorate. Change your seed every two or three years, getting it, if possible, from a more northern latitude.

2. THE TOMATO—*Solanum Lycopersicum*.

This plant belongs to the same family as the potato, and, like that vegetable, is almost universally esteemed and cultivated. It is a native of South America. There are several sorts—yellow and red. The Large Smooth Red and the Pear-

Shaped are the best for table use; but the Large Red, a scolloped or indented variety, is preferred for marketing, as it grows much larger. The Large Yellow differs in flavor from the Red, and is preferred by some. It comes into use somewhat earlier than the other sorts. It is much used for preserves. The Red Cherry-Shaped and the Yellow Cherry-Shaped are beautiful varieties, much used for pickling and preserving.

A light, loamy, and moderately rich soil is best for the tomato. To have early tomatoes, the plants must be started in hot-beds in March. Sow the seeds thinly, or thin out the plants soon after they come up. As they advance in growth, they may be transplanted into a cold frame or walled pit, protected by glass, where they may stand three inches apart to harden for final transplanting into the open air; or they may remain in the hot-bed till settled warm weather—from the middle to the end of May in this latitude—when they may be planted out into a warm, sheltered situation in the open air.

Those who have no hot-bed or pit may very easily forward a few plants in a large pot or box of rich earth placed in the kitchen window, sowing the seeds in it from the middle of March to the first of April. Two or three weeks may be gained in this way over those planted in the open air.

For early tomatoes, we form conical hills, a foot or more in height, and three feet apart, with a little well-rotted manure in the center. Into a little crater-like excavation in the summits of these hills we set the plants, which should be taken up with a trowel in such a way as not to check their growth. A still better way is to sow the seeds in small pots, and in transplanting to transfer the whole ball of earth from the pot to the hill. The advantage of the elevated hills is, that the earth around the roots is more readily and thoroughly warmed by the heat of the sun. For a late crop, or for a hot, dry climate, this plan is not to be recommended.

In the South a plenty of tomatoes may be raised from self-sown seed, which will spring up in the garden, and require little care; but if they are wanted earlier, the plants may be forwarded in a frame, or glass-covered boxes, sowing in February or the first of March, and transplanting when the frosts are over.

The earliest tomato plants should be shortened by taking off a few inches of their tops, so soon as they have set their first fruit, which will cause it to ripen more rapidly. Stir the soil frequently, and keep it free from weeds. Support the plants with branches or a little trellis, as you would peas, to keep the fruit from the ground. The plants, too, when supported, run less to vines, and are much more fruitful. One dozen plants properly supported will yield more and better fruit than three times that number will when allowed to rest on the ground.

3. THE EGG PLANT—*Solanum Melongena.*

This plant also, as may be seen by its botanical name, belongs to the potato family. It is a native of Africa. One of its varieties bears a white fruit resembling an egg, whence its name; but the purple varieties only are used in cookery. Of these the Large Prickley Purple produces the largest fruit, but the Long Purple is superior in flavor, and should be preferred for family use. They may be cultivated in the same way as tomatoes, but are rather more sensitive and tender. They may be sowed in April or the first of May in the open air, selecting a warm border, with a southern exposure.

The fruit is fit for use when two or three inches in diameter, and continues so till the seeds begin to change color. It is cut in thin slices, and fried, and is also sometimes used in stews and soups.

4. THE STRAWBERRY TOMATO—*Physalis Edulis.*

This is a newly-introduced annual plant, producing fruit of the size of a cherry. It is excellent eaten raw, made into pies or simply stewed. We have tried it and esteem it highly. It is cultivated the same as the tomato.

THE KITCHEN GARDEN. 107

5. THE PEPPER—*Capsicum Annum.*

The pepper is a tropical plant, but may easily be matured in the open air in this climate. It is better, however, to start the plants in a hot-bed, if practicable, and transplant in May or June. A warm situation and a light, rich soil suit it best. The plants should stand in rows eighteen inches apart, and a foot apart in the rows. Earth them up a little in cultivation. The Bell or Sweet is the best for pickling. The Cayenne is more used in its ripe state as a seasoning.

6. OKRA—*Hibiscus Esculentus.*

This vegetable, which belongs to the natural family of the cotton plant, was introduced from the West Indies, and is much cultivated in the Southern States. It is often called *gumbo* (Fr. *gombo*), and is used as an ingredient in stews and soups. It is cultivated to a considerable extent in New Jersey, and may be produced still farther north. A light, dry soil is best suited to it. Plant in drills three feet apart, scattering the seeds sparsely, and thin out to eighteen inches apart in the drill. It requires careful culture in a northern climate. Hoe very frequently, and keep the ground free from weeds. The pods must be gathered while quite green and tender. They may be cut into thin slices and dried for winter use.

7. RHUBARB—*Rheum Rhaponticum.*

Rhubarb, sometimes called pie-plant, although it has been cultivated to a small extent for centuries, and used for medicinal purposes, has not till quite recently been popularly appreciated. It certainly deserves a place in every garden. It is a native of Asia. Myatt's Victoria, Myatt's Linnæus, Buist's Early Red, and Downing's Colossal are all excellent varieties.

The soil for rhubarb should be a light loam, rich, and moderately moist. Bone-dust and guano are excellent special manures for it.

Rhubarb is propagated either by seeds or by division of the roots The latter is, in ordinary cases, the preferable method.

From ten to twenty plants will be sufficient for a moderate family, and these may be had by dividing one or two good roots, leaving an eye on each set. The ground should be prepared in October, by spading it at least eighteen inches deep, digging in a large quantity of well-rotted manure, and breaking it up thoroughly in the process. Allow it to settle, and then plant out your sets two feet apart in the row, and four feet between the rows. The crowns or eyes of the sets should be about two inches below the surface, and should be immediately covered with four or five inches of litter, leaves, or straw, to prevent the frost from throwing them out during the winter. In this way a crop may be obtained the first year after planting. The only after-culture required is to cover the ground with a few inches of manure every fall, digging it in with a fork in the spring, and keeping the ground free from weeds. If you wish to raise it from the seed, sow in the spring, transplant in the fall, and treat as just directed. You will get new varieties. It will be ready for the table in three years.

To make the edible leaf-stems of your rhubarb grow long and tender, place barrels, pots, boxes, and so forth over them when they begin to grow in the spring; but the air and light should not be entirely excluded, unless you wish to obtain a very mild flavor.

Rhubarb may easily be forced by inverting boxes, pots, or half barrels over the plants in the autumn, and afterward covering the whole with leaves and hot stable manure. The boxes, etc., should be placed over the plants before the ground shall be frozen, covering the ground with eight or ten inches of litter. The mixture of leaves and manure may be applied about the middle of January or the first of February. By merely covering your plants with six or eight inches of litter, leaves, or almost any dry material, you may forward them from seven to ten days, without further trouble.

To gather, remove a little earth, and, bending down the leaf you would remove, slip it off from the crown without breaking or using the knife. The stalks are fit to use when the leaf is half expanded. A larger, but inferior produce is obtained by letting them remain till in full expansion, as is practiced by the market-gardeners.

For use, peel the stem, and cut it into thin slices, and prepare as you would apples, for pies, tarts, or sauce. The English gardeners say, however, that it should be grown so quickly and be so tender as to require no peeling.

8. PARSLEY—*Apium Petroselinum.*

Parsley is but little cultivated in this country, and is principally used for garnishing. It is a native of Sardinia. The curled variety is most worthy of cultivation. Sow in April, in drills half an inch deep. It may form an edging around beds, borders, or compartments. From the long time the seed lies in the ground without germinating, it has been said that it goes nine times to the devil and back before it comes up! These journeys require ordinarily a month or more; but by soaking the seed twenty-four hours before sowing, the process is somewhat hastened. When the plants are three or four inches high, thin them out to six inches apart. With a little protection, it will grow all winter in this climate. It is esteemed by many as a seasoning for stews and soups.

XI.—SWEET HERBS, ETC.

Of the sweet herbs and medicinal plants more or less cultivated in gardens, a brief mention may properly be here made. They are generally planted in borders, and, to secure their peculiar virtues in perfection, should not be manured. Common garden soil is sufficiently rich for most of them. As a general rule, they are gathered when in bloom, and carefully dried in the shade.

1. *Shrubby Plants.* — Sage (*Salvia officinalis*); Winter Savory (*Saturica montana*); Rosemary (*Rosmarius officinalis*); Thyme (*Thymus vulgaris*); Rue (*Ruta graveolens*); Wormwood (*Artimesia absinthium*); Southernwood (*Artimesia abrotanum*); Lavender (*Lavendula spica*); Hyssop, *Hyssopus* (*offici*

nalis). The foregoing are all propagated by dividing the roots or by cuttings, and require little cultivation.

2. *Perennial Herbaceous Plants.* — Peppermint (*Mentha piperita*); Spearmint (*Mentha viridis*); Pennyroyal (*Mentha pulegium*); Balm (*Melissa officinalis*); Tansy (*Tanacetum vulgaris*); Burnet (*Poterium sanguisorba*); Chamomile (*Anthemis nobilis*); Elecampane (*Iluna helinium*); Fennel (*Anethum fœniculum*); Thoroughwort or Boneset (*Eupatorium perfoliatum*); Liquorice (*Glycirrhiza glabra*). These are all increased by parting the roots.

3. *Biennial and Annual Plants.*—Caraway (*Carum carni*); Coriander (*Coriandrum sativum*); Dill (*Anethum graveolens*); Anise (*Pimpinella anisum*); Sweet Marjoram (*Origonum majorana*); Summer Savory (*Saturega hortensis*); Sweet Basil (*Ocimum basilicum*); Bush Basil (*Ocimum minimum*); Angelica (*Angelica archangelica*); Borage (*Borago officinalis*); Horehound (*Marrubium vulgare*). All propagated by sowing the seeds.

VII.

THE FRUIT GARDEN.

But forward (in the name of God, graffe, set, plant, and nourish up trees in every corner of your grounds, the labour is small, the cost is nothing, the commoditie is great, yourselves shall have plenty, the poore shall have somewhat in time of want to relieve their necessitis, and God shall reward your good mindes and diligence.—Gerarde.

I.—A HINT OR TWO.

THE lamented Downing says: "He who owns a rood of proper land in this country, and, in the face of the pomonal riches of the day, raises only crabs and choke-pears, deserves to lose the respect of all sensible men. Yet there are many in utter ignorance of most of the delicious fruits of modern days—who seem to live under some ban of expulsion from all the fair and goodly productions of the garden."

Such persons are still to be found, but their number is rapidly decreasing; and there are few who will not thoughtfully heed the quaint exhortation which we have chosen for the motto of this chapter.

After what we have said in our third and fifth chapters (which see), but few introductory hints will here be necessary. Let it be remembered that the plot set apart for the fruit garden should be thoroughly prepared before you commence planting; that the soil should be very deep (not less than two feet), and thoroughly broken up; that it must be moderately rich; that it should be well drained if the nature of the soil require it, and that a careful attention to the directions we have given under the heads of transplanting, budding, grafting, pruning, etc., are essential to success. Specific directions, when necessary, will be given under the name of each species.

The best manure for fruit-trees in general is composed of about equal parts of meadow mud, muck, or peaty earth, and common stable manure. A small quantity of wood-ashes, say four bushels to a cart-load of manure, and charcoal-dust in about the same ratio, may be intermixed with this composition to great advantage. This manure should be prepared and well worked over several months before using. Half a peck of bone-dust and a little lime, well mixed with the soil when setting the tree, or from a peck to a bushel of old broken bones, put into the bottom of the hole before setting, will be of great benefit for years. The general manuring of a fruit garden should be performed in autumn; and the holes for setting out the trees in the spring may be dug and filled with compost and earth at the same time with decided advantage. Rotted chips make an excellent manure for fruit-trees, and may be applied either in the holes or as a top-dressing.

Having set out your trees properly in well-prepared ground, the work is rightly *begun*—that is all. If you stop here, you might as well have never commenced—nay, better; for in that case you would have saved the cost of the trees and the labor of preparing the soil.

After your trees are planted, *it is absolutely essential that the ground around them shall be kept loose and mellow by cultivation.* Cultivate potatoes or some other low-growing crop between the rows of trees, keeping an area of more than the diameter of the head around each tree clear from both the crop and the weeds. So far as the tree's roots extend, the ground belongs to them, but it must be kept well stirred.

Newly transplanted trees sometimes, especially if the season be uncommonly dry, require watering; but a little water poured on the surface never reaches the roots, and, by causing the ground to bake, does more harm than good. To produce the desired result, take off a few inches of the surface above the roots, apply the water, and then replace the earth.

Mulching is exceedingly beneficial to young fruit-trees. A sufficient quantity of straw, litter, leaves, or tan-bark applied in a circle covering the whole area of the roots will tend to retain the moisture, and render watering, in ordinary cases, unnecessary. In winter, where the climate is severe, it is still more useful, and often saves young trees from entire destruction by frost. A small space immediately about the trunk may be left uncovered, as it might harbor mice.

Every spring, wash the bodies of your young trees with soft soap, or one of the following preparations:

1. Dissolve one pound of potash in two gallons and one half of water, and then apply with a flat varnish-brush to the limbs and trunks of the trees. A varnish-brush is best, as the bristles are held together by tin bands on them, and not tied together with strings, as paint-brushes are, which the potash soon cuts through, and the brush falls to pieces.

2. Mix fresh cow-dung with urine and soap-suds, and with the mixture wash over the stems and branches of the trees as you would your room with whitewash, first cutting off the cankery parts, and scraping the moss and rough bark off the trunks of the trees before applying it. This is particularly applicable to large and old trees. It will destroy the eggs of insects, and prevent moss growing on the trunks.

The following, it is said, will prevent rabbits [and probably mice] from girdling fruit-trees:

Make a solution of, say half a pound of tobacco to three gallons of water. Mix with clay, a little lime, a little fresh cow-dung, and an ounce or two of glue or paste. Thicken to the consistency of thick whitewash, and put on with a brush.

The following is Bridgeman's recipe for causing trees to thrive:

"The ground where they are planted must be kept well cultivated. Young trees will not thrive if the grass be permitted to form a sod around them; and if it should be necessary to plant them in grass grounds, care must be taken to keep the earth mellow and free from grass for three or four feet distant around them, and every autumn some well-rotted manure should be dug in around each tree, and every spring the bodies of the trees washed or brushed over with common soft-soap, undiluted with water. This treatment will give a thriftiness to the trees, surpassing the expectation of any one who has not witnessed its effect."

II.—POMACEOUS FRUITS.

1. THE APPLE—*Pyrus Malus*.

All the varieties of the apple cultivated in this country have originated from the small, acid crab-apple of Europe. When cultivated with the same care and skill, it seems to succeed even better here than in its native localities. It is well worthy to stand at the head of all the fruits of temperate climates.

The apple-tree requires so much room that, in an ordinary garden, we must confine ourselves to a small number. The choice of our varieties, then, becomes an important affair, and, we may add, a difficult one. 1. In the first place, the varieties are very numerous, being numbered by thousands; 2. Sorts which are considered "best" in one section of our widely extended country, often prove inferior or worthless in another; 3. Soil, seasons, and modes of cultivation modify them greatly in the same climate; 4. Many new and apparently excellent varieties have not yet been sufficiently tested in reference to their adaptation to general cultivation; 5. Tastes differ widely in reference to flavors; 6. Some sorts are known by from three to twenty different names—every neighborhood, almost, having its local appellation for them. The reader must make the necessary allowances, as the circumstances of his locality, soil, and climate, and his own experience and observation may dictate; and none but the best should be allowed to occupy the limited space of a fruit garden.

Apple-trees should be planted thirty feet apart each way. As special manure, lime and ashes are indicated. About half a peck of each, applied annually to each tree, will be useful.

In common management, apple-trees in general bear only alternate years, which are called their bearing years; but by thinning out half the blossoms on the bearing year, you may easily have about an equal quantity of fruit every season. The bearing year may be entirely changed, by taking off all the blossoms or young fruit on that year, and allowing them to remain on the year which we wish to make the bearing one.

To preserve winter apples, gather them carefully by hand on a dry day; lay them gently by hand twelve or fourteen inches deep on the floor of a cool, dry room, and let them dry and season there for three weeks. Then carefully take them up, on a clear day, and pack them by hand in clean, dry barrels, filling the barrels so full that a gentle pressure will be necessary in order to head them up.

Smaller quantities may be put up in common, tight, wooden buckets. The best place for keeping them is a dry, airy room or cellar, of which the temperature ranges from 35° to 45° Fahr.

Thomas recommends packing alternate layers of apples and dry chaff mixed with a small portion of dry, pulverized lime. Apples for exportation are often wrapped each one separately in clean, soft, coarse paper, like oranges, and then put up in boxes or barrels, as above directed.

2. THE PEAR—*Pyrus Communis.*

The pear is second only to the apple in general utility, and superior to that fruit in delicacy and flavor. The pear was cultivated so long ago as the earliest times of the Romans, but it is only in modern times that it has reached a high degree of those delicious qualities for which it is now so much esteemed.

The best soil for the pear is a strong loam on a *dry* subsoil. It requires the same manure as the apple, with the addition of a larger quantity of ashes or potash in some other form. Set standard trees twenty feet apart each way; dwarfs from ten to twelve. Give bearing trees a moderate top-dressing of manure every autumn. Pear-trees require comparatively little pruning.

To dwarf the pear, it is grafted on Anger's quince stocks. The fruit produced by trees thus grafted is usually better than that of those on the pear stock. They also come into bearing sooner, and take up less room in the garden; but they are not so long-lived as on the pear. Quince-bottomed pear-trees must be very carefully cultivated. They will not bear neglect. They should be headed-in more or less every year.

Winter pears are all necessarily ripened in the house; and nearly all summer pears, and a very large proportion of the autumn varieties, are greatly improved by ripening them in the house also. As a general rule, take summer and early autumn pears from the trees, just when some of the earlier full-grown specimens begin to ripen. Gather them carefully by hand on a dry day, spread them on the shelves of your *fruit-room*, or upon the floor of a cool, dry chamber. Here they will ripen by degrees, and without further care.

Late autumn and winter pears should also be gathered very carefully by hand, in dry weather. Put them away very carefully, so as not to bruise or indent them in the least, in tight, clean wooden boxes, buckets, or barrels, and keep them in a cool, dry, airy room or cellar, of which the temperature shall be from about 38° to 45° Fahr. Examine them occasionally, and if they should be sweating, take them out carefully, and dry them on the floor, removing any that may have begun to decay, and re-packing them as before. About ten days before their usual time of ripening, bring them into a warm room. The result of this process will surprise, as well as gratify, one who has never tried it.

3. The Quince—*Cydonia Vulgaris*.

This tree is a native of Germany. It was cultivated, and its fruit much esteemed by the Greeks and Romans. It was used by them, as by the moderns, for preserving.

The quince is easily propagated from seeds, layers, or cuttings. A moist, strong soil suits the quince, as it grows naturally along the borders of streams. Set the trees ten feet apart, and give them the same cultivation as the apple and the pear. Little pruning is required, except to improve the form of the head.

III.—STONE FRUITS.

1. THE PEACH—*Persica Vulgaris*.

The peach derives its name from Persia (It. *persica*, Fr. *pecher*), from which country it originated. It is now cultivated to a greater extent in the United States than in any other country in the world. In its perfection, it does not yield the palm to any other fruit. A Seckel would hardly tempt us to lay aside a Rareripe.

Set peach-trees about sixteen feet apart each way. Bone-dust and wood-ashes are the special manures most likely to be serviceable to them.

The peach is somewhat dwarfed and rendered hardier in a northern climate by grafting on a plum stock. It requires but little pruning, except "shortening-in," which should be done early in the spring every year so long as the tree lives. Cut off half the last year's growth over the whole outside of the tree. This method will increase the size and value of the fruit, and cause the tree to live and continue in bearing several years longer than under the old system.

Every one who cultivates peaches should preserve a quantity for winter use, either in air-tight cans or by drying.

2. THE NECTARINE—*Persica Vulgaris Lævis*.

The nectarine is only a distinct accidental variety of the peach with a smooth skin. The well-known Boston Nectarine originated from a peach-stone. Soil, manure, and culture are the same as for the peach. It is a beautiful fruit, but, on account of its liability to be destroyed by the curculio, is little cultivated. Good crops are rare.

3. THE APRICOT—*Armeniaca Vulgaris*.

The apricot is native of central Asia, and is the most beautiful of all the stone fruits. It ripens about midsummer, or immediately after the cherries. In this country it may be cultivated in the open air, in almost any locality south of Massachusetts. Like the nectarine, it is very liable to be destroyed by the curculio. Let the poultry or pigs have access to the trees when the fruit begins to drop.

The apricot is generally budded on the plum stock. It should be placed on a north, east, or west aspect, and be protected by a wall or fence. It requires no pruning.

4. THE PLUM—*Prunus Domestica.*

Several varieties of the plum are found growing wild in this country, but the original parent of most of our cultivated sorts is supposed to have been brought from Asia. The varieties are numerous. The Green Gage, an old English plum, still keeps its place, in popular estimation, at the head of the list.

The best soil for the plum is a strong loam on a dry subsoil, but it will grow in any tolerably fertile soil. An annual top-dressing of common salt will be found very useful, not only promoting the growth of the tree, but driving away most of the insects to which it is liable. The tree should be set about sixteen feet apart each way. The great enemy of the plum is the curculio, against which you must wage a war of extermination.

The plum is generally propagated by budding, but may be grafted with success, if the operation be skillfully and carefully performed. Little pruning is necessary, except when the tree is young, to improve the form of the head.

5. THE CHERRY—*Cerasus Sylvestris et C. Vulgaris.*

The cherry was brought originally from Asia by the Roman general Lucullus, and has been in cultivation in Europe for more than eighteen hundred years. It was introduced into America on the first settlement of the country.

All sorts of cherries are generally worked on Black Mazzard stocks. They may be either budded or grafted. Set the trees from sixteen to twenty feet apart, and cultivate the same as the plum.

6. The Olive—*Olea Europæa.*

The olive should be more widely cultivated in the Southern States. The seaboard States of the South are well adapted to its culture. It will thrive farther north than the orange. It is a low evergreen tree, and commences bearing in five or six years after being planted. The oil is made by crushing the fruit to a paste, and pressing it through a coarse, hempen bag, into hot water, from the surface of which the oil is skimmed off. The common European olive is the best variety for general cultivation. It is propagated by means of little knots or tumors, which form on the bark of the trunk, and are easily cut out with a penknife. These are planted in the soil like bulbs. It may also be propagated by cuttings or seeds.

OLIVE BRANCH AND FRUIT.

IV.—THE ORANGE FAMILY.

1. The Orange—*Citrus Aurantum.*

This delicious tropical fruit is successfully cultivated in Florida, and to some extent in Louisiana, Texas, Georgia, South Carolina, and other Southern States. With only slight protection, it will succeed so far north as Baltimore. Of the sweet orange, which alone is worthy of garden cultivation, the best varieties are the Havana or Common Sweet, the Maltese, the Blood Red, the Mandarin, and the St. Michael.

The orange requires a deep, rich loam. To procure stocks for budding with the sweet varieties, sow early in the spring the seeds of the wild, bitter orange of Florida. They may be budded the same or the next season.

The great foe of the orange-tree is the scale insect (Coccus

Hesperidum), but the common chamomile is found to be a specific against it. This herb, in bunches, hung on the branches of the trees, drives it away, and by cultivating the plant about the roots of the tree, it is protected against its attacks.

2. THE LEMON—*Citrus Limonum.*

The lemon is cultivated like the orange. Besides the common lemon, there is an Italian variety called the Sweet Lemon. The lime, the citron, and the shaddock belong to the same family, and are subject to the same culture.

V.—BERRIED FRUITS.

1. THE GRAPE—*Vitis* of species.

The grape should undoubtedly head the list of berried fruits. It has been cultivated from the earliest ages, and in almost every country in the temperate zones. The varieties cultivated in Europe are all of one species (*Vitis vinifera*), and originated in Asia. Our native grapes are of different species.

The foreign grapes do not succeed in this country in open-air culture. The Black Burgundy and the Sherry may perhaps be considered as partial exceptions at the South. Under glass they may be successfully cultivated in all parts of the United States; but as our plan does not embrace hot-house cultivation, we must refer the reader to Chorlton's "Grape-Grower's Guide," and other works devoted specially to grape-culture.

"GRAPES AND WINE," a standard work on the cultivation of the native Grape and manufacture of American Wine, by Geo. Husmann, of Missouri, is one of the best authorities on the subject, and we recommend it to all who wish full and practical information on Grape-culture and Wine-making. Published by Geo. E. Woodward, N. Y., and sent, post-paid, for $1 50.

The grape will succeed in most soils, if properly prepared, but dry, rich loam is preferable. It must be deeply worked, and, if at all wet, thoroughly underdrained. Lime, ashes, plaster of Paris, and bone-dust may be added to the common compost, or used as a top-dressing with great advantage. Choose a warm, sunny exposure for your grapery. In the shade the fruit is liable to mildew.

All the varieties of the native grape are very readily propagated by means of layering, and most of them will grow from cuttings. Cuttings—unless struck where they are to remain, which is the better plan—should be left where they are started for two years before planting out. Layers may be planted out the first year. Set the plants from twelve to twenty feet apart, according to the height of the trellis and the mode of training to be adopted. When planted, cut them down to about two eyes from the ground, and allow only one of these to grow the following season.

In garden culture, grape-vines are trained in various ways, as fancy or convenience may dictate. Downing directs as follows:

"The two buds left on the set are allowed to form two upright shoots the next summer, which at the end of the season 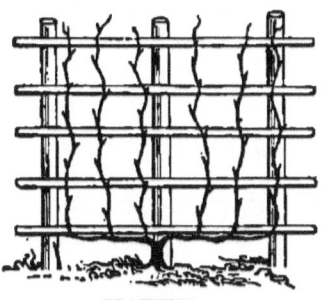 are brought down to a horizontal position, and fastened each way to the lower horizontal rail of the trellis, being shortened to three or four feet, or such a distance each way as it is wished to have the plant extend. The next year upright shoots are allowed to grow one foot apart; and these are stopped at the top of the trellis. The third year, the trellis being filled with vines, a set of lateral shoots will be produced from the upright leaders, with from one to three bunches on each. The vine is now perfect, and it is only necessary at the autumnal or winter pruning to cut back the lateral shoots or fruit-spurs to within an inch of the uprights, and new laterals producing fruit will annually supply their places. If it should

TRAINING.

be found, after several years bearing, that the grapes fail in size or flavor, the vines should be cut down to the main horizontal shoots at the bottom of the trellis. New uprights will be produced, which treat as before."

This is the way to have good crops of perfect grapes. If you desire wood and leaves instead, less pruning will do. The annual pruning should be performed either in November, in February, or early in March—at least a month before vegetation commences. All the other pruning required may be performed with the fingers or a pair of scissors. Only two bunches should be allowed to grow on one shoot; and the end of the shoot should be pinched off, four or five joints beyond the last of these, when the grapes are about half grown. All suckers and supernumerary shoots should be rubbed off so soon as they appear. Beyond this, no leaves must be removed, as they are absolutely essential to the full development and ripening of the fruit. Every third year, at least, the borders where the grapevines are growing should have a heavy top-dressing of manure.

Grapes may be preserved for a considerable time by taking the ripe bunches when free from external moisture, and packing them in jars, filling all the interstices with baked sawdust or bran.

2. The Currant—*Ribes Rubrum.*

The currant is more easily cultivated than any other fruit. The best mode of propagating it is by planting out cuttings in the fall, or quite early in the spring. It is well to procure the cuttings in the fall, and keep them like scions until spring. By taking out all the eyes of a cutting except the three or four upper ones, currants can easily be kept in the form of little trees.

3. The Gooseberry—*Ribes Grossularia.*

The gooseberry requires a deep, strong, rich soil. It is very liable to suffer from drouth, and in dry seasons should be mulched. It is rather shy of bearing in this country, and does not succeed in all localities, even at the North. At the South it is nearly useless, in ordinary localities, to attempt its culture.

HOUGHTON'S SEEDLING.

The tree form is best for the gooseberry; and one half of the top should be thinned out at the winter pruning, so as to admit light and air through the head of the plant. When the berries are fairly set, thin them out, taking away one half or more of them for the benefit of the rest. The best preventive and remedy for mildew is to keep the plants well manured and pruned every year.

4. THE RASPBERRY—*Rubus Idœus.*

A deep, rich loam, rather moist than dry, suits the raspberry best. It is propagated by suckers or offsets. Plant in a sunny quarter of the garden, in rows from three to four feet apart each way. Three or four suckers may be planted together to form a group. This should be done in the autumn or very early in the spring.

All dead wood and the smaller stems should be cut away in the spring, even with the ground. Four or five shoots should be left, and tied to a stake, the tops having about one foot of their upper extremities headed off. A slight top-dressing of manure, with a sprinkling of salt, dug in every spring, is all the further cultivation required.

The raspberry plant is in perfection when it is three years old. When it is about six years old, it should be dug up, and a new plantation made, on a piece of ground where the plant has not recently grown before. It is an excellent mode to make a small plantation every year, so as to continue a supply of the fruit. In extreme cold latitudes, it is necessary to bend the plants down, and cover them with earth or straw through the winter.

To have a fine crop of late raspberries, cut down some of the canes or stems, in the spring, to within a few inches of the ground. The new shoots which will spring up will come into bearing in August or September.

5. BLACKBERRY—*Rubus* of species.

The low blackberry or dewberry (*rubus Canadensis*) has never, we believe, been cultivated, but the fruit, when well exposed to the sun and fully ripened, is sweet, high flavored, and not to be despised. It is also doubtless susceptible of improvement. Of the high blackberry (*rubus villosus*), the following improved varieties are highly esteemed, and the first two much cultivated.

The blackberry requires similar culture to the raspberry.

6. THE STRAWBERRY—*Fragaria* of species.

This is the queen of all berries—delicious, wholesome, and universally esteemed. It is a native of the temperate latitudes of Asia, Europe, and America. The best varieties now cultivated in this country have originated from native species—the Scarlets and the Pines.

In its wild or natural state, the strawberry generally produces hermaphrodite or perfect blossoms. Cultivated varieties have not all retained this property. They are properly divided, with reference to their blossoms, into three classes—hermaphrodite, staminate, and pistillate. Varieties of the first class are, like the wild plants, perfect in themselves, and bear excellent crops. In the second class, the staminate or male

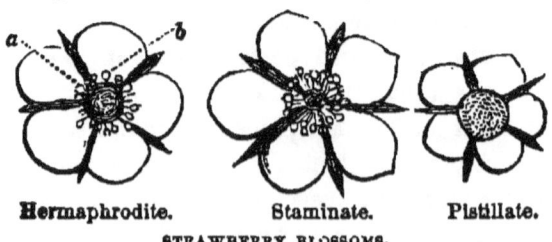

Hermaphrodite.   Staminate.   Pistillate.
STRAWBERRY BLOSSOMS.

organs are perfect, but the female or pistillate organs are more or less imperfect. They bear uncertain and comparatively small crops, because only a part of the blossoms develop the pistils sufficiently to swell into perfect fruit. Plants of the third class bear only pistillate or female blossoms, and are by themselves entirely barren; but when grown near a proper number of the staminate plants, they bear the largest crops and the most perfect berries. In planting a strawberry bed, therefore, it is important to know which are staminate, which pistillate, and which hermaphrodite varieties, and to arrange them accordingly.

Form your strawberry bed in an open exposure, free from the shade of trees or buildings. For an early crop, a slight inclination to the south or east is desirable. The ground must be deeply spaded, and a plenty of decomposed leaves and other *vegetable manure* and ashes well turned under and mixed with the soil. Pulverize the soil thoroughly. Now mark off your bed into rows two feet apart, and set the plants, if of the large growing sorts, two feet apart. For some of the smaller sorts one foot or eighteen inches will do. " Care should be taken that the plants are put into the ground just as they came out of it—that is, with all their laterals spreading, and not all gathered together and crammed into a little hole." If your principal sort is a pistillate, you must plant a sufficient number of staminate plants to impregnate the others. Of less vigorous kinds, more are required. It is well to plant them in alternate strips, thus:

```
P  P  P  P  P  P  P  P  P  P  P  P  P  P  P  P
P  P  P  P  P  P  P  P  P  P  P  P  P  P  P  P
P  P  P  P  P  P  P  P  P  P  P  P  P  P  P  P
P  P  P  P  P  P  P  P  P  P  P  P  P  P  P  P
              PATH
S  S  S  S  S  S  S  S  S  S  S  S  S  S  S  S
              PATH
P  P  P  P  P  P  P  P  P  P  P  P  P  P  P  P
P  P  P  P  P  P  P  P  P  P  P  P  P  P  P  P
P  P  P  P  P  P  P  P  P  P  P  P  P  P  P  P
P  P  P  P  P  P  P  P  P  P  P  P  P  P  P  P
```

The staminate strip may, of course, consist of several rows if desirable.

In planting the hermaphrodite or perfect flowered varieties, as the Woods, Alpines, and Hautbois, of course no such arrangement is required. Planting may be done with success either in autumn or spring. Keep the ground well worked between the rows, to keep it free from weeds, and, unless you want new plants for a future setting, cut off all the runners so soon as they appear. A light mulching with partially decayed leaves or straw, covering the whole ground, but not the plants, will prove highly beneficial, especially in dry seasons and at the South. Before the fruit begins to ripen, cover the ground with a thin layer of straw, hay, or new-mown grass, to keep the fruit clean. Every autumn, if the plants be not sufficiently luxuriant, a light top-dressing of manure should be applied.

A strawberry bed must always be renewed after the fourth year. An easy mode of renewing a strawberry is what is called cultivation in alternate strips. On the third summer from planting, suffer the runners to grow and root into the spaces between the rows; then, in the fall or spring, dig up the old plants, and your new rows are already formed in what were last year the spaces between the rows. At the end of three years repeat the process, and so on, not forgetting to spade in a generous quantity of vegetable manure whenever you dig up the old rows.

"To accelerate the ripening of strawberries," Downing says, "it is only necessary to plant the rows or beds on the south side of a wall or tight fence. A still simpler mode is to throw up a ridge of earth three feet high, running east and west, and to plant it in rows on the south side." Ten days or more may be gained in this way; and if later fruit be desired, rows planted on the north side would probably have their fruiting retarded nearly as much.

Mr. Peabody, of Georgia, one of the most successful strawberry culturists in the world, insists with great emphasis that no animal manure should be used in the cultivation of this plant. The grand secret of success, he says, is *to feed the plant for fruit, and not for vine*—to stint the natural luxuriance of the latter, and turn all the vital forces of the plant to the production of berries. In this way, and by keeping the ground shaded by mulch, and continually watering his plants, he has fine strawberries for nine months out of the twelve. "Let the cultivator remember," he says, "the four great requisites for a profitable strawberry bed: Proper location, vegetable manures, shade to the ground, and WATER, WATER, WATER." The shade to the ground is secured by the mulching we have recommended. The watering is less essential at the North than at the South, but is often very advantageous. Let no reader of this little work neglect to plant a strawberry bed, and enjoy with thankfulness its delicious fruits.

VI.—MISCELLANEOUS FRUITS.

1. THE FIG—*Ficus Carica.*

This delicious southern fruit is a native of Asia and Africa, and has been cultivated from the earliest times. In our Southern States it grows almost spontaneously everywhere. In the Middle States it may be cultivated in the open air, by keeping it low, and covering it well during the winter.

The fig is propagated by cuttings either of the shoots or the root, and planted either in the fall or the spring. Planted in hot-beds in January, they will form handsome plants the same season. Layers also may be made, and suckers taken off for planting. Set them out fifteen feet apart, and the first winter after planting they may be cut off nearly to the ground. The next year they will make vigorous shoots, one or more of which may be allowed to grow, and the rest rubbed off. When young, it is best even at the South to protect the tree during the winter by covering it with evergreen branches. Little pruning is required. North of Philadelphia the branches must be bent down to the ground on the approach of winter, and covered with three or four inches of soil. No one who lives in a climate adapted to their growth, should fail to cultivate a few fig-trees.

2. THE POMEGRANATE—*Punica Granatum.*

This unique and beautiful fruit should receive more attention than has hitherto been given to it in all Southern gardens. It will grow readily so far north as Maryland, but does not always mature its fruit perfectly north of South Carolina. The tree is quite ornamental, and the fruit has a very refreshing acid pulp. Its singular and beautiful appearance renders it a welcome addition to the dessert. It is also used medicinally in fevers, on account of its cooling nature. It might be exported from the South to any extent. It is propagated by cuttings, layers, or suckers, and is very easily cultivated. The finest varieties are the Sweet Fruited, the Sub-acid Fruited, and the Wild Acid Fruited. Besides these, there are several double-flowering varieties, which are very beautiful.

BRANCH AND FRUIT.

3. THE MULBERRY—*Morus* of species.

The mulberry deserves mention here, and a place in the garden or lawn. It is a hardy and handsome tree, and produces a palatable and wholesome fruit.

The Red Mulberry (*morus rubra*) is a native species, but is less desirable for the garden than the Black Mulberry (*morus nigra*), a species much esteemed and widely cultivated in Europe. This sort will hardly succeed, except in very warm and sheltered situations, north of New York. It is propagated by cuttings, and easily cultivated.

A CALENDAR OF OPERATIONS

IN EACH MONTH OF THE YEAR, FOR THE ORCHARD, VINEYARD, FARM, GREENHOUSE AND GARDEN.

JANUARY.

Orchard.

Destroying eggs of insects, protection of trees against the depredations of mice and rabbits, which in some sections do much damage by girdling the trees, is about all that can be done at this season. A wash of cow-dung, lime, and sulphur is recommended as a preventive against the rabbit. Mice work only under the snow, and if this is trodden down occasionally, immediately around the tree, there is little danger from their attacks.

Vineyard.

In the northern sections of the country, vines, if not already protected, should be laid down on the ground and some litter thrown over them; or if the ground is not frozen, cover with three inches of earth. In the latter case, the vines should be raised early in the spring, or the buds will be apt to rot. If vines are not already pruned, do so, selecting a mild day when the temperature is above the freezing-point.

Farm.

The ground being now frozen, out-door operations are in the main suspended; still, the industrious farmer will find plenty of occupation in planning for next season's operations. His cattle, horses, sheep, pigs, cows, and especially the young stock, will require his attention, that they may be in good condition in the spring.

Fences may be repaired, firewood cut, ice-houses filled, manure thrown into heaps and prepared for spring use, and tools of all kinds repaired.

Garden.

There is but little that can be done at this season. If not done already, and the ground is not covered with snow, clear up all rubbish, put away poles, stakes, etc., under cover, and prepare new ones, if required, for next season's use. If there are any cold frames in use, they should be aired when the weather will permit. See that a good stock of seeds is provided for spring use.

Green-house.

Admit air at every favorable opportunity when the thermometer out of doors is above the freezing point; 45° to 50° is high enough as a night temperature for general green-house plants. Camellias and Azaleas do better at 40°. Look out for insects, and fumigate with tobacco as soon as seen. Be careful that the smoke is not too strong. Camellias will soon be in bloom; also some of the early-blooming Azaleas. Avoid wetting the flowers when syringing the plants. Water plants only when needed; perform the operation in the morning, using water five to ten degrees higher than the temperature of the house. A few Achimenes and Gloxinias may be potted and plunged in bottom heat, for early bloom. Keep plants of Calla Ethiopica well watered. Cyclamen persicum will now be in bloom, and make a fine show if the bulbs are large. Scarlet Geraniums will require but little water at this season. Cinerarias should be kept near the glass, and repotted if needed. Keep all plants neat and clean, and tie into neat shape when required.

FEBRUARY.

Orchard.

But little can be added to the directions given last month. Cions may be cut when the wood is not frozen, and may be preserved in damp sand or moss in a cool cellar. Keep a look-out for mice and rabbits. It is the general practice with farmers, and some professed fruit-growers, to prune apples, pears, cherry, and other trees in mid-winter. We do not regard the season as the correct or best one for the labor, and why? because if the operation is correctly performed, that is, the cut made close to the bud or body, it is liable to dry hard, crack, and cause death of the bud in the one case, or decay of the trunk or large limb in the other. It is better to delay pruning until June.

Vineyard.

There is nothing to be done here to which the directions of last month will not apply. If any vines are not pruned, do it when the wood is not frozen.

Garden.

Sketch out plans for flower-beds, and arrange the position of plants therein, so that there may be no delay when the time arrives for commencing work.

Materials should be got ready for starting hot-beds. About the last of the month will be soon enough to make the bed, but in the mean time secure a supply of materials. Fresh horse manure, to which should be added an equal bulk of leaves, may be thrown together in heaps, and turned over every three or four days until it is thoroughly heated. Manure alone gives the greatest heat, but a mixture of leaves and manure the most permanent. Earth should be provided for the bed at the first opportunity, and covered over to prevent freezing up again until wanted. Look over the shrubbery, hardy roses, etc., and if they need pruning, it may be done now. Thin out the old wood of the currant and gooseberry bushes, and thus improve the size and quality of the fruit next season.

Farm.

Our directions for last month will apply to this. The principal business will be the care of the animals, and looking after a supply of wood for next season, as well as getting out posts and rails for new fences, and for the repairs of old ones. While the snow is on the ground, hauling from the wood-lot can be done to great advantage.

Green-house.

The house should now be gay with flowers. Camellias will be in full bloom, and in warm houses Azaleas also. Both should be carefully attended, that they do not lack for water. One of the best plants for winter bloom is the Monthly Carnation, and if a good supply of plants has been secured, there will now be plenty of blooms. Look carefully to the fires, that frost may not get into the house on cold nights. Endeavor to keep the night temperature as regular as possible, and air the house in the daytime at every favorable opportunity. Propagate cuttings of Verbenas, Petunias, Carnations, and such other plants as are wanted for bedding out in the garden, or for the green-house next winter. Cuttings put in now will make fine strong plants by the time for planting out. Cinerarias and Primroses in bloom may be watered occasionally with manure water. The Double-White Chinese Primrose is a splendid object when well grown. It must be propagated by cuttings. If plants of Deutzia Gracilis, Weigelia Rosea, or Double-Flowering Plum were potted in the fall, they may now be started in the warmest corner of the house. Insects will now begin to be busy. Give them occasional doses of tobacco smoke.

MARCH.

Orchard.

If new orchards are to be planted the coming spring, make out lists of trees wanted, and send to a reliable nurseryman at once. You will be able to secure better trees now, than if the order is sent just at the planting season. Continue searching for eggs of insects under the rough bark, and on limbs of trees. It will be advantageous to apply a wash of strong soft soap and water to the body and larger branches, to destroy any eggs that may otherwise escape. Look out for the apple-borer now. Remove the earth for a few inches in depth immediately around the tree. Scrape the bark gently with the back of the pruning-knife, to ascertain where the borer is located, then cut him out. We have found in our practice that a mallet and a half-inch carpenter's gouge are the best instruments.

Don't be satisfied with poking a wire into the holes. We know to our cost that it is not always effectual.

Vineyard.

As soon as the frost is out of the ground, uncover all vines that have been protected by earth or litter. If left covered after the ground begins to get warm, the buds are liable to decay. Tie the vines up to the trellis, and if new vines are to be planted, secure them at once.

Farm.

Improve all the favorable weather this month to haul manure into the fields, ready to be plowed in at the proper time. Manure should be thrown into compact heaps, and spread when the frost is not in the ground. Select the best grain for seed, and see that it is free from seeds of weeds. Considerable work may be done the latter part of this month in picking up and hauling off stone from fields that require it. Fences may be put in repair, and new ones made.

Garden.

Make hot beds for starting seeds of early vegetables, and sow seeds of Pepper, Egg-plant, Tomato, Early Cabbage, Cauliflower, Celery, etc. Hardy vegetable seeds may be sown in the open ground the last of the month—Onions, Beets, Peas, Parsnep, Lettuce, Radish, Spinach, etc. Remove covering from Asparagus, Spinach, Raspberry-canes, etc. Prepare all vacant ground for general planting in April and May. Seeds of hardy flowers may be sown as soon as the ground will admit. Tender annuals should be sown in the hot-bed, and transplanted into open ground in May.

Green-house.

Camellias will be now making their growth, and will need more water than at other times, also an increase of temperature. About the commencement of growth is a good time to graft or inarch with better varieties. Azaleas will be in bloom unless they have been kept very cool; but in a large collection, flowers may be had from December to May, some varieties flowering early, others late.

Cinerarias will now be in bloom; fumigate them if attacked with green-fly.

Start Gloxinias and Achimenes for succession.

Flower seeds may be started in pots and boxes.

Propagate Chrysanthemums. Cuttings make better plants than those procured by division of the old roots. Fuchsias struck now will make fine blooming plants for next summer.

Push the propagating of plants to the utmost now, to have an abundance at time for planting out of doors. Also put in cuttings for next winter's stock. The season is so far advanced that the sun will furnish all the heat by day, and moderate fires only will be required at night. Give air freely in all moderate weather, and close the house early, to retain as much sun-heat as possible.

APRIL.

Orchard.

This is the month when the most of the planting is done, though we prefer doing this in the fall, in this latitude. Prepare your ground thoroughly over the whole orchard, if a new one is to be planted, by plowing, subsoiling, and enriching. If new trees are to be planted in places where old ones have died, dig the holes not less than six feet in diameter, and fill up with fresh soil if possible.

The Garden.

Grafting may now be done. Cions should have been cut during the winter; but if this has been neglected, they should be cut a few days before wanted for use. Don't be in a hurry to graft too early, but wait until the buds begin to start. If your trees are not growing thriftily, give your orchard a good top-dressing of old manure, and plow it in.

Vineyard.

Unless the soil is naturally drained, it is absolutely necessary to success that it should be thoroughly drained. Fifteen to eighteen inches is deep enough to work the soil for a vineyard. Plant only well-tested varieties found to succeed in your locality. Test new varieties, if you have the time and space for experiments.

Farm.

Plow as soon as the ground is in a fit state, which it will be when it will crumble and fall to pieces. In some soils plowing, done when the ground is wet, leaves it to bake hard on becoming dry. Spread the manure hauled out last month, and plow it under. Spring grain of all kinds will need to be sown as soon as the ground is prepared properly. If root crops are cultivated, carrots, parsneps, and beets should be sown at once. A seed drill will be found very useful at this time. Plant potatoes on rich ground, or made so at the time of planting. Do not plant the small potatoes; better cut up the large ones in pieces, if seed is scarce.

Garden.

Uncover the strawberry beds, or rather expose the crowns of the plants. The mulch will be better left to keep the ground moist. Make new beds if needed. Beds made now, and properly cared for, will give a full crop next spring. Fork up the asparagus beds lightly, taking care not to injure the buds or roots. Make new beds now, preparing the ground to the depth of eighteen inches and incorporating with it a considerable amount of old manure. Salt is considered an excellent fertilizer for this vegetable—it may be applied in spring or fall.

Early Cabbage plants may be planted out the latter end of this month. Plants in hot-beds should be thinned out, or better transplanted three to four inches apart into a cooler bed. Plant Peas for a succession. Early Potatoes should now be put in drills. It is rather too soon to plant beans or corn this month.

Plant out flowering shrubs, roses, etc. Seeds of hardy plants may be sown, but all seeds of tender plants should be kept until next month, or sown in a hot-bed. Hyacinths and tulips should have their winter covering removed, and the surface of the soil stirred. Transplant herbaceous plants.

Green-house.

There will be little or no fire heat required this month if care is taken to shut up the house before the sun leaves it. Give all the air possible during favorable weather, to harden the plants for removal out of doors next month. Prepare for a general potting by getting soil, pots, etc., in order, but do not let a plant wait for a *time* when it wants attention. Water for all plants will now be required oftener. Plants that are to be left in the house during the summer will require some shading material to be put upon the glass. Lath-screens made with openings about an inch and a half between, and placed outside of the glass, experience has shown to be an effectual and cheap mode of shading. Propagate by seeds, roots, and cuttings, inarching and grafting; young plants thus get strong before winter. Remove seedlings as soon as possible from seed pans, and put them single into pots. Keep Camellias rather close and warm to promote a vigorous growth.

MAY.

Orchard.

The season for planting is pretty well over by this time, but if any remains to be done, do it as soon as it is possible to do it well. If trees are received in a dry state, bury them root and branch for a few days, then prune severely when planted out. Grafting, if not already finished, may be continued.

If plowing is to be done in the orchard, see that a careful man holds the plow, that as few roots may be injured as possible. Make war on insects this month. Remove nests of tent-caterpillar on their first appearance, and get your neighbor to join you in your efforts for their destruction.

Vineyard.

If vines are not already planted, it may yet be done. Vines, if not tied to the trellis, should be so at once. After the buds start, they are very liable to be rubbed off in handling. The time to tie up vines is while the buds are dormant. Layers may now be made if it is thought desirable to increase vines in this way; preference will generally be given to vines raised from cuttings planted out in well-prepared ground.

Farm.

This will be a busy month. Most of the spring grains will have been sown in April, but the latter part of this month is the time for corn-planting. It is useless to put the seed in until the ground is warm, and equally useless to plant upon any but a rich soil. Some of the larger-growing beets should be sown for feeding the cows and other stock during the fall and winter. The white sugar beet and yellow globe mangel-wurzel are the best for this purpose. Potatoes for the general crop should be put in as early as possible. Let the pastures get a good start before the cattle are turned out. Put in a good supply of corn fodder now, to use in the hot months, when pastures fail.

Garden.

Plant early Valentine and China beans for using green, and Limas for shelling.

Plant sweet corn about first of month, and again in about two weeks, for a succession. The first planting may be cut off by frost, but is often successful. Transplant tomatoes and other plants from hot-beds and frames as soon as danger from frost is past. Cabbage and cauliflower plants should have a very rich soil. Plant cucumbers, melons, and bush squashes in hills at least six feet apart, and manure well. Sow late sorts of peas. In the flower-garden, by the middle of the month, seeds of most flowers may be planted; those kinds that bear transplanting may be sown in a reserve bed, from which they may be taken when wanted.

Plant bulbs of Gladiolus, Tigrida, Tuberose, etc., and prepare beds for the bedding-plants from the green-house.

The Garden. 135

Green-house.

Admit air freely in good weather ; toward the end of the month leave a little air on all night, increasing the quantity by degrees.

Shifting plants into larger pots must be carefully proceeded with. Seedlings and cuttings must be potted off in time, or they will destroy each other.

Bedding-plants of all kinds may be planted out about the middle of the month. Carnations should be planted out, and if required for winter blooming, the flower shoots pinched off frequently. Neapolitan Violets should be divided, and planted out in rich ground, partially shaded. Water and syringe Camellias and Azaleas freely while making their growth.

About the middle of the month some of the most hardy of the plants may be brought from the green-house, and placed in a position where they will be shaded for a portion of the day; they should be carefully attended to for water.

JUNE.

Orchard.

If large limbs are to be removed, this month is the time to do it. The sap is now in active operation, and wounds quickly heal over. Consider well before you remove a branch what is to be gained by it. Never send an ignorant laborer into an orchard to prune if you would not have an indiscriminate cutting of limbs, but study the form of the tree carefully, and if the branches need thinning, use a sharp saw and knife, and leave the wound smooth. Cover the wounds with grafting wax, or shellac dissolved in alcohol. Rub off all shoots from the stock about new-set grafts, and renew the wax if it has melted or cracked off. Continue the war upon the insect tribe, and especially the caterpillars and borers.

Vineyard.

Vines will now be making rapid growth, and will require attention in tying up, pinching, etc. It is the usual practice to stop the shoots at three or four joints or leaves beyond the last cluster of fruit. The bunches will require thinning out, leaving only one bunch to each shoot, if fine fruit and well-ripened wood is to be obtained.

Farm.

Corn is planted in some sections as late as the first of this month, and if an early-maturing kind is selected, and the land is in a good condition, fair crops are often the result. It is not too late to put in a good supply of corn fodder to help out the pastures in the dry weather in August. The plow and hoe must be kept busy in the fields of early planted corn and other hoed crops, to eradicate the weeds.

The latter part of this month haying will commence in many sections. Get everything ready beforehand, that there may be no delay when the time comes.

Garden.

The principal work in the garden this month will be keeping down the weeds. Don't let them get a start. Plant sweet corn for succession, also beans, peas, lettuce. Celery for early use should be set in trenches well manured. Thin out beds of onions, beets, carrots, salsify, etc., and keep them free from weeds.

THE GARDEN.

Green-house.

Green-house plants should be mostly placed out of doors this month. In placing plants out of doors, try to have them so that they will be in shade soon after mid-day. This is especially a point of importance as we go farther south, where the heat of afternoon suns often nearly destroys the plants.

Camellias should remain in the house until growth ceases and the wood becomes brown. Azaleas should be re-potted, if needed, and vigorous shoots pinched to make the plants bushy. Prepare soil for winter use. Neapolitan violets for winter bloom should be divided, and planted out in rich soil. Achimenes, Gloxinias, Caladiums, etc., will now take the place of the plants taken out of doors. The house should be well shaded by the lath screens before recommended, and careful attention given to watering. Torrenia Asiatica will now be a fine object; it looks best in a vase, or hanging basket, the shoots being allowed to droop over the side.

RED ANTWERP.

HORNET.

JULY.

Orchard.

Pruning may be continued as directed last month. Look to the grafts set last spring that they be not robbed by the numerous suckers that are sure to push out about the stocks in which they are set. If any trees were set last spring and not mulched, do it now, that their roots may be preserved from the influence of the sun this month and next. If it is desirable to have large, fine fruit, the crop should be severely thinned now.

Vineyard.

Continue to tie shoots to trellis as growth progresses. Look over the bunches, and see that too many are not left on. An over-crop this season will be followed by unripe wood in the fall, which will be still further weakened by the cold of winter, and a meagre crop the following season will be the certain result.

If mildew makes its appearance, give the vines a dusting of sulphur. De La Vergnes' Sulphur Bellows is the best means of applying it.

Farm.

This month will commence the haying and harvest, and those who would keep up with their work have already secured sufficient assistance. Reapers, Mowing-machines, Hay Tedders, and Horse Pitchforks save an immense amount of hard labor, and even on farms of moderate size will be found to save more than their cost in two or three seasons. Cut hay before it becomes withered and dry. It is frequently left standing too long.

Cut wheat before it is fully ripe, and while it is in the dough state.

Sow buckwheat early in the month to avoid frosts when ripening. Turnips should be sown the latter part of the month. Continue the cultivation of hoed crops, and keep down all weeds.

Garden.

Transplant cabbage and cauliflower plants for a late crop. Continue to transplant celery into trenches, and see that the soil in which they grow is well enriched. Corn for using as green corn may be planted as late as the 15th, to give a supply until frosts. Hoe melons and cucumbers until the vines cover the ground. If melons are thinned on the vines, those remaining will be all the finer. Dig up all the vacant spaces from which early vegetables have been removed, and sow turnips, spinach, and other late crops.

Green-house.

The majority of the plants will be out of doors, as before advised, but will require to be looked over every day or two to see that they are not over or under watered. Those who have large collections will find it to their advantage to construct a sort of shed, with the sides and roof of lath, placed about an inch and a half apart This will admit sufficient light and air on all sides, as well as the rain. Some of our large florists and nurserymen have used such structures much to their advantage, for the protection of Camellias, Azaleas, etc., from the sun. It is important now to prepare plants for winter bloom. Chinese Primroses, Cinerarias, Calceolarias may be sown this month, and cuttings of all desirable plants put in. Carnations from cuttings, planted out, may have the tops pinched off to make them branch freely and prevent bloom now, Look over the plants, and see if any need re-potting. Tuberoses, for late blooming in-doors, may be potted now. Mignonette and Sweet Alyssum seeds may be sown in pots or boxes.

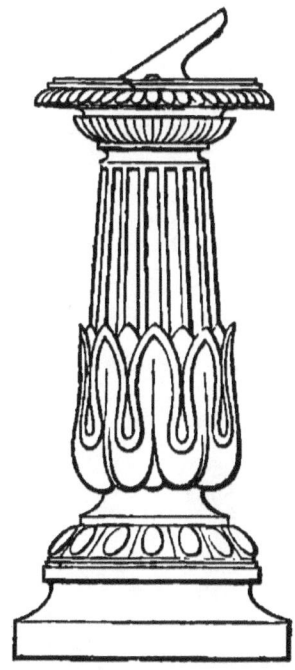

AUGUST.

Orchard.

There will be little remaining to be done in the orchard this month if previous hints have been followed. If pruning is not completed, it is not too late to finish it now. Early fruit should be gathered and marketed as soon as ripe, and all windfalls or wormy apples gathered and taken to the pig-pens. The fruit intended for market should be carefully picked by hand. Fruit bruised by shaking from the tree brings a lower price, and quickly decays.

Vineyard.

The directions given last month apply so well to this, that we can add but little. Some of the fruit of the early varieties will begin to color the last of the month. Continue to tie shoots to the trellis, and use the sulphur remedy for mildew.

Farm.

The harvesting of grass and grain crops will be completed early this month, the time somewhat depending upon the season. See that the grain is properly dried before it is put into barns or stacks. If in stacks, they should be well built, that they may effectually shed the rain. Grass and grain will both keep well in stacks if they are properly put up.

Fall plowing may commence the last of the month. Where farms are large, plowing should be continued at all favorable times, when other work is not pressing.

Garden.

Continue to eradicate the weeds whenever they make their appearance. Provide a good supply of seeds for next season's use, of those varieties found to be successful and of good quality. Select the earliest ripening and best vegetables of the different varieties for seed, and not, as is too often the case, gather them after the crop is nearly over, and the best have been used. Sow turnips on vacant places. Earth up celery wanted for early use, and set out plants for the latest crops.

Green-house.

Green-house plants in general, if healthy, and wood matured, will be now out of doors in a sheltered spot, defending the pots from the sun, which is even of more importance than shading the tops. Finish potting all plants in need of the operation as soon as possible, that they may become well established before winter. Almost everything may now be successfully propagated. Gather seeds of desirable plants as they ripen. Oxalis and Lachenalias should now be potted. Plants out of doors, as well as in the house, will receive much benefit by a syringing every evening. Sow seeds of annuals required for winter bloom. Secure a good supply of soil, pots, etc., for future use.

Now is a good time to look over houses; make any necessary repairs; paint and put in order for the reception of the plants.

The Garden.

SEPTEMBER.

Orchard.

If trees are to be planted in the fall, which is the best time in this latitude, prepare the ground thoroughly beforehand. Order the trees in season, that they may be on hand when wanted. Select only such varieties as are known to succeed in your localities. Look out for the borers this month, and do not leave any to perpetuate the race another season. Gather varieties of fruit maturing this month as soon as fit to pick.

Vineyard.

All the varieties of grapes worth having will mature this month. Let the fruit become fully ripe before picking, which will not be before some days after it is fully colored. If the fruit is intended for wine, the longer it is left on the vine, so that it escapes frosts, the better will be the quality of the wine. If fruit is to be sent to market, pack in boxes about one foot long by six inches wide, and of sufficient depth to hold two layers of bunches; pack the fruit, close that there be no movement of it in transportation.

Farm.

Prepare soil thoroughly for winter wheat, and sow early. Sowing with a drill will be found advantageous on smooth ground. Grass-seed may be sown alone this month on well-enriched soil, or with the winter grain. Early potatoes may be dug and marketed, or put under cover. Cut buckwheat as soon as it ripens. Select the best ears of corn for seed. This is a good time to drain land, dig out muck from the bogs for winter use in the barn-yards, and grub up bushes, briars, etc.

Garden.

Keep the garden clear from rubbish. As soon as one crop is off, even if no other is to be sown, clear off the dead vines, etc., and carry them to the manure heap; dig up the ground and keep clear from weeds. Continue to earth up celery, when the soil is not wet. Sow seeds of early cabbages and cauliflower plants for preserving over winter in frames.

Green-house.

Clear out and repair the house, if not already done, preparatory to bringing in the plants the latter part of this, or early next month. Sow seeds of annuals for winter or early spring blooming. Pot bulbs of Hyacinths, Crocus, Narcissus, Lachenalias, for early bloom. Propagate Geraniums, Fuchsias, Salvias, Petunias, Verbenas, etc.; Primroses, Cinerarias and Chyrsanthemums should be repotted, and encouraged to grow. Water sparingly all plants in a state of rest. Take up such plants as were planted out during the summer, pot and put them in a sheltered place out of the sun for a few days. See that you have a good stock of Monthly Carnations. Heliotropes for winter flowering should not be planted out, but be grown in pots all summer, and the pots plunged. Clean, tie, and arrange plants of all kinds. Where there is not plenty of room, cuttings put in early will answer better than old plants taken up, and will also save much labor. Take up plants of Neapolitan Violets, plant them in frames to be covered with sash and mats on cold nights. With careful management flowers may be had all winter. They may be also potted for the green-house, but will be required to be kept very cool to insure bloom.

OCTOBER.

Orchard.

Pears and apples, usually termed fall varieties, should be gathered a week or ten days before they would naturally drop. Pick them by hand; lay them in barrels or boxes, inclosing them tight, and place them in a cool but dry room or cellar. So cared for they will often keep till near or quite mid-winter. Winter varieties, especially long-keeping sorts, should be left on the tree as long as the weather will permit. Planting may be done the latter part of this month, on ground previously prepared.

Orchards that have been many years in grass, as well as the trees in young orchards, will receive far greater benefit from plowing the ground, and leaving it in a rough state for action of the winter frosts, than if the work is left until spring.

Farm.

Fall plowing should not be neglected this month. Keep the teams going in all favorable weather. Dig potatoes and get in all the root crops before the ground freezes. Turnips can be left out until the last. See that all roots are put away dry. Root crops generally keep better in pits out of doors than when stored in cellars. Those wanted for spring use may be placed in pits and lightly covered with earth at first. When hard freezing is likely to occur, cover with two feet of earth.

Vineyard.

Gather all grapes before frosty nights occur. Prune vines as soon after the fall of the leaf as possible. Grape-cuttings made as soon as the foliage of the vine drops, and planted out in well-prepared land, will start early in the spring, and make a stronger and better growth than when made during winter and planted out in the spring. Plant new vineyards the last of the month, on ground previously well-prepared.

Garden.

Mow off the tops of asparagus, and cover the beds four to six inches deep with manure. Cauliflower and cabbage plants should now be taken up and placed in frames for wintering. Plant deep, and about three inches apart. Leave off the sashes until cold weather. Continue to earth up celery. Turnips and salsify for spring use may be left in the ground all winter; those wanted for use may be taken up and preserved in sand through the winter. Strawberry beds should be looked over and all weeds removed.

Green-house.

Tender plants should be taken in early this month. The house should be abundantly ventilated, care being taken to close up early to avoid frosts. Look over the plants and see that they are free from insects. Fire may be needed at night the latter end of the month. Avoid a high temperature, 45 to 50 degrees should not be exceeded. Hyacinths should be potted early this month; place them under the stage in the house, and keep the soil moist. Chrysanthemums for winter blooming shelter from cold rains and early frosts, water with manure water alternately with clean. Pot all young struck plants. Plants to be taken up from the flower-beds should previously have their roots cut round, and then after potting should be placed in frames or in the green-house, to encourage fresh roots. Water should now be given with a careful hand, and only when necessary. Bear in mind that bad watering is the great cause why pot plants so often languish and die.

The Garden. 141

NOVEMBER.

Orchard.

Tree planting may be continued all this month, or until the ground becomes frozen. All dry soils work better and easier in fall than spring, and all hardy trees succeed as well or better transplanted in the autumn. All apples intended for late keeping should now be taken to the cellar, which should be well ventilated whenever the weather will permit.

Vineyard.

Grapevines should receive their pruning back this month for next spring's growth. As to the number of buds to be left on each cane, and the number of canes to a vine, much depends on the vigor and age of the vine. No universal rule can be laid down for vineyard pruning. After pruning, lay the vines upon the ground, and cover with earth or leaves, in this latitude and farther north.

Farm.

Continue plowing as long as possible. All clayey lands if plowed deeply and turned up rough and exposed to the winter frosts will improve in quality fully as much as the covering of one coat of manure given and worked in in the spring. All the stock should now be taken into the barns and well cared for. Young stock especially should be well fed and kept growing all winter. All root crops left in the ground should be at once secured, either in the cellar or in pits out of doors. Secure a good supply of fire wood.

Garden.

Lose no time in attending to the gathering and storing of roots of all kinds. Cabbages, celery, etc., should at once be trenched and prepared for early obtainment in winter. Leave no fence corners or by-places occupied with heaps of rubbish, old melon vines, bean haulm, etc., for these are almost invariably the harbors of insects, and if left will cause you to regret your neglect another season. Asparagus beds, if not already done, should at once have the old tops mowed and cleared off, a good dressing of salt given, and the whole covered with half-rotted stable-manure, say three inches deep.

Green-house.

Admit air rather freely when the weather will permit. Azaleas for blooming early, keep at the warmest part of the house. If the buds are well set, and prominent, and the heat about 60 degrees, some will be in bloom by Christmas; those once forced will come earlier of their own accord again. Those for spring flowering keep as cool as possible, so that the temperature is above 35 degrees. The buds on the earliest Camellias will now be swelling, and should be placed with the forward Azaleas. Cinerarias, encourage the forwardest to grow in a moist gentle heat; chrysanthemums encourage with manure water. Keep plants clear from dirt and insects by washing and fumigation. Temperature from 40° to 45° at night. Water only when necessary. Clean pots, paths, stages, and tie and train plants in bad weather.

DECEMBER.

Orchard.

All fruit trees should be carefully looked over at this season for the purpose of destroying insects. Borers may have laid themselves up cosily for winter quarters in the bodies of the trees. Search for as recommended before. The eggs of caterpillars should be sought for on the small branches and in the forks of the trees. The cocus, or scale insect, should be destroyed by washing the bodies and limbs of trees to which they have attached themselves. Strong lye water, or a mixture of soft soap and fresh-slacked lime will destroy them. If you have not yet mulched around your newly planted trees, do so at once.

Vineyard.

Pruning, if it has been deferred, should be completed and the vines laid upon the ground and covered. If the wood is wanted for propagation, cut it up into suitable lengths and store away in moist sand in the cellar.

Farm.

The winter is often a comparatively leisure season. It is profitably occupied in most cases in draining wet lands. Make the ditches narrow, two and one half to three feet deep, and use two-inch tiles for the primary drains, and four to six inch tiles for the main or outlets. Cutting wood, getting out fence posts, and fencing will occupy the attention of the farmer now. See that a good stock is now provided, that work may not be interrupted in a hurrying time. All kinds of livestock will now require careful attention; see that they are properly fed, and with a variety of food, if possible.

Garden.

The hints of last month, if heeded, will leave but little to be done now. Look to the roots, celery, cabbages, etc., stored in trenches and pits, and put on the final winter covering, which should be sufficient to exclude entirely the frost. Keep cold frames used for protection of cabbage and cauliflower plants well aired at all favorable opportunities.

Green-house.

Admit air freely when the external temperature is above 35°, especially among plants designed for late blooming. Azaleas for late bloom, keep cool those swelling their buds, not below 45°.

Poinsettia Pulcherima will make a warm green-house gay for several weeks. Chinese Primrose, water with liquid manure when it shows flower buds; give the *Double White* a favorable and warm position. Water seldom; be regulated by temperature, evaporation, and the wants of the plants; when the flower buds are swelling and opening, give it oftener and after breakfast, and with the water rather higher than the temperature of the house.

VIII.

THE FLOWER GARDEN

> God might have bade the earth bring forth
>   Enough for great and small,
> The oak-tree and the cedar-tree,
>   Without a flower at all.
>
> He might have made enough, enough
>   For every want of ours—
> For luxury, medicine, and toil,
>   And yet have made no flowers.
>
> Our outward life requires them not—
>   Then wherefore have they birth?
> To minister delight to man;
>   To beautify the earth;
>
> To comfort man—to whisper hope,
>   Whene'er his faith is dim;
> For whoso careth for the flowers,
>   Will much more care for him.—*Mary Howitt.*

I.—INTRODUCTORY REMARKS.

HE who loves not flowers, and grudges the few square feet of soil which they are grumblingly permitted to occupy in a corner of his garden, may skip over this chapter. We give him our heartfelt pity; and to the wife or daughter, whose more refined and elevated tastes have not allowed him to devote his front yard to the cultivation of potatoes and cabbages, we offer our thanks.

Had we room, we could prove even to the devotee of literal utilitarianism, that the flower garden has its uses—that lilies and dahlias have quite as important a mission in the world as beets and carrots; but we must forego the arguments and illustrations which this course would call for, and confine ourself to the less interesting, but perhaps more useful, details which follow.

A word, however, to the ladies, to whom we most respectfully dedicate this chapter. We shall take it for granted that you love flowers; for we hold that she who does not, is no true woman. But perhaps you are ready to declare that, positively, you have no time to devote to their cultivation, that you have not sufficient strength for such labor; or, possibly, that all out-of-door employments are ungenteel and unfeminine.

Unless you have time to be sick, which you will hardly admit, you have time to take care of your health. To do this properly, you must have *daily exercise in the open air.* Where can you take this more pleasantly or more profitably than in your flower garden? You are not strong enough, do you say? This is just the way to acquire strength. Begin very moderately, allowing some stronger person to do the heaviest work. An hour or two of light, active, and pleasurable employment, out-of-doors, each fair day, take our word for it, will prove more beneficial than the best tonic mixture that your good and much respected doctor, with all his skill, can prepare for you. Try it. You will soon be able to use the light hoe and spade, which we recommend you to procure at once, with ease and pleasure. The quack's Female Pills find few patrons among the wives and daughters who cultivate their own flower gardens. The idea that the employment is unsuited to woman is a preposterous and absurd one. Where is her place if not among the flowers—herself the fairest flower of all? Shall she blush to own that her own fair hands have reared the floral gems with which she adorns her hair? But we rejoice in believing that few of our readers will urge *this* plea. They will, for the most part, fully agree with us that floriculture should have a prominent place among the female "accomplishments."

For her light work, a lady requires implements made specially for her use. A spade; a hoe; a rake; a fork; a trowel; a watering-pot; a pruning-knife; a pair of small shears; a basket, for the weeds and clippings; a small hammer; a ball of twine; a stout apron, with pockets for the pruning-knife, shears, etc.; a pair of strong leather gloves, for handling prickly shrubs; and a pair of overshoes, will make up a very good outfit. The implements should all be light, and of the best quality. The pruning-knife should be kept *very* sharp. Use it for cutting slips, and for removing branches, leaves, etc. The shears are used for clipping hedges, box, borders, etc.

In connection with her gardening operations, we recommend to every lady who has sufficient leisure the study of botany—both structural and systematic.

II.—LAYING OUT A FLOWER GARDEN.

To attempt, within the limits of a few pages, to fully instruct those who have extensive grounds to lay out, would be presumptuous. Such persons will need to study Downing's "Landscape Gardening," or seek the aid of a practical landscape gardener. Our brief hints and suggestions are intended for those whose ornamental grounds are measured by rods instead of acres.

We will suppose that, as is generally the case, you wish to devote a portion of the space immediately around your dwelling-house to the cultivation of flowers.

If the distance between the entrance gate and the house be small, you must be content with a straight walk from the one to the other; but this should be relieved, and its necessary stiffness somewhat modified, by curved side-walks, branching from the main walk near the front door, and running back to the vegetable garden in the rear of the house. Where the space is a little greater, the straight walk should not be tolerated. It may be curved in various ways, as taste may suggest, and the nature of the case permit. The walks may all have edgings of dwarf box. Near these walks we recommend cutting a sufficient number of flower-beds in the turf. This gives a much more beautiful appearance to the yard than it would have if devoted exclusively to flower-beds. If more space be wanted, it may, perhaps, be found behind the house, and next the fruit or vegetable garden. The beds thus cut in the turf may be of various shapes and sizes, but should always be bounded by curved lines. The grass-plots in which they are situated should be kept smoothly shaven.

In arranging the plants in your beds, place the tallest in the center; but very tall growers, like the hollyhocks and sunflowers, should, in general, be disposed as a back-ground in borders next the walls. So arrange all the kinds that the smaller shall not be hidden or too much shaded by the larger, but all be seen in their order, and each contribute to the general effect. Reference must also be had to colors and their proper combination. It is well, so far as is possible, to select plants which appear well through the season, whether in blossom or not. A constant succession of flowers in each bed may be secured by commencing with the early flowering bulbs, following these with the best herbaceous perennials, and closing with a good selection of annuals.

Climbing plants of various kinds, both annual and perennial, if judiciously introduced, add greatly to the beauty of the grounds around a dwelling. Walls may be mantled with them; doors and windows enwreathed; any unsightly object hidden; arbors covered; and posts and the trunks of trees entwined. They may also be permitted to trail among the smaller shrubs—care being taken, of course, that they do not, in their luxuriance, overpower or hide other plants. Various kinds of supports for climbers may be introduced into the portions of the yard devoted to trees and shrubs. The simplest of these is a single upright pillar of cedar or other durable wood in its rough bark, or a sawed piece of timber with holes bored through it at regular intervals, through which the leading shoots may be drawn as they advance in growth. Prairie roses, bignomas, and other hardy climbers, if skillfully trained, make a very handsome appearance on such pillars. Two climbing roses, of unlike colors, may be thus trained together with a fine effect. These posts should be nine or ten feet high.

In some cases it is better to drive strong wooden rods through the holes we have spoken of, for the support of the climber. Slender climbers, like the cypress vine and the morning glory, require a lighter and more elegant support.

In the arrangement of the shrubs and trees the same principle applies as to the herbaceous plants. We should endeavor to produce the effect of banks, and irregular and picturesque conical masses of foliage, rising higher as they recede from the eye. We therefore place the larger growing kinds in the back row, or in the center of a group, as the case may be; somewhat smaller ones next in order, and still smaller ones in front.

III.—GENERAL DIRECTIONS.

Our very limited space will not permit us to go into details in reference to the cultivation of flowers. With a few general directions, however, one may get on very well in the management of a small flower garden. What is most needed is some guide in the selection of plants to be cultivated; and this we shall furnish in the next section.

1. *Soil, etc.*—For most kinds of flowers a rather sandy soil, well enriched with vegetable mold and well-rotted stable manure, is the best. It must be thoroughly broken up or pulverized before planting. This is even more necessary here than in the kitchen garden. The ground should be dug to the depth of fifteen inches, and raised a few inches above the general level of the garden or yard.

2. *Annual and Biennial Plants.*—Annual* and biennial† plants are in general very easy of cultivation, merely requiring, in a majority of cases, to be sown where they are to bloom, thinned out (with a few exceptions, which will be noted in their place) to give them room, and kept free from weeds.

Never sow till the soil has become tolerably warm and dry, as some flower-seeds are very liable to rot in the ground. In

---

* Annual plants are those which live but one year.
† Biennial plants are such as endure two years; blooming on the second.

this climate, from the middle of April to the first of May, in ordinary seasons, will be sufficiently early for most of them. A little farther north, from the first to the middle of May will be the average time. The smaller seeds must be very lightly covered, but larger ones, like the lupines, may be covered to the depth of two inches. It is a good way to sow in small circles—say from four to nine inches in diameter. In the center of this circle place a tally, or label of some kind, with the name, to prevent mistakes. Soon after they come up, the soil must be carefully stirred, the plants thinned out, if they require it, and all weeds removed. A few kinds do better with transplanting than to remain where they are sown. Of this nature are the balsams, the China aster, the marigold, the hibiscus, and the zinnia, and several other very free-growing plants.

3. *Bulbs.*—The best season for planting hardy bulbous roots, such as the lilies, peonies, etc., is late in autumn, but they may be set out in December if the ground be not frozen, and the bulbs remain sound.

"Hyacinths, Amaryllis, Martagon, and other large lilies, and peonies, should be planted at the depth of four inches; Crown Imperials and Polyanthus Narcissus, five inches; Tulips, Double Narcissus, Jonquilles, and Colchicums, three inches; Bulbous Iris, Crocus, Arums, small Fritillarias, Gladiolus Byzantium, and Snowdrops, two inches; Ranunculus and Anemones, one inch; always measuring from the top of the bulb. The roots should be placed from four to six inches apart, according to their size.

"Take up bulbous roots about a month after the blossom is completely over, in the following manner: When the plants put on a yellowish, decayed appearance, take up the roots, cut off the stem and foliage within an inch of the bulbs, but leave the fibers, etc., attached to them; spread them in an airy room for two or three weeks to dry, after which wrap each root carefully in paper (as the air is very injurious to bulbs), or cover them in sand perfectly **dry.**"

4. *Shrubs.*—Flowering-shrubs may be planted out so soon as the frost is out and the ground sufficiently dry, which will generally be in April. The same general directions apply as have already been given for trees. Tall shrubs should be supported for a while by a stake. The roots must not be permitted to dry before planting; and if they are to be carried to a distance, they must be kept from the air by means of moss, or straw mats bound about them.

IV.—LISTS OF FLOWERING PLANTS AND SHRUBS.

We now proceed to give lists of choice herbaceous plants and flowering shrubs. We might make our catalogues much more extensive, and still fail to embrace all that are desirable in particular localities and under particular circumstances. We trust that they will be found useful, if not wholly satisfactory, to the novice. For the professional gardener, of course, we do not write.

HARDY ANNUALS.

1. BLUE FLOWERED AGERATUM (*Argeratum Mexicanum*).—Color, blue; height, one foot; in bloom all the season.
2. SWEET ALYSSUM (*A. calycina*).—White; fragrant; six inches; all season.
3. LOVE LIES BLEEDING (*Amaranthus caudatus*).—Red and yellow; sum.
4. PRINCE'S FEATHER (*A. hypochondriacus*).—Red; summer.
5. THREE-COLORED AMARANTH (*A. tricolor*).—Is most beautiful on rather poor soil; summer
6. PHEASANT'S EYE (*Adonis miniata*).—Red; showy; summer.
7. CHINA ASTER (*A. Chinensis*).—Various colors; some lately imported varieties are very beautiful; eighteen inches; summer.
8. COCKSCOMB (*Celosia cristata*).—Crimson; eighteen inches; autumn.
9. SWEET SULTAN (*Centaurea* of species).—(*C. moschata*), purple; (*C. cretica*), white; (*C. suaveolens*), yellow; two feet; summer.
10. MORNING GLORY (*Convolvulus major*).—Various; climbing; summer and autumn.
11. DWARF MORNING GLORY (*C. minor*).—Blue; eighteen inches; summer.
12. CHRYSEIS (*C. crocea*).—Orange; one foot; all the season; (*C. Californica*) yellow.
13. LUPINE (*Lupinus* of species).—Many varieties; various; one to five feet; some are perennial.
14. CYPRESS VINE (*Ipomœa* of species).—(*I. quamoclit*), crimson; (*I. alba*), white; climbing; summer and autumn. *I. coccinea*, a native Southern plant is generally classed with the morning glories; red; climbing; autumn.

15. PHLOX (*P. Drummondii*).—Crimson; rose, lilac, and white; (*P. Van Houtti*), variegated; two feet; all the season.
16. ZINNIA (*Z. elegans*).—Various; two feet; very showy; should be watered copiously; all the season.
17. BALSAM, OR LADIES' SLIPPER (*Balsamina hortensis*).—Various; two feet summer and autumn.
18. MIGNONETTE (*Reseda odorata*).—Yellowish green; six inches; chiefly valued for its perfume; all the season.
19. NASTURTIUM (*Tropæolum atrosanguineum*).—Crimson; climbing; in bloom all the season.
20. CANARY BIRD FLOWER (*T. aduncum*).—A beautiful climber.
21. PORTULACCA (*P. splendens*).—Purple; splendid; (*P. Thorburnii*), yellow; (*P. alba*), white; (*P. elegans*), crimson; (*P. Thellusonii*), red; should be grown in a mass to give the finest effect.
22. MALOPE (*M. grandiflora*).—Scarlet and white; three feet; summer.
23. TEN-WEEK-STOCK (*Mathiola annua*).—At least a dozen distinct colors; one foot; summer. All the varieties are well worthy of cultivation.
24. MARIGOLD (*Tagetes erecta*).—Orange, yellow, straw-colored; eighteen inches; autumn. French Marigold (*T. patula*), striped with deep brown, purple, and yellow.
25. CLARKIA (*C. elegans*).—Rose-colored; elegant; (*C. Pulchella*), purple; showy; (*C. alba*), white; one foot; all the season.
26. CANDYTUFT (*Iberis amara*).—White; (*I. umbellata*), purple; (*I. violacea*), violet; (*I. odorata*), sweet-scented. All these species are desirable.
27. LARKSPUR (*Delphinum ajacis*).—Many varieties, double flowered, and superb. Branching Larkspur (*D. consolida*), various colors; summer.
28. THREE-COLORED GILIA (*G. tricolor*).—Light-blue margin and dark center; dwarf; summer.
29. POPPY (*Papaver Marseillii*).—White, edged with red; eighteen inches; summer.
30. SWEET PEA (*Lathyrus odoratus*).—Many varieties—white, black, scarlet, and variegated; three or four feet; summer and autumn.
31. HIBISCUS (*H. manihot*).—Yellow; (*H. Africanus major*), buff, with a black center; two feet; summer.
32. CLINTONIA (*C. elegans*).—Blue; six inches; very slender; autumn.
33. VERBENA (*V.* of species).—Every shade of color from white to crimson; procumbent; very pretty; all the season.
34. DWARF SUNFLOWER (*Helianthus Californicus*).—A double flower.
35. SUN LOVE (*Heliophila araboides*).—Blue; very pretty.
36. PANSY (*Viola tricolor*).—Various; all the season. [A perennial, but treated as an annual.]
37. PETUNIA (*P. violacea*).—Every variety of color; dwarf; all the season.
38. YELLOW EVERLASTING (*Xerantheum* of species).—Eighteen inches; aut.
39. EVENING PRIMROSE (*Œnothera macrocarpa*).—Yellow; large flowered dwarf; summer and autumn.
40. LOASA (*L. lateritia*).—Orange colored; a beautiful climbing plant.
41. CALANDRINIA (*C. discolor*).—Rosy purple; very fine; sum. and autumn.

42. CALLIOPSIS (*C. bicolor*).—Three feet; very showy; autumn.
43. MARVEL OF PERU (*Mirabilis Jalapa*).—Many varieties; autumn.
44. GROVE LOVE (*Nemophila maculata*).—Spotted; beautiful.
45. HELIOTROPE (*Tournefortia heliotropioides*.)—White and blue; very fragrant; autumn.
46. LOVE-IN-A-MIST (*Nigella Damascena*).—Showy; autumn.

For twelve sorts, the following would be a good selection: Numbers 1, 2, 7, 9, 10, 14, 15, 21, 23, 25, 33, and 37. To make up twenty sorts add 6, 11, 13, 16, 19, 22, 29, and 41.

HARDY BIENNIALS.

1. ROSE CAMPION (*Agrostemma coronaria*).—Blooms all summer.
2. FOXGLOVE (*Digitalis* of species).—Purple, white, and spotted.
3. CANTERBURY BELL (*Campanula* of species).—Various; blooms in July and August.
4. HOLLYHOCK (*Althea roesa.*)—All its varieties; summer and autumn. Desirable varieties can be propagated by dividing the roots. Biennial-perennial.
5. GERARDIA (*G.* of species).—Yellow, purple, and spotted.
6. DWARF EVENING PRIMROSE (*Œnothera corymbosa*).
7. HUMEA (*H. elegans*).—All the season.
8. CATCH FLY (*Silene multiflora*).
9. MUSK-SCENTED SCABIOUS (*Scabiosa atropurpurea*).
10. NAKED-STEMMED POPPY (*Papaver nudicaule*).

Though all the biennials are generally propagated by seeds, the double ones may also be successfully continued by cuttings and slips of the tops, and by layers and pipings. Biennials, it should be remembered, never flower till the second year.

HARDY PERENNIALS.*

1. HERBACEOUS PLANTS.†

1. COLUMBINE (*Aquilegia vulgaris*).—Single and double, and many colors.
2. HAREBELL (*Campanula* of species).—All the species of this genus are very beautiful. Flowers single and double; many colors. *C. grandiflora* has superb blue flowers.
3. CARNATION (*Dianthus caryophyllus*).—A much noted and very beautiful flower; propagated by seeds and by layers.
4. SWEET WILLIAM (*D. barbatus*).—Many colors and shades of color—white, red, pink, and crimson. The French call it *boquet parfait*.

---

* Perennial plants are those which endure from year to year indefinitely.

† Those which die down to the root every year. In a restricted sense (in which we use it here), the term herbaceous is not made to include the bulbous and tuberous rooted plants.

5. PINK (*D. plumarius*).—Many varieties.

6. CHRYSANTHEMUM (*Pyrethrum* of species).—Varieties and colors numberless; the last showy flower of the season. The following are all very beautiful

LARGE FLOWERED.	SMALL FLOWERED.
Defiance—lemon-yellow.	La Fiancée—white.
Baron de Solomon—rosy-crimson.	Harriette Lebois—rosy-carmine.
Julia Langdale—rosy-purple.	Cybelle—amber and gold.
Liencour—lilac and orange.	Mignonette—rose.
Magnificent—blush.	Vartigene—crimson.
Mrs. Cope—crimson-purple.	Paquerette—white-shaded crimson.
Sphinx—bright claret.	Sacramento—dark yellow, red center.
White Perfection—pure white.	Louise—pale rose.

7. DOUBLE DAISY (*Bellis perennis*).—Many varieties and various shades of white, pink, and crimson.

8. DIELYTRA (*D. spectabilis*).—A very beautiful plant; flowers pink and white; June and July.

9. FOXGLOVE (*Digitalis* of species).—Various and beautiful. Theoretically a biennial; but may be continued by dividing into off-sets.

10. GENTIAN (*Gentiana* of species).—Blue, yellow, and white; very showy.

11. GERANIUM (*Pelargonium* of species).—Species numerous; varieties numberless. For bedding plants the Scarlet, the Nutmeg-scented (white), and the Rose are the most desirable.

12. FORGET-ME-NOT (*Myosotis sylvatica*).—Blue, pretty, and indispensable.

13. HOLLYHOCK (*Althea rosa*).—We have mentioned this among the biennials, where it theoretically belongs; but it is practically a perennial, from the way in which it increases by off-sets. Hollyhocks are very beautiful *in their proper places*—in borders and among shrubbery. The varieties and colors are numberless. Choose the double-flowering sorts.

14. LUPINE (*Lupinus* of species).—Some of the perennial herbaceous sorts are very beautiful; early in summer.

15. DOUBLE RAGGED ROBIN (*Lychnis* of species).—Scarlet and white.

16. PANSY, OR HEARTSEASE (*Viola tricolor*).—Varieties innumerable; sometimes treated as an annual; blooms all the season.

17. VIOLET (*Viola* of species).—Many of the species, both native and foreign, deserve a place in the garden. Of *V. odorata plena*, the white and purple varieties are very beautiful; bloom early.

18. PHLOX (*P.* of species).—Various colors; no garden should be without some of the perennial species; summer.

19. VERONICA (*V. chamædrys*).—Blue flowers; a good border plant; early in summer.

20. VALERIAN (*V. hortensis et V. Pyrenaica*).—White and red; grow and bloom well on walls and rock-work.

Nearly all the foregoing plants are easily propagated by dividing the roots, and will grow in any garden soil. A few of them will not prove hardy north of New York

2. TUBEROUS-ROOTED PLANTS.

1. Dahlia (*D. variabilis*).—Colors and varieties numberless; a splendid autumn flower for large beds and among shrubbery. The following are a few of the finest varieties:

    Amazone—yellow, margined with carmine.
    Anna Maria—violet, tipped with white.
    Belle Amazone—bright yellow, edged with gold.
    Favorite—dark carmine.
    Gazelle—delicate blush.
    Grand Sultan—dark purple, with light edges.
    Emperitrice Eugenie—black brown.
    Madame Becker—maroon, tipped with white
    Malvina—purple, shaded with darker purple.
    Renuncale Imperiale—lilac and purple.
    Prétrose—dark carmine.
    Wonderful—dark yellow, with purple stripes.

2. Iris (*I.* of species).—More than fifty species, some of which are tuberous-rooted; all very beautiful. *I. susiana* is the finest; flowers large and spotted with brown.

3. Marvel of Peru (*Mirabilis Julapa*).—Generally treated as an annual very beautiful; requires a warm border.

4. Everlasting Pea (*Lathyrus* of species).—The common Everlasting Pea is *L. latifolius*. Once planted it will, for the most part, take care of itself. Some of the species are annuals.

5. Peony (*P. officinalis*).—Many varieties. The Chinese Peony (*P. fragrans*) has pinky-purple flowers and a rose-like perfume.

6. Ranunculus (*R.* of species).—Several species are hardy and desirable for border-plants. The Double Buttercup (*R. acris*) is well known.

7. Ladies' Slipper (*Cypripedium* of species).—Several species are natives of our woods; very beautiful, but difficult of propagation.

8. Anemone (*A.* of species).—Many species; white, purple, yellow, and scarlet; succeed best in cool latitudes. Our native Wood Anemone (*A. nemorosa*) deserves mention among the garden flowers.

The tuberous-rooted plants are propagated by tubers, and some of them also by seeds. Dahlias require a sandy soil. Sand and vegetable mold make a good mixture for them. No animal manure should be applied.

3. BULBOUS-ROOTED PLANTS.

1. Crocus (*C.* of species).—Many species, yellow, lilac, white, etc. The Yellow Crocus (*C. luteus*) is the greatest favorite. The Spring Flowering (*C. vernus*) works in well among shrubs and trees, blooms early in the spring.

2. Crown Imperial (*Fritillaria Imperialis*).—Color varies from light yellow to orange red; showy; suitable for borders.

3. HYACINTH (*Hyacinthus Orientalis*).—Varieties innumerable; choose an assortment of various colors.

4. IRIS (*I.* of species).—Of the bulbous species, the Persian (*I. Persica*) is the most beautiful, but does better in a pot or frame, with some protection.

5. LILY (*Lilium* of species).—The species are very numerous, and all very beautiful. The following is a selection:

Common White (*L. candidum*).
Double White (*L. candidum flore pleno*)
Scarlet (*L. chalcedonicum*).
Japan (*L. lancifolium* of var.)—white, red, rose, spotted; very beautiful.
Turk's Cap (*L. martagon*)—various.
Tiger (*L. tigrinum*).

6. NARCISSUS (*N. tazetta*).—Yellow and white variously combined; varieties numerous.

. DAFFODIL *N. pseudo narcissus*).—Many varieties.

8. JONQUIL (*N. jonquilla*).—Bright yel; fragrant; requires copious watering.

9. SNOWDROP (*Galanthus nivalis*).—Double and single; both desirable.

10. SQUILL (*Scilla* of species).—Blue and white; *S. amœna* and *S. Siberica* are exceedingly brilliant and beautiful; blossom early in spring.

11. STAR OF BETHLEHEM (*Ornithogalum* of species).—White and variegated; easy of cultivation.

12. TULIP (*Tulipa Gesneriana*).—Varieties innumerable and of every shade. There are early and late sorts. Choose some of both.

FLOWERING SHRUBS.

1. ROSE (*Rosa* of species).—Multitudinous in species and countless in variety. No two persons would make the same selection. For the few sorts wanted in a common garden, we suggest the following:

HYBRID PERPETUAL ROSES.

Augusta Mie—blush.
Geant des Batailles—brilliant crimson.
Caroline de Sansal—flesh color.
Lord Raglan—fiery crimson.
Matharia Regina—lilac.
General Jaqueminot—crimson-scarlet.
Mrs. Elliott—rosy-purple.
Duchess d'Orleans—rosy-carmine.
Baron Hallez—light crimson.
Sydonie—light pink.
Baron Prevost—deep rose.
La Reine—deep rosy lilac.
Louis Peronny—deep rose, shaded.

PERPETUAL MOSS ROSES.

Madam Edward Ory—rosy carmine.
Marie de Burgoyne—clear red.
Salet—bright rosy red.
General Drouot—purplish crimson.
Perpetual White—pure white.

SUMMER ROSES.

Coupe de Hebe—brilliant pink.
Paul Ricaut—rosy crimson.
Perle de Panche—white and red.
Persian Yellow—deep golden yellow.
Madame Plantier—pure white.

CLIMBING ROSES.

Queen of the Prairies—red, striped with white.
Baltimore Belle—blush, nearly white.
Mrs. Hovey—pale blush.
Perpetual Pink—purple pink.

2. RHODODENDRON (*R. Catawbiense*).—This splendid American flowering shrub is worthy of a place in every garden.

3. AZALIA (*A. vicosa et A. nudiflora*).—White and purple; fragrant; too much neglected.

4. FLOWERING ALMOND (*Amygdalus nana*).—Beautiful pink flowers. Very desirable in every garden. Spring.

5. MAGNOLIA (*M. abovata*).

6. TREE PEONY (*P. Moutan*).

7. JAPAN QUINCE (*Pyrus Japonica* of var.).—Scarlet and white; very early n the spring.

8. JAPAN GLOBE FLOWER (*Kerria Japonica*).—Double yellow flowers. Showy. Spring.

9. SPIRÆA (*S.* of species).—Many very beautiful species. The Lance-Leaved Spiræa (*S. lancolata*) is the most beautiful of all. Flowers, white; blooms in May. Very desirable indeed.

10. DEUTZIA (*D. gracilis et D. scabra*).—Flowers white. *D. scabra* is the more hardy. Both should be cultivated where the climate will permit.

11. GUELDER ROSE OR SNOWBALL TREE (*Viburnum opulus*).

12. GARDEN HYDRANGEA (*H. Hortensis*) —White flowers.

13. LILAC (*Syringia* of species).—Some of the new varieties are very fine.

14. POMEGRANATE (*Granatum flore pleno*).—Beautiful; should be a favorite wherever the climate is sufficiently mild.

15. SWEET SCENTED SHRUB (*Calycanthus Floridus*).

16. ALTHEA OR ROSE OF SHARON (*Hibiscus Syricus*).—Many varieties.

17. HONEYSUCKLE (*Lonicera* of species).—Beautiful shrubs.

18. PINK MEZEREUM (*Daphne mezereum*).—Dwarf, pretty; flowers in March.

19. ROSE ACACIA (*Robina hispida*).

20. MOCK ORANGE (*Philadelphus coronarus*).—White; fragrant. May and June.

21. FORSYTHIA (*F. vividissima*).—A magnificent new shrub from China; flowers bright yellow; very early in spring.

22. CRIMSON CURRANT (*Ribes sanguineum*).—Single and double crimson; early in spring.

23. ASHBERRY (*Mahonia aquifolia*).—Evergreen; bright yellow flowers; blossoms very early in spring.

24. ROSE-COLORED WIEGELA (*W. rosea*).—Delicate rose-colored blossoms.

25. SILVER BELL (*Halesia* of species).—*H. diptera* is much finer than the common Silver Bell (*H. tetraptera*).

CLIMBERS AND CREEPERS.

1. VIRGINIA CREEPER (*Ampelopsis hederacea*).

2. TRUMPET FLOWER (*Tecoma radicans**).

3. CLEMATIS (*C.* of species).—Several species; white, blue, and purple. The Sweet Scented (*C. flamula*) is exceedingly fragrant.

---

* Gray; the *Bignonia* of the old botanists.

4. IVY (*Hedera* of species).

5. HONEYSUCKLE (*Lonicera* of species).—The Sweet Scented (*L. Belgica*) is one of the most desirable species; in bloom through the summer; very fragrant. The Chinese Evergreen (*H. sinensis*) is also a very fine sort.

6. CHINESE WISTARIA (*W. sinensis*).—A very beautiful climbing blue flowers in clusters.

7. CLIMBING ROSE (*Rosa* of species).—For these, see preceding list.

8. JASMINE (*Jasminum revolutum*).—Bright golden flowers; very fragrant. Southern. Deserves a place in every garden at the South.

9. PASSION FLOWER (*Passiflora* of species)—The most beautiful one is the Purple Flowering (*P. incarnata*).

10. BIRTHWORT OR DUTCHMAN'S PIPE (*Aristolochia sipho*).—An excellent arbor vine.

IX.

ORNAMENTAL TREES AND SHRUBS.

> Happy is he who in a country life
> Shuns more perplexing toil and jarring strife;
> Who lives upon the natal soil he loves,
> And sits beneath his old ancestral groves.

I.—GENERAL HINTS.

HAPPY indeed is he

Who lives upon the natal soil he loves,
And sits beneath his old ancestral groves;

but this happiness is the lot of comparatively few in this country. Our forefathers were too deeply absorbed in the work of hewing down forests to think of planting groves, or to appreciate their beauty. They waged a war of extermination against trees, and, so far as they went, nothing but blackened stumps and unsightly skeletons remained. The effects of their indiscriminate "clearing" have been partially remedied in the older portions of the country (for which more thanks to nature than to man); but even there the language of our motto applies to only a few. Each man's natal soil is in the hands of a stranger. What American lives where his father and grandfather lived and died? We have been a migratory people. It will not always be so, however, and if we can not, except in rare cases, "sit beneath our old ancestral groves," we may yet sit beneath those of our own planting—may learn to

> Love our own cotemporary trees,

and die with the hope that our children and grandchildren may enjoy their shade after we have ceased to need it.

The exhortation, "Plant trees! plant trees!" which has gone forth of late, and been so often reiterated, has not fallen upon heedless ears. Thousands have obeyed it, and tens of thousands stand ready, and only wait to be told what trees to plant, and how to plant them.

For planting trees, we have already given such general directions as the limits of our work would permit. With a careful attention to the fundamental principles set forth in the first and second chapters, these directions will be found sufficient. It remains for us to add a few hints on arrangement, etc., and to give lists of the most desirable species for common use, as ornamental and shade trees and shrubs.

As a border for a straight road or street, we must, of necessity, have a straight row of trees, if any; but in laying out the road or street, simple utility, and not beauty, was the end in view. In laying out ornamental grounds, straight lines and a geometrical arrangement of objects must be avoided; and any necessary straight line, like a boundary fence, should be wholly or partially hidden, and its effect neutralized, by curving rows and irregular groups of trees and shrubs.

This principle applies to the smallest village plot as well as to the extensive park. Something may be done in arrangement and grouping to produce a pleasing and beautiful or picturesque effect, in a very limited space. To tell the reader how, in detail, would require a volume. The hint we have just dropped will at least lead him to think and inquire. His own taste, once awakened, will do the rest.

Do not, we beg of you, distort and deform your ornamental trees by trimming. If any accident or unnatural condition may have caused a tree to grow into an ungraceful and unnatural shape, you may, by a judicious use of the pruning-knife, aid it to return to its natural form; but you can not improve a free-growing and symmetrical tree. If it put out branches near the ground, do not, by any means, remove them. Therein consists much of the beauty of many of our handsomest trees, especially the evergreens.

Other things being equal, preference should be given to native trees and shrubs, and we have so many beautiful species that but few foreign ones need be placed on our lists.

Trees taken from the nursery or forest before they can be used must be "heeled in"—that is, their roots must be placed in a trench prepared for the purpose, and covered with earth. Roots left exposed to the sun and winds soon lose their vitality. Avoid the common error of too deep planting. The tree should be set only two or three inches deeper than it stood before, in the nursery or forest, to allow for the settling of the soil.

II.—LISTS OF TREES AND SHRUBS.

Those who desire more extensive lists to select from than our space allows us to give, can readily obtain them from the nurserymen. Our object is to aid the novice in making a selection of a few kinds.

LARGE-GROWING TREES.

DECIDUOUS.*

1. OAK (*Quercus* of species).—Well known; indispensable in extensive grounds—especially the White Oak (*Q. alba*).

2. AMERICAN ELM (*Ulmus Americana*).

3. MAPLE (*Acer* of species).—In an article condemnatory of the ailanthus, the lamented A. J. Downing says: "Take refuge, friends, in the American maples; clean, sweet, cool, and umbrageous are the maples." For the Middle and Western States the Silver Maple (*A. dasycarpum*) is the best. For the North and East the Sugar or Rock Maple (*A. saccharinum*) is better. The Red Flowering (*A. rubrum*) and the Norway (*A. platanoides*) are beautiful trees, but of slower growth.

4. BLACK WALNUT (*Juglans nigra*).—Adapted to extensive grounds.

5. ASH (*Fraxinus Americana*).—Fine to group with other trees.

6. HORSE CHESTNUT (*Æsculus* of species). The White Flowering (*Æ. hippo-castanum*) and the Red Flowering (*Æ. rubicundo*) are desirable.

7. TULIP TREE (*Liriodendron tulipifera*).—Lofty and magnificent

8. CUCUMBER TREE (*Magnolia acuminata*).—A large, beautiful tree, with bluish-white flowers. All the magnolias are desirable where they will succeed. The most magnificent of them all (*M. grandiflora*) will flourish only at the South, where it is deservedly a favorite.

9. LARCH (*Larix* of species).—The European (*L. Europea*) is the best. The

---

* Deciduous trees are those whose leaves fall in autumn—not evergreens.

American or Black Larch Tamarac (*L. Americana*) resembles it, but grows only in very moist soils.

10. AMERICAN CYPRESS (*Taxodium distictium*).—Lofty and magnificent, but requires a moist, rich soil. For the Middle and Southern States.

11. CATALPA (*C. a ringœfolia*).—Makes a large, round head, and large leaves and showy flowers.

12. AMERICAN WHITE BIRCH (*Betula alba*).—A tall, slender, and beautiful tree; has a fine effect for grouping.

13. HONEY LOCUST (*Gladitschia triacanthos*).—Highly ornamental; fine for lawns and for grouping.

14. PAULOWNIA (*P. imperialis*).—Rapid growing; large-leaved; large blue flowers in clusters; blooms in June. Suitable for Middle and Southern States.

15. WEEPING WILLOW (*Silex Babalonicum*).

EVERGREENS.

1. SPRUCE (*Abies* of species).—The Hemlock Spruce (*A. Canadensis*) is one of the most beautiful of all evergreen trees. Fine for a lawn. The Norway Spruce (*A. excelsa*) is also a stately and magnificent tree.

2. WHITE PINE (*Pinus strobus*).

3. BALSAM FIR (*Picea balsamea*).

4. DEODAR CEDAR (*C. Deodara*).—Graceful and beautiful; rapid growing; not perfectly hardy at the North.

5. CEDAR OF LEBANON (*C. Libani*).—Scarcely hardy at the North, but exceedingly desirable where it will succeed.

6. AMERICAN ARBOR VITÆ (*Thuja occidentalis*).

SMALL TREES AND LARGE SHRUBS.

DECIDUOUS.

1. WEEPING ASH (*Fraxinus excelsior pendula*).—Very graceful.

2. JUDAS TREE (*Cercis Canadensis*).

3. LABURNUM (*Cytissus laburnum et C. Alpinus*).

4. MOUNTAIN ASH (*Pyrus* of species).—European and American. The Weeping Mountain Ash (*P. aucuparia pendula*) is a beautiful drooping variety of the European.

5. FRINGE TREE (*Chionanthus Virginica*).—Covered in spring with a profusion of white flowers.

6. HAWTHORN (*Cratægus oxyacantha* of var.).—White, scarlet, and rose-colored flowers; single and double.

7. MAGNOLIA (*M. conspicua* & *M. Soulangiana*).—The first has white and the second purple flowers.

8. BURNING BUSH (*Euonymus atropurpureus*).

9. LARGE FLOWERING SYRINGA (*Philadelphus grandiflorus*).

10. CORNELIAN CHERRY (*Cornus mascula*).

EVERGREENS.

1. TREE BOX (*Buxus aborescens*).

2. COMMON JUNIPER (*Juniperus communis*).

3. IRISH YEW (*Taxus Hibernicus*).
4. MOUNTAIN LAUREL (*Kalmia latifolia*).
5. AMERICAN HOLLY (*Ilex opaca*).

HEDGE PLANTS.

DECIDUOUS.

1. OSAGE ORANGE (*Maclura aurantiaca*).
2. BUCKTHORN (*Rhamnus Catharticus*).
3. HAWTHORN (*Cratægus oxyacantha*).
4. ALTHEA OR ROSE OF SHARON (*Hibiscus Syriacus*).
5. BERBERRY (*Berberis vulgaris*).

EVERGREENS.

1. AMERICAN ARBOR VITÆ (*Thuja occidentalis*).
2. AMERICAN HOLLY (*Ilex opaca*).
3. HEMLOCK SPRUCE (*Abies Canadensis*).
4. NORWAY SPRUCE (*Abies excelsa*).
5. WHITE CEDAR (*Cupressus thyoides*).
6. HOLLY-LEAVED BERBERRY (*Mahonia aquifolia*).
7. DWARF BOX (*Buxus suffruticosa*).—For edging.
8. EVERGREEN THORN (*Cratægus pyracantha*).—For the South.
9. CHEROKEE ROSE (*Rosa lævigata*).—Southern.
10. WHITE MACARTNEY ROSE.—The best of all hedge plants for the South.

Live hedges must gradually take the place of our unsightly fences in the older parts of the country, where timber is already scarce. On the prairies of the West there seems to be no other resource. See "The Farm" for directions for their cultivation. Some of the foregoing hedge plants have not been well proved, but are all more or less perfectly adapted to the purpose. The Osage Orange seems as yet to be most generally approved.

For further information on the culture of forest trees, for shade, for shelter, for timber, for fuel and for profit, see "Fuller's Forest Tree Culturist." And for the selection and management of ornamental, deciduous and evergreen trees, see "Elliot's Lawn and Shade Trees." Both published by GEO. E. WOODWARD, and sent post paid for $1.50 each.

APPENDIX.

A.
THE BEARING YEAR.

This arises simply from the tendency in the apple, when left to itself, to bear so large crops one year as to require the next year to recover sufficient strength to bear again. This becomes a kind of fixed constitutional habit in a given variety, and is continued by grafting, so that whole orchards bear one year, and are unfruitful the next, with great regularity. On the other hand, certain sorts, like the Belle-fleur and Holland Pippin, which bear but moderate crops, in strong soils bear every year.

The habit itself may be corrected or changed, when the tree or orchard is young, by picking off all the fruit that sets the first year the tree bears a good crop, thus forcing it to take its bearing year the next season.—*A. J. Downing.*

B.
CAUSE OF DIMINISHED FERTILITY.

The first colonists of Virginia found a country the soil of which was rich in alkalies. Harvests of wheat and tobacco were obtained for a century from one and the same field, without the aid of manure; but now whole districts are converted into unfruitful pasture land, which without manure produces neither wheat nor tobacco. From every acre of this land there were removed in the space of one hundred years 1,200 lbs. of alkalies, in leaves, grain, and straw. It became unfruitful then because it was deprived of every particle of alkali which had been reduced to a soluble state, and because that which was rendered soluble again in the course of a year was not sufficient to supply the demands of the plants. . . . It is the greatest possible mistake to suppose that the temporary diminution of fertility in a soil is owing to the loss of vegetable mold. It is the mere consequence of the exhaustion of the alkalies.—*Liebig.*

C.
REMOVING LARGE TREES—"BALLING."

Late in the autumn, dig a circular ditch at a distance of from two to five feet, according to its size, from the trunk of the tree, and from eighteen to thirty inches deep, smoothly cutting off all the lateral roots close to the central mass of earth. This ditch must be kept free from snow, until the inclosed ball containing the roots of the tree is thoroughly frozen. With iron bars and levers force up this circular mass of earth, and place two or more strong skids under it. By means of a strong set of pulleys, with oxen attached, if necessary, the mass of earth, and the tree altogether, must be drawn over the skids up out of the hole, upon a stone-boat or sled, the tree standing vertically, just as it grew. Thus loaded and secured, it may easily be drawn to the spot selected for it.—*George Jaques.*

D.

NEW VARIETIES OF THE POTATO FROM THE SEED.

The plants from the seeds are about as hardy as tomatoes [and may be sown in the same way either in a hot-bed or in the open air. The former is the preferable way.] They should be hoed often, and dug early, or before the fall rains and cold nights. Some years they will grow large enough for the table, but are not fit to eat until three or four years old.

Each hill should be dug by itself, and all small and unhealthy tubers thrown away, and the good ones labeled and put away carefully for another year's planting. Any plants that have been well cultivated, and only produce small tubers the first year, will never afterward ripen in season.

The second planting will need care and close attention through its growth. Observe the time of flowering, and time of the decay of the vines, that when digging them you may have the history of every hill, for almost every hill is a family by itself.

At this time many sorts can again be rejected, reserving only those that promise good, or indicate the object in view. I threw away a great many varieties at every digging till the fourth year. I had but three families, all white skin and flesh, to which I gave the name of "Stone Hill," the quality of which has been well tested by use, as they have gone into almost every State in the Union, and have been exhibited at very many fairs, and always attracted notice; and a premium.—*A. D. Bulkeley.*

E.

LUXURIES OF A FRUIT GARDEN.

A friend of ours, in whose reliability we have implicit confidence, has a small plot of ground, of which he tells us the following facts:

From a row of currant bushes, about eight rods long, he and his neighbors gathered over two bushels of currants this year. The currant season, from the first picking to the last, was, from June 1st to August 15th, two and a half months.

From a row of gooseberry bushes, two rods long, he gathered about a bushel of gooseberries.

From a plot of strawberry vines, four rods long and one rod wide, he gathered nearly three bushels of strawberries. The strawberry season lasted about three weeks, ending about the middle of July.

Then his raspberries came on, and lasted about three weeks. Of these he had about half a bushel. They stood next to the strawberries in point of delicacy.

He has a number of cherry-trees. They yielded well this year. His family and friends used a bushel or so, and the children of the neighborhood fed themselves upon them, without stint, for two weeks.

Soon after the raspberries were gone, his peaches began to ripen. One of the trees ripened its fruit late, and it has lasted till within a few days past; of these he has had two or more bushels.

All along since the first of August his apples and pears have been ripening, and have furnished an abundant supply for his family, for the cow and pig, and some to sell or give away besides. He will have a large quantity of excellent winter apples. He has just gathered from two or three grapevines as many bushels of fine grapes. Some of these his wife made into marmalade, and some she has preserved in paper, for use hereafter. The best—and greater portion of the whole—were eaten as a dessert, or given to children or friends, all of whom enjoyed them much.

These are some of the enjoyments drawn from a small plot of ground during the season just closing. They were at small cost, but they sweetened many a meal, ministered to health, and added to the comfort of many guests.

Why may not nearly every man have as large a plot of ground, and as many comforts? Simply because he is negligent.—*Ohio Farmer.*

F.

HYACINTHS IN GLASSES.

Hyacinths intended for glasses should be placed in them during October and November, the glasses being previously filled with pure water, so that the bottom of the bulb may just touch the water; then place them for the first ten days in a dark room, to promote the shooting of the roots, after which expose them to the sun and light as much as possible. They will blow, however, without any sun, but the color of the flowers will be inferior. The water should be changed as it becomes impure; draw the roots entirely out of the glasses, rinse off the fibers in clean water, and wash the inside of the glass well. Care should be taken that the water does not freeze, as it would not only burst the glass, but cause the fibers to decay. Whether the water be hard or soft is not of much consequence—soft is preferable—but must be perfectly clear to show the fibers to advantage.—*Thorburn's Catalogue.*

INDEX.

	PAGE
Ashes	88
Asparagus	89
Apple	114
Apricot	127
Annuals	149
Bulbs	19
Budding	63
Beet	78
Bean	81
" Pole	82
" Lima	83
Borecole	86
Broccoli	86
Blackberry	136
Biennials	151
Bulbous Rooted Plants	153
Composts	89
Crops, Rotation of	60
Cuttings	62
Carrot	78
Cabbage	83
" Savoy	85
Cauliflower	86
Chive	95
Cress	96
Celery	97
Cucumber	100
Corn Salad	100
Cape Gooseberry	106
Cherry	128
Currant	133
Climbing Plants	155
Draining	32, 44
Exogen	20
Endogen	20
Endive	96
Egg Plant	106
Flowers	28
" Annual	149
" Biennial	151
" Perennial	151
" Tuberous Rooted	153
" Bulbous Rooted	153
Flower Garden, Laying Out	145
" " Cultivation of	147
Fruit	24
" Ripening of	24
" Gardening	111
Food of Plants	25, 28
Fencing	43
Fixtures	48
Forcing	52
Frost, Protection from	57
Fig	141

	PAGE
Garden, Situation of a	41
" Size of a	41
" Shape of a	41
" Laying Out	42
Garlic	94
Grape	130
Grape Vines, How to Train	132
Germination	13
Growth, Conditions Essential to	27
Guano	89
Grafting	65
Grafting Wax	68
Gooseberry	134
Hot Beds	49
Hoeing	57
Horse Radish	100
Hedge Plants	161
Implements	46
" for Ladies	144
Insects, Destruction of	58
Indian Corn	104
Leaves	21
Lime	88
Layers	61
Leek	94
Lettuce	95
Lemon	130
Lime, The	130
Manures	36
" Application of	51
Marls	88
Mulching	58
" Potatoes	76
" Trees	58
Mustard	96
Melon	102
Mulberry	142
Nectarine	126
Onion	92
" Top	93
" Potato	93
Okra	107
Olive	129
Orange	130
Pits	48
" Sunk	48
" Walled	49
Propagation	61
Pruning	68
Potato	73
" Rot	75
" Sweet	76
Parsnep	79
Pea	80

INDEX.

	PAGE		PAGE
Pea, Sweet	150	Suckers	61
" Everlasting	153	Slips	62
Pea-Nut	83	Salsify	79
Pumpkin	102	Spinach	88
Peach	124	" New Zealand	89
" Trees, Pruning	126	Sea Kale	90
" " Heading-in	126	Shallot	93
" " Training	71	Shrubs	154–160
Pomegranate	141	" Lists of	154
Pepper	107	" Flowering	154
Parsley	109	Squash	103
Plum	127	Sweet Herbs	109
Perennials	151	Sweet Potato	76
Quince	128	Strawberry	136
Roots	16	Trenching	44
Radish	99	Trellises	50
Rhubarb	107	Transplanting	53
Raspberry	134	Training	71
Seed-Leaves	16	Turnip	77
Stem	19	Tomato	104
Seeds	24	Trees	157
" Sowing	58	" Transplanting	54
" Saving	60	" Washes for	118
Soils	80	" Protection of, against Rabbits	118
" Improvement of	82	" Lists of	159
" Depth of	84	" Large Growing	159
" Preparation of	44	" Small	160
" Stirring	51	" Deciduous	159, 160
Situation	41	" Evergreen	160
Subsoils	82	Vegetable Marrow	103
Subsoil Plowing	45	Wheat, Analysis of	27
Stirring the Soil	51	Watering	57
Sowing Seeds	58	Water Melon	108

THE FARM:

A MANUAL

OF

Practical Agriculture;

OR, HOW TO CULTIVATE

ALL THE FIELD CROPS:

EMBRACING

A THOROUGH EXPOSITION OF THE NATURE AND ACTION OF SOILS AND MANURES THE PRINCIPLES OF ROTATION IN CROPPING; DIRECTIONS FOR IRRIGATING, DRAINING, SUBSOILING, FENCING, AND PLANTING HEDGES; DESCRIPTIONS OF AGRICULTURAL IMPLEMENTS; INSTRUCTIONS IN THE CULTIVATION OF THE VARIOUS FIELD CROPS, ORCHARDS, ETC., ETC.;

WITH A MOST VALUABLE

Essay on Farm Management.

BY D. H. JACQUES,

AUTHOR OF "THE GARDEN," "THE HOUSE," "DOMESTIC ANIMALS," "HOW TO DO BUSINESS," "HOW TO BEHAVE," ETC.

To render agriculture more productive and beneficial to all, it is necessary that its principles should be better understood, and that we should profit more from the experience of each other.
JUDGE BUEL.

REVISED EDITION.

NEW YORK:
THE AMERICAN NEWS COMPANY,
39 AND 41 CHAMBERS STREET.

Entered, according to Act of Congress, in the year 1870, by

GEO. E. WOODWARD,

In the Clerk's Office of the District Court of the United States for the Southern District of New York.

PREFACE.

BELIEVING that good books on farming can hardly be too greatly multiplied, and that a cheap manual, embodying not only comprehensive practical directions for the cultivation of the various field crops, but also a brief exposition of the fundamental principles which underlie all the operations of the farm, is a special want at the present time, we have essayed, in the work now before the reader, to supply this lack. How well we have succeeded, we leave it for the public to judge.

In the details of cultivation we have been intentionally brief, because we believed that the mass of those into whose hands this book would fall, stand less in need of these than of the information condensed into the first six or seven chapters.

Having a correct notion of the fundamental principles of agricultural science, and with clear outlines of the common practical operations of farming before him, any intelligent man will readily, by means of observation and experience, make himself master of the minor details. Without the theoretical part, the rules of practice laid down in most agricultural works are liable constantly to lead astray.

In the preparation of this little book we have consulted a large number of the best agricultural works—American, English, French, and German—to some of which we have been largely indebted for facts and suggestions. In addition to the formal credit given in the body of the work, we take pleasure in mentioning the following works as among those from which we have received more or less valuable aid:

    Stephens' Book of the Farm.
    The American Farmer's Encyclopedia.
    Allen's American Farm Book.
    Agricultural Reports of the Patent Office.
    Fessenden's Complete Farmer.
    Thaer's Principles of Agriculture and Manures.
    Beatty's Southern Agriculture.
    White's Gardening for the South.
    Norton's Scientific Agriculture.
    Dana's Muck Manual.
    Boussingault's Economie Rurale.
    Downing's Fruits and Fruit Trees.
    Munn's Practical Land Drainer.
    Tucker's Annual Register.
    Harris' Rural Annual.
    The Country Gentleman.
    The American Agriculturist.
    The Southern Cultivator.

Hoping that his little book will aid largely, in its humble way, in the promotion of agricultural progress, and prepare the way for many a larger and better work, the author most respectfully dedicates it

    TO THE YOUNG FARMERS OF AMERICA.

INTRODUCTION.

AGRICULTURE may be said to have had its origin when it was ordained that man should earn his bread by the sweat of his brow. From that time to the present, among all nations and tribes of men, more or less attention has been given to the cultivation of the earth; although in the earlier stages of social progress the principal reliance of mankind for subsistence has been first upon the chase, and then upon flocks and herds. Man is first a hunter, then a shepherd or herdsman, and then a farmer.

Of the existence of agriculture as one of the prominent occupations of the people among the ancient Israelites, we have many notices in the Bible. We gather from various scattered passages in the books of sacred history and prophecy that they had plows; that they turned the soil up into ridges; that they plowed with two oxen; that they sowed the seed broadcast from a basket and plowed it in; that they used hoes or mattocks for extirpating the weeds; that when the grain was ripe they cut it with a sickle or a scythe; that it was bound into sheaves and carried in carts immediately to the threshing floor or to the barn; that threshing was variously performed by means of a threshing-machine or instrument (Isaiah xviii. 27, 28), cart wheels, the treading of horses and cattle, and beating with poles; and that the grain was winnowed by being thrown up against the wind by means of a shovel.

Among the ancient Greeks, agriculture received great attention, and was evidently conducted with great skill and success; in fact, it seems to have been much the same thing as at the present day, our superiority consisting more in the improved implements we use than in our better knowledge of the art and science of cultivation.

The Romans probably derived their knowledge of agriculture from the Greeks and other older nations, adding to it from their own experience. They well understood the nature of soils and the use of manures, and practiced irrigation and underdraining. The Roman farmers, Pliny tells us, were very particular in drawing straight and equal-sized furrows. They always plowed three times at least before they sowed. The furrows in the first plowing were usually nine inches deep.

In the early days of Rome, when they praised a good man they called him an agriculturist and a good husbandman; and he was thought to be very greatly honored who was thus praised.

The first of modern countries to improve the practice of agriculture was Flanders; and the Flemings or Belgians have continued to this day the model farmers of Europe. Their whole country resembles a series of gardens. Their farms are small, and they devote their efforts to three grand points—the accumulation of manures, the destruction of weeds, and the frequent and deep pulverization of the soil. They were the first among the moderns to raise crops for the purpose of plowing them in.

Nowhere at the present time is agriculture pursued with greater skill and success than in England; and there is in that country a steady and continued progress both in the science and the art of cultivation.

American agriculture commenced at the point which that of England had reached at the time her colonies were planted on the shores of the Western Continent. It has not kept pace, we are sorry to say, with that of the mother country. A virgin soil, abounding in all the elements of the highest fertility, and requiring at first but slight tillage to produce large crops, the abundance and cheapness of new lands, and the lack of persistent, steady effort, which soon became an American characteristic, led at once to a superficial and exhausting mode of cultivation which has resulted in reducing thousands of acres of once fertile soil to a barren wilderness.

But there has been a reaction. American husbandry is now

rapidly improving, and we shall not long be left behind by the leading agricultural nations of Europe. The old or exhaustive system is giving place to the new or fertilizing system, under which the productiveness of lands is constantly increased instead of being diminished. The worn-out lands of Virginia and the other old States have, in many instances, under the new system, been restored to more than their original fertility. This will go on till the older States will rival, if not excel, the new in productiveness.

The conditions requisite for the improvement of agriculture, and the elevation of the agriculturist to the high social position to which his contributions to the general welfare and the prosperity of the State entitle him, are thus happily stated by Hon. L. Chandler Ball, in a late agricultural address:

"1. By adopting a higher standard of education, both general and professional.

"2. By a more thorough cultivation of the soil, by which its fertility shall be increased, and permanently maintained.

"3. By the more general introduction of improved implements of husbandry, by which farm and household labor may be more easily and more economically performed.

"4. By improving the breeds of domestic stock, and rearing only those animals which are the best of their respective kinds.

"5. By growing only those roots, grains, grasses, and fruits which are the most nutritious and the most productive.

"6. By pursuing that particular branch of industry which gives the strongest probabilities of success; having reference to climate, soil, markets, and amount of foreign and domestic competition.

"7. By making the business of farming attractive to educated men, and the farm-house and all its surroundings pleasant to refined taste and cultivated manners."

The extensive demand for books on farming, and the wide circulation of agricultural papers and magazines, show that " a redeeming spirit" is truly abroad among our farmers. The vast amount of sound agricultural teachings which is now being almost universally diffused, can not fail to show itself everywhere in a rapid and permanent improvement of our system of cultivation.

But much still remains to be done. Ignorance and prejudice are obstinately blind and deaf. There is much of both to be yet overcome. We send this little book out into the world to aid as it may in the work.

CONTENTS.

I.—SOILS.

Importance of the Subject—The Organic and the Inorganic Parts of Soils—Origin of Each—Classification of Soils—Heavy Soils—Light Soils—Crops adapted to Each -Sandy Soils—Clayey Soils—Limy Soils—Loamy Soils—Marly Soils—Alluvial Soils—Vegetable Molds—Subsoils—Analysis of Soils—Professor Johnson's Tabular View—The Causes of Fertility and of Barrenness—How to Ascertain the Per-centage of Sand in any Soil—A Test for Lime—Physical Properties of Soils—Texture—The Value of the impalpable Powder in Soils—A Mechanical Analysis—Consistency of Soils—Depth of Soil—Colors of Soils—Humidity—Influence of Subsoils—Position and Form of Surface—Improvement of Soils—Management of Clayey Soils—Draining—The Addition of Sand, Lime, Plaster of Paris, etc.—Fall Plowing—Paring and Burning—Management of Sandy Soils—Vegetable or Peaty Soils—Management of Subsoils—Subsoil Plowing—Benefits of Subsoiling......Page 13

II.—MANURES.

Necessity of Manures—Why the Soil of a Forest does not become Exhausted—Exhaustion of Cultivated Soils—Decrease of Productiveness of the Soils of New York—Instructive Facts—Land, like Animals and Plants, must be Fed—Food of Plants—Organic and Inorganic Substances found in Plants—Both made up from their Food—Where Plants obtain their Food—What the Different Crops Take from the Soil - A Tabular View—Classification of Manures—Vegetable Manures—Green Crops as Manures—Advantages of Green Manures—Straw, Leaves, etc.—Sea-Weed—Composition of Sea-Weed—Cotton Seed—Turf—Swamp Muck—Great Value of Muck—Muck and Ashes—How to Compost Muck—Animal Manures—Stable Manures—Value of Urine—How to Preserve and Apply it—Waste of Manures by Fermentation—How to avoid it—Hog Manure—The Manure of Fowls—How to Treat it—Guano—Composition of Guano—Fish Manures—Night Soil—How to Preserve and Compost Night Soil—Flesh, Blood, etc., as Manures—Bones—Process of Dissolving Bones—Mineral Manures—Lime—Marls—Green Sand—Gypsum—Major Dickinson's Method of Applying Mineral Manures to Seeds—Common Salt—Other Salts—Ashes—Management of Manures—Fermentation—Overhauling Manures—Drawing Manure in Winter—A Caution in reference to Quicklime—Burying Manure—Importance of Texture—Composts—Irrigation............ 25

III.—ROTATION OF CROPS.

Theory of Rotations—The Three Grand Classes of Crops—The Grain Crops—The Root Crops—The Grass Crops—Systems of Rotation—Benefits of Rotation in Cropping—Astonishing Neglect of a Great Source of Profit..Page 43

IV.—DRAINING.

Bad Effects of Excess of Moisture—How Draining remedies them—Ten Reasons for Underdraining—Conditions Requiring Drainage—Practical Directions—Examination of the Field—Draining Springy Ground—Direction of Drains—Depth and Distance Apart—Digging—Implements—A Ditcher's Level—Materials and Construction—Brush-Wood Drains—Stone Drains—Different kinds of Stone Drains—Tile Drains—Rationale of their Action—Will Draining Pay?—A Farmer's Reply—Some Facts—Estimates—Economy of Tiles 51

V.—FENCES.

Requisites of a Good Fence—Various kinds of Fence—Stone Fence—The Zig-zag Fence—Posts and Rails—The best Wood for Posts—Board Fence—The Sunken Fence—The Wire Fence Illustrated—Cost of Wire Fence—Wire Netting—Hurdle Fence—Hedges—Causes of Failure in Cultivating Hedges—The best Hedge Plants—Directions for Planting and Trimming—Hedges for the South—How to Form a Hedge of Cherokee or Macartney Rose—A Hint or Two—Are Fences Necessary?—No Fences in France, Belgium, etc.—The Ohio Farmer's Opinion 61

VI.—AGRICULTURAL IMPLEMENTS AND THEIR USE.

The Plow—Ancient Plows—Modern Improvements—The Eagle Plow—The —Michigan Plow—The Double Mold-Board Plow—The Subsoil Plow—The Harrow—The Cultivator—The Horse Hoe—The Field Roller—Seed Sowers—The Horse Rake—Mowers, Reapers, etc.—Conclusion................ 78

VII.—FARM MANAGEMENT.

Introductory—Capital—Livestock—Implements—Seeds—Labor—Recapitulation of Estimates—Size of Farm—Laying Out Farms—Fences—Gates—Buildings—Choice of Implements—Choice of Animals—Soils and their Management—Manures—Rotation of Crops—Operations in Order of Time—Conclusion 82

VIII.—FARM CROPS.

Indian Corn—Wheat—Rye—The Oat—Barley—Rice—Buckwheat—Millet—How to Shock Grain—Potato—Sweet Potato—Turnip—Kohl Rabi—Carrot—Parsnep—Beet—Chinese Yam—The Grasses—Timothy—Meadow Grass—Red Top—The Fescue Grasses—Orchard Grass—Egyptian Grass—German Millet or Hungarian Grass—The Clovers—Other Grasses—Cotton—Sugar-Cane—Chinese Sugar-Cane—Imphee—Broom Corn—Flax—Hemp—Hops.... 100

IX.—THE ORCHARD.

Laying Out Orchards—Squares—Quincunx—Soil and Situation—Planting—Cultivation—Profits of Apple Culture................................... 140

THE FARM

I.
SOILS.

For the reason that a plant would die in a vacuum, for the same reason it would die in a soil destitute of the bases necessary for its organic constitution. . . . . for to live is to combine, and without elements no combination would be possible.—Raspail.

I.—CLASSIFICATION OF SOILS.

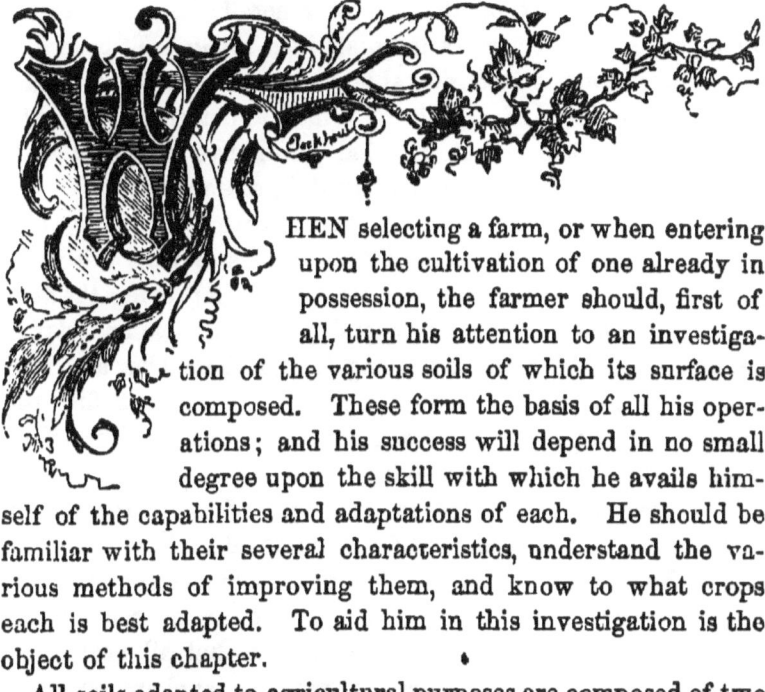

WHEN selecting a farm, or when entering upon the cultivation of one already in possession, the farmer should, first of all, turn his attention to an investigation of the various soils of which its surface is composed. These form the basis of all his operations; and his success will depend in no small degree upon the skill with which he avails himself of the capabilities and adaptations of each. He should be familiar with their several characteristics, understand the various methods of improving them, and know to what crops each is best adapted. To aid him in this investigation is the object of this chapter.

All soils adapted to agricultural purposes are composed of two classes of substances—organic and inorganic. The inorganic parts are derived from the decay of animal and vegetable matter. There must have been a time, in the geological history of the earth, when the soil was destitute of these elements. A low grade of animal and vegetable life was possible without them. Living things found nourishment in the crumbled rocks, which formed the primitive soil. Enriched by their decay, it became capable of sustaining a higher order of existence. The result gradually attained, we see in the present condition of the earth's surface.

The organic part of the soil is generally called vegetable mold, but scientific writers designate it as *humus*. To be fertile, a soil must contain a considerable portion of this organic matter; but we know of no rule by which to determine precisely what quantity is essential. Probably from five to ten per cent. must be present in all permanently rich, strong soils.

Besides ministering directly to the growth of plants, by furnishing them with a portion of their necessary food, this vegetable mold or *humus* promotes fertility by improving the texture of the soil, making sandy land more tenacious and clayey land more friable; and by giving it a darker color, and thus increasing its power of absorbing heat. More than fifty per cent. of *humus*, however, in a moist soil has an injurious effect, rendering it what is called *sour*.

We have already hinted at the origin of the inorganic portions of the soil, in speaking of the crumbled rocks which nourished the first living things. The process of decomposition or crumbling down is still going on under our eyes. Some rocks crumble very slowly, others more rapidly; but all wear away more or less. Each rock gives its own peculiar character to the soil which it forms.

Of the various soils several distinct classifications may be made. It will be well for us, at the outset, to consider them all as embraced in two grand classes—*heavy* or *light*. The distinction indicated by these terms is familiar to every farmer. He knows, too, that it is a predominance of clay which constitutes a soil heavy, and that an excess of sand or gravel makes a soil what is called light. We will look at these two classes of soils a little more in detail.

1. *Heavy Soils.*—Heavy soils, also often denominated cold and wet, are distinguished for their affinity for water, their tenacity, their softness when wet, and their hardness when dry. They are comparatively difficult to cultivate, and require more skill and caution in their management than light soils; but they are generally fertile, and not easily exhausted. They not only hold securely the various solid manures applied to them, till they are required for the support of the growing crops, but greedily absorb the fertilizing gases brought within their reach by the air and the rains. They are admirably adapted to wheat, oats, Indian corn, and the various grasses; hence they are sometimes styled *grass lands*. They of course exist in great diversity, and vary much in value, but are generally susceptible of being made highly productive.

2. *Light Soils.*—Light soils are easily cultivated, friable, dry, and warm; but their porousness facilitates the escape of both the water and the manure applied to them, and renders them liable to drouth and exhaustion. They are particularly adapted to rye, barley, buckwheat, and the tap-rooted plants. The English farmers sometimes distinguish them as *turnip soils*.

Although soils contain small quantities of a large number of substances, they are chiefly made up of what are sometimes called the three primitive earths—silex (including sand and gravel), clay, and lime. As either of these predominates, it gives its peculiar character to the soil, whence we have the arrangement into three grand classes—silicious, argillaceous, and calcareous, or, in other words, sandy, clayey, and limy soils.

1. *Sandy Soils.*—A soil containing not less than seventy per cent. of sand may be considered sandy, in the sense in which the term is here used.

2. *Clayey Soils.*—Clay with a mixture of not more than twenty per cent. of sand forms a clayey soil.

3. *Limy Soils.*—Limy or calcareous soils are those in which lime, exceeding twenty per cent., becomes the distinguishing

characteristic. Calcareous soils may be either calcareous clays, calcareous sands, or calcareous loams, according to the proportions of clay or sand that may be present in them.

4. *Loamy Soils.*—Loamy soils are intermediate between those denominated sandy and those with predominant clayey characteristics. There are sandy loams, clayey loams, calcareous loams, and vegetable loams.

5. *Marly Soils.*—Soils containing lime, but in which the proportion does not exceed 20 per cent., are sometimes called marly.

6. *Alluvial Soils.*—Soils made up of the washings of streams are called alluvial. They contain portions of every kind of soil existing in the surrounding country, and are generally loamy and very fertile.

7. *Vegetable Molds.*—When decayed vegetable and animal matter or *humus* exists in so great a proportion as to give the predominant character to a soil, it sometimes receives the name of vegetable mold.

8. *Subsoils.*—The stratum or bed on which a soil immediately rests is called the subsoil. Subsoils, like soils, may be either silicious, argillaceous, or calcareous.

II.—ANALYSIS OF SOILS.

Chemical analysis shows that the organic parts of a soil are composed of *carbon, oxygen, nitrogen,* and *hydrogen*. The inorganic parts of a fertile soil, in addition to the silex, clay, and lime, of which we have already spoken, contain smaller quantities of magnesia, potash, soda, sulphur, phosphorus, chlorine, oxyd of iron, and oxyd of manganese. All these are essential to independent fertility.

It may be remarked here, that while chemical science is a highly useful ally of agriculture, its decisions must, for the present, be held subject to reversal by practical experiments. This lack of perfect and universal reliability comes from the imperfection of the most careful analyses, and from the influence of conditions of which chemistry can not take cognizance; and not from the unsoundness of chemical theories.

Professor J. F. W. Johnson has given the following tabular view of the composition of soils of different degrees of fertility:

IN ONE HUNDRED POUNDS.	Fertile without Manure.	Fertile with Manure.	Very Barren.
Organic matter...............................	9.7	5.0	4.0
Silica...	64.8	83.3	77.8
Alumina (the base of clay)................	5.7	5.1	9.1
Lime...	5.9	1.8	.4
Magnesia......................................	.9	.8	.1
Oxyd of iron	6.1	3.1	8.1
Oxyd of manganese........................	.1	.8	.1
Potash...	.2		
Soda..	.4		
Chlorine.......................................	.2		
Sulphuric acid...............................	.2	.1	
Phosphoric acid.............................	.4	.2	
Carbonic acid................................	4.0	.4	
Loss during the analysis..................	1.4		.4
	100.0	100.0	100.0

The soil of which the composition is given in the first column contained all the elements required for the growth of plants, and so long as these remain unexhausted will produce good crops without manure.* Some of the alluvial soils of the West are of this character. They will all be found to contain every one of these constituents. The proportions may vary in soils of equal fertility. This is immaterial, so long as there shall be a sufficient quantity of each to supply the wants of the crop. The soil the analysis of which is recorded in the second column lacked potash, soda, and chlorine. These are essential, and therefore the soil, in its natural condition, was barren; but as these constituents are all supplied in considerable quantity by ordinary manuring, fertility was thus easily attained. In the third column half the inorganic substances present in the first are entirely lacking, and two others—lime and magnesia—are greatly reduced in their proportion. No ordinary manuring would supply all these deficiencies, and therefore the soil was, in a practical point of view, hopelessly barren.

Does not this illustration make the cause of fertility on the

---

* See "The Garden," Chapter I.

one hand and of barrenness on the other perfectly obvious! Here it is in the compass of a nut-shell. A soil is fertile (as a general rule) when it contains in sufficient quantity all the substances which plants require, and barren when some of these substances are either entirely wanting or deficient in quantity. The exceptions to the first part of this rule are an unfavorable physical condition and the presence of certain substances in hurtful excess.

The time is coming when every farmer, thoroughly educated at an agricultural college, will possess both the knowledge and the apparatus necessary for making any required analysis of soils, but at present we must, in general, be content with the knowledge of their composition which we are able to obtain by a few simple processes.

To ascertain the per-centage of sand which a soil may contain, dry a quantity thoroughly; weigh it; boil it in water; stir it in a convenient vessel, and when the sand has settled pour off the liquid, which will hold the fine clay, etc., in suspension; after doing this a few times nothing will remain in the bottom of the vessel but nearly pure sand, which may be dried and weighed, and the quantity will show whether the soil be sandy, loamy, or clayey.

Any considerable quantity of lime in a soil is readily detected by pouring upon it a little muriatic acid, which may be obtained at any apothecary shop. So soon as this acid comes in contact with lime, if there be any, a brisk effervescence will take place, owing to the bubbling up and escape of carbonic acid gas. This simple test would save many a farmer from the expensive mistake of applying lime to land which already contains a sufficient quantity of that important element of fertility.

III.—PHYSICAL PROPERTIES OF SOILS.

In judging of the value of a soil, the nature and proportions of the elements of which it is composed are not the only circumstances to be considered. Its physical properties must also be taken into account.

1. *Texture of Soils.*—Considered in reference to texture, a soil may be described as essentially a mixture of an impalpable powder with a greater or smaller quantity of visible particles of all sizes and shapes. Now, although the visible particles are absolutely essential, their effects are, as it were, indirect; the impalpable powder alone exerting a direct influence upon vegetation, by entering into solution with the water and acids with which it comes in contact; for *plants are incapable of taking in solid matter however minutely divided;* and it is in a liquid or gaseous form only that their food can be received.* From this it will be readily understood how a soil may possess all the elements of fertility and yet be barren, as stated in a previous section, on account of some of these elements being locked up in it, as it were, in an insoluble condition. The stones and smaller visible portions of the soil are gradually but constantly crumbling down under the action of air, moisture, and other chemical agents, thus adding, from year to year, new impalpable matter to the soil. The greater the proportion of this impalpable matter, all other things being equal, the greater will be the fertility of the soil. This proportion may be ascertained with considerable accuracy by the following simple experiment:

"Take a glass tube about two feet long, closed at one end; fill it about half full of water, and put into it a sufficient quantity of the soil to be examined to fill two or three inches of the tube at the bottom; then put in a cork, and having shaken the tube well, to mix its contents thoroughly, set it in an upright position for the soil to settle. Now, as the largest particles are of course heaviest, they fall first, and form the undermost layer, and so on in regular gradation, the impalpable powder forming the upper stratum. By examining the various layers and noting their proportions you may make a very good mechanical analysis of soils."

Soils must also be examined in reference to their consistency or tenacity, which is nothing more than the strength with which their molecules or particles are bound to each other by what is

---

* See "The Garden," Chapter I.

called, in the language of natural philosophy, the attraction of cohesion. Clayey soils have the greatest degree of consistency, and sandy soils the least. Both extremes are unfavorable, a medium in this respect agreeing best with vegetation.

2. *Depth of Soil.*—Another very important point is depth of soil. A deep soil has not only the advantage of giving the roots of plants a wider range and a greater mass of food, but it retains moisture better in seasons of drouth, and is not so readily saturated in rainy weather. For the tap-rooted plants, such as beets, carrots, parsneps, etc., depth of soil is particularly important.

3. *Colors of Soils.*—Soils are of various colors—black, white, gray, yellow, red, etc., and the effects and indications of these hues are not to be disregarded in estimating the value of land for agricultural purposes. The brown and red soils are generally best. They are termed warm, and are mostly loamy and fertile. Yellow and gray indicate clayey soils, which are cold in their nature. Black generally indicates peat or deep vegetable mold. Dark-colored earths absorb heat more rapidly than others, but they also allow it to escape with equal readiness.

4. *Humidity of Soils.*—Too great moisture is not less injurious to a soil than extreme dryness. The proper medium should be sought, and where land is too wet, thorough underdraining should be practiced. But more on this point in another chapter.

5. *Influence of Subsoils.*—A subsoil of clay beneath a clayey soil is unfavorable; but beneath a sandy soil it is beneficial, especially if deep plowing and subsoiling be resorted to, for the purpose of improving the latter. On the same principle a sandy or gravelly subsoil is desirable under clayey soils, as it permits the infiltration of any superabundant moisture, and may ameliorate the soil by mixing with it. A calcareous or limy subsoil is beneficial to both clayey and sandy soils.

6. *Position and Form of Surface.*—The position in which a piece of land lies and the form of its surface increases or detracts from its value according to its composition. Sandy soils are

most fertile when flat and situated lower than the surrounding country. On the declivities of hills, such soil is of less value, as it is liable to become parched by drouths and washed away by rains. Clayey soils, on the contrary, especially where the subsoil is impermeable, are favorably situated when on a hillside. Southern and eastern exposures are favorable to early vegetation, and in a cold climate or with a clayey soil are very desirable for many crops.

IV.—IMPROVEMENT OF SOILS

Even the most valuable farms generally contain many acres which require considerable amelioration, aside from ordinary culture and manuring, to bring them into the highest state of fertility of which they are capable; and the farmer should be well acquainted with the various means and methods to be made use of in improving each kind of soil.

The means of ameliorating soils may be divided into two classes, mechanical and chemical. The former includes draining, trenching, subsoil plowing, paring, the addition of various substances to improve texture, etc.; the latter embraces the various kinds of manures. Practically, however, the two classes run into each other, the mechanical processes leading to chemical changes, and the addition of manures to mechanical improvement.

To draining and manures, separate chapters will be devoted. We will speak here briefly of a few other means of improvement which should not be neglected.

1. *Improving Clayey Soils.*—One of the principal defects of clayey soils, especially where they rest upon a subsoil of the same nature, is the excess of water which is held in them. The only effectual way, in a majority of cases, to get rid of this is by thorough underdraining. This draws off by imperceptible degrees all the excess of water and opens the soil to the free admission of the air, which in its passage through it imparts warmth and such fertilizing gases as it may contain. Open drains or ditches, though less effectual, are useful. In some

cases "water furrows," terminating in some ravine or ditch, serve a very good purpose.

To break the too great tenacity of clayey soils, sand seems to be the ingredient indicated; but so large a quantity is required to produce the desired effect, that its application on a large scale is generally considered impracticable. Lime is exceedingly useful as an ameliorator of clayey soils, inducing chemical combinations the mechanical effect of which is to break up the too great tenacity of the clay, while it adds, at the same time, an element of fertility which may perhaps be wanting. Gypsum or plaster of Paris has the same effect in a still more powerful degree. Ashes, coarse vegetable manures, straw, leaves, chips, etc., are also very useful, adding new materials to the soil and tending to separate its particles and destroy their strong cohesion. In cold climates, plowing clayey lands in the fall, and thus exposing them to the action of the frosts and snows, has a beneficial effect. At the South, where there is little frost, and frequent and heavy rains occur during the winter, the effect of fall plowing is very injurious. Clayey lands must never be plowed when wet.

Where a clayey soil rests upon a sandy subsoil its improvement is easier, as deep plowing, by which a portion of the subsoil is turned up and mixed with the soil, soon modifies it very sensibly.

In Europe, paring off the surface containing vegetable matter, drying, and burning it, and spreading the charred mass to which it is thus reduced upon the surface, to become again mixed with it, is frequently resorted to for the improvement of clayey soils; but this process is too expensive to be generally applicable in this country, where labor is so dear and land so cheap.

2. *Improving Sandy Soils.*—Sandy soils require a treatment in most respects the reverse of that applied to clayey soils. Clay is the great ameliorator, and as the quantity required to produce a decided beneficial effect is not great, it may generally, when it can be obtained in the immediate neighborhood, be applied with profit. It should be thinly spread in the fall upon sward

land previously plowed, so that the frosts of winter may act upon it and separate its particles. The land should be thoroughly harrowed in the spring and subsequently plowed, if necessary.

Lime and gypsum, which render clayey soils more friable, increase the adhesiveness of sandy soils, and when cheaply obtained furnish a profitable dressing. Ashes may also be applied with great benefit, as may vegetable manures and vegetable mold. Sandy soils are plowed to the greatest advantage when wet, and are improved by the frequent use of a heavy roller. Pasturing sheep upon them is very beneficial.

Gravelly soils (except calcareous gravels) are more difficult of improvement than sandy soils, and are most profitably appropriated to pasturage. Sheep will keep them in the most useful condition of which they are capable.

3. *Improvement of Vegetable Soils.*—Soils composed mainly of *humus* or vegetable mold, such as are found on low, swampy levels, and sometimes called peaty soils, are generally, in their natural state, totally unfit for any profitable vegetation. When it is desirable to cultivate such a soil, the first process is to drain from it all the excess of water which it may contain. Then the hommocks, if any, must be cut off, dried, and burned, and the ashes spread over the surface; after which sand, fine gravel, ashes, air-slacked lime, and barn-yard manure should be liberally added. These soils, thus ameliorated, make valuable grass lands, but require subsequent dressings of sand, lime, ashes, etc., as their fertility decreases.

4. *Management of Subsoils.*—We have already spoken of the benefits resulting from mixing the soil and subsoil by deep plowing, in cases where they are of a different nature. To break up the subsoil and prepare it for mixing, and also to deepen soils and give the roots of plants a greater scope, a variety of subsoil plows have been invented. In subsoil plowing a common plow goes first and is followed in the same furrow by the subsoil plow, which thoroughly breaks up the subsoil to the depth of from twelve to sixteen inches, without displacing it. At subsequent plowings portions of this subsoil are turned up by

allowing the common plow to run more deeply than before; but care should be taken not to bring it up too rapidly or in too large quantities.

Besides allowing the roots of plants to penetrate more deeply in search of nutriment and moisture, subsoil plowing, by opening the stratum broken up to the action of the atmosphere, gradually prepares it to become an integral part of the soil, increases its warmth by making it a better conductor of heat, and renders it far less liable to suffer from drouth. This last point is particularly important, as subsoiled lands frequently produce excellent crops in seasons in which those subjected to common plowing alone fail to return even the seed deposited in them. Subsoil plowing should be repeated once in five or six years; going each time a little deeper than before, till the greatest practical depth is attained.

Subsoil plowing is not applicable, however, to all lands. Where the subsoil is loose and leachy, consisting of an excess of sand or gravel, it is not only unnecessary but positively injurious.

The gradual mixing of the subsoil with the soil which results from subsoil plowing is especially beneficial to lands which have been for a long time under cultivation, and have become partially exhausted. A fresh supply of the inorganic elements is thus furnished for the nourishment of vegetation, and new avenues opened to those powerful agents of fertilizing decomposition, the air and the rains.

Where underdraining is required, it should precede the subsoiling, and the surface of the drains should be sufficiently below the surface not to be disturbed by the subsoil plow.

With the exception we have noted, where the subsoil is loose and leachy, subsoil plowing, though expensive, will most certainly "pay," as experience has amply proved.

The subject of improving soils will be continued in the next two chapters, under the heads of Manures and Draining.

II.

MANURES.

Manures, in some form, must be considered absolutely essential to sustaining soils subjected to tillage.—Allen.

I.—NECESSITY OF MANURES.

WHILE soils remain covered by unbroken forests, they not only retain their fertility, but actually grow richer and richer from year to year, notwithstanding the vast amount of nutritive matter annually absorbed by the roots of the growing trees. Everything thus taken from them is ultimately returned with interest. The leaves and broken twigs, and eventually the branches, trunk, and roots, in their decay, give back not only what they received from the soil, but much, in addition, that they have elaborated from the atmosphere. We receive from the hands of nature no worn-out lands; but her system of tillage is very different from ours.

The productive power of soils subjected to cultivation is gradually exhausted by the process. Some of the alluvial lands of Virginia produced large annual crops of corn and tobacco for more than a century, without any return being made to them for the elements of fertility abstracted; but these lands are now nearly valueless. The secondary "bottoms" of the Scioto and

Miami may retain an apparently undiminished fertility for a still longer period, but they must ultimately fail, and unless a system of cultivation radically different from that now pursued be adopted, become like the worn-out lands of some of the older portions of the country. Reliable statistical tables prove beyond a doubt that, notwithstanding our improved farm implements and superior methods of cultivation, the average yield, per acre, of the cultivated lands of the State of New York has decreased considerably since 1844, when the records on which these tables are founded were commenced. In corn the decrease is nearly four bushels per acre; in wheat nearly two bushels; and in potatoes, partly owing to the rot, no doubt, twenty-two and a half bushels. The falling off would have been still greater had not deeper tillage and better husbandry furnished a partial offset to the decreased fertility of the soil.

These are instructive facts, and should cause the farmer to pause and reflect.

The fruitfulness of a soil is decreased or increased according to inexorable laws. With each crop that is taken from a plot of ground a greater or less amount of each of the elements of fertility—silex, potash, lime, soda, magnesia, chlorine, etc.—is necessarily removed. Another portion is lost in the process of cultivation independently of what is taken up by the plants. Continue this process year after year, and what must be the result? Ultimate barrenness, of course. There is no remedy but to supply in the form of manures what is thus taken away. The farmer must feed the land which feeds him and so many others, or in the end all must starve together. In the older portions of our country at least, the time has come when the importance of manuring should be more fully appreciated.

II.—THE FOOD OF PLANTS.

In burning a dried plant of any kind, we find that the greater portion of it is dissipated in the process. Generally only from three to ten per cent. is left. This is in the form of ash or ashes. The portion driven off has evidently disappeared in the air, in a gaseous form. It is found by a method of analysis which we can not here stop to describe, that it was composed of four elements—carbon, hydrogen, nitrogen, and oxygen. These are called the organic parts of plants.

An analysis of the incombustible portion remaining shows it to be composed, as a general rule, of these ten substances— potash, soda, magnesia, lime, oxyd of iron, oxyd of manganese, silica, chlorine, sulphuric acid, and phosphoric acid. All these substances are generally present in our cultivated crops, but not invariably; one or two of them being sometimes absent. In some species of plants one of these is wanting and in other species another, and the proportions vary greatly in different species of plants. Of these differences we shall have occasion to speak further under the head of rotation of crops.

Both the organic and inorganic parts of plants are made up from their food, which must of course consist of both organic and inorganic materials. The former are obtained partly from the soil and partly from the air; the latter come exclusively from the soil. A fertile soil must therefore contain, in sufficient quantity and in an available form, all the constituents of plants; and to maintain its fertility under cultivation, these constituents must be supplied in the form of manures so fast as they are taken up by the crops produced.

The food of plants, so far as it is derived from the soil, is all received through the roots in a state of solution; and the roots have, to a certain extent, the power of selecting their food and of rejecting whatever would prove hurtful to the plant. Deleterious agents brought in contact with them may, however, under certain circumstances, be taken up by mere capillary attraction, and the plant thereby poisoned.

III.—WHAT THE DIFFERENT CROPS TAKE FROM THE SOIL.

In examining the ash of the different cultivated plants, we observe, as we have already hinted, great differences in the proportions in which the various elements exist. The ash from the stem or the leaves of a plant and from the seeds of the same plant also varies considerably. The following table gives the composition of our most common cultivated crops:

	Indian Corn.	Wheat.	Wheat Straw.	Rye.	Oats.	Potatoes.	Turnips.	Hay.
Carbonic acid.....	a trace	—	—	—	—	10.4	—	—
Sulphuric acid....	.5	1.0	1.0	1.5	10.5	7.1	13.6	2.7
Phosphoric acid ..	49.2	47.0	8.1	47.8	43.8	11.3	7.6	6.0
Chlorine	0.3	a trace	0 6	—	0.3	2.7	3.5	2.6
Lime..............	0.1	2.9	8.5	2.9	4.9	1.8	18.6	22.9
Magnesia	17.5	15.9	5.0	10.1	9.9	5.4	5.8	5.7
Potash	28.2	29.5	7.2	32.8	27.2	51.5	42.0	18.2
Soda..............	8.8	a trace	0.3	4.4	27.2	a trace	5.2	2.3
Silica.............	0.9	1.3	67.6	0.2	2.7	8.6	7.9	37.9
Iron	0.1	a trace	1.0	0.8	0.4	0.5	1.3	1.7
Loss..............	4.5	2.4	5.7	—	0.8	0.7	—	—
	100.0	100.0	100.0	100.0	100.0	100.0	100.0	100.0

With reference to the character of their ash, we may arrange these crops into three grand classes:

1. The grains in which phosphoric acid predominates
2. The roots in which potash and soda abound.
3. The grasses in which lime is an important element.

In straw and the stems of the grasses silica is abundant, constituting from one half to two thirds of the whole weight. The wood of trees gives an ash in which lime is a prominent ingredient. There are particularly large quantities in that of fruit-trees.

The foregoing facts furnish hints toward a sound system of manuring, and show how important to the farmer is a knowledge of the composition and mode of action of the various manures.

IV.—CLASSIFICATION AND DESCRIPTION OF MANURES.

Manure, in the broadest sense of the word, is anything which added to the soil, either directly or indirectly, promotes the growth of plants. All manures might be considered under two heads—*organic* and *inorganic;* but it will better serve our present purpose to arrange them in three grand classes, *vegetable, animal,* and *mineral.*

1. VEGETABLE MANURES.

Vegetable manures are not so energetic in their action as

those of animal or mineral origin, but their effects are more durable; and the wise agriculturist will avail himself largely of the cheap means of ameliorating his soil which they afford.

1. *Green Crops.*—Plowing in green crops, such as clover, spurry, sainfoin, buckwheat, cow-peas, turnips (sown thickly), Indian corn, etc., is one of the best modes of renovating and sustaining a soil. Worn-out-lands, unsalable at ten dollars an acre, have by this means, while steadily remunerating their proprietors by their returning crops for all the outlay of labor and money, been brought up in value to fifty dollars an acre.

For the Northern States red clover has been found best fitted for a green manure; but in particular cases some other crop may be used with greater advantage. At the South, the cow-pea (which is no pea, but a bean) is considered the best fertilizer. R. L. Allen, in the "American Farm Book," says, "The advantages of green manures consist mainly in the addition of organic matter which they make to the soil. The presence of this aids in the liberation of those mineral ingredients which are there locked up, and which, on being set free, act with so much advantage to the crop. The roots also exert a power in effecting this decomposition, beyond any other known agents, either of nature or art. Their minute fibers are brought into contact with the elements of the soil and they act upon them with a force peculiar to themselves alone. Their agency is far more efficacious for this purpose than the intensest heat or strongest acids, persuading the elements to give up for their own use what is essential to their maturity and perfection. By substituting a crop for a naked fallow, we have all the fibers of the roots throughout the field, aiding the decomposition which is slowly going forward in every soil.

"Clover and most broad-leaved plants draw largely for their sustenance from the air, especially when aided by the application of gypsum. By its long tap roots, clover also draws much from the subsoil; as all plants appropriate such saline substances as are necessary to their maturity, and which are brought to their roots in a state of solution, by the up-welling moisture from beneath. This last is frequently a great source of improvement to the soil. The amount of carbon drawn from the air in the state of carbonic acid, and of ammonia and nitric acid, under favorable circumstances of soil and crop, is very great; and when buried beneath the surface, all are saved and yield their fertility to the land; while such vegetation as decays on the surface loses much of its value by evaporation and drainage. In the green state, fermentation is rapid, and by resolving the matter of plants into their elements, it fits the ground at once for a succeeding crop."

The proper time to turn in most plants used as green manure is at the season of blossoming.

The same effects follow the plowing of grass lands, and turning under the turf; and the thicker and heavier the sward the better, since then a larger amount of organic matter in the form of roots is added to the soil.

1. *Straw, Leaves, etc.*—Straw, leaves, hay are usually applied to the lands after they have either been worked over by animals and mixed with their manures, or composted with other substances and decomposed; but clayey soils are benefited by their application in an undecayed state.

Potato tops or haulm; bean haulm; weeds, pulled before they have seeded, and all kinds of vegetable refuse, are readily decomposed by the addition of a small quantity of animal substances or lime, and should be carefully composted.

3. *Sea-weed.*—Sea-weed and pond-weed form valuable manures. The former is particularly rich in the substances most needed by our crops, the ash containing, according to Professor Johnston, the following constituents and proportions:

Potash and soda	from 15 to 40	per cent.
Lime	" 8 " 21	"
Magnesia	" 7 " 15	"
Common salt	" 8 " 85	"
Phosphate of lime	" 8 " 10	"
Sulphuric acid	" 14 " 81	"
Silica	" 1 " 11	"

Farmers who live near the coast should embrace every opportunity of getting it. It may be plowed in green or applied as a compost. In either case, it decomposes very rapidly, and its effects are immediately seen.

4. *Cotton Seed.*—At the South, cotton seed is much used as a manure, and is very valuable for that purpose. It is applied at the rate of from eighty to a hundred bushels per acre. It may be sown broadcast and plowed in during the winter, when it will rot before spring, or it may be left in heaps to heat till its vitality is destroyed, when it may be thrown upon the corn hills and covered with the hoe or plow.

5. *Turf, Muck, Mud, etc.*—Rich turf, full of the roots of the grasses and decayed vegetable matter, is valuable as an absorbent of animal or other manures in compost heaps. Mixing it with lime, and leaving it several weeks to decompose, is a good preparatory process.

Swamp muck, pond mud, and the scourings of old ditches, are exceedingly rich in vegetable matter, and may as well be mentioned here as anywhere else. These are all exceedingly useful as manures; but differ in richness according to the circumstances under which they have been formed. When there is no outlet for the water and sediments, and the mud, besides containing a large proportion of salts, the result of ages of evaporation, is the receptacle of the remains of myriads of minute shell-fish, animalculæ, infusoriæ, and the spawn and exuvia of frogs and other occupants, the mud is especially valuable. Such reservoirs of vegetable nutrition are mines of wealth to the farmer, if judiciously applied.

Dana, in his valuable "Muck Manual," says:

"The salts of geine* in a cord of peat are equal to the manure of one cow for three months. It is certainly very curious that Nature herself should have prepared a substance whose agricultural value approaches so near to cow-dung, the type of manures. Departing from cow-dung, and wandering through

---

* Geine, in its agricultural sense, includes all the decomposed organic matters of the soil. In some form it is absolutely essential to agriculture.

all the varieties of animal and vegetable manures, we land in a peat-bog. The substance under our feet is analyzed, and found to be cow-dung, without its musky breath of cow odor, or the power of generating ammonia, except some varieties of peat. . . . . . The power of producing alkaline action on the insoluble geine is alone wanting to make it equal to cow-dung."

According to this statement, we have but to add an alkali in the proper proportion, to produce a manure equally valuable with cow-dung. From sixteen to twenty-four bushels, according to their strength, of wood ashes, or about sixty pounds of soda ash, will supply in full the lacking elements; but as clear cow-dung may profitably be mixed with two parts of loam or muck, so two thirds of the alkali may be omitted from the muck mixture, to make it correspond with the cow-dung compost.

"The best plan," Dana says, "for preparing the artificial manure, is to dig the peat in the fall, and mix it in the spring with eight bushels of common house ashes or twenty pounds of soda ash to every cord of muck, estimating the quantity when fresh dug, and making no allowance for shrinkage. If ashes be used, they may be mixed at once with the muck, but the soda ash should be dissolved in water and the heap evenly wet with it. In either case it must be well shoveled over. If leached or spent ashes be used, add one cord to three cords of the muck."

The salt and lime mixture, described in another section, may be added to muck in the proportions of four bushels of the mixture to one cord of the muck, making a very effective manure; or the latter may be composted with stable manure or any animal matter found about the house or barn.

2. ANIMAL MANURES.

These comprise the flesh, blood, hair, bones, horns, excrements, etc., of animals. They contain more nitrogen than vegetable manures, and are far more powerful.

1. *Stable Manures.*—The standard manure of this country is that from the stable and barn-yard. The principal varieties

are those of the ox, the cow, the horse, and the sheep. Of these, that of the horse is the most valuable in its fresh state, but is very liable, as ordinarily treated, to lose much of its value by fermentation; that of the sheep comes next; while that of the cow is placed at the bottom of the list, because the enriching substance of her food goes principally to the formation of milk. That of the ox is better. The value of each of these manures varies also with the food and condition of the animals from whom it is obtained.

The manure of any animal is richer than the food given to it, because it contains, in addition to the residuum of the food, certain particles belonging to the body of the animal. The extent to which it is animalized depends upon the thoroughness of the digestion, fatness of the animal, and the drain made upon the elements of nutrition by the system. The manure of well-kept cattle, it is readily seen, is far more valuable than that from those which are barely kept alive.

All the urine, as well as the solid excrements of animals, should be carefully preserved. It is very rich in nitrogen and the phosphates, and some writers on agriculture contend that its value, if properly preserved and applied, is greater than that of the dung. From an experiment made in Scotland, it appears that in five months each cow discharges urine which when absorbed by loam furnishes manure enough of the richest quality and most durable effects for half an acre of ground. Think of this, ye American farmers, who are accustomed to allow so much of this richness to run to waste! *The urine of three cows for one year is worth more than a ton of guano, which would cost from fifty to sixty dollars!* Will you continue to waste urine and buy guano? Various methods of preserving and applying it will suggest themselves to the intelligent farmer. Stables may be so constructed that the liquid discharges of the cattle, together with the wash of the barn-yard, may be conducted to a tank or cistern, to be pumped out and applied directly to the land, or absorbed by saw-dust, charcoal dust, turf, etc., and used in that form. If allowed to stand long in the tank, in a liquid form, fermentation is liable to take place, and the ammonia to pass off; but a few pounds of plaster of Paris occasionally thrown in will cause the formation of the sulphate of ammonia, which will not evaporate.

But the waste of manures is not confined to those of the liquid form. The solid excrements of the animals are often left to drain, bleach, or ferment, till the greater portion of their most valuable elements have disappeared. *Stable manures should be sheltered from the sun and rain, and fermenting heaps so covered with turf or loam as to prevent the escape of the fertilizing gases.* Plaster, as in the case of urine, will aid in retaining the ammonia. Boussingault, one of the most accurate of experimenters in agricultural chemistry, states that while the nitrogen in fresh horse-dung is two and seven tenths per cent., that in the fermented and dried dung is only one per cent. Horse-dung should be mixed at once with other manures, or with turf or loam, to retain its full value. The manure of sheep is strong and very active, and, next to that of the horse, is most liable to heat and decompose.

2. *Hog Manure.*—The manure of swine is strong and valuable. Swamp muck, weeds, straw, leaves, etc., should be thrown into the sty in liberal quantities, to be rooted over and mixed with the dung. In this way from five to ten loads of manure per annum may be obtained from a single hog.

3. *The Manure of Fowls, etc.*—The excrements of birds contain both the feces and urine combined, and are exceedingly rich in nitrogen and the phosphates. The manure of hens, turkeys, geese, ducks, and pigeons should be carefully collected and preserved. Do not think that because the quantity is small, it is hardly worth the trouble of collection. Professor Norton says that three or four hundred pounds of such manure, *that has not been exposed to the rain or sun,* is equal in value to from fourteen to eighteen loads of stable manure! It may be kept dry, reduced to a powder, and applied as a top dressing, or formed into a compost with muck, turf, decayed leaves, charcoal dust, or other absorbents. If exposed to the

weather uncovered, much of its value is quickly destroyed. The custom adopted by some farmers of mixing the excrements of fowls with unleached ashes, quick-lime, etc., is not founded on correct principles, and inevitably deteriorates the manure.

4. *Guano.*—Guano is formed from the excrements of sea-birds, mixed with the remains of the fish on which they prey, their own carcasses, and other animal matters. It is found in tropical latitudes, where it seldom rains, and where immense numbers of sea-birds have resorted for ages, to build their nests and rear their young. Here their excrements, etc., have accumulated till beds of from fifteen to thirty feet in thickness have in some instances been formed. Of its value as a manure there can be no doubt; but circumstances must determine whether in any given case it can profitably be purchased and applied at the prices at which it is held.

Professor Norton gives the composition of a few of the leading varieties of guano as follows:

VARIETY.	Water, per cent.	Organic Matter and Ammoniacal Salts.	Phosphates.
Bolivian	5-7	56-64	25-29
Peruvian	7-10	56-66	16-28
Chilian	10-13	50-56	22-30
Ichaboe	18-26	36-44	21-29

The guano of commerce is often adulterated, and great caution should be exercised in buying it. That purchased directly from the agent in Peru, in New York, may, it is said, be relied upon as absolutely pure.

In applying guano, care should be taken that it do not come in contact with any seed, as it might destroy its vitality.

5. *Fish Manures.*—These are available near the sea-coast only, where they furnish an important source of fertility, which should not be neglected. The flesh of fish acts with great energy in hastening the growth of plants. It decomposes rapidly, and should be at once plowed under, or made into a well-covered compost heat.

6. *Night Soil.*—From the analysis of Berzelius, the excre-

monts of a healthy man yielded—water, 733; albumen, 9; bile, 9; mucilage, fat, and the animal matters, 167; saline matters, 12; and undecomposed food, 70, in 1,000 parts. When freed from water, 1,000 parts left, of ash, 132; and this yielded—carbonate of soda, 8; sulphate of soda, with a little sulphate of potash and phosphate of soda, 8; phosphate of lime and magnesia, and a trace of gypsum, 100; silica, 16.

Human urine, according to the same authority, gives in every 1,000 parts—of water, 933; urea, 30.1; uric acid, 1; free acetic acid, lactate of ammonia, and inseparable animal matter, 17.1; mucus of the bladder, .3; sulphate of potash, 3.7; sulphate of soda, 3.2; phosphate of soda, 2.9; phosphate of ammonia, 1.6; common salt, 4.5; sal-ammoniac, 1.5; phosphates of lime and magnesia, with a trace of silica and of fluoride of calcium, 1.1.

Urea is a solid product of urine, and, according to Pront, gives—of carbon, 19.99; oxygen, 26.63; hydrogen, 6.65; nitrogen, 46.65, in 100 parts. The analyses of Wœhler and Liebig differ immaterially from this. Such are the materials, abounding in every ingredient that can minister to the production of plants, which are suffered to waste in the air, and taint its purity and healthfulness. Boussingault considers the excrements of a single man during a year sufficient to produce fourteen and a half bushels of wheat.

Doubtless much of the waste of night-soil, which has been permitted in this country, has resulted from the offensive odor it imparts and the supposed difficulty of managing it. These difficulties are easily obviated in various ways. Allen, in his "American Farm Book," recommends that tight wooden boxes, with hooks on the outer side, to which a team may be attached for drawing them out, be placed under the privy. These boxes should have a layer of charcoal dust, charred peat, or plaster of Paris at the bottom, and others successively as they become filled. These materials are cheap, compact, and readily combine with the volatile gases. Sulphuric acid is more efficient than either, but more expensive. Quick-lime will neutralize the odor, but it expels the enriching qualities; and if it be intended to use the night-soil, lime should never be mixed with it. Both the charcoal and peat condense and retain the gases in their pores, and the sulphuric acid of the gypsum leaves the lime, and like the free acid, combines with the ammonia, forming sulphate of ammonia, an inodorous and powerful fertilizer. Raw peat, turf, dry tan-bark, saw-dust, and leached ashes are all good; but as more bulk is needed to effect the object, their use is attended with greater inconvenience. From its great tendency to decompose, night soil should be immediately covered with earth when exposed to the air.

7. *Flesh, Blood, Hair, etc.*—Dead animals, the blood and offal from slaughter-houses, are among the most powerful of fertilizers—equal to guano and the other costly manures; and yet it is not uncommon to see horses or cattle that die from disease drawn out into the wood to decay on the surface of the ground. Every animal that dies should be made into compost at once. Covered with a few inches of turf or loam, decomposition goes on without the loss of the fertilizing element, and a manure of the most valuable kind is produced. In large animals the flesh should be separated from the bones, and the latter be subjected to one of the processes described in the next section.

Hair, woolen rags, leather shavings from the shoe-shops, and all other refuse animal matters, should be carefully preserved and composted, as they make very rich manure.

8. *Bones.*—The value of bones as a manure is just beginning to be appreciated in this country. "They unite," Professor Norton says, "some of the most efficacious and desirable organic and inorganic manures." Boiled bones have lost most of their organic parts, but are still very valuable, being rich in phosphate of lime. They are generally crushed to fine fragments in mills, and thus applied to the land. Another way of applying them is in a state of solution, by sulphuric acid (oil of vitriol). Professor Norton thus describes the process of dissolving them:

"To every hundred pounds of bones, from fifty to sixty pounds of the acid is taken; or if bone-dust be used, from twenty-five to forty-five pounds of the acid will be sufficient. The acid must be diluted with three times its bulk of water. The bones are placed in a tub and a portion of the acid, previously diluted, poured upon them. After standing a day, another portion of the acid may be poured on; and finally the last on the third day, if they be not already dissolved. The mass should be often stirred. It will dissolve into a kind of paste, which may be mixed with twenty or thirty times its bulk of water, and applied to the land by means of an ordinary water cart; but a more convenient method, in most cases, is to thoroughly mix the pasty mass with a large quantity of coal ashes, earth, sawdust, or charcoal dust. It can then be sown by hand or dropped from a drill machine. Two or three bushels of these dissolved bones, with half the usual quantity of yard manure, will be sufficient for an acre."

Bones make a cheap as well as a rich manure, and no thoughtful farmer will suffer one to be wasted about his house.

3. Mineral Manures.

1. *Lime.*—Lime is applied to land in three different states—as quick-lime, slaked lime, and mild or air-slaked lime. To cold, stiff, newly drained land, especially if there exist in it much of acid organic compounds, it is best to apply quick-lime or caustic hydrate (slaked lime), as it will have a more energetic effect in ameliorating it. On light soils mild or air-slaked lime is considered most beneficial. It is best to apply lime frequently and in small quantities, so as to keep it near the surface and always active.

Lime, as we have seen, is an essential ingredient in soil, being constantly needed by the plants in all their parts. It may always be added with profit wherever it does not already exist in sufficient quantity.

2. *Marls.*—In true marl the principal element of fertility is the lime which it contains; but its value is increased by the greater or less proportion of magnesia and phosphoric acid which are usually combined with it.

A valuable mineral fertilizer generally called marl, but which contains comparatively little lime, abounds in parts of New Jersey and Delaware. Its predominant characteristic is a green granular mineral or sand. The carbonate of lime in shells, scattered through it, varies from ten to twenty per cent. in some specimens, while others are almost entirely destitute of it. The secret of its value lies chiefly in the from ten to twelve per cent. of potash which the best specimens contain. Magnesia is also often present. Its effects upon the light sandy soils of New Jersey are very striking indeed.

3. *Gypsum.*—Gypsum, or plaster of Paris, is a sulphate of lime, and has been found one of the cheapest and most powerful fertilizers derived from the mineral kingdom. In reference to the manner in which plaster acts there has been some controversy among agricultural chemists; some contending that it serves as a direct food of certain plants, while others maintain that its utility is due to its power of absorbing gases and holding them in contact with the roots of plants. Late experiments seem to prove that it acts in both these modes. When scattered over compost heaps, it is known to absorb ammonia and prevent its escape. On grass lands it is best to sow it in damp weather or while the dew is on. Sow broadcast at the rate of a bushel to the acre. Seed potatoes may be wet and rolled in plaster before planting with decided advantage; and we know of no better way of applying it to corn than to give the seed a coat before putting it in the ground. Hon. A. B. Dickenson's mode of applying plaster, lime, etc., is an excellent one. We insert his directions as given in one of his inimitable agricultural addresses: "I will tell you how you can put a coat of tar over all kinds of seed as evenly as a painter could put a coat of paint over a board with his brush. An iron kettle is the best to mix the tar and water. Have sufficient boiling water to cut the tar; mix it with the hot water; then pour in sufficient cold to make it near blood heat. Have sufficient water to stir whatever grain you put in, that the water and tar may come into contact with every part and particle; it will then be coated

evenly and is ready to be taken out. Shovel it into a basket—for economy the basket may be placed over a tight barrel to catch the water; as soon as it is done draining, throw into a tight box, where you can mix and put on whatever your soil lacks. If wheat or barley, you need not fear to apply lime and salt. If oats, corn, or buckwheat, plaster and salt. And on the soils of Yates County it would be beneficial to all of the above-named grains, to steep in strong brine over night. Every species of grass seed I sow with a heavy coat, and fasten as much plaster as possible, which draws moisture in a dry season, and prevents rotting in an excessively wet one, and I never fail to have my grass seed take well."

4. *Common Salt, etc.*—Common salt or chloride of sodium has been in use for ages as a fertilizer, and its great value can not be disputed. As an ingredient in compost, it is of great service, and operates with an influence upon the soil which can be produced by no other stimulant, either mineral or vegetable. As to top dressing for grass lands—especially those of a loamy texture—it is invaluable. Mixed with wood ashes and lime, in the proportion of one bushel of salt to three of ashes and five of lime, it constitutes a very energetic manure for Indian corn—producing an early and vigorous germination of the seed, and acting as an efficient protection against the ravages of the various insectivorous enemies by which the young plants are too frequently infested and destroyed.

A very useful and energetic mixture is made by the following simple process:

"Take three bushels of unslaked lime, dissolve a bushel of salt in as little water as will dissolve it, and slake the lime with it. If the lime will not take up all the brine at once—which it will if good and fresh burned—turn it over and let it lie a day and add a little more of the brine; and so continue to do till it is all taken up."

This mixture will supply plants with chlorine, lime, and soda, all of which are essential; destroy the odor of putrefying animal matters, while it retains the ammonia, and promotes the decomposition of vegetable and animal matters in the soil or compost heap to which it may be applied. The farmer should keep a quantity of this mixture constantly on hand.

Brine which has been used for salting meat or fish is still more valuable than that newly made, as it contains a portion o' blood and other animal matter.

Whenever refuse nitrate of potash—that is, common saltpeter—or refuse liquid in which it has been dissolved for pickling meat, can be procured, it should be carefully preserved and mixed into a compost heap.

There are various other salts which are valuable as manures, but the high price at which they are sold precludes their use in ordinary cases.

5. *Ashes.*—Ashes, as we have seen, compose the entire inorganic parts of plants. Returned to the soil, they may again be taken up by the growing vegetation. Their great usefulness as a manure is evident and undisputed. The ashes from different trees differ materially in composition and value; but all are highly useful applications to every kind of soil and crop. Johnston gives the composition of the ash from oak and beech as follows:

PER-CENTAGE OF	Oak.	Beech.
Potash	8.43	15.83
Soda	5.64	2.79
Common salt	0.02	0.28
Lime	74.63	62.37
Sulphate of lime	1.98	2.31
Magnesia	4.49	11.29
Oxyd of iron	0.57	0.79
Phosphoric acid	3.46	8.07
Silica	0.78	1.32
	100.00	100.00

"Ashes," Allen observes, "are to the earthy part of vegetables what milk is to the animal system, or barn-yard manures to the entire crop; they contain every element, and generally in the right proportions, to insure a full and rapid growth."

Leached ashes have lost some of their value, being deprived

of the greater portion of their potash and soda, but are still very useful as manures.

Coal ashes are less valuable than wood ashes, but are by no means to be neglected by the farmer.

Soot is exceedingly valuable as a manure, and the small quantity produced should be carefully saved.

IV.—MANAGEMENT OF MANURES.

Great skill and care are requisite in the management of manures, in order to preserve them from waste and secure their greatest efficiency. Some hints on this point have already been dropped in speaking of the different kinds of manure. We have room for only a few additional suggestions.

1. *Fermentation.*—The comparative advantages of using fermented and unfermented manure is still under discussion among scientific agriculturists; but that great loss takes place when manure ferments *uncovered by some absorbent* of the fertilizing gases is clear to every observer and thinker. See to it, then, that all fermenting manure is covered with turf, muck, charcoal dust, saw-dust, or plaster, to take up and retain the ammoniacal gases as they arise.

2. *Digging over Manures.*—The frequent digging over of barn-yard manure, practiced by some farmers, while it promotes decomposition, also leads to great waste.

3. *Hauling Manure in Winter.*—The opinion is now gaining ground that when it can be conveniently done, the best way to secure to the land the greatest possible benefit from stable and barn-yard manure is to draw them at once, so fast as they are produced, to the fields where they are to be used, and either spread them at once or deposit them in heaps so small that no putrefactive fermentation will take place. In many cases, manures may be hauled in the winter with great economy, as the labor of the teams and hands is in less demand elsewhere. A correspondent of one of our agricultural journals, who hauled and spread a part of his manure in the winter and a part immediately before planting, in May, says:

"Where the manure was applied in the winter, the corn *started* earlier and continued ahead through the season; it also yielded the heaviest growth and the *largest, soundest ears*. I have followed this plan at different times, and have always been pleased with the result. In hot weather, I plow the manure under immediately after spreading."

4. *A Caution.*—*Never mix quick-lime with any animal manure*, as it will cause the escape of ammonia and greatly deteriorate the manure.

5. *Burying Manure.*—Here again doctors disagree. Some advocate burying manure very deeply, others slightly, and still others would leave it upon the surface. The best general rule, we believe, is to mix it so thoroughly as possible with every part of the soil. The roots will then be sure to find it. A few crops—onions and some of the grasses, for instance—must find their nutriment near the surface, as the roots do not extend deeply; for these a top dressing may be best.

6. *Importance of Texture.*—J. J. Thomas, in an excellent article on the "Effective Action of Manures," says:

"Far more important than the mere presence of fertilizing ingredients, or even the *chemical condition* of those ingredients, in many cases, is their mechanical texture and degree of pulverization. We have elsewhere given an instance, furnished by one of the most eminent scientific and practical cultivators of our country, where the complete crushing of the clods of an adhesive soil, and the grinding together with them into powder the manure applied to the land, produced an effect upon the subsequent crop *five times* as great as the ordinary operation of manure. How absurd it must be to make strict calculations on the result of a given quantity of yard manure, without ever inquiring into the mode of application—whether, on the one hand, by spreading in large, unbroken lumps, carelessly and imperfectly plowed under, and in a condition wholly useless for plants, or even detrimental in case of drouth—or, on the other, by a thorough harrowing of the soil and manure together, before turning under and a repetition of the operation when necessary afterward for complete intermixture. We have known the most admirable results by this practice, where nothing but fresh, coarse manure could be obtained for succulent garden crops, and nearly a total failure under like circumstances without its performance. Even the time of year that manure has been carted on the land, has sometimes had an injurious bearing on the success of its application, simply by the packing and hardening resulting from traveling over its surface when in a wet and adhesive condition. It is a perfectly self-evident truth, that a mixture of unburned bricks and clods of manure, would afford immeasurably less sustenance to the fine and delicate fibers of growing plants, than the same mixture ground down together into a fine powder. Hence it may be reasonably believed that the general introduction and free use of pulverizers, as the most effective harrows, clod-crushers, and subsoilers, assisted by tile-draining, may be of greater benefit to the whole country than the importation of a million tons of guano."

V.—COMPOSTS.

Composts of various kinds have already been recommended and described; but a few words more:

Let nothing that is capable, when decomposed, of furnishing nutriment to your growing crops be permitted to go to waste about your premises. A compost heap should be at hand to receive all decomposed refuse. The best basis for this heap is well-dried swamp muck; but where this is not readily obtained, procure rich turf scraping from the roadside, leaves and surface soil from the wood lands and the sides of fences, straw, chips, corncobs, weeds, etc., aiding the decay of the coarser materials by the addition of urine or the lime and salt mixture mentioned in a previous section. Let this be composted with any animal matter found about the premises, or in the vicinity: the carcasses of all dead animals, large or small, offal of every kind, woolen rags, bones, old boots, shoes, and waste leather of every description, the droppings of the hen-roost, soap-suds, salt, brine, all drainings from the sink spout, slops from the chambers, and cleanings from the privy: let all go to the compost heap. And whatever will not decay there, with sufficient rapidity, without assistance, aid its decay by the addition of such substances as will facilitate the object. Bones, leather, etc., may be softened so as to pulverize readily, by being packed in ashes and kept moist a few months; and if the whole be sufficiently covered with muck during the process, there will be no loss of any element; or they may be packed in an old cask in a strong solution of potash, or may be prepared with sulphuric acid in the most scientific manner, and when thus prepared in either of these ways, will add greatly to the value of the compost heap. And if it still is not strong enough, add wood ashes to any extent, from one to ten or twelve bushels per cord.

When thus prepared, our compost heap should be carefully worked over, thoroughly mixing all the different ingredients. It may then be applied to the soil in the same manner with that from the barn-cellar, or in any other way desirable.

In addition to the foregoing general compost and the various special compounded manures already referred to, every farmer who has swamp muck or peat on his farm should compost it extensively with his stable manure; for it is believed, on the evidence of careful experiment, that two cords of compost prepared by mixing daily one cord of dry muck with the same quantity of the solid excrements of animals is fully equal, for all practical purposes, to two cords of the latter preserved and applied without the muck; and also that two cords of compost, prepared by using that quantity of dry muck, to absorb all the liquid voided by the same animals, during the time required to obtain one cord of solid excrement, to be equal in value to two cords of the former compost. Thus we have four cords of equal value by this process, to every one cord obtained where the manure is thrown out of doors and left exposed to sun, wind, and rain, and all the liquid allowed to run to waste.*

These are a few of the ways in which your stock of manures

---

* W. G. Wyman, in *Country Gentleman.*

may be greatly and cheaply increased. Your own experience, observation, and study will suggest others.

VI.—IRRIGATION.

Irrigation is manuring by means of water. "The manner of irrigating must depend on the situation of the surface and the supply of water. Sometimes, reservoirs are made for its reception from rains or inundations; and at others, they are collected at vast expense, from springs found by deep excavations, and led out by extensive subterraneous ditching. The usual source of supply, however, is from streams or rivulets, or copious springs, which discharge their water on elevated ground. The former are dammed up, to turn the water into ditches or aqueducts, through which it is conducted to the fields, where it is divided into smaller rills, till it finally disappears. When it is desirable to bring more water on to meadows than is required for saturating the ground, and its escape to fields below is to be avoided, other ditches should be made on the lower sides, to arrest and convey away the surplus water."

Irrigation contributes to the growth of plants in several ways. 1. It causes the deposit on the surface of the soil of more or less fertilizing matter brought from a distance by the stream; 2. It brings the gases—oxygen, nitrogen, and carbonic acid, to the roots of plants in different proportions from those in which they exist in the air (but if the water be permitted to remain stagnant on the surface this effect ceases); 3. It disposes the soil to those changes, both mechanical and chemical, which are essential to its greater fertility.

"The advantages of irrigation are so manifest that they should never be neglected, when the means for securing them are within economical reach. To determine what economy in this case is, we have to estimate, from careful experiment, the equivalent needed in annual dressing with manures to produce the same amount of grass as would be gained by irrigation; and to offset the cost of the manure, we must reckon the interest on the permanent fixtures of the dam and sluices, etc.

"The increase from the application of water is sometimes fourfold, when the soil, the season, and the water are all favorable, and it is seldom less than doubled. Many fields which, in their natural condition, scarcely yield a bite of grass for cattle, when thoroughly irrigated will give a good growth for years, and without the aid of any manures.

"Light, porous soils, and particularly gravels and sands, are the most benefited by irrigation. Tenacious and clay soils are but slightly improved by it unless first made porous by underdraining. It is not only important that water be brought on to the ground, but it is almost equally important that it should pass off immediately after accomplishing the objects sought."*

---

* R. L. Allen, in the "American Farm Book."

III.

ROTATION OF CROPS.

Manuring is the steam-engine which propels the vessel, rotation is the rudder which guides its progress.—J. J. Thomas.

I.—THEORY OF ROTATION.

THE following statements and illustrations of the principles on which rotation in cropping has its foundation, are condensed from Professor Norton's "Elements of Scientific Agriculture."

"Suppose the farmer to have a soil which requires, as almost all soils do, the application of manure to render it fertile. He adds a good coating of manure, and then takes off a crop of corn or wheat. This crop will carry away the largest part of the phosphates that were added in the manure. In most cases, therefore, a second crop of the same kind would not be so good as the first; and the third would be still less. There yet remains, however, from the manure, considerable quantities of other substances, which the grain crops did not so particularly require, such as potash and soda. With this a good crop of potatoes, turnips, or beets may be obtained; and after this there is probably still enough lime, etc., left to produce an excellent crop of hay, if the ground be seeded down with another crop of grain of a lighter character than Indian corn or wheat.

We perceive, then, that any good rotation must be founded upon the principle that different classes of crops require different proportions of the various substances which are present in soils, and in the numerous fertilizers which are applied for the purpose of enriching them. Thus the crops may be made to succeed each other with the least possible injury to the soil, and with the greatest economy in the use of manures.

It would be useless to recommend here any particular system of rotation as *best;* for that must be determined by experience in each section of country, under the various circumstances of climate, location, and value of crops. Attention may, however, be again called to the fact that there are several distinct classes of crops, considered with reference to the substances which they take from the soil, and that these classes of crops should bear a part in every system of rotation. The principal of these are grain crops, root crops, and grass crops. See table and remarks in section 11 of the previous chapter.

II.—BENEFITS OF ROTATION.

J. J. Thomas, in speaking of rotation in cropping, says:

"There are other very important requisites in good farming, but they are all accomplished with an increase of expenditure and labor. Manuring, for example, is a most powerful means for improvement; but both manures and their application are expensive in proportion to the amount applied. Underdraining has wrought wonderful results, but the cost is always a large item, and the same may be said in some degree of deep plowing and subsoiling. But in the arrangement of a rotation, no additional expenditure or labor is necessary; it costs no more to cultivate crops which are made to succeed each other judiciously, than to cultivate those arranged in the worst manner possible. The former may bring triple the successful results of the latter—not by the expenditure of five hundred extra days in drawing manure, or five hundred dollars' worth of ditching, but simply by making a proper use of one's brains.

"It seems surprising, under the circumstances, that so small a number seize the golden prize thus completely placed within their reach—that there are so few, even of those reckoned good farmers, who pursue anything like a systematic succession, to say nothing of such a rotation that shall accomplish its peculiarly beneficial results, namely, preservation of the riches of the soil, destruction of weeds, destruction of insects, and the most advantageous consumption by each successive crop of all the means for its growth within reach. As a consequence of this neglect, we see land overcropped with wheat, the soil worn out for this particular grain, and those troublesome weeds, chess and red-root, taking its place. We see pastures, left unplowed for a long series of years, become filled with "buttercups" and ox-eye daisy. A disproportion of spring crops facilitates the spread of wild mustard, and among insects, grubs and wire worms increase according to the cultivation that favors their labors. It appears to be but little understood how great is the assistance to clean cultivation afforded by a good rotation. The best example of this sort we ever witnessed, where every field of the symmetrically laid-out farm, except a wet meadow, was brought under a regular, unvarying system, scarcely a weed was ever to be seen; and we ascertained that not one third of the labor usually expended was required for the hand dressing of hoed crops."

For something more on this topic, see chapter on "Farm Management."

IV.

DRAINING.

If one of our railroads should be known to pay thirty per cent. dividend annually, from its regular earnings, and the stock could be bought at par, what a furious rush would be made for it. Yet there is a way that farmers may invest in stocks at home, on their own lands, that will pay thirty to fifty per cent. yearly. This is in systematic tile-draining. We have known many who have tried it, and they generally say that it is paid for by the increased crops in two years. They are good farmers, however.—Annual Register of Rural Affairs.

There is not one farm out of every seventy-five in this State but needs draining—yes, much draining—to bring it into high cultivation.—Com. Report to N. Y. State Ag. Soc.

I.—EFFECTS OF DRAINING.

SOME of the unfavorable effects of an excess of moisture in a soil have already been adverted to, and the proper remedy—thorough drainage—pointed out. Thorough drainage implies *covered* drains, and it is to the advantages of these mainly that we now desire to call the reader's attention; although, as we have said in a previous chapter, open ditches and water-furrows are very useful in certain situations.

The rain which falls upon a piece of land prepared with properly constructed covered drains never remains to stagnate or to run over the surface, washing off the best of the soil, but sinks gradually down, yielding to the roots of plants any fertilizing matter which it may contain, and often washing out some hurtful substances. As it descends, air and consequently warmth follow it. Under these new influences the proper decompositions and preparations of compounds fit for the sustenance of plants go on, the soil is warm and sufficiently dry, and plants flourish which formerly would never grow on it in perfection, if at all. It is a curious fact, too, that such soils resist drouth better than ever before. The reason is, that the plants are able to send their roots much farther down in search of food without finding anything hurtful. Every part being penetrated by the air, and consequently dryer and lighter, these soils do not bake in summer, but remain mellow and porous. Such effects can not, in their full extent, be looked for in a stiff clay in a single season; the change must be gradual, but it is sure.*

The principal benefits of a system of covered drains are succinctly and clearly stated in the following—

"TEN REASONS FOR UNDERDRAINING.

"1. It prevents water which falls from resting on or near the surface, and renders the soil dry enough to be worked or plowed at all times.

"2. By rendering the soil porous or spongy, it takes in water without flooding in time of rain, and gives it off again gradually in time of drouth.

"3. By preventing adhesion and assisting pulverization, it allows the roots to pass freely through all parts of the soil.

"4. By facilitating the mixture of manure through the pulverized portions, it greatly increases its value and effect.

"5. It allows water falling on the surface to pass downward, carrying with it any fertilizing substances (as carbonic acid and ammonia), until they are arrested by the absorption of the soil.

"6. It abstracts in a similar manner the heat contained in falling rains, thus warming the soil, the water discharged by drain-mouths being many degrees colder than ordinary rains.

"7. The increased porosity of the soil renders it a more per

---

* Norton's "Elements of Agriculture."

fect non-conductor of heat, and the roots of plants are less injured by freezing in winter.

"8. The same cause admits the entrance of air, facilitating the decomposition of enriching portions of the soil.

"9. By admitting early plowing, crops may be sown early, and an increased amount reaped in consequence.

"10. It economizes labor, by allowing the work to go on at all times without interruption from surplus water in spring, or from a hard-baked soil in summer."*

II.—CONDITIONS REQUIRING DRAINAGE.

The conditions from which arise the principal causes of mischief to undrained land are thus stated by Munn in "The Practical Land-Drainer :"

"1. Where water has accumulated beneath the surface and originated springs.

"2. Where, from the close nature of the substrata, it can not pass freely downward, but accumulates and forms its level, or water-line, at a short distance below the surface; and

"3. Where, from the clayey or close texture of the soil, it lies on the surface and becomes stagnant."

Farmers are apt to consider land in which the second condition mentioned exists, to be too dry to need draining, yet it is *cold* and *sour*, late in spring, apt to bake hard in summer, and very liable to suffer from early frosts in autumn. There is no remedy but underdraining. The necessity of this operation in the other two cases named is obvious.

III.—PRACTICAL DIRECTIONS.

1. *Preliminary.*—The first thing to be done is to examine the field to be drained and determine the plan of drainage best adapted to effect the object in view, and the materials which may most economically be used in constructing the drains.

2. *Draining Springy Soils.*—Where the wetness to be remedied results from springs having their source in higher grounds

---

* "Annual Register of Rural Affairs."

above the field to be drained, the desired result is generally attained by making one or more drains across the declivity about where the low grounds of the valley begin to form, thus intercepting or cutting off the springs. These transverse drains must be connected with others, made for the purpose of conveying the water collected in them into some brook, ravine, or other outlet which may be near.

3. *Direction of Drains.*—In cases characterized by either of the other conditions specified in the previous section, parallel drains should be cut *directly up and down the inclination of the field*, and emptying into a main cross drain at the lower side.

4. *Depth and Distance Apart.*—In reference to depth and distance apart, differences of opinion and of practice prevail. Some cut their drains only about two and a half feet deep and from twelve to twenty feet apart, while others make them from three and a half to five feet deep and from thirty to fifty feet apart. The experience of some of the most extensive drainers both in this country and in Europe seems to indicate, however, that for very heavy, clayey soils, from two and a half to three feet in depth and from twelve to thirty feet apart, generally produce the most satisfactory results. More porous and friable soils may be successfully drained at greater depth and distance.

5. *Digging.*—Having marked out your drains at the distance apart decided upon, and got your tiles or other materials ready for laying down the ducts, you may begin to dig, commencing at the lower end, cutting the main drain into which the others are to empty, and then working upward on the parallel drains. Their dimensions must depend mainly upon the material to be used for the ducts. Where they are to be filled with broken stone or brush, they are made wider than where the small, oval tile, tube, or pipe is to be laid. Where tiles of any kind are to be used, their size must determine the width of the bottom of the drain. The top must be wider for convenience of digging. A narrow spade and a peculiar hoe are necessary for digging and smoothing the bottom of the drain. There must

be a gradual fall, of course, from end to end, of which the regular flow of water will be a test. For the purpose of keeping a uniform grade of descent in cutting drains, a common mason's level will answer; but the A or span level, represented by the accompanying cut, is better. Such a level may easily be constructed of wood. The span should be either sixteen feet six inches, or half that length. The two feet being placed on a perfectly level floor, the

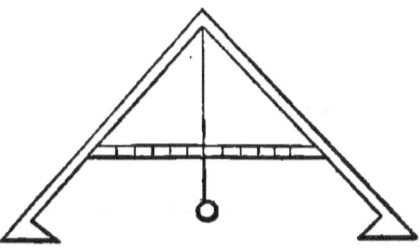

plumb-line will hang in the center, where a notch should be cut in the cross-bar. Then place a block of wood, exactly an inch thick, under one leg, and mark the place on the cross-bar that the plumb-line touches. Put a second block of one inch under the same leg, and mark the place of contact of the line with the bar as before, and so on so far as is necessary. Then mark the other side in the same way. When thus prepared, if the span of the level be sixteen feet and six inches, the plumb-line will indicate upon the bar, by the number of spaces at which it hangs from the center, the number of inches per rod of the descent. If its span be eight feet and three inches. it will, in the same way, indicate the number of inches of descent in half a rod.*

6. *Materials and Construction.*—The ditch thus excavated must now be furnished with a permanent duct through which water may at all times freely pass off. This may be constructed of various substances—brushwood, straw, turf, clinkers from furnaces, wood, brick, stone, and tiles of burned clay. Of these, stone and tiles in their various forms, when they can be procured, are the only materials which we can unconditionally recommend.

Brushwood Drains.—Where no better materials are avail-

---

* Munn.

able these will be found, while they last, quite effective; and they are far more permanent than might be supposed. An instance is recorded where they have been found after twenty years in as good condition apparently as when constructed. They are formed by laying down branches or brushwood in the bottom of the drain to form the duct for the passage of the water. The brush are put into the cutting in a slanting direction with the descent of the ground, their root or large ends being toward the bottom. They should be trodden down and covered with inverted turf before filling in.

Stone Drains.—In reference to their mode of construction, stone drains are of various kinds. The simplest form is that in which the ditch or cutting is filled, to the depth of nine or ten inches, with small stones, covered with inverted turf, shavings, or something of the kind. The stones should be about the size of a hen's egg. Where larger ones are used, the earth is apt to fall into the cavities, or mice or rats make their burrows there, and the drain becomes choked. Some, however, make use of larger stones,

THE STONE SCREEN.

merely covering them with a layer of small stones or gravel, before putting on the sod. When the stones are procured, whether in a natural state or broken, it is desirable to screen them in order to get them assorted as to size. The accompanying cut represents an excellent portable harp or screen for that purpose. Having filled the ditch to the required depth, and covered the surface carefully with inverted sods, the earth should be thrown in and trampled hard upon them. *The water should find its way into the drain from the sides, and not from the top.*

Fig. 1.

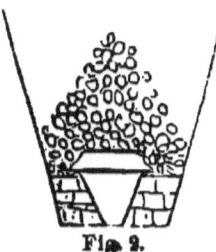
Fig. 2.

The accompanying cuts represent other forms of stone drains, in which flat stones are used to form a regular and continuous duct. A drain well constructed in either of these forms may be considered permanent. Where the earth is hard and the quantity of water is not large, the form represented by Fig. 4 is the best and cheapest in which a stone drain can be constructed. In making stone drains in swampy or

Fig. 3.

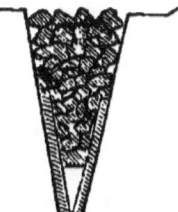
Fig. 4.

very soft ground it is sometimes necessary to lay a plank or slab on the bottom, before putting in the stones, to prevent them from sinking before the soil shall become dry enough to be firm.

But in large portions of the country stones can not be procured, and where they can be had, and require to be broken and screened, the expense is considerable; and it is now found that, in many cases, tiles made of clay and burned are much cheaper.

Tile Drains.—The first form of tile drain used was arched

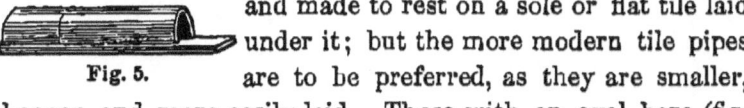
Fig. 5.

and made to rest on a sole or flat tile laid under it; but the more modern tile pipes are to be preferred, as they are smaller, cheaper, and more easily laid. Those with an oval bore (fig.

Fig. 6.

Fig. 7.

7) are considered better than those with a round one. The

tiles are, of course, placed in the bottom of the ditch, which must be smooth and straight. They are simply placed end to end and wedged a little with small stones, if necessary, and the earth packed hard over them. *The water very readily finds its way in through the pores of the material and at the joints.* Collars or short outer tiles are sometimes used to go over the joints, to secure them against getting displaced. An inch pipe is sufficient for most situations. It may seem impossible for the water freely to reach a tile pipe with the earth packed close about it, especially where the soil is clayey; but practically no difficulty occurs. The portion of earth next the drain first dries; and as it shrinks on drying, little cracks begin to radiate in every direction, and to spread until they penetrate the whole mass of the soil within their influence, allowing the superfluous oisture to pass off, and rendering the ground, in the course a season or two, light, mellow, and wholesome for plants.*

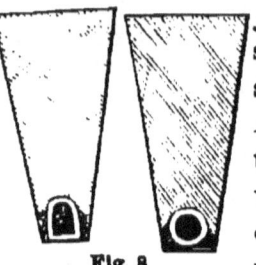

Fig. 8.

For main drains (where the parallel drains do not discharge directly into some open ditch, ravine, or brook, and the former are not constructed of stone or brick), two horse-shoe or arched tiles may be used, one inverted against the other.

The drains should be connected at the upper end of the field by a small drain running at right angles with them. It should be of the same depth as the other drains.

Where the ground is firm and the drain is made in the summer, and when the length is not great, begin at the upper end to lay the tiles or put in the stones; but where the ground is liable to fall down at the sides, the safest way is to build the conduit or duct immediately after the earth is taken out of the bottom.†

IV.—WILL UNDERDRAINING PAY?

The *Genesee Farmer* thus answers this question: This de-

---

* Norton.   † Munn.

pends on circumstances. If good naturally underdrained land can be obtained in your neighborhood for from $15 to $20 per acre, it would not pay in all probability to expend $30 per acre in underdraining low, wet, or springy land; but in all districts where land is worth $50 per acre, nothing can pay better than to expend from $20 to $30 per acre in judicious underdraining. The labor of cultivation is much reduced, while the produce is generally increased one half, and is not unfrequently doubled; *and it must be remembered that the increase is net profit.* If we get $15 worth of wheat from one acre and $20 worth from the other, and the expense of cultivation is $10 in both cases, the *profit* from the one is twice as much as from the other. That judicious underdraining will increase the crops one third, can not be doubted by any one who has witnessed its effects. If it should double the crops, as it often does, the *profit* would be four-fold."

It has been remarked, that "to apply manure to undrained land, is to throw money away," an illustration of which is furnished by a statement in the Transactions of the New York State Agricultural Society, where seven acres of low, wet land, manured annually at the rate of 25 loads to the acre, produced 31 bushels of oats per acre; but after being thoroughly underdrained at a cost of about $60 for the whole, the first crop of oats without manure was 89½ bushels per acre.

Gov. Wright, in his address before the Wayne County Agricultural Society, estimates the amount of marshy lands in Indiana at three million acres. These were generally avoided by early settlers as being comparatively worthless, but when drained they become eminently fertile. He says: "I know a farm of 160 acres that was sold five years ago for $500, that by the expenditure of less than $200, in draining and ditching, the present owner refuses now $3,000."

No estimates of the cost of draining that we could give would be of much practical value. The character of the soil, the cost of the materials, the price of labor, and other circumstances, must be taken into the account, and these vary so much in different localities that they can not be made the basis of any useful general estimates. The following table, showing the number of tiles, of the different lengths made, which are required for an acre, will be useful to those who may desire to purchase just enough for a particular piece of ground. We extract it from Munn's "Practical Land-Drainer:"

DISTANCE APART.	12-Inch Tiles.	13-Inch Tiles.	14-Inch Tiles.	15-Inch Tiles.
Drains 12 feet apart require	3,630	3,351	3,111	2,9 4
" 15 " " "	2,904	2,681	2,489	2,323
" 18 " " "	2,420	2,234	2,074	1,936
" 21 " " "	2,074	1,914	1,777	1,659
" 24 " " "	1,815	1,675	1,556	1,452
" 27 " " "	1,613	1,480	1,383	1,291
" 30 " " "	1,452	1,340	1,245	1,162
" 33 " " "	1,320	1,218	1,131	1,056
" 36 " " "	1,210	1,117	1,037	968

In reference to tile-pipe drains, it must be remembered that the ditch may be much narrower than when stones are used, thus making a considerable saving in the expense of digging. The upper part of the earth is taken out with a common spade, and the lower part with one made quite narrow for the purpose, being only about four inches wide at the point.

V.

FENCES.

<small>Have an eye upon your fences!—*Farmer's Almanac.*</small>

I.—REQUISITES OF A GOOD FENCE.

THE first essential in a farm fence is perfect efficiency as a barrier against such animals as it is desired to shut in or exclude. Without this quality it is worse than useless. In the second place, it must be so cheap that its cost will not exceed, to say the least, the profit to be derived from its existence. Thirdly, it must not require too frequent renewal. It is desirable, also, that it occupy little space, and that it do not present an unsightly appearance. The best fence, therefore, for any given place and time, is the one which combines most perfectly all these qualities. In one place this may be stone fence, in another one of posts and rails, in a third a live hedge, etc. In one period of a country's history it may be made of logs, in another of rails, in a third of growing Osage orange or holly, and in a fourth of wire.

II.—VARIOUS KINDS OF FENCE.

1. *Stone Fence.*—Wherever there is plenty of stone, and especially where loose stones abound, and must be removed before the land can be properly cultivated, stone fences are the

best and most economical that can be constructed. When well built, broad, and high, they are perfectly efficient and very permanent. In an esthetic point of view they are far less offensive to the eye of taste than our wooden fences, even of the least objectionable form. After a few years, as we judge from the sober livery of moss with which she decks them, Nature adopts these structures as her own, and they become a legitimate portion of the landscape.

Where stone is not very abundant, a combination of stone and rail fence is often economically constructed. A substantial foundation of stones is laid, reaching two or two and a half feet above ground, in which posts are placed at proper distances, with two or three bar holes above the wall, for the insertion of an equal number of rails, which for convenience should be put in when the posts are set.

2. *The Zig-zag or Worm Fence.*—In large portions of our country, where there is a superabundance of timber, and economy of space is of little importance, the common zig-zag or worm fence of the West and South is probably the most economical that can be erected. When well built, it is firm and durable, but unsightly and inconvenient, occupying a great deal of space, harboring vermin, and encouraging the growth of weeds and bushes.

3. *Post-and-Rail Fences.*—As timber becomes somewhat more valuable, it ceases to be economical to use it so lavishly as the worm fence requires, and the post-and-rail fence takes its place. This is, in many respects, the best of all the wooden farm fences.

"The posts," Allen says, "should be placed from two and a half to three feet below the surface, in the center of a large hole and surrounded by fine stone, which must be well pourded down by a heavy, iron-shod rammer, as they are filled in. The post will not stand so firmly at first as if surrounded by dirt, but it will last much longer. The lower end should be pointed, which prevents its heaving with the frost. If the position of the post while in the tree be reversed, or the upper end of the split section of the trunk which is used for a post, be placed in the earth, it will be more durable. Charring or partially burning the part of the post which is buried, will add to its duration. So also will imbedding it in ashes, lime, charcoal, or clay; or it may be bored at the surface with a large auger, diagonally downward and nearly through, then filled with salt, and closely plugged.

"The best timber for posts, in the order of its durability, is red cedar, yellow locust, white oak and chestnut, for the Northern and Middle States. I recently saw red cedar posts in use for a porch which, I was assured, had been standing exposed to the weather previous to the Revolution, a period of over 70 years, and they were still perfectly sound. The avidity with which silicious sands and gravel act upon wood, renders a post fence expensive for such soils."*

In some cases, boards may be economically substituted for rails, and firmly nailed to suitably prepared posts.

4. *The Sunken Fence.*—The sunken fence or wall consists of "a vertical excavation on one side, about five feet in depth, against which a wall is built to the surface of the ground. The opposite side is inclined at such an angle as will preserve the sod against sliding, from the effects of frost or rain, and is then turfed over. A farm thus divided presents no obstruction to the view, where it is everywhere properly walled in, besides affording good ditches for the drainage of water." Such a fence, properly constructed, might be considered absolutely permanent; and it would scarcely need repairing at all.

5. *Iron Fences.*—Wire and other forms of iron fence are coming into extensive use in some portions of the country. Where there is a deficiency of both timber and stone, the wire fence is probably the best and most economical that can be made. With the improvements lately introduced, especially those made by the New York Wire Railing Company, these fences are entirely efficient, and in every way satisfactory.

---

* The "American Farm Book."

The fences are made with horizontal wires, tightened by means of an effective arrangement, so that *the whole tension of the rod is obtained.* The posts are furnished with contrivances of different patterns for security in the ground. The size of the rods varies in accordance with the uses for which the fence is designed. No ordinary domestic animal will break through fences of considerably less than ¼-inch wrought wire, while still larger sizes may be used with the same facility if required. The bright or hard wire is now generally used.*

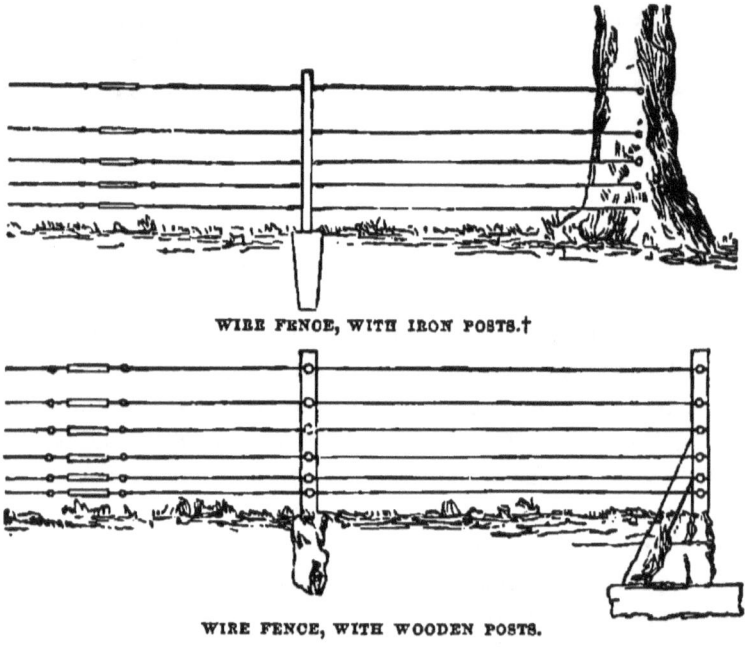

WIRE FENCE, WITH IRON POSTS.†

WIRE FENCE, WITH WOODEN POSTS.

* We are indebted for the accompanying illustrations of wire fences to the Descriptive Catalogue of the New York Wire Railing Company. John B. Wickersham, Superintendent.

† As it may be useful to some of our readers, we give the prices per rod at which this fence may be procured (packed and shipped) at the warehouse of the New York Iron Railing Company, in New York.

For cattle and horses, 3 wires, with iron posts and screws..............$1 66
   "   "   "   4   "   "   "   "   "...............1 84
   "   "   "   5   "   "   "   "   "...............2 00
   " Hogs, sheep, etc. 7   "   "   "   "...............2 40
   " Turkeys, geese, etc. 10   "   "   "   "...............3 00
Each additional wire, 20 cents per rod.

The accompanying cut exhibits the natural size of the wires most commonly used for farm fences, and shows the manner in

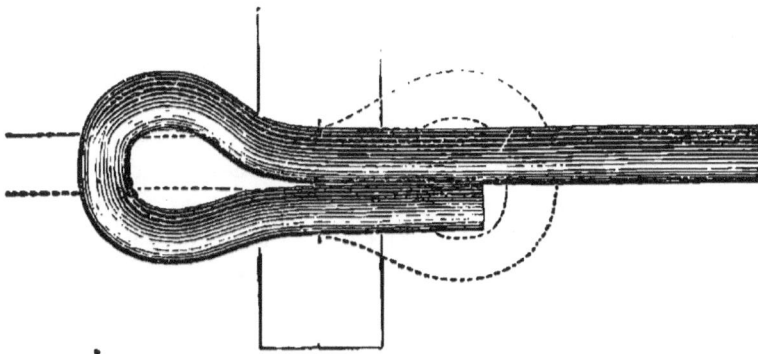

which they pass through and support the post and are supported by it. The following are the manufacturer's directions for putting up the fence:

"It is absolutely necessary that the straining pillar, or starting post, of wood or iron, at the extreme ends of the fence, should be perfectly firm, as the wires can not otherwise be made tight. Commencing from a tree is recommended, if possible. Plant the posts 12 feet apart, hook in the rails, and at the distance of 150 feet place a screw on each wire. Place the next set of screws at the distance of 300 feet, and so continue.'

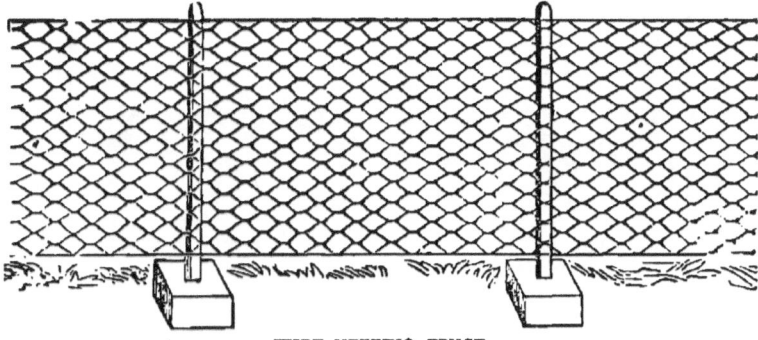

WIRE NETTING FENCE.

The wire netting fence furnishes an admirable barrier against small animals, poultry, etc. It costs from $1 50 to $2 75 per rod, according to the height and the size of the wire and meshes.

Another style of iron farm fence is called the "Corrugated Flat Rail Fence." It is in some respects preferable to the round rail or wire, being visible at a greater distance and less liable to sagging.

6. *Hurdle Fence.*—The hurdle, or light, movable fence is formed in short panels, and firmly set in the ground by sharpened stakes at the end of each panel, and these are fastened together. This is a convenient addition to farms where heavy green crops of clover, lucern, peas, or turnips are required to be fed off in successive lots, by sheep, swine, or cattle. It is variously constructed of wood or iron, and is much less expensive than might be supposed, "Wickersham's Corrugated Hurdle Fence" being furnished by the Wire Railing Company at from $2 50 to $5 per rod, according to weight and quality.

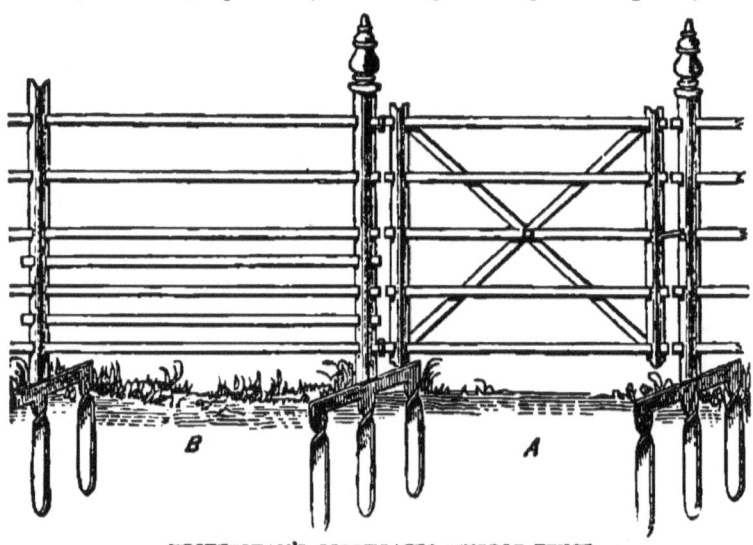

WICKERSHAM'S CORRUGATED HURDLE FENCE.

7. *Hedges.*—The live fence, almost universal in England, is still an experiment here. There have been a few successes and many failures in the cultivation of hedges. The causes of failure have been various—a wrong choice of trees, the dryness

of our climate, lack of experience in planting, neglect of proper after cultivation and pruning, etc. But the few examples of complete success which may be pointed out prove conclusively that, under proper and easily attainable conditions, live fences are perfectly practicable in this country; and in some parts of it they are doubtless economical. When well kept, they are certainly very beautiful.

Among the plants employed in this country with more or less success for hedges are the buckthorn, the hawthorn, the barberry, the althea or rose of Sharon, the Osage orange, the American arbor vitæ, the American holly, the hemlock spruce, the white cedar, the evergreen thorn (*Cratægus pyracantha*), the Cherokee rose, and the white Macartney rose.

For the Middle, Western, and some of the Northern States, the Osage orange seems to be, on the whole, the best. It also succeeds at the South; but there the evergreen thorn, the Cherokee rose, and especially the single white Macartney rose, are preferable.

The soil for a hedge row must be deeply plowed or spaded, and, if poor, manured a little. The space thus prepared should be at least two feet wide, and with a soil from eighteen inches to two feet deep. The best way is to open a trench of the required width and depth, throw some well-rotted manure in the bottom, and then fill up with the surface earth. Along the middle of this filled trench stretch a line, and make holes under it in the soft earth every six or eight inches, with a "dibble" or pointed stick. Set your plants in the holes precisely as you would plant cabbages, pressing the earth around the roots, and leaving only one inch of the top visible above the surface. The plants may be either one or two years old, and the tops should be cut off within two inches of the root. The young hedge must be well cultivated for several years, and cut back once or twice a year till it shall be four feet high. The conical shape is best for a hedge, as it admits every shoot to the benefit of the air and light. Where vacancies occur, vigorous shoots may be "layered"—that is, fastened to the ground with hooked pegs, when they will take root and send up sprouts to fill the open spaces.

The editor of the *Country Gentleman* very truly says: "*Not one Osage orange hedge in twenty succeeds, simply because it is expected to take care of itself after setting out.* Constant culture and cutting are as essential as air and food to animals."

Evergreens make the handsomest hedges; and although less stout, yet by shutting out *sight* are usually quite safe. The Norway fir is the fastest grower—the hemlock most beautiful, and the best of any for the shade of trees; the growth is, however, rather slow. It shears finely, and its *interior* is dense. The Norway fir also does well on these points.

At the South we should choose the single white Macartney rose for general cultivation; although the Cherokee rose, when properly treated, the evergreen thorn, the honey locust, the jujube, and the Spanish bayonet (*Yucca gloriosa*) all form efficient and beautiful hedges.

Mr. Redmond, one of the editors of the *Southern Cultivator*, gives the following directions for the cultivation of rose hedges; and no one is better qualified to speak on this point:

"As a general rule, both the Macartney and Cherokee roses are improperly planted. To succeed with them, it is necessary to open two parallel ditches or trenches about four feet apart, heaping the earth along the center in the form of a sloping bank. At the *base* of this bank, on each side, plant 12-inch cuttings in December or January, training the tops *over* the bank from each side. Having this bank as a foundation, they will constantly layer themselves and grow *close at the bottom*, and will interlace their thorny branches so intricately that no animal can pass through. The ditch on each side forms an additional obstruction to the passage of animals, and forms a definite boundary or limit to the hedge—to which limit only the ends of the branches must be allowed to extend. In trimming, a man passes rapidly along the bottom of the ditch, clipping off even with the inner side all the straggling ends of the plants. In order to explain this system of rose hedges more fully, we will endeavor to give a drawing hereafter. In the mean time, let it be remembered that the cuttings *must always be planted at the bottom*, never at the top of the bank—the latter situation being too dry to make them grow off vigorously."

SECTION OF MODEL HEDGE.

A really good and perfect hedge should form a rounded pyramid, similar to the accompanying cut, branching out broadly and close to the ground, and tapering up either sharply or obtuse, as the taste of the cultivator may determine. This is a fundamental principle in all hedging, and unless it is secured at the outset by proper trimming, it can never be done afterward.

III.—A HINT OR TWO.

But let your fence be of what kind it may, it is necessary, in the words of our motto, to "keep an eye" upon it. Some accident may cause a breach in the best fence, and a fence that is not perfectly efficient is worse than none. A fence, to accomplish the purpose of a fence, must not only be able to "stand alone," but must bear a little jostling. Your cattle may very innocently rub themselves against it. If it tumble down, who can blame them if they walk into the adjoining field, or into the highway, as the case may be? And you underrate their sagacity if you suppose that they will not take a hint from the accident, and rub again for the express purpose of producing the result obtained before without a purpose. Rail bars are often slipped out in this way. Gates are much better. "When bars are used, they should be let down so near the ground that every animal can step over conveniently; nor should they be hurried over so fast as to induce any animal to jump. In driving a flock of sheep through them, the lower bars ought to be taken entirely out, or they be allowed to go over the bars in single file. Animals will seldom become jumpers, except through their owner's fault, or from some bad example set them by unruly associates; and unless the fences be perfectly secure, such ought to be stalled till they can be disposed of. The farmer will find that no animal will repay him the trouble and cost of expensive fences and ruined crops."

IV.—ARE FENCES NECESSARY?

The burden and expense of fence-making is so great that the question has very naturally been raised whether it would not be better, in an economical point of view, to dispense with them entirely. It is said that the greatest investment of capital in this country is in the common fences which divide the fields from the highway, and separate them from each other. Do they pay?

In France, Belgium, Germany, Italy, and other parts of Europe, fences are seldom seen. When cattle or sheep are pastured in these countries, they are placed under the care of a herdsman or shepherd, who, with the aid of his sagacious and well-trained dog, easily keeps a large herd or flock within prescribed limits, which are marked by a slight ditch, or in some other simple way. Does the labor of the herdsman and his dog cost more than the fences which would have been required without him? In those countries undoubtedly not. In reference to the United States we have not the necessary estimates or the exact data on which to base them; but, according to the figures given in the following extract from an article published in the *Ohio Farmer*, it appears that fences do not always pay, even here, where labor costs so much more than in Europe. After mentioning the fact that the ancients had no fences, and that there are none in France, and declaring them wholly unnecessary here, the writer goes on:

"The fences in our State cost more than its railroads. Now, this huge amount of capital is, to all intents and purposes, dead. More, it is a decaying capital; annually a large amount of its depreciated stock must be replaced. These repairs cost immense sums of timber, time, and hard work. But the evil does not stop here: timber is decreasing in quantity and quality; for rails, posts, and stakes require a great deal, and that of the best kind, while our vast prairies have no timber at all hardly for fencing.

"And there are other evils connected with this expensive and stupid modern invention. Fences become the refuge of vermin and all manner of noxious weeds. Then, too, they act as natural and annual distributors of these weeds. The fence protects the weed till it is ripe, and then furnishes the seed to the first high winds of winter and spring.

"In addition to these objections to fences, we might mention that they occupy a great deal of ground.

"Now, what are their advantages? They keep cattle in their proper places, protecting the farmer against his own and other people's cattle. But what need is there for anybody's cattle to run at large? There are laws now prohibiting some kinds of animals from running abroad; why not extend it to all? It is our impression that it would be much more economical to hire help to attend them in the field and in the stable than to pay for fences, fencing, and waste lands occupied by fences.

"We will append a few figures, from our own experience, in order to present to the farming community the importance of looking at this matter. We claim no special accuracy for our statistics, but they are, in the main, correct; and if they will call out from one or more of our farmers and agricultural professors the facts in the case, as they exist in our State, we shall feel that our object has been accomplished.

"Taking our own observations as a guide, these are the figures: Chestnut rails are worth six dollars per hundred; oak stakes, about three dollars per hundred. It takes fourteen rails and four stakes per rod for a worm fence; in round numbers, it costs one dollar per rod. This would be three hundred and twenty dollars per mile, and there were seven miles of fence, making two thousand two hundred and forty dollars for the fencing material. Now, add to this first cost the price of hauling, of setting up, or keeping in repair, of decay, and of the waste of land occupied. If you pay for bringing these rails to their proper places and putting them up, the first cost of material will be three thousand dollars. First cost of material and work, three thousand dollars; interest at six per cent., one hundred and eighty dollars; annual decay, six per cent., one hundred and eighty dollars; annual repairs, three per cent., ninety dollars; loss of land, five per cent., one hundred and fifty dollars. Annual cost, five hundred dollars.

"Could not this sum be better used?"

We suspect that in reference to large portions of the West, at least, the writer's closing question may be answered in the affirmative.

VI.

FARM IMPLEMENTS AND THEIR USE.

'Tis time to clear your plowshare in the glebe.—Graham.

I.—THE PLOW.

HISTORY does not inform us when plows were first used; but there are traces of them in the earliest of all written authorities—the Bible. By consulting the sacred records (Deut. xxii. 10) we find that in very early times they plowed with two oxen, and that their plow had a coulter and plowshare (Sam. xiii. 20); and drawings of early Greek plows show that they were furnished with wheels. The plows of Rome were of the most simple form. "Nothing," J. J. Thomas says, "shows the improvements of modern agriculture more conspicuously than the difference between the old and new plows." The "old plow" is still used in many countries where farmers do not enjoy the benefit of agricultural periodicals. The accompanying cut represents the plow at present used in Morocco. It would hardly receive the premium of the State Agricultural Society, and has probably never been patented. It may, however, be made very cheaply, the point only being shod with iron. In the less civilized regions of Morocco the plow consists only of a crooked limb of a tree, with a projecting branch sharpened to a point for scratching up the ground. The Moors do not take the agricultural papers.*

A MOORISH PLOW.

Compare the rude implement of the Moor with the improved Eagle Plow of Nourse, Mason & Co., here represented. This

THE EAGLE PLOW.

is a No. 2, and is a medium-sized two-horse or cattle sod or stubble plow. It is adapted to turn sod furrows from four to seven inches deep by from twelve to fourteen inches wide, and will work somewhat deeper in stubble plowing. It is rigged with the lock coulter, wheel, draft-rod, and dial clevis, as represented by the cut, and with these fixtures is a very strong, and at the same time light plow for two cattle or horses, in plowing stony, stumpy, or rough, uneven land. Or it is rigged with wheel and cutter, for flat furrows in smooth land. There are other sizes, both larger and smaller than this, and for general use no plow has given better satisfaction.

An admirable plow for turning under sward deeply is the Double Michigan. "It has two mold-boards. The forward or small one skims the surface, taking off a few inches of the top of the sod, and laying it in the bottom of the previous furrow;

---

* Annual Register of Rural Affairs.

and the second or large mold-board turns up what is left, and completely buries the former. Three strong horses will draw this plow when of the smaller size, and will run a furrow eight or nine inches deep; but the larger sized plow requires nearly double this force, and will cut a furrow a foot deep.

"The Michigan plow prepares sod ground in the best manner for planting corn, the mellow soil which is thrown on the sod being deep enough to allow a coat of manure to be buried afterward a few inches by means of a gang-plow.

"When the subsoil is of such a nature as not to enrich the top soil when thrown up and mixed with it, or when it is desirable to loosen up a deep bed of mellow earth to serve as a reservoir for moisture, the *subsoil plow* serves a valuable purpose. It is also useful for loosening the soil to allow the trench or Michigan plow to enter more fully to a greater depth.

"The subsoil plow merely loosens the earth, but does not turn it up to the surface. It is made to follow in the furrow of a common plow. It runs much deeper than the trench plow, with the same force of team. Four horses attached to a strong plow, running in a furrow seven inches deep, will loosen the earth to a depth of fifteen to eighteen inches. The benefit of subsoiling depends essentially on keeping the ground well drained; for if the loosened earth is afterward allowed to become thoroughly soaked or flooded with water, it soon becomes compacted together again, and the operation proves of no permanent advantage. This is one fruitful source of failure."*

The ridging or double mold-board plow is a very useful implement. It is used for opening drills to plant

DOUBLE MOLD-BOARD PLOW.

potatoes, corn, etc.; in plowing between narrow rows; in dig-

---

* J. J. Thomas.

ging potatoes, etc. No farmer should be without it. It is a light one-horse plow.

The side-hill or swivel-plow is so constructed that the moldboard is easily and instantly changed from one side to the other, which enables the plowman to perform the work horizontally upon hillsides, going back and forth on the same side, and turning all the furrow slices downward. This prevents the washing of the soil by heavy rains, to which all hillsides are more or less liable when plowed up and down the slope. Such a plow should be considered indispensable at the South.

II.—THE HARROW.

Next to the plow in the order of description, as well as of use, comes the harrow. Like the plow, it was anciently a very

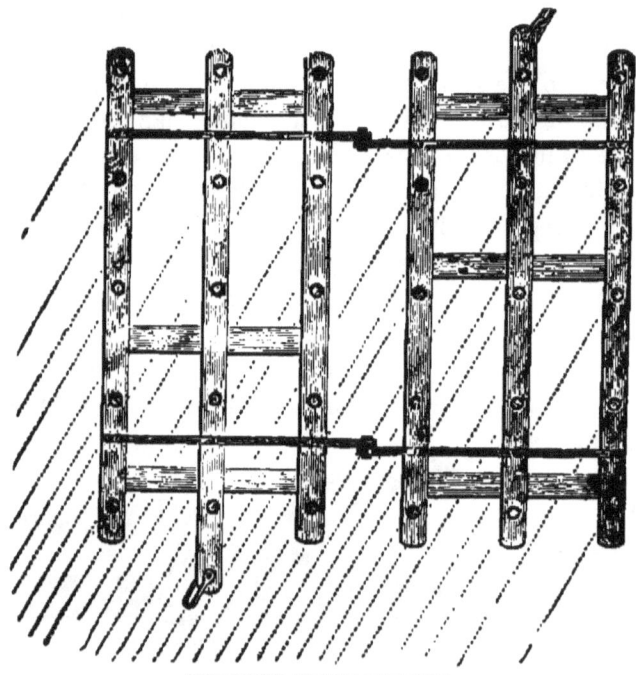

IMPROVED HINGE HARROW.

rude implement; and it is only quite recently that it has reached the high degree of efficiency and facility of action which char-

Farm Implements and Their Use. 77

acterize the best implements of the present day. "He must have lived to little purpose who is content to use the clumsy, coarse harrow of former days."

One of the best of the improved harrows is the hinge harrow represented by the accompanying cut. This harrow may be folded double, or separated into two parts, for the convenience of transportation or other purpose. Either half may be lifted for any purpose while the implement is in motion; and the easy and independent play of the parts up and down upon the hinges enables the instrument to adapt itself to the surface of the ground in all places, so that whether going through hollows, or over knolls or ridges, it is always at work, and every tooth has an operation upon the soil.

The Geddes harrow and the Hanford harrow, triangular in shape, are also excellent implements; and for light grounds, free from stones and other obstructions, the Scotch or square harrow serves its purpose admirably.

The accompanying engraving represents a harrow recently patented by Samuel J. Orange, of Grayville, Ill. It involves the rotary principle, the rotation being produced by the pressure of the rollers g g upon the wheels A A. It has the important advantage, that while it secures the rotation of the wheels, it at the same time avoids side draft.

III.—THE CULTIVATOR

This is a useful implement for stirring the soil and killing weeds. It is generally made to be drawn by one horse, and is mostly used between the rows of corn, potatoes, cotton, etc. It is made so as to expand or contract, according to the width of the rows. It saves a great deal of hard labor; but must not be allowed to usurp the place of the plow where deep cultivation is required.

IV.—THE HORSE HOE.

Allied to the cultivator is the horse hoe in its various forms. "Knox's patent has four teeth. The forward one is simply a coulter, to keep the implement steady and in a straightforward direction; the two side or middle teeth are miniature plows, which may be changed from one side to the other, so as to turn the earth from the rows at first weeding, when the plants are small and tender, or toward them in later cultivation—at the option of the operator; the broad rear tooth effectually disposes of grasses and weeds, cutting off or rooting up all that come in its way. It is a thorough pulverizer of the surface, sifting the earth

HORSE HOE FOR COTTON.

and weeds through its iron prongs or fingers in the rear, leaving the weeds on the surface to wilt and die, and the ground level and mellow. For hoeing carrots, turnips, etc., where the rows are narrow, the side teeth are taken out, and the rear tooth, with the forward one as a director to guide the instrument, hoes and mellows the ground between the rows very perfectly." Our engraving represents a modification of Knox's horse hoe, adapting it particularly to the cultivation of cotton.

V.—THE FIELD ROLLER.

No good farmer will omit this useful implement from his list. It levels and smooths the plowed land on sowing down to

WOODEN FIELD ROLLER.

grass, forcing sods and small stones into the soft ground, pulverizing all lumps of earth, pressing the light, loose soil of the surface around the seeds of grain, grass, etc., securing a sure and quick germination and growth of the seeds, and preparing a smooth, even surface for the reaper, scythe, and rake. By making the earth compact at the surface, insects are deprived of shelter; otherwise the sods, loose stones, and lumps of earth afford them convenient habitations. In spring there is frequently great advantage in rolling lands recently sowed to grain and grass, as the earth that has been raised by the frost, exposing the roots of plants, is replaced by the operation, with benefit to the growing crop. The roller is particularly beneficial on light lands, of soil too loose and porous to retain moisture and protect the manure from the effects of drying winds and a scorching sun, and too light too allow the roots of plants a firm hold in the earth; for on such lands its compressing effect, especially in dry seasons, very much increases the product of crop as well as preserves the manure from undue evaporation, thus saving a greater portion of its fertilizing properties for the benefit of the land and succeeding crops.

VI.—SEED SOWERS.

Every farmer or gardener needs a seed-sower of some sort; but one of the smallest and simplest of the many kinds manufactured will serve the purpose of the majority of agriculturists. The light hand-drill represented by the accompanying cut will be found entirely satisfactory where the work to be performed by such an implement is limited.

A SMALL HAND-DRILL.

The seed sower represented by the next engraving is larger, and rather more effective, but still light and cheap. With proper care, either of these little implements will do the work required of them, in garden and field, for many years, without requiring renewal or repair.

SEED-SOWER.

VII.—THE HORSE RAKE.

The utility of this simple implement is not fully realized, we are sure, or it would be more generally employed. One man, with a horse and a boy (and with some of the implements the boy is not required), will, upon a favorable surface, perform the work of eight men with hand-rakes. A horse-rake is not an expensive implement, and every farmer should have one. The old revolver is perhaps the best for general use.

VIII.—MOWERS, REAPERS, ETC.

Of the expensive labor-saving agricultural implements, like the mower, the reaper, and the thrasher, it does not fall within our purpose to speak, further than to recommend our readers to avail themselves of the grand economies which they afford, whenever they can, by combinations with their neighbors for joint ownership of such machines, or by employing those kept for the purpose of being hired out. The small farmer can not afford to invest capital, of which he generally has too little, in these implements for himself alone. Those who are engaged in cultivation on a large scale, and have adequate capital, should, of course, own these labor-saving machines.

For a complete list of farm implements, with an approximate estimate of their cost, see the next chapter.

VII.

FARM MANAGEMENT.

A little farm well tilled;
A little barn well filled;
A little wife well willed.

I.—INTRODUCTORY.

BY the permission of our much respected friend, the author, we here present, unabridged, the interesting and valuable Essay on Farm Management, by J. J. Thomas, which obtained the prize from the New York State Agricultural Society, in 1844. The author, in according permission to use this document, expresses his regret that he has not the leisure to rewrite it, as it was written many years ago, under much disadvantage, and is consequently less perfectly adapted to its purpose than he might now make it. The reader will, however, find it, in its present form, worth more than anything else that we could condense into the same space.

II.—THE PRIZE ESSAY.

ON FARM MANAGEMENT.

BY J. J. THOMAS.

The great importance of performing in the best manner the different operations of agriculture is obvious to every intelligent mind, for on this depends the success of farming. But a good performance of single operations merely does not constitute the best farming. The perfection of the art consists not only in doing everything well individually, but in a proper adjustment and systematic arrangement of all the parts, so that they shall be done not only in the best manner and at the right time, but with the most effective and economical expenditure of labor and money. Everything must move on with clock-work regularity, without interference, even at the most busy seasons of the year.

As this subject includes the whole routine of farming in a collected view as well as in its separate details, a treatise upon it might be made to fill volumes; but this being necessarily confined to a few pages, a general outline, with some remarks on its more essential parts, can only be given.

CAPITAL.—The first requisite in all undertakings of magnitude is to "count the cost." The man who commences a building, which to finish would cost ten thousand dollars, with a capital of only five thousand, is as certainly ruined as many farmers are who, without counting the cost, commence on a scale to which their limited means are wholly inadequate. One of the greatest mistakes which young farmers make in this country, in their anxious wish for large possessions, is, not only in purchasing more land than they can pay for, but in the actual expenditure of all their means, without leaving any even to *begin* the great work of farming. Hence, the farm continues for a long series of years poorly provided with stock, with implements, with manure, and with the necessary labor. From this heavy drawback on the profits of his land, the farmer is kept long in debt; the burden of which not only disheartens him, but prevents that enterprise and energy which are essential to success. This is one fruitful reason why American agriculture is in many places in so low a state. A close observer, in traveling through the country, is thus enabled often to decide from the appearances of the buildings and premises of each occupant, whether he is in or out of debt.

In England, where the enormous taxes of different kinds imperiously compel the cultivator to farm well or not farm at all, the indispensable necessity of a heavy capital to begin with is fully understood. The man who merely *rents* land there, must possess as much to stock it and commence operations as the man who *buys* and pays for a farm of equal size in some of our best farming districts. The result is, that he is enabled to do everything in the best manner ; he is not compelled to bring his goods prematurely to market to supply his pressing wants ; and by having ready money always at command, he can perform every operation at the very best season for product and economy, and make purchases when necessary at the most advantageous rate. The English farmer is thus able to pay an amount of tax often more than the whole product of farms of equal extent in this country.

The importance of possessing the means of doing everything at exactly the right season can not be too highly appreciated. One or two illustrations may set this in a clearer light. Two farmers had each a crop of ruta-hagas of an acre each ; the first, by hoeing his crop early while the weeds were only an inch high, accomplished the task with two days' work, and the young plants then grew vigorously and yielded a heavy return. The second, being prevented by a deficiency of help, had to defer his hoeing one week, and then three days more by rainy weather, making ten days in all ; during this time the weeds had sprung up six to ten inches high ; so as to require, instead of two days, no less than six days to hoe them ; and so much was the growth of the crop checked at this early stage that the owner had 150 bushels less in his acre than the farmer who took time by the forelock. Another instance occurred with an intelligent farmer of this State, who raised two fields of oats on land of similar quality. One field was sown very early, and well put in, and yielded a good profit. The other was delayed twelve days and then hurried ; and although the crop was within two thirds of the amount of the former, yet that difference was just the clear profit of the first crop ; so that with the latter the amount yielded only paid the expenses.

Admitting that the farm is already purchased and paid for, it becomes an object to know what else is needed and at what cost, before cultivation is commenced. If the buildings and fences are what they should be, which is not often the case, little immediate outlay will be needed for them. But if not, then an estimate must be made of the intended improvements, and the necessary sum allotted for them. These being all in order, the following items requiring an expenditure of capital will be required on a good farm of 100 acres of improved land.

Farm Management.

I. LIVESTOCK.

The amount will vary with the fertility and products of the land, its quality, and situation with regard to market. The following will approximate the average on good farms taken at the spring of the year or commencement of work :*

3 Horses, at $100	$300
1 Yoke oxen	150
8 Milch cows, at $30	240
10 Steers, heifers, and calves	100
10 Pigs, at $3	80
150 Sheep, at $2 50	375
Poultry—say	5
Total	**$1,200**

II. IMPLEMENTS.

2 Plows fitted for work	$20 00
1 Small plow, do.	6 00
1 Cultivator, best kind	7 00
1 Drill-barrow	5 00
1 Roller	5 00
1 Harrow	10 00
1 Fanning-mill	20 00
1 Straw-cutter	15 00
1 Root-slicer	8 00
1 Farm-wagon, with hay-rack etc.	70 00
1 Ox-cart	50 00
1 Double farm harness	30 00
1 Horse-cart	45 00
1 Horse-cart harness	18 00
1 Root-steamer, or boiler	20 00
1 Shovel and one spade	2 50
3 Steel-plate hoes	1 50
2 Dung-forks	2 00
3 Hay-forks	2 25
2 Hand-rakes	25
1 Revolving horse-rake	8 00
1 Grain-cradle	4 00
2 Scythes	4 00
1 Wheelbarrow	4 00
1 Pointed shovel	1 25
1 Grain-shovel, or scoop-shovel	1 25
1 Pick	1 50
Carried forward	$361 50

* We allow the figures to stand as in our first edition. If we add to each sum the premium on gold, we shall approximate present prices.

	Item	Cost
	Brought forward	$361 50
1	Mall and wedges	2 50
2	Axes	4 00
1	Hammer	50
1	Wood-saw	1 00
1	Turnip-hook	75
1	Hay-knife	1 00
2	Apple-ladders (for gathering)	1 50
2	Large baskets	1 25
2	Hand-baskets	50
1	Tape-line (for laying off land)	2 00
2	Sheep-shears	2 00
1	Grindstone	3 00
1	Steel-yard, large, and one small	2 00
1	Stable lantern	50
1	Curry-comb, and one brush	75
1	Half-bushel measure	1 00
20	Grain-bags	5 00
1	Ox-chain	3 00
1	Crow-bar	2 00
1	Sled and fixtures	30 00
	Total	$425 75

Other articles might be included, as subsoil plow, sowing machine, threshing machine, etc. To the preceding amount ought to be added one-tenth the expense of fencing the farm, as fences need renewing at least once in ten years. Every farmer should also be supplied with a small set of carpenter's tools, which would cost about $12, for repairing implements in rainy weather and other useful purposes. This set should include saw, hammer, augers, planes, adze, mallet, chisel, square, breast-bits, etc., and by the convenience and economy afforded, would soon repay their cost.

III. SEEDS.

Quantity	Item	For	Cost
2½	Bushels clover seed	for 10 acres	$15 00
2	" corn	" 6 "	1 00
20	' potatoes	" 2 "	10 00
2	" carrot	" 1 "	1 00
40	Bushels seed wheat	" 20 "	40 00
10	" oats	" 4 "	4 00
10	" barley	" 5 "	6 00
	Total		$77 00

IV. LABOR.

Supposing the owner to labor with his own hands, as every owner should, so far as is consistent with a general superintend ence of all parts, which would probably amount to one half the time, he would need besides through the season two men and one boy, and in the winter one man; during haying and harvest he would require two additional hands. The men boarding themselves, could be had for twenty dollars per month in summer and sixteen in winter; if boarded, the cost of their meals would make up the deficiency in the wages to the same amount. The expenditure needed, then, would be,

2 Hired men, eight months, $20 per month	$320 00
1 " boy, " " 10 "	80 00
Day labor in harvest	30 00
Total	$430 00

V. MAINTENANCE OF ANIMALS.

Cattle and sheep would need hay till fresh pasture, and horses hay, and also a good supply of oats till after harvest. All would be benefited by a liberal feeding of roots, including swine. The amount of all these supplies needed would be about,

7 Tons of hay	$42 00
200 Bushels oats	80 00
400 " roots	50 00
Total	$172 00

RECAPITULATION.

Livestock	$1,200 00
Implements	425 75
Seeds	77 00
Labor	430 00
Maintenance of animals	172 00
Total	$2,304 75

—the amount of capital needed the first year, in stocking and conducting satisfactorily the operations of one hundred acres of improved land, several items being doubtless omitted.

If this is a larger sum than the young farmer can command, let him purchase only fifty acres, and reserve the rest of the purchase money which would be needed for the one hundred acres, to commence with on a smaller farm, and he will scarcely fail to make more than on a larger, with every part subjected to an imperfect, hurrying, and irregular management. He may calculate, perhaps, on the return of his crops in autumn, at least to pay his hands. But he must remember that the first year of farming is attended with many expenses which do not usually occur afterward, which his crops may not repay, besides supporting his family and paying his mechanics' and merchants' bills. The first year must always be regarded with uncertainty; and it is better to come out at the end on a moderately sized farm, well tilled and in fine order, with money in pocket, than on a larger one, in debt, and hired hands—a class of men not to be disappointed, and who ought not to be—waiting for their pay. There are a far greater number of farmers embarrassed and crippled by placing their estimate of expenses too low, than of those who swing clear and float freely by a full previous counting of cost.

SIZE OF FARMS.—After what has just been said, the cultivator will perceive in part the advantages of moderately sized farms for men in moderate circumstances. The great disadvantage of a superficial, skimming culture is obvious with a moment's attention. Take the corn crop as an illustration. There are a great many farmers, to my certain knowledge, whose yearly product per acre does not exceed an average of *twenty-five* bushels. There are other farmers, whom I also well know, who obtain *generally* not less than *sixty* bushels per acre, and often eighty to ninety-five. Now observe the difference in the profits of each. The first gets 250 bushels from *ten* acres. In doing this, he has to plow ten acres, harrow ten acres, mark out ten acres, find seed for ten acres, plant, cultivate, hoe, and cut up ten acres, besides paying the interest on ten acres, worth from three to five hundred dollars. The other farmer gets 250 bushels from *four* acres at the farthest; and he only plows, plants, cultivates, and hoes, to obtain the same amount, *four acres*, which from their fine tilth, and freedom from grass and weeds, is much easier done, even for an equal surface. The same reasoning applies throughout the farm. Be sure, then, to cultivate no more than can be done in the best manner, whether it be ten, fifty, or five hundred acres. A friend who owned a four-hundred-acre farm told me that he made less than his next neighbor, who had only seventy-five. Let the man who applies a certain amount of labor every year to his farm reduce its dimensions until that labor accomplishes everything in the very best manner. He will doubtless find that the amount of land will thus become much smaller than he supposed, more so than most would be willing to reduce it; but, on the other hand, the net proceeds from it will augment to a greater degree than perhaps could possibly be believed.

But let me not be misunderstood. Large farms are by no means to be objected to, provided the owner has capital enough to perform all the work as well as it is now done on the best farms of small size.

As an example of what may be obtained from a small piece of land, the following products of fifty acres are given, and are not more than I have known repeatedly to be taken from good land by several thorough farmers:

10 Acres wheat,	35 bushels per acre, at $1 00....				$350 00
5 " corn,	90 " "			40....	180 00
2 " potatoes,	300 " "			20....	120 00
1 Acre ruta-bagas,	800 " "			10 ...	80 00
6 Acres winter apples,	250 "	•		25....	375 00
6 " hay,	2½ tons		"	6 00....	90 00
10 " pasture, worth...............................					60 00
5 " barley,	40 bushels per acre			40....	80 00
5 " oats,	50 "	"		20....	50 00
Total products of fifty acres of very fine land....					$1,385 00

This aggregate yield is not greater than that obtained by some who might be named, from a similar quantity of land. Good land in most localities could be brought to that state of fertility very easily, at a total cost of one hundred dollars per acre, and then it would be incomparably cheaper than many large good farms at nothing; for, while the fifty acres could be tilled for three hundred and eighty-five dollars, leaving one thousand dollars net profits, large poor farms hardly pay the work spent upon them. One proprietor of such a farm declared, "It requires me and my hired man all summer hard at work to get enough to pay him only."

LAYING OUT FARMS.—This department is very much neglected. The proper disposition of the different fields, for the sake of economy in fencing, for convenience of access, and for a full command of pasture and protection of crops at all times, has received comparatively little attention from our agricultural writers and from farmers.

Many suppose that this business is very quickly disposed of; that a very few minutes, or hours at most, will enable a man to plan the arrangement of his fields about right. But this is a great error. Even when a farm is of the simplest form, on a flat, uniform piece of ground, many things are to be borne in mind in laying it out.

In the first place we all know that the *fencing* of a moderately sized farm costs many hundred dollars. It is very desirable to do it well, and use at the same time as little material as possible. To do this much will depend on the shape of the fields. A certain length of fence will inclose more land in the form of a *square* than in any other practical shape. Hence fields should approach this form as nearly as possible. Again, the disposition of lanes is a matter of consequence, so as to avoid unnecessary length and fencing and occupy the least quantity of ground.

But these rules may be materially affected by other considerations. For instance, it is very desirable that land of a similar quality may be in the same inclosure. Some may be naturally too wet for anything but meadow or pasture: some may be much *lighter*, and susceptible of plowing, while others are not: some may be naturally sterile, and need unusual manuring with green crops. All these should, as far as practicable, be included each in its own separate boundary. The situation of surface drains, forming the boundaries of fields, may influence their shape; facilities for irrigation may have an essential bearing: convenience for watering cattle is not to be forgotten. Where, in addition to all these considerations, the land is hilly, still more care and thought are required in the subdivision, which may possibly require years of experience; but where fixed fences are once made, it is hard to remove them; hence a previous thorough examination should be made. A farm road, much used for heavy loads, should be made hard and firm, and can not easily be altered; it consequently should be exactly in the right place, and be dry, level, and short; the shape of adjoining fields even conforming with these requisitions; but a road little used should not interfere with the outlines of fields.

✿ ✿ ✿ ✿ ✿ ✿ ✿

In laying out a farm with a very uneven surface or irregular shape, it would be best to draw, first, a plan adapted to smooth ground, and then vary the size and shape of the fields, the distance of the lane from the center, its straightness, etc., according to the circumstances of the case.

FENCES.*—The kind of fence used, and the materials used for its construction, must depend on circumstances and localities. A good fence is always to be preferred to an imperfect one; though it will cost more, it will more than save that cost, and three times the amount in vexation besides, by keeping cattle, colts, and pigs out of fields of grain. A thriving farmer whose whole land, except a small part with stone wall, is inclosed by common rail fence, with upright cedar stakes, and connecting caps to the tops, finds that it needs renewing once in six years. He accordingly divides his whole amount of fences into six parts, one of which is built new every year. All is thus kept systematically in good repair. Stone walls, if set a foot below the surface to prevent tumbling by frost, are the most durable fence. Hedges have not been sufficiently tried. The English hawthorn is not well adapted to our hotter and drier climate, and though sometimes doing well for a time, is not to be depended on.

GATES.—Every field on the farm should be entered by a good self-shutting and self-fastening gate. A proper inclination in hanging will secure the former requisite, and a good latch, properly constructed, the latter. Each field should be numbered, and the number painted on the gate-post. Let the farmer who has *bars* instead of gates, make a trial of their comparative convenience, by taking them out and replacing them without stopping as often as he does in one year on his farm, say about six hundred times, and he can not fail to be satisfied which is the cheapest for use.

BUILDINGS.—These should be as near the center of the farm as other considerations will admit. All the hay, grain, and straw being conveyed from the fields to the barn, and most of it back again in manure, the distance of drawing should be as short as possible. This will also save much traveling of men and cattle to and from the different parts of the farm. The buildings should

---

* Strange as it may seem, the greatest investment in this country, the most costly production of human industry, is the common fences which divide the fields from the highway, and separate them from each other. No man dreams that when compared with the outlay of these unpretending monuments of art, our cities and our towns, with all their wealth, are left far behind. You will scarce believe me when I say that the fences of this country have cost more than twenty times the specie there is in it. In many of the counties of the Northern States the fences have cost more than the farms and fences are worth.—*Burnap.*

not, however, be too remote from the public road, and a good, dry, healthy spot should be chosen. The dwelling should be comfortable, but not large; or it should rather be adapted to the extent of the lands. A large, costly house with a small farm and other buildings, is an indication of bad management. The censure of the old Roman should be avoided, who, having a small piece of land, built his house so large that he had less occasion to plow than to sweep.

The barn and out-buildings should be of ample extent. The barn should have space for hay, grain, and straw. It is a matter of great convenience to have the straw for littering stables housed and close at hand, and not out of doors, under a foot of snow. There should be plenty of stables and sheds for all domestic animals. This provision will not only save one third of the fodder, but stock will thrive much better. Cows will give much more milk, sheep will yield more and better wool, and all will pass through the winter more safely. The wood-house, near or attached to the dwelling, should never be forgotten, so long as comfort in building fires and economy in the use of fuel are of any importance.

A small, cheap, movable horse-power should belong to every establishment, to be used in churning, sawing wood, driving washing machine, turning grindstone, cutting straw, and slicing roots.

There should be a large root-cellar under the barn, into which the cart may be *dumped* from the outside. One great objection to the culture of roots, in this country—the difficulty of winter keeping—would then vanish.

Both barns and house cellars should be well coated, on the bottom and sides, with water-lime mortar, which is a very cheap and effectual way to exclude both water and rats.

CHOICE OF IMPLEMENTS.—Of those which are much used, the very best only should be procured. This will be attended with a gain in every way. The work will be easier done and it will be better done. A laborer who, by the use of a good hoe for one month, can do one quarter more each day, saves, in the whole time, an entire week's labor.

CHOICE OF ANIMALS.—The best of all kinds should be selected, even if costing something more than others. Not "*fancy*" animals, but those good for use and profit. Cows should be product

Ive of milk, and of a form adapted for beef; oxen hardy, and fast-working; sheep, kept fine by never selling the best; swine, not the *largest* merely, but those fattening best on least food. A Berkshire at 200 pounds, fattened on 10 bushels of corn, is better than a "*land pike*" of 300, fattened on 50 bushels.

Having now taken some notice of the necessary items for commencing farming, it remains to glance a little at

SOILS, AND THEIR MANAGEMENT.—Soils are of various kinds, as heavy and light, wet and dry, fertile and sterile. They all require different management in a greater or less degree.

Heavy soils are often stronger and more productive than light; but they require more labor for pulverization and tillage. They can not be plowed when very wet, nor so well when very dry. Although containing greater or less portions of clay, they may be distinguished, as a class, from lighter soils, by the cloddy surface the fields present after plowing in dry weather, by their cracking in drouth, and by their adhesiveness after rains.

Sandy and gravelly loams also contain clays, but in smaller quantity; so that they do not present the cloddiness and adhesiveness of heavy soils. Though possessing, generally, less strength than clay soils, they are far more easily tilled, and may be worked without difficulty in wet weather. They do not crack or break in drouth. Indian corn, ruta-bagas, and some other crops, succeed best upon them. Sandy soils are very easily tilled, but are generally not strong enough. When made rich, they are fine for some succulent crops. Peaty soils are generally light and free, containing large quantities of decayed vegetable matter. They are made by draining low and swampy grounds. They are fine for Indian corn, broom corn, barley, potatoes, and turnips. They are great absorbers, and great radiators of heat; hence they become warm in sunshine and cold in clear nights. For this reason they are peculiarly liable to frosts. Crops planted upon them must, consequently, be put in late, after spring frosts are over. Corn should be of early varieties, that it may not only be planted late, but ripen early.

Each of these kinds of soil may be variously improved. Heavy soils are much improved by draining; open drains to carry off the surface-water, and covered drains, that which settles beneath. An acquaintance covered a low, wet, clayey field with under-drains, and from a production of almost nothing but grass, it yielded the first year forty bushels of wheat per acre, enough to pay the expense, and admitted of much easier tillage afterward. Heavy soils are also made lighter and freer by manuring; by plowing under coatings of straw, rotten chips, and swamp muck; and, in some rare cases, by carting on sand, though this is usually too expensive for practice. Subsoil plowing is very beneficial both in wet seasons and in drouth; the deep loose bed of earth it makes, receiving the water in heavy rains, and throwing it off to the soil above, when needed; but a frequent repetition of the operation is needed, as the subsoil gradually settles again.

Sandy soils are improved by manuring, by the application of lime, and by frequently plowing in green crops. Leached ashes have been found highly beneficial in many places. Where the subsoil is clayey, which is often the case, and especially if marly clay, great advantage is derived from shoveling it up and spreading it on the surface. A neighbor had twenty bushels of wheat per acre on land thus treated, while the rest of the field yielded only five.

MANURES.—These are among the first of requisites in successful farm management. They are the strong-moving power in agricultural operations. They are as the great steam-engine which drives the vessel onward. Good and clean cultivation is, indeed, all important; but it will avail little without a fertile soil; and this fertility must be created or kept up by a copious application of manures; for these contribute directly or assist indirectly to the supply of nearly all the nourishment which plants receive. It is these which, produced chiefly from the decay of dead vegetable and animal matter, combine most powerfully to give new life and vigor; and thus the apparently putrid mass is the very material which is converted into the most beautiful forms of nature, and plants and brilliant flowers spring up from the decay of old forms; and thus a continued succession of destruction and renovation is carried on through an unlimited series of ages.

Manures possess different degrees of power, partly from their inherent richness, and partly from the rapidity with which they throw off their fertilizing ingredients, in assisting the growth of plants. These are given off by solution in water, and in the form of gas; the one as a liquid manure, which, running down, is absorbed by the roots; and the other, as air, escaping mostly into the atmosphere, and lost.

The great art, then, of saving and manufacturing manure consists in retaining and applying, to the best advantage, those soluble and gaseous portions. Probably more than one half of all the materials which exist in the country are lost, totally lost, by not attending to the drainage of stables and farmyards. This could be retained by a copious application of straw; by littering with sawdust, when saw-mills are near; and, more especially, by the frequent coating of yards and stables with dried peat and swamp muck, of which many parts of our States furnish inexhaustible supplies. I say *dried* peat or muck, because, if it is already saturated with water, of which it will often take in five sixths of its own weight, it can not absorb the liquid portions of the manure. But if it will absorb five sixths in water, it will, when dried, absorb five sixths in liquid manure, and, both together, form a very enriching material. The practice of many farmers shows how little they are aware of the hundreds they are losing, every year, by suffering this most valuable of their farm products to escape. Indeed, there are not a few who carefully, and very ingeniously, as they suppose, place their barns and cattle-yards in such a manner, on the sides of hills, that all the drainage from them may pass off out of the way into the neighboring streams; and some one mentions a farmer who, with pre-eminent shrewdness, built his hog-pen directly across a stream, that he might, at once, get the cleanings washed away, and prevent their accumulation. He, of course, succeeded in his wish; but he might, with almost equal propriety, have built his granary across the stream, so as to shovel the wheat into the water when it increased on his hands.

The loss of manure, by the escape of gas, is often very great. The proof of this was finely exhibited by Humphrey Davy, in an experiment performed by filling a large retort from a heap of fermenting manure, and placing the beak among the roots of some grass. Nothing but vapor left the vessel, yet in a few days the grass exhibited greater luxuriance around the beak of the retort than any of the surrounding portions. Hence the superiority of unfermented manures; the rich portions are not yet lost. And hence, too, the importance of preventing this loss by an immediate application, and ploving into the soil, or by mixing it in composts with muck, peat, swamp mud, and even common earth, in a dry state—and of preventing its escape, from stables and yards, by a daily strewing with dried peat, lime, or plaster.

Fresh manure is generally in a state not readily mixed with soils. It is thrown into large lumps over the surface, some of which are plowed in, others not; but none of them prove of immediate use to the crops. But, on the other hand, fermented manure, from its ready pulverization, admits of an easy admixture. But let fresh manure be thoroughly ground down and worked into the soil by repeated harrowings and two or three plowings, and its influence will be like magic.

Swamp muck has often been spoken of as manure; but those who expect great and striking results from its application will be disappointed. Even with ashes, it is much less powerful than stable manure, not only because it possesses less inherent richness, but because it has less soluble parts, and, consequently, imparts its strength more slowly to growing plants. But this quality only makes it the more enduring. By decoction in water, vegetable mold loses a small portion of its weight by solution; but if the remaining insoluble part is exposed to the air and moisture a few months, another part may be again dissolved. Thus, peat, muck, and all decayed vegetable fiber, become a slow but lasting source of nourishment to plants.

But it is when shoveled out and dried, to be mixed with farm-yard manure, as a recipient for its evanescent parts, that peat or muck becomes pre-eminently valuable. Some parts of the State abound with inexhaustible supplies in almost every neighborhood; many land-owners have from twenty to a hundred thousand cubic yards on their farms, lying untouched, while half-starved crops are growing in the adjacent fields. There are whole counties so well supplied with it that, if judiciously applied, it would, doubtless, double their aggregate products.

All neat farming, all profitable farming, and all satisfactory farming must be attended with a careful saving of manures. The people of Flanders have long been distinguished for the neatness and excellence of their farms, which they have studied to make like gardens. The care with which they collect all refuse materials which may be converted into manures, and increase their composts, is one of the chief reasons of the cleanliness of their towns and residences; and were this subject fully appreciated and attended with a corresponding practice generally, it would, doubtless, soon increase, by millions, the agricultural products of the State.

But there is another subject of scarcely less magnitude. This is a systematic

ROTATION OF CROPS.—If manuring is the steam-engine which propels the vessel, rotation is the rudder which *guides* it in its progress. Unlike manuring, rotation does not increase the labor of culture: it only directs the labor in the most effective manner by the exercise of judgment and thought.

The limits of this paper do not admit of many remarks on the principles of rotation. The following courses, however, have been found among some of the best adapted to our State:

I. 1st year—Corn and roots, well manured.
   2d year—Wheat, sown with clover-seed; 15 lbs. an acre.
   3d year—Clover, one or more years, according to fertility and amount of manure at hand.
II. 1st year—Corn and roots, with all the manure.
   2d year—Barley and peas.
   3d year—Wheat, sown with clover.
   4th year—Clover, one or more years.
III. 1st year—Corn and roots, with all the manure.
   2d year—Barley.
   3d year—Wheat, sown with clover.
   4th year—Pasture.
   5th year—Meadow.
   6th year—Fallow.
   7th year—Wheat.
   8th year—Oats, sown with clover.
   9th year—Pasture or meadow.

The number of the fields must correspond with the number of the changes in each course; the first needing three fields to carry it out, the second four, the third nine. As each field contains a crop each, in the several successive stages of the course, the whole number of fields collectively comprise the entire series of crops every year. Thus, in the list above given, there are two fields of wheat growing at once, three of meadow and pasture, one of corn and roots, one of barley, one of oats, and one in summer fallow.

OPERATIONS IN THE ORDER OF TIME.—The vital consequence of doing every thing in the right season is known to every good farmer.

To prevent confusion and embarrassment, and keep all things

clearly and plainly before the farmer at the right time, he should have a small book to carry in his pocket, having every item of work for each week or each half month laid before his eyes. This can be done to the best advantage, to suit every particular locality and difference of climate, by marking every successive week in the season at the top of its respective page. Then as each operation severally occurs, let him place it under its proper heading; or if out of season, let him place it back at the right time. Any proposed improvement can be noted down on the right page. Interesting experiments are often suggested in the course of reading or observation, but forgotten when the time comes to try them. By recording them in such a book, under the right week, they are brought at once before the mind. Such an arrangement as this will prevent a great deal of the confusion and vexation too often attendant on multifarious cares, and assist very essentially in conducting all the farm work with clock-work regularity and satisfaction.

In reviewing the various items which are most immediately essential to good farm management, some of the most obvious will be—capital enough to buy the farm and to stock it well; to select a size compatible with these requisites; to lay it out in the best manner; to provide it well with fences, gates, and buildings; to select the best animals, and the best implements to be had reasonably; to bring the soil into good condition, by draining, manuring, and good culture; to have every part under a good rotation of crops; and every operation arranged so as all to be conducted systematically, without clashing or confusion. An attention to all these points would place agriculture on a very different footing from its present condition in many places, and with most farmers. The business, then, instead of being repulsive, as it so frequently is to our young men, would be attended with real enjoyment and pleasure.

But in all improvements, in all enterprises, the great truth must not be forgotten, that success is not to be expected without diligence and industry. We must sow in spring and cultivate well in summer, if we would reap an abundant harvest in autumn. When we see young farmers commence in life without a strict attention to business, which they neglect for mere pleasure, well may we in imagination see future crops lost by careless tillage—

broken fences, unhinged gates, and fields filled with weeds—tools destroyed by heedlessness, property wasted by recklessness, and disorder and confusion triumphant; and unpaid debts, duns, and executions already hanging over the premises. But, on the other hand, to see cheerful-faced, ready-handed industry, directed by reason and intelligence, and order, energy, and economy, guiding the operations of the farm—with smooth, clean fields, and neat, trim fences—rich, verdant pastures, and fine cattle enjoying them; and broad, waving meadows and golden harvests, and waste and extravagance driven into exile, we need not fear the success of such a farmer; debts can not stare him in the face, nor duns enter his threshold.

It is such enterprise as this that must place our country on a substantial basis. Agriculture, in a highly improved state, must be the means which, next to the righteousness which truly exalts a nation, will contribute to its enduring prosperity. All trades and commerce depend on this great art as their foundation. The cultivation of the soil and of plants was the earliest occupation of man. It has, in all ages, been his chief means of subsistence; it still continues to furnish employment to the great majority of the human race. It is truly the great art of peace, as during wars and commotions it has languished and declined, but risen again, in strength and vigor, when men have lived at peace with each other; it has then flourished and spread, converted the wilderness into life and beauty, and refreshed and adorned nature with embellished culture. For its calm and tranquil pleasures—for its peaceful and healthful labors—away from the fretful and feverish life of crowded cities, "in the free air and beneath the bright sun of heaven" —many who have spent the morning and noon of their lives in the anxious cares of commercial life, have long sighed for a scene of peace and of quietude for the evening of their days.

VIII.

FARM CROPS.

Let it rain potatoes.—Shakspeare.

I.—THE EDIBLE GRAINS

1. INDIAN CORN—*Zea Mays*.

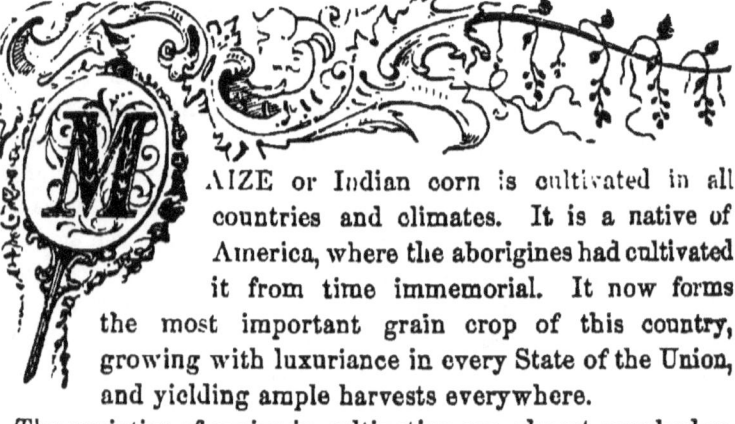

MAIZE or Indian corn is cultivated in all countries and climates. It is a native of America, where the aborigines had cultivated it from time immemorial. It now forms the most important grain crop of this country, growing with luxuriance in every State of the Union, and yielding ample harvests everywhere.

The varieties of maize in cultivation are almost numberless, and new sorts are constantly being produced. No plant, perhaps, is equally susceptible of modification by hybridizing, cultivation, soil, and climate. At the North it is dwarf in its habit, and requires but three or four months to bring it to maturity, while at the South it reaches a magnificent height, and is much longer in maturing. A kind of corn cultivated in Oregon has a separate sheath or envelop for every distinct kernel; but in the climate of New York it soon loses this characteristic, and assumes the more comprehensive husk. So the low growing, early Northern corn, if cultivated for a few years at the South, becomes taller, larger, and later; thus approximating to the Southern varieties.

The principal varieties of Indian corn in extensive use for field culture in the United States are the Big White, Big Yellow, Little White, Little Yellow, and Virginia Gourd Seed (yellow and white). Of each of these there are many sub-varieties. The King Philip or Brown Corn, a very early and small-growing, but productive variety, is much approved in the more Northern States; and Peabody's Prolific or Tillering Corn, said to be a wonderfully productive sort, is adapted to the Southern and Middle States; but it has not yet been extensively tested. In the selection of varieties, choose for general planting those that have been *proved* in your own vicinity, as the best sort of one locality may prove inferior in another. For trial, get new sorts from a more northern latitude, especially where earliness is particularly desirable.

The best soil for corn is a rich loam, but good crops are produced, with proper manuring, on light, sandy land. A strong clay, or a poor, wet soil, will not produce a good crop. Corn is a gross feeder, and, except on very light, sandy soils, fresh, unfermented manure is best for it. Ashes may be added, or applied as a top-dressing, with great advantage; also the salt and lime mixture.

Indian corn should always be planted in hills, and in straight rows, both ways, for convenience of cultivation. The distance apart of the hills should be from three to five feet, varying with the sort of corn and the quality of the land. From three to five stalks in a hill is better than a larger number. Soak the seed one or two days in a solution of common salt, or, better still, of saltpeter, after which apply a coat of tar and plaster, according to the directions given in Chapter II. This will not only accelerate the growth of the plant, but also afford an efficient protection against both worms and birds. As to the proper depth for covering the seed, much difference of opinion exists. We think a depth of one inch, in soil of medium consistency and humidity, and of two or two and a half inches in a dry, sandy soil is sufficient. Plant so soon as the ground is sufficiently warm and dry, without respect to the day of the month. The blossoming or leafing of certain trees may be taken as a guide. Our time is when the flower-buds on the apple-trees begin to burst open.

The after-culture of Indian corn may mostly be performed with a light plow and a good cultivator. It should be commenced soon after the plants show themselves above ground; but deep culture of every kind should be discontinued after the roots have spread through the soil, as they can not be disturbed without great injury. Hilling or heaping the earth about the plants is an absurd and injurious process, which, instead of helping to support them, as many suppose, greatly weakens the stalks, by destroying or covering up the prop-roots with which Nature has supplied them. This compels them to partially exhaust themselves by putting forth others, which after all can not efficiently perform their office. Indian corn requires very little, if any, earthing.

In reference to harvesting Indian corn, a variety of opinions prevail. Some advocate topping it soon after the kernels have become glazed or checked, believing that such a course hastens the ripening of the grain, and that the fodder thus cut is much more valuable than when left till the corn is fully ripened. In these opinions the advocates of topping are undoubtedly correct; but, on the other hand, experiments seem to prove that the weight of the grain and the number of bushels per acre is considerably lessened by thus cutting the stalks. The more common practice at present, except at the South, is to let the crop stand till the kernels are principally glazed, and then cutting all near the surface of the ground, and shocking in the field, to remain till dry enough to husk. The grain loses a little in weight, no doubt, by this process, but the fodder is more valuable than when it stands till fully ripened, and the crop thus treated is placed beyond injury from frost. This, for the Northern and Middle States, we consider the best way to harvest Indian corn; although a somewhat greater bulk and weight of grain may be obtained, if the frosts be long enough deferred, by allowing nature to take its course.

Corn should be perfectly dried in the field, husked, and stored in an airy loft, or in a properly constructed granary or crib.

The proper selection and saving of seed is of great importance. It should be selected in the field from the earliest and largest ears of the most prolific stalks. In this way astonishing improvements in a variety may be gradually made. Thomas N. Baden, Esq., of Prince George County, Md., by carefully selecting the best seed in his field for a long series of years, having special reference to those stalks which produced the greatest number of ears, ultimately obtained a variety which yields from four to ten ears to the single stalk.

In husking seed corn, leave a few of the husks upon the ears, with which to braid several of them together, for convenience in hanging them up. They should be hung in a dry, airy loft. In shelling, reject both extremities of the ear where the kernels are imperfect or misshapen.

The expense per acre of cultivating corn varies greatly in different parts of the country, being influenced by soil, climate, cost of manure, price of labor, etc. For New York, Judge Buel estimates as follows:

One plowing (suppose a clover lay)	$2 00
Harrowing and planting	2 00
Two hoeings	3 75
Harvesting	3 00
Rent of land	5 00
Total	$15 75

This estimate does not include manure, which is generally essential, and would add from five to ten dollars to the expense. In New England the whole expense varies from twenty-five to fifty dollars. A farmer near Philadelphia estimates it at twenty-three dollars in his neighborhood; another, at Ripley, Ohio, gives the following:

"I subjoin my account with a corn-field of eighteen acres. The ground and the corn have been measured—there is no guess work about it.

"Timber—originally walnut, ash, sugar maple, and beech—has been under cultivation twenty years—last year was in wheat, and the year before in corn. The soil dark—ten inches deep, with a clay bottom—was broken up eight inches deep with a span of horses:

Team and hand, 12¼ days' breaking, $2............................	$25 50
Cost of seed, laying off, and planting.............................	18 05
30¾ days' work, harrowing, plowing, hoeing, etc., 87½ cents.......	26 90
Use of team, equal to 26¼ days single, 52 cents...................	13 91
Repairing tools...	1 00
Entire cost, board, labor, and all................................	$80 86

"The yield is 1,350 bushels, costing before gathering not quite six cents per bushel."*

Here no manure is used, we presume, and the soil requires less cultivation than at the East, in order to produce good crops. The expense per acre, exclusive of harvesting, according to this estimate, is less than $4 50.

But, leaving these estimates out of the account, the fact that corn is generally one of the most profitable crops that a farmer can cultivate, may be set down as an established fact.

2. WHEAT—*Triticum* of species.

The origin of wheat is unknown; but it is certain that it was cultivated upward of a thousand years before the Christian era, and that more than one sort was known at that time, for it is stated in the book of Ezekiel (xxvii. 7) that "Judah traded in wheat of *Minnith*." Columella, who wrote about the time of Christ, observes that, "The chief and the most profitable corns for men are common wheat and bearded wheat."

Botanists describe about thirty species of wheat, and some

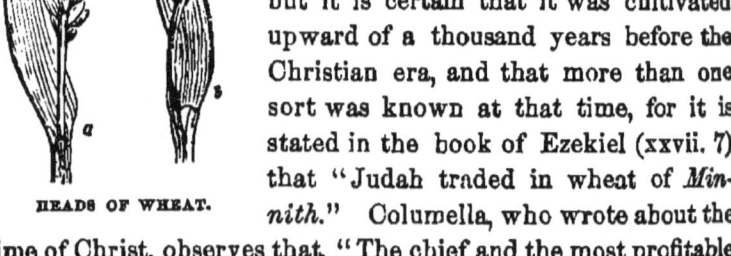

HEADS OF WHEAT.

---

* "W. G. A." in *Country Gentleman*.

hundreds of varieties. The species mainly cultivated in the United States are the Winter Wheat and the Spring Wheat, in their numerous varieties.

In your choice of varieties it is best to be governed, as in the case of Indian corn, by the experience either of yourself or others. From the ever-varying character of the various kinds of seed, their superiority at one time and locality, and their inferiority at other times and in other situations, it would be worse than useless for us to recommend any particular variety. Depend upon known and tried sorts till, by experiments on a small scale, you are satisfied that you have obtained something better.

Wheat thrives best on a strong, clayey loam, but many light and all calcareous soils, if in a proper condition, will give a good yield. A glance at the table on page 28 will show that potash, lime, and phosphoric acid enter largely into the composition of the grain, and that both lime and silica abound in the straw; for this reason, rich vegetable soils generally, being deficient in these elements, are not well adapted to wheat. On such soils there is always a tendency to rapid growth, large but weak straw, and light grain; and a liability both to lodge and to rust. A remedy, however, may be found in the application of ashes, lime, bone-dust, etc. The soil should be deep and well pulverized with the plow and the harrow. Underdraining and subsoil plowing add greatly to the amount of the crop.

Select seed that is free from the seeds of weeds and from smut, if this be possible; but, in any event, it is well, previous to sowing, to wash it in a strong brine made of salt and water, taking care to skim off all light and foreign seeds. If the grain be smutty, repeat the washing in another clean brine, when it may be taken out and intimately mixed with about one twelfth of its bulk of pulverized quicklime.

The time for sowing in the Northern States is from the tenth to the twentieth of September, but it is often successfully sown both earlier and later. Sow broadcast, at the rate of from three to five pecks to the acre, and harrow thoroughly. Rolling is beneficial, especially on light soils.

"Wheat is subject to the attack of the Hessian fly, if sown too early in the fall, and again the ensuing spring, there being two annual swarms of the fly, early in May and September. When thus invaded, harrowing or rolling, by which the maggots or flies are displaced or driven off, is the only remedy of much avail. Occasionally, other flies, and sometimes wheat worms, commit great depredation. There is no effectual remedy known against any of these marauders, beyond rolling, brushing, and harrowing."

Smut is a parasitic fungus, of a brown or blackish color, which grows upon the head and destroys the grain. We have indicated the only remedy with which we are acquainted, in speaking of the preparation of the seed.

"The grain should be cut immediately after the lowest part of the stalk becomes yellow, while the grain is yet in the dough state, and easily compressible between the thumb and finger. Repeated experiments have demonstrated that wheat cut at this time will yield more in measure, of heavier weight, and a larger quantity of sweet, white flour. If early cut, a longer time is required for curing before storing or threshing."

Spring wheat should be sown so early as the ground will admit. The best crops are raised on land that has been plowed the previous fall, and sown without additional plowing, but harrowed-in thoroughly.

Propagation may be extended with incredible rapidity by dividing the plant. The English Philosophical Transactions give the result of a trial, made by planting a single grain on the 2d of June. "On the 8th of August it was taken up and separated into eighteen parts, and each planted by itself. These were subdivided and planted, between 15th of September and 15th of October, and again the following spring. From this careful attention, in a fertile soil, 500 plants were obtained, some containing 100 stalks bearing heads of a large size; and the total produce within the year was 386,840 grains from the single one planted."

3. RYE—*Secale Cereale.*

This plant is supposed to be a native of the Caspian Caucasian desert. It is more hardy than wheat, and will flourish on soils too poor or too destitute of lime for wheat. It has taken the place of wheat in many portions of the country, where repeated crops of the latter have exhausted the soil of some of the requisite elements for its growth. The best soil for it is a rich, sandy loam, but it grows freely on the lightest sandy and gravelly soils that are capable of sustaining any kind of vegetation. The directions for the preparation of soil and seed, and for cultivation, harvesting, etc., are the same as for wheat; but it is sometimes sown among standing corn and hoed in, the ground being left as level as possible. So soon as the corn is matured, it is cut up by the roots and removed to the sides of the field, when the ground is thoroughly rolled.

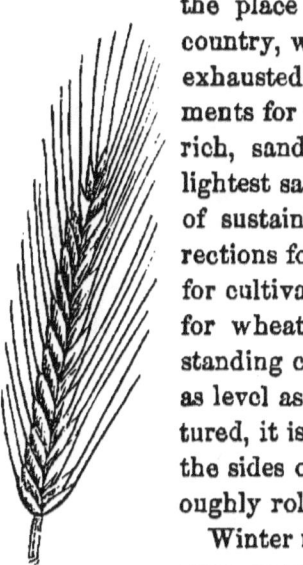

EAR OF RYE.

Winter rye and spring rye are varieties of the same species, and may readily be transformed into each other. Sow from five pecks to two bushels to the acre, according to the quality of the soil, the richest lands demanding most. Winter rye may be sown from the 20th of August to the 20th of September, and spring rye so soon as the state of the soil will permit in the spring.

Rye, when ground and unbolted, is much used in New England to mix with Indian corn meal, for bread-making. The corn meal is scalded, and the loaves baked for a long time. The product is known as "rye-and-Indian bread," and is much esteemed and very wholesome. There is a peculiar aroma and flavor connected with the husk of the grain, which is lost in the bolted flour. Dr. Thaer, the distinguished German physician and agricultural writer, says that "this substance has a singularly strengthening, refreshing, and beneficial effect on the animal frame."

4. The Oat—*Avena Sativa*.

This grain will grow on any soil and in almost any climate. It is affected less by disease, and has fewer insect enemies than most of the cereals. The wire worm, however, occasionally proves destructive to it, when sown on fresh sod. The remedy in this case is to turn over the sod late in the fall, just before the severe winter frosts.

There are many varieties and sub-varieties of the oat. Loudon describes the following:

"The White or Common Oat is in most general cultivation in England and Scotland, and is known by its white husk and kernel.

"The Black Oat, known by its black husk, and cultivated on poor soils in the north of England and Scotland.

HEAD OF THE OAT.

"The Red Oat, known by its brownish-red husk, thinner and more flexible stem, and firmly-attached grains. It is early, suffers little from winds, meals well, and suits windy situations and a late climate.

"The Poland Oat, known by its thick, white husk, awnless chaff, solitary grains, short, white kernel, and short, stiff straw. It requires a dry, warm soil, but is very prolific.

"The Black Poland Oat is one of the best varieties; it sometimes weighs 50 lbs. to the bushel.

"The Friesland or Dutch oat has plump, thin-skinned, white grains, mostly double, and the large ones sometimes awned. It has longer straw than the Poland, but in other respects resembles it.

"The Potato Oat has large, plump, rather thick-skinned,

white grains, double and treble, with longer straw than either of the two last. It is now almost the only kind raised in the north of England and south of Scotland, and brings a higher price in London than any other variety.

"The Georgian Oat is a large-grained, remarkably profitable variety, and on rich soil, in good tilth, has produced more than any other variety.

"The Siberian or Tartarian is by some conceded a distinct species. The grains are black or brown, thin and small, and turned mostly to one side of the panicle, and the straw is coarse and reedy. It is little cultivated in England, but is found very suitable for poor soils and exposed situations.

"The Winter Oat is sown at the rate of two bushels per acre in October, the plants are luxuriant and tiller well, and afford good winter and spring pasture for ewes and lambs, and when these are shut out, it affords an ample crop of grain in August."

The heaviest oat cultivated in the United States is the Imperial; and it is preferred by many to all others. It is bright and plump, and yields a large proportion of nutritive matter. It has proved very productive in the Northern and Middle States. But the variety most cultivated is the common White Oat, which is hardy and a good bearer.

The only oat that will mature with certainty in the Southern States is the Egyptian. It is sound, hardy, and moderately productive. It is sown in autumn.

At the North, oats may be sown from the first of March till the last of May; but the earliest sown usually yield the best crops. From two to four bushels to the acre are sown in this country; but in England they sow from four to six. The land should be prepared by plowing and harrowing, after which the seed should be sown broadcast, and harrowed in. On most soils rolling is beneficial.

Oats may be mowed or cut with the cradle or the sickle. They are fit to harvest when they begin to turn yellow.

As an article of diet, the oat is not properly appreciated in this country, oatmeal being little eaten except by foreigners.

In Ireland and Scotland it is a common article of diet. It would be well for us if it were so here. It is wholesome and strengthening. It is prepared by grinding the kiln-dried seeds, which have been previously deprived of their husks and outer skin.

5. BARLEY—*Hordeum* of species.

In Europe this grain ranks next to wheat in importance; but it is much less extensively cultivated in the United States.

HEADS OF BARLEY.

Professor Lowe enumerates six species of barley, but two only are in general cultivation—the Two-Rowed and the Six-Rowed. In England, the latter is preferred for its superior hardiness and productiveness; but the former is more generally cultivated in this country, the Six-Rowed being, with us, more subject to the smut.

Like rye, it may be made either a winter or a spring grain; but in this country it is almost universally sowed in the spring. Sow so soon as the ground is sufficiently dry, on land plowed the previous fall. If sown on sod, it may be lightly plowed in, and afterward harrowed or rolled. Sow about two bushels to the acre, on soil of medium richness. If sown very early, a smaller quantity of seed will suffice. A loam of medium consistency, between light and heavy, is best for it. Barn-yard manures must never be applied directly to this grain. Steeping the seed twenty-four hours in a weak solution of saltpeter is beneficial. The roller is sometimes applied to the field, when the plants are two or three inches high, with great benefit.

It is of great importance to harvest barley at the proper time.

Farm Crops.

If cut too early, the kernels shrink very much, and if suffered to stand too long, the grain wastes at the slightest touch, the heads breaking off and falling to the ground. It is known to be ripe by the disappearance of the reddish cast from the ear, the drooping of the heads, and the yellowish color of the stalks. It may be stacked like wheat.

Barley is very useful as an article of human food, but, like oats, is too much neglected in the United States, being used principally for malting and brewing. In the form of *pearl* barley, which is the small, round part of the kernel that remains after the skin and a part of the seed are ground off, it is excellent when cooked in the same way as rice—either simply boiled or in puddings.

6. Rice—*Oryza Sativa*.

Rice probably affords food for more human beings than any other plant. In China, and nearly the whole length of the southern part of Asia; throughout the innumerable and densely populated islands of the Pacific and Indian oceans; in the southern part of Europe, and a large extent of Africa; and through no inconsiderable portion of North and South America and the West Indies, it is extensively grown, and forms the staple food of the inhabitants.

The varieties of rice most grown in South Carolina and Georgia, which have hitherto been the greatest rice-producing States of the Union, are the Gold-seed rice, the Guinea, the Common White, and the White-bearded. There are several other varieties, but generally inferior to the foregoing. The best are produced by careful cultivation on soils suited to this grain, and by a careful selection of seed.

HEAD OF RICE.

The method of cultivation pursued on the rice lands of the lower Mississippi, as detailed by Dr. Cartwright, a practical planter, is as follows:

"The seed is sown broadcast about as thick as wheat, and harrowed-in with a light harrow, having many teeth; the ground being first well plowed and prepared by ditches and embankments for inundation. It is generally sown in March, and immediately after sowing, the water is let on, so as barely to overflow the ground. The water is withdrawn on the second, third, or fourth day, or as soon as the grain begins to swell. The rice very soon after comes up and grows finely. When it has attained about three inches in height, the water is again let on, the top leaves being left a little above the water. Complete immersion would kill the plant. A fortnight previous to harvest the water is drawn off to give the stalks strength, and to dry the ground for the convenience of the reapers.

"The same measure of ground will yield three times as much rice as wheat. The only labor after sowing is to see that the rice is properly irrigated; except in some localities, where aquatic plants prove troublesome, the water effectually destroying all others. The rice grounds of the lower Mississippi produce about seventy-five dollars' worth of rice per acre. The variety called the Creole white rice is considered to be the best."*

Upland rice is cultivated entirely with the plow and harrow, and grows well on the pine barrens. A kind of shovel plow, drawn by one horse, is driven through the unbroken pine forest, not a tree being cut or belted, and no grubbing being necessary, as there is little or no undergrowth. The plow makes a shallow furrow about an inch or two deep, the furrows about three feet apart. The rice is dropped into them and covered with a harrow. The middles, or spaces between the furrows, are not broken up until the rice attains several inches in height. One or two plowings suffice in the piney woods for its cultiva-

---

* The "American Farm Book."

tion—weeds and grass, owing to the nature of the soil, not being troublesome.

Rice prepared according to the following recipe makes a dish which we prefer to the richest rice pudding, and which is certainly far more wholesome:

Slowly simmer the rice in milk three or four hours, or til the grains burst and absorb the milk; add a little sugar; put the whole into a wide dish, and bake till slightly brown. Eat with milk or butter.

7. BUCKWHEAT—*Polygonum Fagopyrum.*

Buckwheat is extensively cultivated in the United States; as it affords a flour which is much esteemed as an article of food. It will grow with considerable luxuriance on the poorest land. It comes to maturity so quickly that it is frequently sowed upon ground from which wheat or some other crop has been taken. When intended for seed it should be sown sufficiently early to allow the kernel to become perfectly ripe—say from the middle of June to the first of July. In New York it is often sown in August with winter wheat, affording a ripe crop in the fall, without injury to the wheat, except so far as it may exhaust the soil. It is sown broadcast, at the rate of from a bushel to a bushel and a half per acre. In harvesting it is usually mowed with a scythe, and made into small stacks.

BUCKWHEAT PLANT.

Buckwheat is often used for plowing under as a green manure.

This can be done where the land is too poor to produce clover for that purpose. When in flower, it should be first rolled, and then plowed in.

8. Millet—*Panicum* of species.

The species generally cultivated for the seed is the *P. milliaceum*. As a forage crop, the German millet (*P. Germanicum*) is preferable, and is coming into extensive use, especially at the West. The common species is sown, either broadcast or in drills, from the first of May to the first of July. If for hay, it is best sown broadcast about five pecks to the acre. In drills, which is the best way when cultivated for the grain, eight quarts will suffice.

Of the German millet or Hungarian grass we shall have more to say, under the head of the grasses.

II.—HOW TO SHOCK GRAIN.

Many a valuable harvest may be preserved from ruin by taking heed to the following hints from a practical farmer. They are from that excellent paper, the *Ohio Farmer*. The readers of this little manual shall have no excuse for the too common awkward and inefficient modes of shocking grain. Here are our sensible farmer's rules:

"1. Grain should be firmly bound in smaller sheaves than it is almost universally found. Loosely bound sheaves can not be well shocked. They also admit more rain than tightly bound ones.

"2. Two men can shock better and more advantageously than one.

"3. Let the shocker always take two sheaves at a time, holding them with his elbow against his side, bringing the heads together with hands well spread upon them. Lift them as high as possible, bringing them with force, in as nearly a perpendicular position as can be, to the ground. Never make the second *thrust*, if the sheaves stand erect, for every one after the first, by breaking the butts, makes the matter worse.

"4. Then let two persons bring down *two sheaves each at the same time*, as before described, being extremely careful to keep them perpendicular. The form of shock at this period may be represented thus:

"5. As lastly stated, two more each, thus: The reader will perceive we now have ten sheaves, forming a circle as nearly as can be.

"6. While one man presses the head of the shock firmly together, let the other *break*, not bend, the *two* cap sheaves, and place them on, well spreading heads and butts.

"The main points are, to have grain *well bound*, sheaves made to stand in an *erect position*, and then to put cap sheaves on *firmly*, and every gust of wind will not demolish your work.

"Grain is usually shocked in this manner: One sheaf is made to stand alone, another is *leaned* against it, and another, sometimes at an angle of forty-five degrees, 'to make them stand up,' until a sufficient number is thought to be *leaned up*.

"Now the probability is, that there is but *one* sheaf in the whole shock that has its center of gravity within its base; as a matter of course, each depends on some other to hold it up Consequently they twist; and if the shock does not fall down before the hands get the next one up, it most certainly will during the first rain, just when the perpendicular position is most necessary."

III.—THE LEGUMES.

1. THE KIDNEY BEAN—*Phaseolus Vulgaris*.

The bush or dwarf kidney bean is frequently cultivated as a field crop. There are many sorts that may be profitably used for this purpose, but the Small White is generally preferred, as it is very prolific, quite hardy, will grow in light, poor soil, and is more delicately flavored than the colored varieties. The Long White garden bean is also good. See "The Garden" for a list of the best varieties for horticultural purposes.

The bean succeeds best on a light, warm, and moderately fertile soil. A strong soil, or too much manure, induces a tendency to run to vine, without a corresponding quantity of fruit.

Plant either in hills or in drills. If you have a sower, or drill for putting them in, the latter is the best mode. The drills may be from two to three feet apart, the hills from eighteen inches to two feet each way. From five to eight plants are enough for a hill. They must be kept clear from weeds by the use of the hoe or cultivator; but should be earthed up very slightly, if at all. The first of June is sufficiently early to plant them. They are sometimes planted with corn, putting three or four beans in each hill. This may be done either at the time of planting the corn, or at the first hoeing.

The best mode of harvesting beans with which we are acquainted is thus described by a correspondent of the *Country Gentleman:*

"Place a small pole or stick a foot in the ground, and five or six above ground; around this stick lay some stones, say from four to six inches high, and from twenty to thirty inches in diameter; then place your beans, with the stems against the pole, allowing the roots to be on the opposite side; your next handful you lay with the top on those last laid roots, and the roots of this on the pod and leaves, and so on to the top, forming, as you proceed, a sugar-loaf, keeping it round, or as you would build a stack, tying the top with a straw band. Thus you throw the water all to the outside, the beans being so compact as not to admit water. You can by this means allow them to remain in the field until you are ready to thresh them in November or December, the stones at bottom keeping them dry. In carting to the barn I loosen the pole by shaking, and take hold bottom and top, and throw pole and beans into the wagon; by doing so you do not shell the beans."

As an article of food, the bean has been undervalued. It is, when properly cooked, very palatable and exceedingly nutritious. It abounds in *legumin,* which is analogous to *casein,* the animal principle in milk, and is essentially the same as the *fibrin* of lean meat.

Sheep are very fond of beans, and the straw or haulm makes an excellent fodder for them. No other animal, we believe, will eat beans raw; but cattle, hogs, and poultry thrive on them when cooked.

2. THE PEA—*Pisum Sativum.*

The Marrowfat and Small Yellow peas are the sorts generally used for field culture. The Marrowfat is the richer and better pea, and is to be preferred for good soils. The Small Yellow thrives on poorer soils, and is therefore, in some cases, more profitably cultivated. In some parts of the South a very prolific bush pea is cultivated and much esteemed for the table, both green and dry.

Prepare the ground as for any other spring crop, by plowing and harrowing, and sow broadcast, at the rate of two or two and a half bushels to the acre. Cover them with the harrow or the cultivator, the latter implement being preferable, and smooth the ground by the use of the roller.

In harvesting the pea, some farmers hook them up with a scythe, and some rake them up by hand with the common rake; but the most expeditious and best way, by far, is to use the horse-rake in gathering this crop.

Peas are easily threshed and prepared for market, and may be made a very profitable crop; from thirty to forty bushels per acre being not an uncommon yield. As an article of food, they are excellent "both for man and beast."

The great enemy of the pea is the pea-weevil or pea-bug, which is too well known to require description. It deposits its egg in the growing pea, by piercing the tender pod. As a remedy, some recommend keeping the seed in tight vessels over one year. This plan, if universally adopted, would probably lead to the total extermination of this destructive insect; but as this is not likely to be the case, the only practicable way to avoid its ravages is by late sowing. It has been ascertained that it is limited to a certain period for depositing its eggs; peas, therefore, which are planted sufficiently late in the season to postpone their seeding beyond this period, are not injured. The time for planting to avoid the bug ranges, in different latitudes where experiments have been made, from May 20th to June 10th.

The Chinese Prolific pea and the Japan pea are new sorts, which seem to promise valuable additions to our leguminous crops.

The plant called Cow-pea or Indian pea, and sometimes Stock pea, is extensively cultivated in some of the Southern States, both as a forage crop and a fertilizer. It is sown broadcast, in drills, or hoed in among Indian corn, when the latter is laid by for the season. When intended for cattle, it is harvested before the seed is fully ripe. It may be harvested in the same way as the common pea.

3. THE PEA-NUT—*Arachis Hypogæa.*

This is a legume bearing its pods under the surface of the ground. It was originally brought from Africa.

A North Carolina planter thus describes the mode of cultivation: "So soon as the frost is out of the ground, the land is broken up, and about the middle of April laid off with the plow thirty-three inches each way; two or three peas are then dropped in the crosses thus made. The plants are kept clean with hoes and plows until the vines cover the ground; but no dirt is put on the vines. In October they are dug with a rake or plow. Hogs are then turned into the field, and they soon fatten upon the peas left upon the ground. When the vines are left upon the land for the hogs to feed upon, there is no crop that improves the land so much.

IV.—ESCULENT ROOTS.

1. THE POTATO—*Solanum Tuberosum.*

This most valuable of all the esculent roots is a native of the American continent, and is now found in a wild state in parts of South America. It was probably introduced into southern

Europe by the Spanish adventurers, and into England by Sir Walter Raleigh. In this country it has been cultivated from the first settlement; but until a comparatively recent period only to a limited extent.

In reference to the choice of varieties for planting, the best advice we can give will be simply a repetition of our recommendations in respect to several other plants: Choose such as have been well tested by yourself or others, and found adapted to the soil and purposes for which they are to be cultivated. Try your experiments with new sorts, on a small scale, and with close observation of the results. Experiment also, if leisure serve, in the production of new varieties from the seeds found in the balls. See directions in "The Garden."

A fair crop of potatoes may be produced on almost any soil, properly manured and prepared and well cultivated, but a rich loam, of medium humidity, is best. If fresh or unfermented manures be used, they should be spread on the land, and plowed under, and not scattered in the drills or hills, as they are apt to injure the flavor of the potatoes. Lime, crushed bones, gypsum, salt, and ashes are excellent special manures for the potato. The soil should be made loose and mellow before planting.

In reference to seed, planting, and cultivation, opinions and practices differ widely. We have not room to discuss the various points in controversy between different scientific and practical agriculturists. All that our plan will permit is to give our own mode of cultivation, leaving our readers to try it in connection with other methods, and adopt the best.

We choose for seed good, well ripened, medium-sized potatoes, such as we would select for the table. These we should prefer to plant whole, but, seed being scarce and dear, we think it economical to cut each into two or four pieces, according to the size. We cut them three or four days, at least, before they are wanted for planting, roll them in plaster of Paris, and spread them on the floor in an airy loft to dry.

We plant in drills from two and a half to three and a half feet apart, according to the strength of the soil and the sort of potatoes planted, some varieties producing much larger tops than others. On some soils we should plant in hills, for convenience of cultivation with the plow and cultivator, but on light and loamy soils tolerably free from weeds and unobstructed by stones, we prefer the drills. We drop our sets from six to nine inches apart in the drills, and cover to a depth of three or four inches.

When the shoots have fairly made their appearance above ground, we run a plow between the rows, throwing the earth well to the plants, and following with a hoe, if necessary. This plowing, or plowing and hoeing, are repeated once or twice before the blossoms appear, but not afterward.

The harvesting is commenced so soon as the tops are mostly dead. We allow only sufficient exposure to the sun to dry the tubers, and then store them at once in bins or barrels, where they will be secure against frost, covering them with straw or dry sand, to prevent the circulation of air.

For an early crop we plant only the seed ends, but for the earliest possible crop we should proceed as follows:

Select medium-sized or large tubers early in February, and prepare them by carefully cutting out all the eyes, except the crow-eye or eyes (for there are sometimes two of them), and then place them in a layer, on some dry sand, in a shallow box, and cover them with sand, chaff, or straw, and keep them in a warm room, where light can be freely admitted. When the shoots appear, they must be exposed to the light as much as possible, by partially removing the covering during the day, but keeping them carefully covered at night, when there is any danger from cold. The leaves soon become green and tolerably hardy. Early in March they may be planted out in a warm southern exposure, covering them so as to just expose the leaves above ground. Give them a covering of straw or litter at night, whenever there is danger from frost. By this means you may have potatoes fit for the table two or three weeks earlier than by planting in the ordinary way. A modification of this plan is to forward the sets prepared, as before, on a heap of fermenting manure, in some warm exposure in the open air, covering them well at night when the weather is cold.

In "The Garden" (page 76) we have given a description of the method pursued by Mr. Peabody, of Georgia, for raising potatoes under straw. We are convinced that his plan is a good one for the South, and late experiments seem to prove that it works well at the North also. A correspondent of the *Ohio Valley Farmer*, for instance, says:

"Having a quantity of wheat straw near a piece of ground I was planting with potatoes, I concluded to try the straw-covering process. The *soil*, if I may so call it, was hard yellow *clay*. On the surface, and *without any preparation* of the ground, I distributed my potatoes, covering them some six or eight inches with straw, and did nothing more to them. They grew finely, and in the fall I took hold of the tops and "*drawed*" my crop. I found the tubers of a good size, and nice, bright, and clean enough for the boiler! and the yield much greater than of those planted in sod ground in the usual way."

Another correspondent of the same paper makes the following strong statement:

"We have the three last years planted our potatoes under straw, *and have got more than double the quantity*, on the same ground, with less work in planting and gathering. Our plan is to prepare the ground as thoroughly as possible, then mark it out with the plow, as close as we can; drop the potatoes six inches apart in same, cover as lightly as possible with the soil, then take the wagon containing the straw, and spread lightly to cover the ground. In this manner the work is done till harvest-time. We then take the potato-hook, and rake the straw into winrows, and our crop is nearly all in sight, ready to be gathered."

We have not ourself sufficiently tested this mode of planting, to speak with confidence from our own experience. Let our thousands of readers try it, and report through the papers!

"Of the potato disease or rot," as we have remarked in "The Garden," "little can profitably be here said. Its cause and remedy have yet to be made known. As preventives, a dry, or an underdrained soil; the use of lime, salt, and ashes; the absence of fresh stable manure; early planting; and new, healthy varieties, may be confidently recommended." Thorough underdraining alone is, we believe, generally effective in preventing the disease.

2. The Sweet Potato—*Convolvulus Batatas.*

This is *the* potato of the South, and is much cultivated in the Middle and Western States. In its perfection, as it grows in South Carolina and the other extreme Southern States, it is the best of all the esculent roots.

The varieties most cultivated are the Small Spanish, long, purplish color, grows in clusters, very productive, and of good quality; Brimstone, sulphur-colored, long, large, and excellent; Red Bermuda, the best early potato; Common Yam, root oblong and large, the best keeper, and very productive.

A dry, loamy soil, inclining to sand, is best for the sweet potato. The manure should be plowed in, and the ground well pulverized. A top-dressing of wood ashes is very beneficial.

The Spanish varieties are generally planted where they are to remain, either whole or cut up into sets. But these may, and the yams must be, propagated by slips, as they grow larger and yield more abundantly.

To raise slips, select a sunny spot, sheltered by fences or buildings, and lay it off in beds four feet wide, with alleys of the same width between them. Slope the beds a little toward the sun, and add plenty of well-rotted manure, if the soil be not already rich. Do this in February or early in March. Choose large, smooth, healthy-looking potatoes, and lay them regularly over the bed, an inch or two apart, and cover them with three or four inches of soil from the alleys. It requires ten bushels of potatoes, thus bedded, for an acre of ground.

Lay off your ground in low, horizontal ridges or beds, the crowns of which should be three feet apart, and about six inches high, on which, when the slips are ready, which will be about the middle of April, plant them out eighteen inches apart, one plant in a place, choosing a wet or cloudy day for the operation. Draw the slips when from three to four inches high, by placing the left hand on the bed, near the sprout, to steady the root and prevent it from being pulled up with the sprout. This is loosened with the right hand from the parent tuber, which will continue, if undisturbed, to produce a succession of slips till the first of July. Stir the soil frequently, keeping the weeds well subdued. Be careful not to cover the vines, but if they become attached to the soil, loosen them from it, so that the whole vigor of the plant may go to the formation of tubers. Make the hills large and flat. When they have been laid by, it is a good plan to fill up the spaces between the rows with litter, when the ground is wet, to retain the moisture.

So soon as the tops are dead or touched by the frost, the crop should be gathered.

Sweet potatoes are difficult to keep. The following is Mr. Peabody's plan:

"Let the small heaps dry during the day. In handling them, take care not to bruise or injure the skin, as the least bruise produces rapid decay. Put them up in hills containing thirty or forty bushels each. Make a circular trench as large as the hill you wish to make. Elevate the earth surrounded by it six inches, or at least sufficiently to prevent the access of moisture. Cover this with straw, and heap the potatoes upon it in a regular cone. If the weather be good, cover them only with pine or other straw for two or three days, that the potatoes may be well dried before earthing up. The covering of straw should be three or four inches thick. Cover this with strips of pine bark, commencing at the base, and covering as in shingling, leaving a small aperture at the top for the escape of the heat and moisture generated within. Cover this, except the aperture, with earth, to the thickness of four or five inches. Some cover the opening in the top with a piece of pine bark, to keep out the rain, but a board shelter for the whole heap is preferable. In the spring take up the potatoes, rub off the sprouts, and keep them on a dry floor. If put up with care, they will keep till July."*

Baked, or roasted in hot ashes, the sweet potato is one of the most delicious and nutritive of all vegetables. They are also used for pies and puddings, and sweet-potato rolls are excellent.

3. THE TURNIP—*Brassica Repa.*

In England the turnip crop is one of the most extensive and important in the whole compass of agricultural production. Fields of hundreds of acres are sometimes seen, and inclosures of fifteen or twenty are common. Here they are cultivated to a more limited extent, differences of opinion existing in reference to the profit of their cultivation as a crop for feeding stock.

"In the corn-growing regions of the fertile West, from the facility with which Indian corn can be grown, and the low price of it in many sections of the country, and its nutritive value over that of roots is such, that it is doubtless more profitable growing corn than roots for feeding purposes. But in the Northern States, where corn is usually worth from 80 cents to $1 per bushel, we believe farmers would generally find it for their interest to grow a certain amount of roots, proportioned to the number of cattle and other stock they winter. Aside from the actual amount of nutritive food that roots afford, we think there can be no doubt that the winter condition of our farm stock would be greatly improved by a daily feed of succulent food, even if it were but four quarts per day to each animal, with their dry hay and straw; but with a larger allowance of roots, cattle can be kept in good condition through our long winters on hay of poor quality, or on straw, and so they can in freely feeding Indian meal or oil cake; but in sections of the country where corn is worth one dollar per bushel, and oil cake in a similar ratio, it is presumed roots would be found the cheapest."†

The varieties of the turnip are numerous. The flat English

---

* White's "Gardening for the South." † *Country Gentleman.*

turnip has been longest in cultivation, and still holds its place among most farmers as a field crop. It thrives best on new land and freshly turned sod, but will grow wherever Indian corn can be raised.

The English turnip may be sown from the middle of June to the first of August, either broadcast or in drills. If sown broadcast, about two pounds of seed per acre will be required. The seed should be lightly harrowed or bushed in. Drilling it in with the seed sower and cultivating with the cultivator or hoe is the better way. The crop will be materially assisted by a top-dressing of lime, ashes, and plaster, at the rate of fifteen or twenty bushels of the first two, and from one and a half to three of the last.

English turnips are often sowed among Indian corn at the last hoeing, producing, in many cases, a fair crop.

The Ruta Baga or Swedes turnip is a far more valuable root than the English, but requires a little more attention in cultivation. It will grow on a heavier soil, yield as good a crop, furnish a more nutritive root, and keep longer.

"The Swedes turnip is generally sown in drills about two feet apart, and on heavy lands these should be slightly ridged. The plants must be successively thinned, to prevent interfering with such as are intended to mature, but enough should remain to provide for casualties. Where there is a deficiency, they may be supplied by transplanting during showery weather. They should be left six or eight inches apart in the drills. The Swede turnip is a gross feeder, and requires either a rich soil or heavy manuring; though the use of fresh manures has been supposed to facilitate the multiplication of enemies. Bones, ground and drilled in with the seed, or a dressing of lime, ashes, gypsum, and salt, are the best applications that can be made. The Swede should be sown from the 20th May to the 15th June, and earlier than the English turnip, as it takes longer to mature; and two or three weeks more of growth frequently adds largely to the product. An early sowing, also, gives time to plant for another crop, in case of failure of the first.

"The turnip is exposed to numerous depredators, of which the turnip flea-beetle is the most inveterate. It attacks the plant so soon as the first leaves expand, and often destroys two or three successive sowings. When the fly or bug is discovered, the application of lime, ashes, or soot, or all combined, should be made upon the leaves, while the dew or a slight moisture is on them."*

Harvesting should be deferred till the approach of severe frosts, and at the South the crop may remain in the ground till wanted in the winter.

The Purple-Topped Swede, Skirving's Swede, and Ashcroft's Swede are approved varieties.

4. KOHL RABI—*Brassica Oleracea.*

In England and Ireland, where the turnip has, in some places, shown signs of degeneracy, the Kohl Rabi has been proposed as a substitute, and has already come into somewhat extensive cultivation. It seems to possess all the good qualities of the turnip, with the addition of some excellences peculiar to itself. It has been proved to be perfectly hardy, to stand severe frosts better, and to keep in store for a longer period than the Swedish turnip. It also resists the attacks of the fly and grub. Its feeding qualities have been fully tested, and all kinds of stock are exceedingly fond of it. When fed to milch cows it does not impart that turnip taste to the milk and butter, as is frequently the case when cows are freely fed with turnips.

The average weight per statute acre has been from 27 to 31 tons, of tops and bulbs.

The seeds of the Green and Purple-Topped varieties have been extensively distributed through the agency of the Patent Office, during the past two or three years. So far as we have learned, they have fallen short of the Swedes in productiveness or weight per acre. But in all cases that have come to our knowledge, the seed of the Kohl were sown at the time of

---

* Allen.

sowing the turnips. This is too late for sowing Rabi seed. The *Irish Farmer's Gazette* says: "The seed is sown in a well-prepared seed-bed; about the end of February, in drills about a foot apart; and in May they are transplanted in the field (when the plants are six or eight inches high), in rows about two feet asunder, and eighteen inches apart in the rows."

5. The Carrot—*Daucus Carota*.

The carrot is looked upon with much favor as a field crop in some parts of the United States. It is preferred by many farmers to every other vegetable for feeding cattle, horses, and swine. A bushel of carrots cut and mixed with an equal quantity of oats is thought to be equivalent to two bushels of oats; and five or six hundred bushels may easily be raised on an acre of good land. Rev. Mr. Coleman, of Massachusetts, says that he has raised them at the rate of more than a thousand bushels to the acre.

The varieties mostly used for field culture are the Altringham, the Orange, and the White Belgian. The last-named is very productive, and, growing high out of ground, is more easily harvested than the other sorts; but, on the other hand, it is considered below the others in nutritive value.

"It is very important to have both the soil and the manure for carrots free from the seeds of weeds and grasses; the plants in the early stages of their growth are small and feeble, which makes it a slow and expensive process to eradicate the weeds, if abundant. Well manured sandy, or light, loamy soils are best adapted to the carrot crop. The ground should be deeply worked, and brought to a fine tilth before sowing the seed. For field crops, the drills should be eighteen inches distant; the plants in the rows should be thinned to six or eight inches apart. This 'thinning out' is a matter too frequently neglected. We have frequently seen carrots growing so thickly that they would average a dozen or more plants to the foot; when left to grow in this crowded manner, the roots must necessarily be small, and the expense of harvesting greatly increased."

6. The Parsnep—*Pastinaca Sativa*.

This root is nearly equal to the carrot in value, and large crops may be obtained on deep, rich, well-pulverized soil. The best variety for field culture is the Isle of Jersey. The cultivation is similar to that of the carrot. The harvesting should be deferred till spring, unless the roots may be wanted for winter's use, as they keep best in the ground.

The parsnep is one of the best of all our table vegetables, and is also excellent for cattle, sheep, and swine. The leaves of both parsneps and carrots are good for cattle, either green or dried.

7. The Beet—*Beta Vulgaris*.

The varieties most in use for field culture are the Sugar beet and the Mangold-Wurzel, of both of which there are several sub-varieties.

Beets do well in any soil of sufficient depth and fertility, but they are perhaps most partial to a strong loam. If well tilled, they will produce large crops on a tenacious clay. We have raised at the rate of 800 bushels per acre, on a stiff clay, which had been well supplied with unfermented manure. The soil can not be made too rich; and for such as are adhesive, fresh or unfermented manures are much the best.

The beet should be planted in drills from twenty to twenty-four inches apart, at the rate of six pounds of seed to the acre. Cover about an inch deep. The seed should be early planted, or as soon as vegetation will proceed rapidly; but it must first be soaked by pouring soft, scalding water on it, allowing it to cool to blood-heat, and remain for three or four days, then roll in plaster and drill it in. The culture is similar to that of carrots and parsneps.

As an article of human food, the beet is a universal favorite. Domestic animals are very fond of it, and swine prefer it to any other root except the parsnep; and on no vegetable can they be kept in a better condition.

8. CHINESE YAM—*Dioscorea Batatas*.

This root was introduced into France seven or eight years ago, and seems to have won a considerable degree of public estimation there. It has not had so long a period of trial here, but has been experimented with more or less in all parts of the United States, generally with ill or indifferent success. We can speak of it only as an object of experiment.

The mode of culture required by the Chinese yam is not yet well determined. It evidently needs a deeply spaded or trenched soil, and probably should be cut into sets and planted in rows three or four feet apart, and one foot apart in the row, and treated like the sweet potato, except that it requires no earthing up. The plants may be forwarded in a hot bed or in a cold frame under glass.

V.—THE GRASSES.

The grasses cultivated for the food of animals are too numerous to admit of a description in such a work as this. It is said that no less than two hundred varieties are cultivated in England. In this country we make use of fewer sorts for cultivation; but the number and excellence of our natural grasses are probably unsurpassed in any quarter of the globe.

We will speak briefly of a few of the leading species cultivated among us, noting some of their peculiar excellences and adaptations.

1. TIMOTHY—*Phleum Pratense*.

Allen says: "For cultivation in the northern portion of the United States, I am inclined to place the Timothy first in the list of the grasses. It is indigenous to this country, and flourishes in all soils except such as are wet, too light, dry, or sandy; and it is found in perfection on the rich clays and clay loams which lie between 38° and 44° north latitude. It is a perennial, easy of cultivation, hardy and of luxuriant growth, and on its favorite soil yields from one and a half to two tons of hay per acre at one cutting."

It may be sown either in August or September with the

winter grains, or in the spring. "Twelve quarts of seed per acre on a fine mellow tilth are sufficient; and twice this quantity on a stiff clay." This is the Herds grass of New England.

2. THE SMOOTH-STALKED MEADOW GRASS—*Poa Pratensis*.

This is one of the best of grasses, both for hay and for pasture. It is a native species, and is found almost everywhere, but does not grow in its greatest perfection north of the valley of the Ohio. It is seen in all its glory on the fertile soils of Kentucky and Tennessee. Every animal that eats grass is fond of it. "The seed ripens in June, and is self-sown upon the ground where the succeeding rains give it vitality and it pushes out its long slender leaves two feet in length, which in autumn fall over in thick winrows, matting the whole surface with a luscious herbage."

The Roughish Meadow grass (*P. trivialis*) has the appearance of the smooth variety, but is rough to the touch, and prefers moist situations and clayey soils. This, also, is an excellent grass.

3. RED TOP—*Agrostis Vulgaris*.

A hardy and luxuriant species, much relished by cattle, but possessing only a moderate nutritive value. It is much cultivated in some portions of New England and elsewhere; but where better grasses will grow, this should be rejected. It is sometimes called Foul Meadow and Bent Grass.

4. TALL OAT GRASS—*Avena Elatior*.

An early and luxuriant grass, flourishing in a loamy or clayey soil, and making good hay. It grows to the height of four or five feet on good soils. It is well suited to pasture.

5. THE FESCUE GRASSES—*Festuca* of species.

The Tall Fescue grass (*F. elatior*), according to some experiments made in England, yields more nutritive matter per acre, when cut in flower, than any other grass cut either in flower or seed. It is an American grass, but has found less favor at home than abroad.

The Meadow Fescue (*F. pratensis*); the Spiked Fescue (*F. loleacea*); the Purple Fescue (*F. rubra*); and the Floating Fescue (*F. fluitans*), are all indigenous grasses of fine qualities and great value.

6. ORCHARD GRASS—*Dactylis Glomerata.*

The Orchard or Cock's Foot grass is excellent for shaded situations. It should be cut before it is ripe, and will furnish three or four crops a year. Twenty or thirty pounds of the seed should be sown per acre. It will grow in almost any climate, being found in this country from the extreme north to the extreme south.

7. THE EGYPTIAN GRASS—*Sorghum Halpense.*

A cane-like grass which grows in profusion in some of the Southern States. It is a superior stock-sustaining plant; but as it is difficult to remove when once embedded in the soil, its introduction into cultivated fields is considered a great evil.

8. GERMAN MILLET—*Panicum Germanicum.*

This plant, known at the West as Hungarian grass, seems to have been introduced into Iowa by a Hungarian immigrant, and to have spread thence to other parts of the country. It had, however, been previously cultivated in small quantities under its proper name of German Millet. As a forage crop, for the West, at least, its value seems to be well proved. It has been less extensively tested at the East.

An Iowa farmer thus describes the mode of cultivation pursued in his vicinity:

"We prepare the ground the same as for oats, and sow about eleven quarts to the acre when we want grass; but if seed is the object, eight quarts to the acre. Good seed will weigh fifty pounds to the bushel. I will say in general terms that wherever a crop of Indian corn will grow, the Hungarian grass will succeed. It loves warm weather, but it requires but about six weeks to mature. If cut green, it will put out an excellent second growth, making the richest kind of pasturage. I have seen, this season, one plant that stood rather isolated produce seventy shoots, and each shoot produce a head. It is a great thing to stool, or send out suckers; so if you sow thin or thick, you are sure of a crop. It usually grows from three to four and a half feet high with us. The best time for sowing is about the 20th of May, or when the ground gets warm, on clean ground, harrowed both ways.

"The usual yield of this grass with us is from four to six tons to the acre, according to the pains taken in its cultivation; but the premium crop of this county, as returned to our last fall's fair, was *eight* tons and some two hundred pounds to the measured acre of good, dry hay, suitable to put in stack, duly sworn to by disinterested parties, to the satisfaction of the committee, in order to receive the premium."

9. The Clovers—*Trifolium* of species.

According to botanical arrangement, the clovers belong among the *legumes*, and not among the grasses; but we find it more convenient to speak of them in connection with the other common forage plants.

The Common Red clover (*T. pratense*) is a hardy and easily cultivated species, of which there are several varieties. It grows luxuriantly on every well-drained soil of sufficient strength to afford it nutriment.

It may be sown broadcast either in August or September, or early in the spring, with most of the grains. Sow from ten to twelve pounds per acre on well-prepared loams, and from twelve to sixteen on clayey lands. It should be very slightly covered. A top-dressing of plaster, at the rate of three or four bushels to the acre, has a most beneficial and striking effect upon this plant.

Clover should be cut after having fully blossomed and assumed a brownish hue.

Southern Clover (*T. medium*) is a smaller species than the common Red, and matures earlier. It succeeds better on a light soil than the latter, and should be sown more thickly.

The White or Creeping clover (*T. repens*), of which there are several varieties, is a self-propagating plant, and adds greatly to the richness of many of our pastures, especially on clayey soils. It is very nutritious, and cattle, sheep, and horses are all fond of it.

10. OTHER GRASSES.

The Muskeet Grass, found growing on the plains of Mexico and Texas, is considered one of the best of the indigenous grasses. We have seen it growing on the plantations of Louisiana, where it has been successfully transplanted.

Winter Grass is known on the low, moist fertile soils of Mississippi and adjoining States. It springs up in the autumn, grows all winter, and seeds in the spring. It fattens all animals that feed upon it.

Grama (*La Grama*, or the grass of grasses) is held in the highest estimation by the Mexicans. It attains a medium height, and is deemed the most nutritious of the natural grasses in our southwestern frontier prairies, in California, and parts of Mexico. It grows on dry, hard, gravelly soils, on side hills, and on the swells of the prairies.

The Prairie Grasses abound in the Western prairies, and are of great variety, according to the latitude and circumstances under which they are found. They afford large supplies of nutritive food, both as pasturage and hay. They possess different merits for stock, but as a general rule they are coarse when they have reached maturity, and are easily injured by the early frosts of autumn. Some of the leguminose or wild pea vines, which are frequently found among them, yield the richest herbage. We are not aware that any of these grasses have been cultivated with success.

Dr. Darlington, of Pennsylvania, gives the following as the

species of grasses most valuable in our meadows and pastures, naming them in the order of their excellence:

1. Meadow or green grass (*Poa pratensis*). 2. Timothy (*Phleum pratense*). 3. Orchard grass (*Dactylis glomerata*). 4. Meadow Fescue (*Festuca pratensis*). 5. Blue grass (*Poa compressa*). 6. Ray grass (*Lolium perenne*). 7. Red top (*Agrostis vulgaris*). 8. Sweet-scented vernal grass (*Anthoxanthum odoratum*).*

VI.—MISCELLANEOUS OBJECTS OF CULTIVATION.

1. COTTON—*Gossypium* of species.

As cotton is generally cultivated on large plantations, and does not strictly come under the head of farm crops, we shall content ourself with a few words only upon this grand object of culture and commerce.

Cotton can not be profitably cultivated north of Tennessee. It requires a dry, rich loam to produce the largest and most profitable crops.

"During the winter, the land intended for planting should be thrown up in beds by turning several furrows together. These beds may be four feet from center to center for a moderate quality of upland soil, and five feet for the lowlands. But these distances should be increased with the increasing strength of the soil, to seven and eight feet, and in some instances even to a greater distance for the strongest lands. These may lie until the time of planting, from 20th of March to 20th of April, when no further danger from frost is apprehended; then harrow, and with a light plow mark the center of the beds, and sow at the rate of two to five bushels per acre. A drilling-machine might be made to answer this purpose better, and save much time. An excess of seed is necessary, to provide for the enemies of the plant and other contingencies. If all the seed germinates, there will be a large surplus of plants, which must be removed by thinning. There is an advantage

---

* Allen.

in mixing the seed, before it is sown, with moistened ashes or gypsum, as it facilitates sowing and germination. It should be buried about an inch deep, and the earth pressed closely over it."

Harvesting is commenced when the bolls have begun to expand and the cotton is protruded, and is continued as the bolls successively ripen and burst their capsules.

2. THE SUGAR-CANE—*Saccharum Officinarum.*

This is another plantation crop, and lies beyond the scope of this little book. It is indigenous both in the Old and the New World, but is restricted in its cultivation to a belt or zone extending from 35° to 40° on each side of the equator. In the United States the cultivation can not be profitably carried on advantageously higher than about 32°.

3. CHINESE SUGAR-CANE—*Sorghum Saccharatum.*

Although the value of this plant as an object of general cultivation is not universally conceded, we think it may be safely set down as worthy the farmer's attention, both as a forage crop and for making syrup. Its habits and mode of cultivation are similar to those of Indian corn. It may be planted at the same time as corn, about three feet apart each way, and two or three plants in a hill; or in drills three feet apart, and the plants, one in a place, two feet apart in the row. When the plants are from six inches to a foot high, turn over the earth on each side of the row with a plow and afterward keep the weeds down with the hoe. On good soil it will grow from six to twelve or fourteen feet high, furnishing a very heavy and nutritious crop of fodder; and one hundred and seventy-five gallons of syrup, equal to the best molasses, and worth at least one dollar per gallon, have been made from an acre of the cane, and that with very imperfect apparatus. A correspondent of one of the agricultural journals, in closing a narrative of his experiments, says:

" The result, therefore, of my experiments lead me to the conclusion that the accounts heretofore published, as to the value of the Chinese Sugar-Cane, are not exaggerated; that it may be grown upon almost any ordinary soil, requiring no more attention than is profitably bestowed upon a crop of Indian corn; that as a soiling crop it is *far superior* both in quantity and quality to Indian corn, producing as a first crop more than can be obtained from any other plant in cultivation; and after once cut, again producing a valuable crop; and that a superior article of syrup can be produced at little cost or trouble."

An African sorgho, called *Imphee*, has been experimented with both in Europe and America, in connection with the Chinese. It has the advantage of maturing earlier, but in reference to its value as a sugar-producing plant, in comparison with the other, opinions, founded probably on imperfect experiments, differ widely. M. Velmarin, of Paris, who has experimented largely with the various saccharine plants, pronounces it greatly inferior. It has hardly had a fair trial yet in this country.

4. Broom Corn—*Sorghum Saccharatum.*

Broom corn requires similar soil to Indian corn. A green sward turned over late in the fall is best. Well-rotted horse or sheep manure and wood ashes may be liberally scattered in the drills or hills. A situation not subject to early or late frosts should be chosen. Clayey lands are not suitable.

Plant so soon as danger from frosts will permit, in drills three feet apart; or in hills from two to two and a half feet apart each way, from twelve to fifteen seeds in a hill, thinning out to ten plants at the first hoeing. The after-culture consists in frequent stirring of the soil with a light plow or cultivator, and keeping the crop clear of weeds with the hoe.

"Break the tops before fully ripe, or when the seed is a little past the milk; or if frost appears, then immediately after it. This is done by bending down the tops of two rows toward each other for the convenience of cutting afterward. They should be broken some fourteen inches below the brush, and allowed to hang till fully ripe, when they may be cut and carried under cover, and spread till entirely dry."

5. FLAX—*Linum Usitatissimum.*

A deep, rich loam or alluvial soil is best for flax. The proper fertility should be secured by a surplus of manure applied to a previous crop, as fresh manures are injurious to it. It is sown broadcast, on well-prepared soil, at the rate of from sixteen to thirty quarts when wanted for seed, and two bushels when cultivated for the fiber.

6. HEMP—*Cannabis Sativa.*

This is a plant of the nettle tribe, and came originally from India. The Russians are at present its chief cultivators; but in our Western States, and especially in Kentucky, it is beginning to be widely raised.

A rich loam or a vegetable mold suits the hemp plant. The ground should be carefully prepared by plowing and harrowing till it is perfectly pulverized, smooth, and even. The seeds are sown broadcast at the rate of a bushel and a half to the acre, and plowed or harrowed in. Plowing is best on ground liable to bake. In Kentucky they sow any time from the first of April to the tenth of May. It is desirable to sow just before a rain.

For a full description of the mode of cultivation, harvesting, and preparing hemp, as practiced in Kentucky, see the "American Farmer's Encyclopedia;" article "Hemp."

7. THE HOP—*Humulus Lupulus.*

The hop is found growing spontaneously on the banks of rivers and brooks in various parts of this country.

The best soil for the cultivation of hops is a sandy loam, rather low and moist; but they will grow on soils very different from this. New lands are to be preferred.

The following is the mode of cultivation recommended by Allen in the "American Farm Book:"

"If the land has been long in use, it should be dressed with a compost of alkaline manures; or, what is nearly equivalent, with fresh barn-yard manures, on a previously well-hoed crop, and made perfectly free from all weeds, and deeply plowed and harrowed. Then mark out the ground at intervals of six feet each way and plant in the intersection of the furrows, and unless the ground be already rich enough, place three or four shovels of compost in each hill. The planting is done with the new roots taken from the old hills, which are laid bare by the plow. Each root should be six or eight inches long, and must contain two or more eyes, one to form the root, and the other the vine. Six plants are put in a hill, all of which should be within the compass of about a foot, and covered to a depth of five inches, leaving the ground level when planted. The first season the intermediate spaces between the hills may be planted with corn or potatoes, and the ground carefully cleared of weeds, and frequently stirred. No poles are necessary the first year, as the product will not repay the cost. The ground should receive a dressing of compost the following spring, and the plants be kept well hoed and clean.

"Poles may be prepared at the rate of two or three to each hill, twenty to twenty-four feet long, and selected from a straight, smooth undergrowth of tough and durable wood, from four to seven inches diameter at the butt end. These are sharpened and firmly set with an iron bar, or socket bar with a wooden handle in such a position as will allow the fullest effect of the sun upon the hills or roots. When the plants have run to the length of three or four feet in the spring, train them around the poles, winding in the direction of the sun's course, and fasten below the second or third set of leaves, where there is sufficient strength of vine to sustain themselves. They may be confined with rushes, tough grass, or more easily with woolen yarn. This operation is needed again in a few days, to secure such as may have got loose by the winds or other causes, and to train up the new shoots.

"The gathering of hops takes place when they have acquired

a strong scent, at which time the seed becomes firm and brown, and the lowest leaves begin to change color. This precedes the frosts in September. The vines must first be cut at the surface of the ground, and the poles pulled up and laid in convenient piles, when they may be stripped of the hops, which are thrown into large, light baskets; or the poles may be laid on long, slender boxes with handles at each end (to admit of being carried by two persons), and as the hops are stripped they fall into the box. Be careful to select them free from leaves, stems, and dirt.

"After gathering in the fall, the hops should be hilled or covered with compost, and all the vines removed. The following spring, when the ground is dry, the surface is scraped from the hill, and additional compost is added, when a plow is run on four sides, as near as possible without injury to the plants. All the running roots are laid bare and cut with a sharp knife within two or three inches of the main root, and the latter are trimmed, if spreading too far. It is well to break or twist down the first shoots and allow those which succeed to run, as they are likely to be stronger and more productive. Cutting should be avoided, unless in a sunny day, as the profuse bleeding injures them. The poles will keep much longer, if laid away under cover till again wanted the following spring. Drying may be done by spreading the hops thinly in the shade and stirring them often enough to prevent heating; but when there is a large quantity, they can be safely cured only in a kiln."

IX.

THE ORCHARD.

There hang the red-cheeked apples, blushing in the sun.—Ponous.

I.—"THE GARDEN."

IN a previous number of this series of manuals ("The Garden") we have devoted a long chapter to the subject of fruits, giving instructions for planting, grafting, cultivation, and gathering; with lists of the best varieties, etc. As the larger portion of our readers will possess that volume also, it will not be profitable to go over the same ground again here; but some additional hints on several points not sufficiently dwelt upon in the work referred to will be useful in this.

II.—LAYING OUT ORCHARDS.

We copy from Tucker's "Annual Register of Rural Affairs," for 1857, the following useful directions for laying out orchards:

We have often observed a good deal of inconvenience and perplexity in measuring off and laying out orchards, from a want of accuracy at the commencement. If the rows are begun crooked, stake after stake may be altered, without being able to form straight lines, and with only an increase of the confusion. If the first tree, in a row of fifty, be placed only six inches out of the way, and be followed as a guide for the rest, the last one will deviate fifty times six inches, or twenty-five feet from a right line, even if the first error is not repeated. We have seen large apple orchards with rows nearly as crooked as this. To say nothing of the deformed appearance to the eye, they proved exceedingly inconvenient every time the crooked space between the rows was plowed, and every time the ground was planted and cultivated with crops in rows.

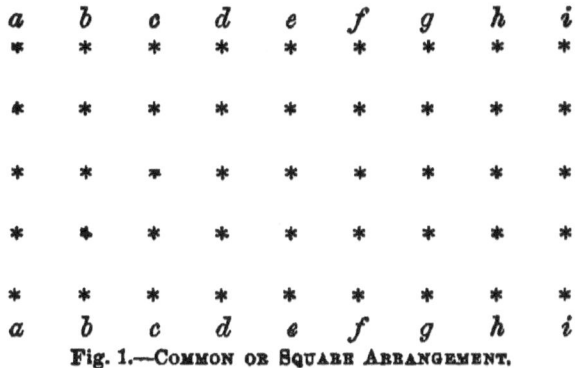

Fig. 1.—Common or Square Arrangement.

The most simple and convenient arrangements for orchards in all ordinary cases is in squares, as shown in fig. 1. But planters are often puzzled to know how to lay out such orchards, with trees at equal distances throughout, and in perfectly straight rows. The easiest and most successful mode is first to measure off one side along the boundary, with a chain or tape-line (a chain is best), and drive in a stake perpendicularly at equal distances (say two rods or 33 feet), *in a straight line*, and at a proper distance from the fence for the first row of trees. Then measure off each end in the same way; and between the last two stakes in these end rows, form another line of stakes like the first, which will be parallel and opposite to it. The more accurately the measuring is done, the less labor will be required in rectifying small errors—no stake should stand half an inch out of a straight line. These rows are represented by the letters *a, b, c, d, e, f, g, h, i*. Then measure off the distance between *a* and *a*, driving in a small stake or peg at each distance of two rods, and then in the same way between * * * *, etc. If accurately done, these will all form perfectly straight rows. The holes may then be dug without the least difficulty or embarrassment, and the trees set out. But a difficulty arises, as the stakes must be removed in digging the holes; this is at once obviated by the plan here proposed, by placing the tree in a line with the row of stakes on one side, and with the newly-set trees on the other, as the holes are successively dug and the trees set.

These directions may seem quite simple, but from want of being generally understood, a great many crooked lines of trees are seen through the country.

The second mode of arranging trees is in the old *quincunx* form (fig 2), which is nothing more than a series of squares laid off diagonally, and has no special advantage to recommend it except novelty.

Fig. 2.—OLD QUINCUNX ORDER.

The *hexagonal* or *modern quincunx* (fig. 3) possesses two important advantages. One is its more picturesque appearance,

Fig. 3.—HEXAGONAL OR MODERN QUINCUNX.

and its consequent fitness for proximity to ornamental plantations; and the other is its greater economy of space, as the trees are more evenly distributed over the ground. This is shown in fig. 4, where each tree stands in the center of a circle, surrounded at equal distances by six other trees, and each single circle leaves but little vacant space beyond it. If cultivated with horses, the furrows may be drawn in three different directions, instead of only two, as in the square arrangement.

One principal reason why the hexagonal mode is so little adopted, is the supposed difficulty in laying out the ground. But like many other apparent difficulties, it becomes very simple and easy when once understood.

To lay off a piece of ground for this purpose, measure off one side of the field at equal distances, as already described for squares, as at *a, b, c, d, e,* fig. 4. These distances must be the distance apart at which the trees are to stand, because they form the sides of the equilateral triangles into which the whole

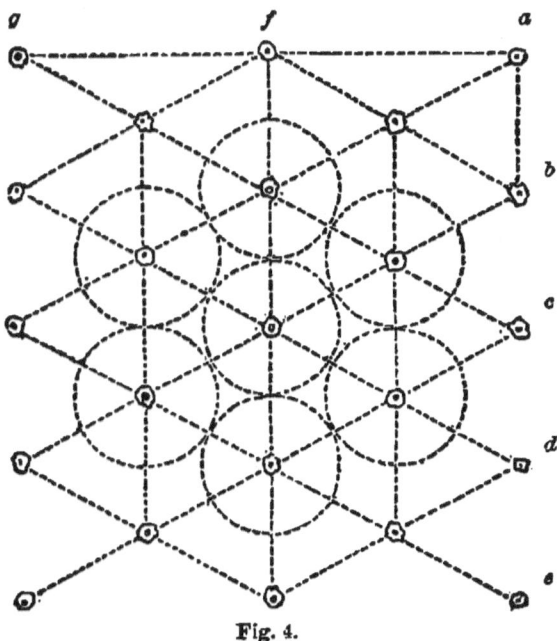

Fig. 4.

ground becomes divided. The next thing is to find the distances, *a, f, g,* for the line of trees at right angles to the first-mentioned row. An arithmetician will easily determine this, for the triangle, *b a f,* being a *right* one, the square of *b a* (which is 33 feet) subtracted from the square of *b f* (which is 66 feet) will leave the square of *a f,* the root of which extracted will give the distances of *f, f, g,* etc., which is 57 feet and half an inch. Divide this and the opposite side of the field, therefore, into distances of 57 feet and half an inch, and the side opposite the first, at 33 feet distances, and proceed to stake off all intermediate intersections, as described for squares. If the distances are less than 33 feet, as they would be for any other kind of fruit-trees, a corresponding proportion is of course to be taken, and which is easily determined as above.

III.—SOIL AND SITUATION.

Downing says that strong loams, by which is meant loams with only just sufficient sand to render them friable and easily worked, are, on the whole, by far the best for fruit in this country. The trees do not come into bearing so soon as on a light, sandy soil, but they bear larger crops, are less liable to disease, and are much longer lived. Clayey loams, when *well drained,* are good, and trees growing on them are generally free from insects.

It is difficult to give any precise rules in reference to aspect. Good orchards may be found in all aspects; but a gentle slope to the southwest is generally to be preferred to any other. Where fruit is very liable to be killed by late spring frosts, and the season is long and warm enough to ripen it in any exposure, planting on the north sides of hills is practiced with advantage. Deep valleys with small streams of water should be avoided, as the cold air settles down in such places, and frosts are apt to prove fatal; but the borders of large rivers and lakes are favorable for orchards, as the climate is rendered milder by the presence of large bodies of water.

IV.—PLANTING AND CULTIVATING AN ORCHARD.

At the risk of repeating in part what has already been published in "The Garden," we will add a hint or two under this head.

The first thing is to prepare the ground by underdraining (if it require it, as most land does), subsoiling, or trench plowing, harrowing, manuring, etc.

Choose sound, healthy trees for planting, and set them out carefully, as directed in "The Garden." Apple-trees should be thirty feet apart in orchard culture. Set the same kind in rows together. This will facilitate the gathering of the fruit, and improve the appearance of the orchard.

"It is an indispensable requisite in all young orchards to keep the ground mellow and loose by cultivation; at least for the first few years, until the trees are well established. Indeed, of two adjoining orchards, one planted and kept in grass, and the other plowed for the first five years, there will be an incredible difference in favor of the latter. Not only will these trees show a rich, dark, luxuriant foliage, and clean, smooth stems, while those neglected will have a sickly look, but the size of the trees in the cultivated orchard will be treble that of the others at the end of this time, and a tree in one will be ready to bear an abundant crop before the other has commenced yielding a peck of good fruit. Fallow crops are best for orchards—potatoes, beets, carrots, bush beans, and the like; but whatever crops may be grown, it should be constantly borne in mind that the roots of the tree require the sole occupancy of the ground, so far as they extend, and therefore that an area of more than the diameter of the head of the tree should be kept clean of crops, weeds, and grass."*

To keep your trees in a healthy, bearing state, regular manuring is requisite. They exhaust the soil, like any other crop.

---

* Downing.

Top-dressings of marl, or mild lime, may alternate with barn-yard manure, muck composts, etc.

To prevent the attacks of the apple-borer, place about the trunks early in the spring a small mound of ashes or lime. Nursery trees may be protected by washing the stems in May, quite down to the ground, with a solution of two pounds of potash in eight quarts of water.

V.—THE PROFITS OF APPLE CULTURE.

"There is no question of the propriety and necessity of the farmer planting apples enough to supply abundantly his own table with the best of this fruit through the whole year; but further than this, we require to know whether a large extent of land may be usefully applied to raising apples for sale; and about what returns may be expected from such orchards, with good management; and what 'good management' is.

"There are some varieties, which, although possessing superior qualities for home use, and therefore necessary in the family orchard, are not salable, and, of course, worthless for marketing. A fruit for *sale* must at least be fair and good looking; it *ought*, also, to be of fine quality, to bring the best price; it must also be a sure and good bearer, and one that keeps long enough to insure carriage to market, and a reasonable period for selling. We find among all the sorts which are known to our nurserymen and orchardists, that there are few that have all these qualifications to such an extent that they can safely be recommended. A close inquiry will show that, in all mixed orchards, the *profit* has been derived from a very few sorts. Other kinds are found to yield some superior specimens, and to be well worth raising for one's own satisfaction, but, so far as money is concerned, the soil would be more profitably employed if planted with other crops.

"Soil and situation fit for an apple orchard must always be valuable for other purposes; and as none but the best of lands can be depended upon, the value of such lands is consequently high. We are safe in assuming that land fit for such use, in

Western New York, is worth, on an average, one hundred dollars per acre, the annual rent of which should be at least ten dollars per acre.

"This is more than would generally be realized net profit from the crops for some years after the planting of an orchard upon it; and at the end of ten years (at which time we might presume the trees to be in a bearing state), there would be a balance due from the orchard to the planter. After this time, the crops from the orchard should not be reckoned worth much, as the trees will occupy the whole soil with their roots, and the sun and air with their branches.

"Ten years from planting, Baldwin and Rhode Island Greening apple-trees can be relied upon to bear about three barrels per tree, each bearing year, which occurs each alternate year with the Baldwin, and generally so with the Greening. This gives us sixty barrels of fine winter apples per year, from trees planted two rods apart, or forty trees per acre. The whole annual expense of cultivation, and the gathering and barreling, will scarcely amount to twenty-five dollars, leaving the net proceeds, if sold at one dollar per barrel, about thirty-five dollars per acre. This sum per acre will soon repay any balance due the planter, and the rapidly increasing produce of the trees, for many years, will satisfy any reasonable man of the expediency of planting large orchards, where the conditions of success are observed; but it will readily be seen that an orchard of any but the best varieties will not pay interest and care.

"It is important that the fruit-grower should base his expectations entirely upon the results to be derived from a *series of years*, and not from any less period of time; otherwise he will be found wide from the truth."*

---

* "Rural Annual."

APPENDIX.

A.

MEASURING LAND.

FARMERS often desire to lay off small portions of land for the purpose of experimenting with manures, crops, etc.; but sometimes find difficulty in doing it correctly, for the lack of a few simple rules. The following table and accompanying explanation, which we copy from the *New England Farmer* carefully studied, will make the whole matter perfectly clear.

ONE ACRE CONTAINS
160 square rods; 4,840 square yards; 43,560 square feet.

ONE ROD CONTAINS
30.25 square yards; 272.25 square feet.
One square yard contains nine square feet.

THE SIDE OF A SQUARE TO CONTAIN

One acre	208.71 feet	12.65 rods	64 paces.
One-half acre	147.58 "	8.94 "	45 "
One-third acre	120.50 "	7.30 "	37 "
One-fourth acre	104.36 "	6.32 "	32 "
One-eighth acre	73.79 "	4.47 "	22½ "

```
                  208.71 feet.
                  12.65 rods.
        ┌─────────────────────────────┐
        │                             │
        │                             │
        │              ↓         104.36│
        │                             │
        │  104.36                     │ 208.71 feet.
        ├──────────┐  · · · · ·       │
        │          ·                  │
        │ 52.18.   ·                  │
        │      ┌───┤· · · ·           │
        │      │   │         ↓        │
        │ 1-16.│   │                  │
        │      │   │                  │
        │ 52.18│52.18│    104.36      │
        └──────┴───┴──────────────────┘
                  208.71 feet.
```

It will be seen by reference to the plan that a practice sometimes followed by farmers is very erroneous; if the side of a square containing one acre measures 208.71 feet, one half that length will not make a square containing one half an acre, but only one fourth an acre, and one third the length of line will inclose a square of one ninth an acre, and one fourth the line, squared, will contain one sixteenth an acre, and so on.

B.

HOW TO ESTIMATE CROPS PER ACRE.

A friend communicates the following method of making an estimate of the yield per acre of a growing crop, of wheat, rye, oats, or barley, which he says has been found correct in England. As it seems easy of application, and approximately correct, we give the plan, and hope it will be tried at the next harvest-time.

Frame together four light sticks, measuring exactly a foot square inside, and, with this in hand, walk into the field and select a spot of fair average yield, and lower the frame square over as many heads as it will inclose, and shell out the heads thus inclosed carefully, and weigh the grain. It is fair to presume that the product will be the 43,560th part of an acre's produce. To prove it, go through the field, and make ten or twenty similar calculations, and estimate by the mean of the whole number of results. It will certainly enable a farmer to make a closer calculation of what a field will produce, than he can do by guessing.—*New York Tribune.*

C.

NUMBER OF PLANTS PER ACRE.

NUMBER OF PLANTS OR TREES THAT CAN BE PLANTED ON AN ACRE OF GROUND, AT THE FOLLOWING DISTANCES APART, IN FEET.

Distances apart.	No. of Plants.	Distances apart.	No. of Plants
1 by 1	43,560	7 by 7	888
1½ " 1½	19,360	8 " 8	680
2 " 1	21,780	9 " 9	537
2 " 2	10,890	10 " 10	435
2½ " 2½	6,969	11 " 11	360
3 " 1	14,520	12 " 12	302
3 " 2	7,260	13 " 13	257
3 " 3	4,840	14 " 14	222
3½ " 3½	3,555	15 " 15	193
4 " 1	10,890	16 " 16	170
4 " 2	5,445	17 " 17	150
4 " 3	3,630	18 " 18	134
4 " 4	2,722	19 " 19	120
4½ " 4½	2,151	20 " 20	108
5 " 1	8,712	24 " 24	75
5 " 2	4,356	25 " 25	69
5 " 3	2,904	27 " 27	59
5 " 4	2,178	30 " 30	48
5 " 5	1,742	40 " 40	27
5½ " 5½	1,417	50 " 50	17
6 " 6	1,210	60 " 60	12
6½ " 6½	1,031	66 " 66	10

APPENDIX.

Multiply the distances into each other, and divide it by the square feet in an acre, or 43,560, and the quotient is the number of plants.

D.

WEIGHTS AND MEASURES.

WEIGHT OF GRAIN, ETC.

ARTICLES.	New York.	Ohio.	Pennsylvania.	Indiana.	Wisconsin.	Iowa.	Illinois.	Michigan.	Connecticut.	Massachusetts.	Rhode Island.	Kentucky.	New Jersey.	Vermont.	Missouri.	Canada.
Wheat, lb......	60	60	60	60	60	60	60	60	56	60	..	60	60	60	60	60
Rye	56	56	56	56	56	56	56	54	56	56	..	56	56	56	56	56
Corn..........	58	56	56	56	56	56	56	56	56	56	..	56	56	56	52	56
Oats..........	32	32	32	32	32	35	32	32	28	30	..	33	30	32	m	34
Barley........	48	48	47	48	48	48	44	48	..	46	..	48	48	46	m	48
Buckwheat....	48	..	48	50	42	52	40	42	45	46	..	52	50	46	m	48
Clover-seed....	60	64	..	60	60	60	..	60	..	..	..	60	64	..	m	60
Timothy-seed..	44	42	..	45	..	45	..	m	..	m	..	45	..	..	m	48
Flax-seed	55	56	..	56	..	56	..	m	..	m	..	56	55	..	m	56
Hemp-seed	44	..	..	44	..	44	..	..	..	..	..	..	..	..	..	..
Blue-grass seed.	14	..	..	14	..	14	..	..	..	..	..	..	..	..	..	..
Apples, dried..	22	25	..	..	23	24	..	28	..	..	..	..	..	..	..	22
Peaches, dried.	32	33	..	..	28	33	..	28	..	..	..	..	..	..	..	22
Coarse salt.....	56	50	55	50	..	50	..	..	..	70	..	50	..	..	50	56
Fine salt.......	56	50	62	50	..	50	..	..	..	70	..	50	..	..	50	56
Potatoes........	60	..	..	60	..	60	..	..	60	60	60	..	..	60	..	..
Peas	60	..	..	..	..	..	..	..	..	60	..	..	..	..	..	60
Beans	62	56	..	60	..	60	..	..	..	60	..	60	..	..	..	60
Castor beans...	46	..	..	46	..	46	..	..	..	..	..	..	..	..	..	..
Onions.........	57	..	..	57	..	57	..	..	..	50	50	..	..	..	..	..
Corn meal.....	..	..	..	50	..	..	..	..	..	..	50	..	..	..	..	..
Mineral coal...	..	..	..	70	..	..	..	..	..	..	..	..	..	..	..	..

A law of New York, in force at the present time, adopts the United States *bushel of measure*, viz.: 2150.42 cubic inches per bushel, 1075.21 half bushel; and the wine gallon, 281 cubic inches.

To reduce cubic feet to bushels, struck measure, divide the cubic feet by 56, and multiply by 45.

BOX MEASURES.

Farmers and market gardeners will find a series of box measures very useful; and they can readily be made by any one who understands the two-foot rule, and can handle the saw and the hammer. The following measurements, it will be seen, vary slightly from the United States bushel adopted by some of the States, but are sufficiently accurate for all ordinary purposes:

A box 16 by 16¼ inches square, and 8 inches deep, will contain a bushel, 2150.4 cubic inches, each inch in depth holding one gallon.

A box 24 by 11.2 inches square, and 8 inches deep, will also contain a bushel or 2150.4 cubic inches, each in depth holding one gallon. A box 12 by 11.2 inches square, and 8 inches deep, will contain half a bushel, or 1075.2 cubic inches, each inch in depth holding half a gallon.

A box 8 by 8.4 inches square, and 8 inches deep, will contain half a peck, or 298.8 cubic inches. The gallon, dry measure.

A box 4 by 4 inches square, and 4.2 inches deep, will contain one quart, or 67.2 cubic inches.

WEIGHT PER CUBIC FOOT.

Weights of a Cubic Foot of various Substances, from which the Bulk of a Load of one Ton may be easily calculated.

Cast iron ....450 lbs.	Common soil, compact, about..124 "
Water........................ 62 "	Clay, about...................185 "
White pine, seasoned, about .. 30 "	Clay with stones, about........160 "
White oak, " " .. 52 "	Brick, about..................125 "
Loose earth, about............ 95 "	

Bulk of a Ton of different Substances.

23 cubic feet of sand, 18 cubic feet of earth, or 17 cubic feet of clay, make a ton. 18 cubic feet of gravel or earth, before digging, make 27 cubic feet when dug; or the bulk is increased as three to two. Therefore, in filling a drain two feet deep above the tile or stones, the earth should be heaped up a foot above the surface, to settle even with it, when the earth is shoveled loosely in.

E.

UNPROFITABLE FARMING.

Manure is a necessary application, in order to bring an impoverished soil into a productive state. Nothing is more certain, all agree. And yet how much of the unprofitable farming of the country results from the attempt to grow crops on worn-out soils without manure! Plant corn on such land—the crop is a meager one, both from want of strength in the soil to grow it, and length of the season to mature it. A rich or well-manured soil will ripen this crop weeks earlier than a poor one. An acre of land, rich, deeply tilled, planted in good season, and thoroughly and cleanly cultivated, will produce more corn than five acres poor, shallow-plowed, late-planted, and half-cultivated, and at perhaps one half the expense of the latter.

Stagnant water, either in or upon the soil, is another cause of unprofitable farming. A soil which has no escape or outlet for the water which falls upon it save evaporation, can not be made to produce a paying crop. In a dry season it is baked and hard—in a wet one it is often flooded with stagnant water, and is never in a condition very favorable to the growth of cultivated crops, however well suited it may be to the production of wild grass, flag, and rushes. And partially drained land of this character is little better. Flooded in spring, the water passes off but slowly; nothing can be done upon it until the "subsiding of the waters," which, as they must in great part go cloudward, is a tedious process.

Poor manure—made so by exposure and leaching while yet in the yard—is another source of loss to the farmer. The contents of the barn-yard are generally dignified with the name of manure; even if they consist of little more than a leached mass of straw and excrement, the real strength of which has long ago passed off into some stream, or floated down the roadside ditch, and into some provident neighbor's field, it is still "manure," and is carted to the field and offered to the crop, with the expectation that it will find therein nutriment, and the material for large productiveness. One thought will show how futile this expectation. How does manure benefit a plant? By its soluble constituents—they receive only *liquid* food. This leached manure has lost the greater share of the soluble elements of fertility, and acts in great part only mechanically upon the soil.

Attempting too much is another great cause of loss to the farmer. "Much labor on little land" is the secret of success—enough labor, at least, to do every thing in the best manner. Look at it—is it good policy to expend the labor of putting in a crop over six acres, when, at the same cost, a like result may be realized from three or four? Will you be content with thirty bushels of corn per acre, at an expense of, say $12, when, by adding $3 in manure and better culture, you may realize sixty or one hundred bushels? Will you grow inferior stock with the same amount of food, when by a larger outlay at first you may have the best—those always salable at good prices—while the unimproved scarcely find purchasers at any price? Is it not best, either to concentrate your labor on less land, or increase your expenditure so as to embrace the whole farm in a thorough system of cultivation?

The acknowledged causes of unprofitable farming are not exhausted, and it is a proper subject for the examination of the farmer. Let him look into the matter, and see *where* and *why* he has failed.—*Country Gentleman.*

F.

FACTS ABOUT WEEDS.

Dr. Lindley estimates as a low average the following number of seeds from each of these four plants:

1 plant of Groundsel produces............ 2,080
1   "   Dandelion   "   2,740
1   "   Sow Thistle "   11,040
1   "   Spurge   "   540

16,360 plants,

or enough seed from these four plants to cover three acres and a half, at three feet apart. To hoe this land, he says, will cost 6s. (sterling) per acre, and hence a man throws away 5s. 8d. a time, as often as he neglects to bend his back to pull up a young weed before it begins to fulfill the first law of nature. He recommends every farmer, whose vertebral column will not bend, to count the number of dandelions, sow thistles, etc., on the first square rod he can measure off.

This operation may be repeated in this country by applying all the above estimates to pig-weed, burdock, fox-tail, chick-weed, and purslane.

G.

SUCCESSFUL FARMING.

James Gowen, of Mount Airy, near Philadelphia, raised, in 1845, a ten-acre field of corn, which averaged 95 bushels of shelled corn per acre. It had been in grass without manure, five years; it was plowed, and the field manured with a ton of guano, costing $40. The rows were 3½ feet apart, and the plants 12 inches. (This distance would be too great for small Northern corn.) Judicious harrowing, in preparation, cleared the ground thoroughly of grass and weeds, and it was kept perfectly clean afterward at little cost. There were 7 acres of winter wheat, and one of spring wheat, the whole computed to average over 40 bushels per acre. The spring wheat was after an acre of carrots, of 900 bushels, and was followed by an acre of turnips of 1,000 bushels; the whole worth over $500—from one acre in two years. The carrot crop the same year was 1,000 bushels per acre; sugar-parsnep, 800 bushels; ruta-baga, over 600 bushels; potatoes, 3 acres, over 200 bushels each. These were only part of the crops. Besides, there were more than 100 tons of excellent hay, though the season was unfavorable. All on an upland farm of about 100 acres, which maintained during the summer over 60 head of cattle. So much for manure, subsoiling, fine culture, draining, rotation, etc.—*Annual Register.*

H.
STIRRING THE SOIL.

Every observant farmer must have noticed the crust which forms on the surface of newly-stirred soils, after lying a few days to the action of the dews. A much heavier crust is formed by each shower of rain which falls. Good and successful cultivation requires that this newly-formed crust be often and repeatedly broken by the hoe, harrow, or other instrument.

A striking instance in proof of the importance of this practice has just been stated by an extensive farmer. He planted a field of broom corn, and, by way of banter, told the man who assisted him that each should choose a row as nearly alike as possible, and each should hoe his row, and the measured amount of crop on each should be the proof which was hoed best. Our informant stated the result in substance as follows: "Determined not to be beaten, I hoed my row, well, once a week the summer through. I had not seen my assistant hoe his at all, but had observed that for a long time he was up in the morning before me. At length I found him before sunrise, hoeing his broomcorn, and I asked him how often he hoed it; he answered, 'Once a day, regularly.' The result of the experiment was, his row beat mine by nearly double the amount."—*Ibid.*

INDEX.

A.
	PAGE
Agriculture History of	9
" Improvement of	11
Ashes	41
Apple Culture, Profits of	146

B.
Bones, how to prepare them	87
Barley	110
Buckwheat	113
Beans	115
Beet	128
Broom Corn	136

C.
Crops, What they take from the Soil	27
" Rotation of	48, 97
" Farm	100
" How to Estimate	150
Composts	45
Capital	83
Corn, Indian	100
Carrot	127
Cotton	134
Chinese Sugar-Cane	135

D.
Drains, Construction of	55
Draining	51
" Ten Reasons for	52
" Conditions requiring	53
" Practical Directions for	58
" Will it Pay?	58

F.
Fences	61, 91
" Iron	63
" Hurdle	66
" Are they Necessary?	70
Facts about Weeds	158
Farm Management, Essay on	82
Farm Crops	100
Farming, Unprofitable	152
" Successful	153
Flax	137

G.
	PAGE
Guano	85
Gypsum	39
Gates	91
Grains, Edible	100
Grain, How to Shock	114
Grasses	129

H.
Hedges	66
Harrow	76
Hoe, Horse	78
Hemp	137
Hop	137
How to Estimate Crops	150

I.
Irrigation	46
Implements	78
" List and prices of	85
" Choice of	92
Indian Corn	100

K.
Kohl Rabi	126

L.
Lime	38
Livestock	85
" Maintenance of	87
Land, How to Measure	149

M.
Manures, Necessity of	25
" Classification and Description of	28
" Management of	42, 94
Marl	38
Mowers	81
Millet	114, 131
Measuring Land	149
Measures, Weights and	151
Maintenance of Livestock	87

N.

	PAGE
Night Soil	35
Number of Plants to the Acre	150

O.

Oat	108
Orchards, Laying out	140
" Soil and Situation for	144

P.

Plants, Food of	26
" Number to the Acre	150
Plow	78
Pea	117
Pea-nut	118
Potato	118
" Sweet	122
Parsnep	128

R.

Rotation, Theory of	48
" Benefits of	49, 97
Roller, Field	79
Rake, Horse	80
Reapers	81
Rye	107
Rice	111

S.

	PAGE
Soils, Classification of	13
" Analysis of	16
" Physical Properties of	18
" Improvement of	21, 93
" Importance of stirring the	154
Subsoils	23
Salt	40
Seeds	86
Seed-Sowers	80
Sweet Potato	122
Sugar-Cane	135
" Chinese	135
Successful Farming	153
Stirring the Soil	154

T.

Turnip	125

U.

Urine	88
Unprofitable Farming	152

W.

Wheat	104
Weights and Measures	114
Weeds, Facts about	158

THE BARN-YARD:

A MANUAL

OF

Cattle, Horse and Sheep Husbandry;

OR, HOW TO BREED AND REAR

THE VARIOUS SPECIES OF DOMESTIC ANIMALS:

EMBRACING

DIRECTIONS FOR THE BREEDING, REARING, AND GENERAL MANAGEMENT OF HORSES, MULES, CATTLE, SHEEP, SWINE AND POULTRY; THE GENERAL LAWS, PARENTAGE, AND HEREDITARY DESCENT, APPLIED TO ANIMALS, AND HOW BREEDS MAY BE IMPROVED; HOW TO INSURE THE HEALTH OF ANIMALS; AND HOW TO TREAT THEM FOR DISEASES WITHOUT THE USE OF DRUGS;

WITH A

Chapter on Bee-Keeping.

BY D. H. JACQUES,

AUTHOR OF "THE HOME," "THE GARDEN," "THE FARM," "HOW TO WRITE," "HOW TO DO BUSINESS," ETC.

Our power over the lower animals, if rightly exercised, redounds to their elevation and happiness no less than to our convenience and profit.—THE AUTHOR.

REVISED EDITION.

NEW YORK:
THE AMERICAN NEWS COMPANY,
39 AND 41 CHAMBERS STREET.

Entered, according to Act of Congress, in the year 1870, by

GEO. E. WOODWARD,

In the Clerk's Office of the District Court of the United States for the Southern District of New York.

PREFACE.

We commenced this little manual with the intention of making the most useful compilation possible, within the space allowed us, from the great number of larger works on the subjects treated to which we had access. In the progress of our work, however, we found occasion to depart, in some degree, from our original plan, and introduce more new matter and re-write and condense more that is, in substance, derived from others, than we at first intended; but our claims on the score of originality will not be large. If the matter and arrangement of our book shall prove acceptable to the public, and serve the purposes intended, we shall be satisfied. The humble merit of having presented, in an attractive and available form a mass of useful information, practical hints, and valuable suggestions, on a number of important topics, is all that we purpose to insist upon. This the great public, for whose good we have labored, will, we are sure, readily accord to us.

We have given credit in the body of the work, whenever practicable, to the authors from whom we have derived aid in the various departments of our labor; but we here gladly make an additional record of our indebtedness to the works of Youatt, Martin, Stuart, Randall, Wingfield, Dixon, Bement, Browne, Quimby, etc. The *Country Gentleman*, the *American Agriculturist*, the *Southern Cultivator*, and other agricultural papers, have been examined with satisfaction to ourselves and with profit to our readers.

We have endeavored to make our little work thorough and reliable, so far as it goes, and to give the largest possible amount of useful information that can be condensed into so small a number of pages. We have occupied a large field, we are aware, and can not hope to have been so full on all points as many readers will desire. We have not aimed, of course, to render the larger works on the special topics to which our chapters are devoted unnecessary. We hope rather to create a demand for them; but there are thousands whom this little manual will furnish with all the information they desire on the subjects on which it treats, and on whom the details with which the larger and more expensive works are filled would be thrown away. To such, in an especial manner, we commend it, hoping that it will not wholly fail to meet their expectations.

CONTENTS.

I.—THE HORSE.

A Historical Sketch—Range of the Horse in Reference to Climate—Effects of Climate and Food—Varieties or Breeds—The Race-Horse—Origin and Characteristics—Half-bred Horses—The Arabian Horse—Wonderful Genealogies—Description—The Arabian "Tartar"—The Morgan—Opinions in Reference to the Morgans—Sherman Morgan—The Canadian Horse—The Norman—"Louis Philippe"—The Cleveland Bay—The Conestoga—The Clydesdale Horse—The Virgioian—Wild Horses—American Trotting Horses—Points of a Horse Illustrated—Color, and what it Indicates—Common Terms Denoting the Parts of a Horse—Stables—Stables as they are—Situation of Stables—Size—Windows—Floors—Draining—Racks and Mangers—Ventilation of Stables—Warmth, etc.—The best Food for Horses—Work and Digestion—Bulk of Food—Quantity—Water—General Management of the Horse—Air—Litter—Grooming—Exercise—Vices and Habits—Restiveness—Backing and Balking—Biting—Kicking—Running Away—Rearing—Overreaching—Rolling—Shying—Slipping the Halter—Tripping—Hints to Buyers—Warranty—Form of a Receipt Embodying a Warranty—What a Warranty Includes—What constitutes Unsoundness .... Page 9

II.—THE ASS AND THE MULE.

Why the Ass has been Neglected and Abused—Eastern Appreciation—The Ass compared with the Horse—The Ass in Guinea and Persia—The Mule—Adaptation as a Beast of Burden—Trade in Kentucky—Use on a Farm—How to have large and handsome Mules 45

III.—CATTLE.

Historical Sketch—Breeds—The Devons—New England Cattle—The Hereford Breed—The Sussex Breed—The Ayrshire Cattle—The Welsh Breeds—Irish Cattle—The Long Horns—The Durham or Short-Horned Breed—Alderney or Jersey Cattle—The Galloway Breed or Hornless Cattle—Other Polled Cattle—The Cream-Pot Breed—Points of Cattle—General Management of Cattle—The Cow-House Feeding—Rearing Calves—Milking—How to Estimate the Weight of Livestock 49

IV.—SHEEP.

Characteristics of the Sheep—Mutton—Breeds in the United States—The Native Breed—The Spanish Merino—American Merinos—Saxon Merinos—The New Leicester Breed—The South-Downs—Mr. Taylor's Facts and Figures—The Cotswold Breed—New Oxfordshire Sheep—The Cheviot Breed—The

Lincoln Breed - On the Choice of a Breed—The Improved English Varieties as Mutton Sheep—The Merinos as Wool-Producers—General Management—Barns and Sheds—Feeding Racks—Feeding—Salt—Water—Shade—Lambs—Castration - Docking—Washing—Shearing—Value of Sheep to the Farmer—An Anecdote. 78

V —SWINE.

Natural History of Swine—The Wild Boar—Opinions Respecting the Hog—The Hog among the Greeks and Romans—Swine Breeding in Gaul and Spain—Abhorrence toward Swine's Flesh among the Jews, Egyptians, Mohammedans, and Others—Cuvier's Opinion—Unwholesomeness of Swine's Flesh in Warm Climates—Breeds of Swine—The "Land Pike"—The Chinese Hog—The Berkshire Breed—The Suffolk Breed—The Essex Breed—The Chester Hog—Points of the Hog—Feeding—The Piggery........... 95

VI.—IMPROVEMENT OF BREEDS

Selection of the Sire and Dam—How the Cream Pot Breed was Produced—In-and-In Breeding—Youatt's Opinion—Crossing—Origin of La Chamois Sheep—The best Breeds most Profitable—How to Improve One's Stock—How Improvements may be bred Out as well as In 108

VII.—DISEASES AND THEIR CURE.

About throwing Physic to the Dogs—Wild Animals seldom Sick – The Reason why—Causes of Disease among Domestic Animals—How they may be kept in Perfect Health—Treatment of their Diseases—The Water-Cure for Animals.. 114

VIII.—POULTRY.

The Domestic Fowl—Wild Origin Unknown—General Characteristics of the Domestic Fowl—The Spanish Fowl—The Dorking—The Polish Fowl–The Hamburg Fowl—The Dominique Fowl—The Leghorn Fowl—The Shanghais and Cochin Chinas—The Bantam—The Game Fowl—Mongrels—Choice of Breed—Accommodations –Incubation—Rearing Chickens—Five Rules—The Guinea Fowl—The Domestic Turkey—The Principal Requisites in Turkey Rearing—General Directions—The Domestic Goose – How to Rear Geese—Shearing instead of Plucking--The Domestic Duck—Best Varieties—How to Rear Ducks –Fattening—Preparing Poultry for Market 118

IX.—BEE-KEEPING.

Wonders of the Bee-Hive—The three kinds of Bees—The Queen and her Duties—Curious Facts—How the Cells are Made—Bee-Bread—Ventilation by the Bees on Scientific Principles—The Apiary—Bee-Hives—How to Make them—Sectional Hives—Mr. Luda's Hive- Swarming—Robbing the Hive—Wintering—Feeding—Killing the Drones............................. 148

APPENDIX.

Horse Taming 161

DOMESTIC ANIMALS.

I.

THE HORSE.

A horse! a horse! My kingdom for a horse!—Shakspeare.

I.—HISTORY.

THE horse is probably a native of the warm countries of the East, where he is found wild in a considerable state of perfection. Its use, both as a beast of burden and for the purposes of war, early attracted the attention of mankind. Thus when Joseph proceeded with his father's body from Egypt into Canaan, "there accompanied him both chariots and horsemen" (Gen. xix.); and the Canaanites are said to have gone out to fight against Israel "with many horses and chariots" (Joshua ii. 4). This was more than sixteen hundred years before Christ.

The horse was early employed on the course. In the year 1450 B. C. the Olympic games were established in Greece, at which horses were used in chariot and other races.

No horses were found either on the continent or on the islands of the New World; but the immense droves now existing in parts of both North and South America, all of which have descended from the two or three mares and stallions left by the early Spanish voyagers, prove very clearly that the climate and soil of these countries is well adapted to their propagation.

Professor Low says: "The horse is seen to be affected in his character and form by the agencies of food and climate, and it may be by other causes unknown to us. He sustains the temperature of the most burning regions; but there is a degree of cold at which he can not exist, and as he approaches this limit his temperament and external conformation are affected. In Iceland, at the Arctic Circle, he has become a dwarf; in Lapland, at latitude 65°, he has given place to the reindeer; and in Kamtschatka, at 62°, he has given place to the dog. The nature and abundance of his food, too, greatly affect his character and form. A country of heaths and innutritious herbs will not produce a horse so large and strong as one of plentiful herbage; the horse of the mountains will be smaller than that of the plains; the horse of the sandy desert than that of the watered valley."*

II.—BREEDS.

The genus *Equus*, according to modern naturalists, consists of six different animals—the horse (*E. caballus*); the ass (*E. asinus*); the quagga (*E. quagga*); the dziggithai (*E. hemionus*); the mountain zebra (*E. zebra*); and the zebra of the plains (*E. burchelli*).

Of the horse there are many varieties or breeds. Ineffectual attempts have been made to decide which variety now existing constitutes the original breed; some contending for the Barb and others for the wild horses of Tartary. It is of the latter that Byron thus speaks in "Mazeppa:"

> With flowing tail and flying mane,
> With nostrils never streaked with pain,
> Mouths bloodless to the bit or rein,
> And feet that iron never shod,
> And flanks unscarred by spur or rod,
> A thousand horse—the wild, the free—
> Likes waves that follow o'er the sea,
> Came thundering on.

The principal breeds of horses now bred in the United States are the Race-Horse, the Arabian, the Morgan, the Canadian,

---

* Illustrations of the Breeds of Animals.

the Norman, the Cleveland Bay, the Conestoga, the Virginia Horse, the Clydesdale, and the Wild or Prairie Horse.

1. *The Race-Horse.*—"There is much dispute," Mr. Youatt says, "with regard to the origin of the *Thorough-bred Horse*. By some he is traced through both sire and dam to Eastern parentage; others believe him to be the native horse, improved and perfected by judicious crossings with the Barb, the Turk, or the Arabian. The Steed Book, which is an authority with every English breeder, traces all the old racers to some Eastern origin; or it traces them until the pedigree is lost in the uncertainty of an early period of breeding.

"Whatever may be the truth as to the origin of the race-horse, the strictest attention has for the last fifty years been paid to pedigree. In the descent of almost every modern racer not the slightest flaw can be discovered."

The racer is generally distinguished, according to the same authority, by his beautiful Arabian head; his fine and finely-set neck; his oblique, lengthened shoulders; his well-bent hinder legs; his ample muscular quarters; his flat legs, rather short from the knee downward, although not always so deep as they should be; and his long and elastic pastern.

The use of thorough-bred and half-bred horses for domestic purposes is becoming common in England. The half-bred horse is not only much handsomer than the common horse, but his speed and power of endurance are infinitely greater.

"The acknowledged superiority of Northern carriage and draught stock," the editor of the New York *Spirit of the Times* says, "is owing almost entirely to the fact that thorough-bred horses have found their way North and East from Long Island and New Jersey, where great numbers are annually disposed of that are unsuited to the course."

For the farm, the pure thorough-bred horse would be nearly useless. He lacks weight and substance to give value and power for draught. For road work the same objections will apply, although not to the same extent, perhaps. The best English road horse is a cross of the thorough-bred and the Cleveland.

2. *The Arabian Horse.*—The genealogy of the Arabian horse, according to Arab account, is known for two thousand years. Many of them have written and attested pedigrees extending more than four hundred years, and, with true Eastern exaggeration, traced by oral tradition from the stud of Solomon. A more careful account is kept of these genealogies than of those of the most ancient family of the proudest Arab chief, and very singular precautions are taken to prevent the possibility of fraud, so far as the written pedigree extends.

The head of the Arabian horse is inimitable. The broadness and squareness of the forehead, the shortness and fineness of the muzzle, the prominence and brilliancy of the eye, the smallness of the ears, and the beautiful course of the veins, are its characteristics. In the formation of the shoulders next to the head, the Arabian is superior to any other breed. The withers are high and the shoulder-blades inclined backward, and so nicely adjusted that in descending a hill the point or edge of the ham never ruffles the skin. The fineness of the legs and the oblique position of the pasterns may seem to lessen his strength; but the leg, although small, is flat and wiry, and its bones uncommonly dense.*

Richardson says: "Often may the traveler in the desert, on entering within the folds of a tent, behold the interesting spectacle of a magnificent courser extended upon the ground, and some half dozen little dark-skinned, naked urchins scrambling across her body, or reclining in sleep, some upon her neck, some on her body, and others pillowed upon her heels; nor do the children ever experience injury from their gentle playmate. She recognizes the family of her friend, her patron, and toward them all the natural sweetness of her disposition leans, even to overflowing."

The Arabian horse Tartar, whose portrait we give on the next page, is thus described in the *New England Farmer:* "This beautiful horse was bred by Asa Pingree, of Topsfield, Mass.

---

* Youatt.

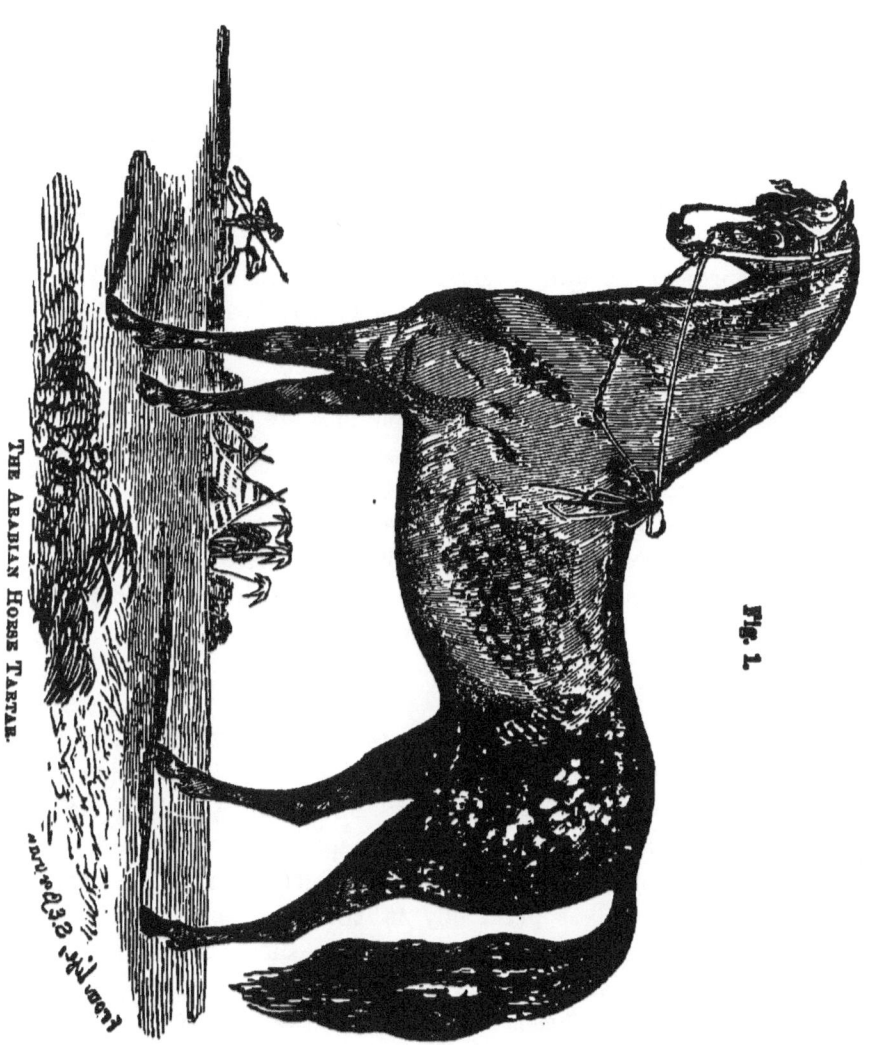

Fig. 1.

THE ARABIAN HORSE TARTAR.

He now stands fifteen and one fourth hands high; weighs nine hundred pounds; is of dark-gray color, with dark mane and tail. He was sired by the imported, full-blood Arabian horse 'Imaum,' and is seven years old this spring. This engraving, copied from life, gives the figure of 'Tartar,' but can not represent the agile action, flashing eye, and cat-like nimbleness of all his movements. It shows the beautiful Arabian head and finely-set-on neck; his ample muscular quarters; his flat legs, rather short from the knee downward; and his long and elastic pastern. All his motions are light and exceedingly graceful, and his temper so docile that a child may handle him."

3. *The Morgan Horse.*—This celebrated American breed is probably a cross between the English race-horse and the common New England mare. It is perhaps, all things considered, the very finest breed for general usefulness now existing in the United States. Mr. S. W. Jewett, a celebrated stock breeder, in an article in the *Cultivator*, says:

"I believe the Morgan blood to be the best ever infused into the Northern horse. The Morgans are well known and esteemed for activity, hardiness, gentleness, and docility; well adapted for all work; good in every spot except for races on the turf. They are lively and spirited, lofty and elegant in their action, carrying themselves gracefully in the harness. They have clean bone, sinewy legs, compactness, short, strong backs, powerful lungs, strength, and endurance. They are known by their short, clean heads, width across the face at the eyes, eyes lively and prominent; they have open and wide under jaws, large windpipe, deep brisket, heavy and round body, broad in the back, short limbs in proportion to size (of body); they have broad quarters, a lively, quick action, indomitable spirit, move true and easy in a good, round trot, and are fast on the walk; color dark bay, chestnut, brown, or black, with dark, flowing, wavy mane and tail. They make the best of roadsters, and live to a great age."

All do not agree, however, with this estimate of the Morgans.

A distinguished judge of horses in Vermont, quoted by Randall in his Introduction to Youatt on the Horse, says:

"They [the Morgans] are good for an hour's drive—for short stages. They are good to run around town with. They are good in the light pleasure-wagon—prompt, lively (not spirited), and 'trappy.' There is no question among those who have had fair opportunities of comparing the Morgans with horses of purer blood and descended from different stocks, in regard to the relative position of the Morgan. He is, as he exists at the present day, inferior in size, speed, and bottom—in fact, in all those qualities necessary to the performance of 'great deeds'

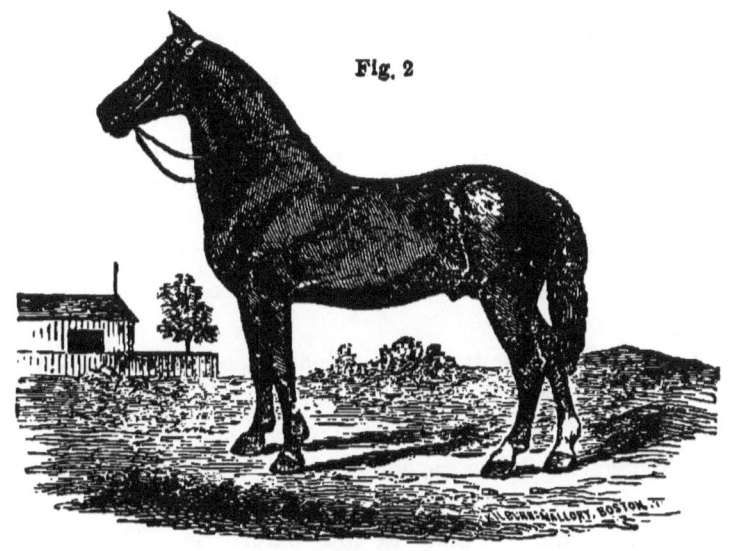

Fig. 2

SHERMAN MORGAN.

on the road or the farm, to the descendants of Messenger, Duroc, imported Magnum Bonum, and many other horses of deserved celebrity."

Sherman Morgan, whose portrait we are permitted to copy from Linsley's "Morgan Horse," was foaled in 1835, the property of Moses Cook, of Campton, N. H. Sired by Sherman, g sire, Justin Morgan. The pedigree of the dam not fully established, but conceded to have been a very fine animal, and said to be from the Justin Morgan. Sherman Morgan is fifteen hands high, weighs about 1,050 lbs., is dark chestnut, and very much resembles his sire Sherman, but heavier, stockier, and not as much action. A fine horse, and is now kept in the stable at Lancaster, N. H., where the Sherman died. He is owned by A. J. Congdon.

4. *The Canadian Horse.*—This horse abounds in the Canadian Provinces and in the Northern States of the Union, and is too well known to require a particular description. It is mainly of Norman-French descent. It is a hardy, long-lived animal, is easily kept, and very useful on a farm, although generally too small for heavy work. A cross between stallions of this breed and our common mares produces a superior horse, and such crosses are finding favor among farmers.

5. *The Norman Horse.*—The French or Norman horse, from which the Canadian is descended, is destined to take a more prominent place than has hitherto been assigned to it among our working horses. We introduce an engraving of one of this breed, called Louis Philippe, which was bred by Edward Harris, of Moorestown N. J., by whom the breed was imported from France.

The Norman horse is from the Spanish, of Arabian ancestry, and crossed upon the draught horses of Normandy. Mr. Harris had admired the speed, toughness, and endurance of the French stage-coach horses, and resolved to import this valuable stock, and deserves the thanks of the American public for his perseverance and sacrifices in this enterprise. The Norman horses are enduring and energetic beyond description, and keep their condition on hard fare and brutal treatment, when most other breeds would quail and die. This variety of horse is employed in France to draw the ponderous stage-coaches, called "diligences," and travelers express astonishment at the extraordinary performances of these animals. Each of these huge vehicles is designed for eighteen passengers, and when thus loaded are equal to five tons weight. Five horses are attached to the clumsy and cumbrous carriage, with rude harness, and

Fig. 3.

THE FRENCH OR NORMAN HORSE LOUIS PHILIPPE

their regular rate of speed with this enormous load is seven miles an hour, and this pace is maintained over rough and hilly regions. On some routes the roads are lighter, when the speed is increased to eight, nine, and sometimes to ten miles an hour.

6. *Cleveland Bay.*—According to Mr. Youatt, the *true* Cleveland Bay is nearly extinct in England. They were formerly employed as a heavy, slow coach-horse. Mr. Youatt says: " The origin of the better kind of coach-horse is the Cleveland Bay, confined principally to Yorkshire and Durham, with perhaps Lincolnshire on one side and Northumherland on the other, but difficult to meet with pure in either county. The Cleveland mare is crossed by a three-fourths or through-bred horse of sufficient substance and height, and the produce is the coach-horse most in repute, with his arched crest and high action. From the thorough-bred of sufficient height, but not of so much substance, we obtain the four-in-hand and superior curricle-horse.

Cleveland Bays were imported into western New York a few years since, where they have spread considerably. They have often been exhibited at our State fairs. They are monstrously large, and for their size are symmetrical horses, and possess very respectable action. Whether they would endure on the road at any but a moderate pace, we are not informed, and have some doubts. Whether they spring from the genuine and unmixed Cleveland stock, now so scarce in England, we have no means of knowing. The half-bloods, the produce of a cross with our common mares, are liked by many of our farmers. They are said to make strong, serviceable farm beasts—though rather prone to sullenness of temper.*

7. *The Conestoga Horse.*—This horse, which is found chiefly in Pennsylvania and the adjacent States, is more remarkable for endurance than symmetry. In height it sometimes reaches seventeen hands; the legs being long and the body light.

---

* Randall.

The Conestoga breed makes good carriage and heavy draft horses.

8. *The Clydesdale Horse.*—The Clydesdale horse is descended from a cross between the Flemish horse and the Lanarkshire (Scotland) mares. The mare is derived from the district on the Clyde where the breed is chiefly found. Horses of this breed are deservedly esteemed for the cart and for the plow on heavy soil. They are strong, hardy, steady, true pullers, of sound constitution, and from fourteen to sixteen hands high. They are broad, thick, heavy, compact, well made for durabil-

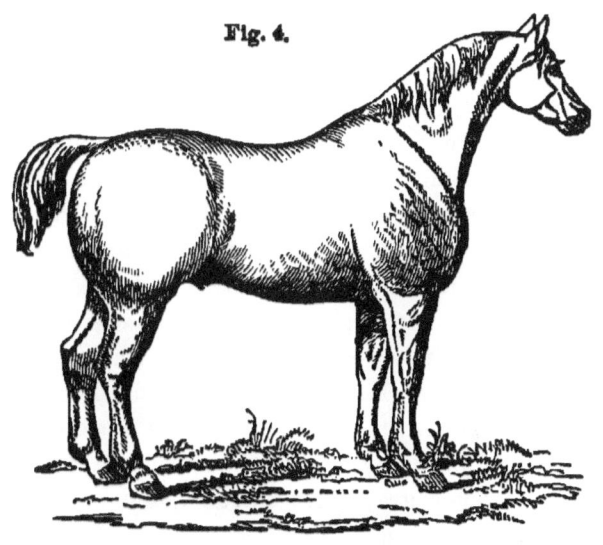

Fig. 4.

THE CLYDESDALE HORSE.

ity, health, and power. They have sturdy legs, strong shoulders, back, and hips, a well-arched neck, and a light face and head.

9. *The Virginia Horse.*—This breed predominates in the State from which it takes its name, and abounds to a greater or less extent in all the Southern, Western, and Middle States. It derives its origin from English blood-horses imported at various times, and has been most diligently and purely kept in the South. The celebrated Shark, the best horse of his day,

was sire of the best Virginian horses, while Tally-ho, son of Highflyer, peopled the Jerseys.*

10. *The Wild or Prairie Horse.* — In the Southwestern States wild horses abound, which are doubtless sprung from the same Spanish stock as the wild horses of the pampas and other parts of the southern continent, all of which are of the celebrated Andalusian breed, derived from the Moorish Barb. The prairie horses are often captured, and when domesticated are found to be capable of great endurance. They are not, however, recommended by the symmetry or elegance of appearance for which their type is so greatly distinguished, being generally rather small and scrubby.†

11. *The American Trotting-Horse.*—" We can not refrain," H. S. Randall says, in the Introduction to Youatt on the Horse, already referred to, " from calling attention to our trotting-horses, though in reality they do not, at least as a whole, constitute a breed, or even a distinct variety or family. There *is* a family of superior trotters, including several of the best our country has ever produced, the descendants of Abdallah and Messenger, and running back through their sire Mambrino to the thorough-bred horse, old Messenger. But many of our best trotters have no known pedigrees, and some of them, without doubt, are entirely destitute of the blood of the race-horse. Lady Suffolk is by Engineer, but the blood of Engineer is unknown (she is a gray mare, fifteen hands and two inches high). Dutchman has no known pedigree. Other celebrated trotters stand in the same category—though we are inclined to think that a decided majority of the best, especially at long distances, have a greater or less infusion of the blood of the race-horse.

" The United States has undoubtedly produced more superior trotters than any other country in the world, and in no other country has the speed of the best American trotters been equaled."

---

* Farmers' Register. † Farmers' Encyclopedia.

III.—POINTS OF HORSES.

Every one who has anything to do with the horse should know something of the "points" by means of which a good animal is distinguished from a bad one. It is necessary to understand this, no matter for what particular service the horse may be required; and the qualities indicated by these points are universal in all breeds.

To illustrate this subject and teach the uninstructed how to correctly judge the horse, we introduce the accompanying lettered outlines.

It is evident that to be a good judge of a horse, one must have in his memory a model by which to try all that may be presented to his criticism and judgment.

Fig. 5 represents such a model. It is a thorough-bred horse, in which the artist has endeavored to avoid every fault. Fig. 6 is designed to represent a horse in which every good point is suppressed. It may not be common to see a horse totally destitute of every good point; but injudicious breeding has so obliterated the good ones, that the cut fig. 6 is not a caricature, though we confess that its original is little less than a caricature on the true ideal of a horse. Such a head is common, so is such a shoulder, such a back, quarters, and legs; and if they are not very often all combined in one animal, they are, unfortunately, often found distributed among the common breeds in such abundance as to mar the beauty and the service of three quarters of all the horses in ordinary use. The letters are alike on both figures, and will enable the reader to draw a comparison between the respective points of each. We copy the description of the cuts from the *Farmer's Companion:*

"The most important part of all is probably the direction of the shoulder, from A to B. Next to this, the length from the hip to the hock, C to D. The point which next to these probably most contributes to speed and easy going, is the shortness of the canon bone between the knee and the pastern joint, E to F, a point without which no leg is good. A horse which has all these three points good will necessarily and infallibly stand over a great deal of ground, W to X, that is, the distance between his fore and hind feet will be great; while one which is deficient in all of them, or, indeed, in the two first, will as

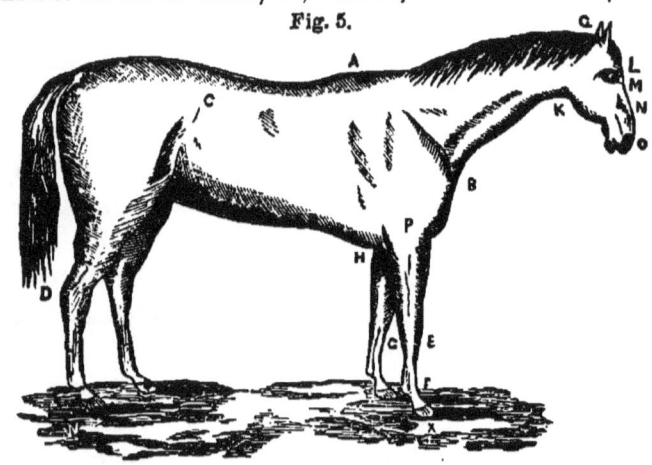
Fig. 5.

assuredly stand like a goat with all its feet gathered under him, and will never be either a fast horse or safe under saddle. A

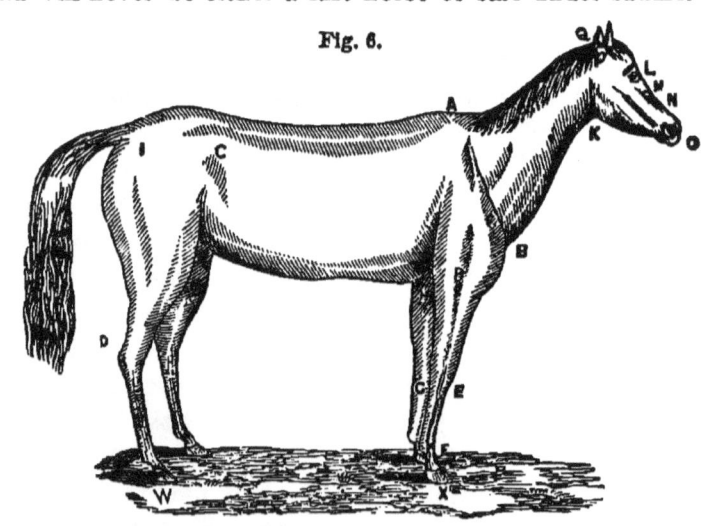
Fig. 6.

horse, not in motion, may be more speedily judged of by this feature than by any other. One consequence of a fine receding shoulder is to give length in the *humerus*, or upper arm, from

B to P, without which a great stride can hardly be attained, but which will seldom if ever be found wanting if the shoulder-blade be well placed. A prominent and fleshy chest is admired by some, probably because they think it indicative of powerful lungs and room for their use. We object to it as adding to what it is so desirable to avoid—the weight to be lifted forward in the act of progression—while all the space the lungs require is to be obtained by *depth* instead of *breadth*, as from A to H, in which point, if a horse be deficient, he will seldom be fit for fast work. The other points which we have marked for comparison are G to E, or the width of the leg immediately below the knee, which in a well-formed leg will be equal all the way down; in a bad one it will be narrowish immediately below the knee, or what is called '*tied in.*' The shape of the neck is more important than might at first thought be supposed, as affecting both the wind and the *handiness* of the mouth; no horse with a faulty neck and a head ill-attached to it, as at Q to K in fig. 6, ever possesses a good or manageable mouth. The points of the face are not without significance, a feebly developed countenance generally showing weakness of courage if not of constitution. We therefore like to see a large and bony protuberance above the eye, as at L in fig. 5, giving the appearance of a sinking immediately below, followed by a slightly *Roman* or protruding inclination toward the nose. These when present are generally signs of 'blood,' which is in some proportion or other a quality without which no breed of horses will ever improve or long entitle itself to rank as other than a race of drudges, fit only for sand or manure carts."

Bearing these points in mind, you may, by observing and comparing the different animals which fall under your eyes, soon qualify yourself to give an intelligent opinion of a horse. One can not become perfect in this branch of knowledge in a week or in a year. Certainly no careful student of this little book will allow himself to be imposed upon in the purchase of an animal having many of the bad points represented in fig. 6. The perfect horse (fig. 5) you will not expect to meet every day.

A badly formed horse is not profitable for any purpose; because, if so formed, they are either clumsy, inactive, dull in mind, or tender and easily broken down. It costs just as much to breed, raise, and keep a poor horse as a good one, and the poor one is low in value and unsalable; besides, he is unable to do good service in any sphere, or to endure.

We copy from Lavater six heads of horses, which indicate different temperaments and a great diversity of character and disposition. The accompanying remarks are from the *American Phrenological Journal:*

Fig. 7.

"Fig. 7 has a slow, heavy temperament; is without spirit, awkward in motion, lazy, stupid in intellect, difficult to teach, bears the whip and needs it, though it is soon forgotten. He is too lazy to hold up his ears or under lip, and is a regular hog-necked, heavy-footed animal.

Fig. 8.

"Fig. 8 has more intelligence and spirit, a more active temperament, and is disposed to anger, will not bear the whip, and shows his anger, when teased or irritated, in a bold, direct onset with the teeth.

"Fig. 9 is a very active temperament; is a quick, keen, active, intelligent animal, but is sly, cunning, mischievous, and trickish; will be hard to catch in the field, inclined to slip the bridle, will be a great shirk in double harness, and will require a sharp eye and steady hand to drive him, and will want something besides a frolicsome boy for a master."

Fig. 9.

"Fig. 10 is obstinate, headstrong, easily irritated, deceitful, and savage; will be hard to drive, unhandy, unyielding, sour-tempered, bad to b.ick, inclined to balk, disposed to fight and crowd his mate, and bite and kick his driver."

Fig. 10.

"Fig. 11 has a noble, proud disposition, and a lofty, stately carriage, but he is timid, restive, and easily irritated and thrown off his mental balance. Such horses should be used by steady, calm men, and on roads and in business which have little variety, change, or means of excitement.

Fig. 11.

Fig. 12.

"Fig. 12 is a calm, self-possessed animal, with a noble, elevated disposition, trustworthy, courageous, good-tempered, well adapted to family use, but not remarkable for sharpness of mind or activity of body.

Fig. 13.

"Figs. 13 and 14 show a great contrast in shape of head, expression of countenance, temperament, disposition, and intelligence. The first is a most noble animal.

"Fig. 13 is broad between the eyes, full, rounded, and prominent in the forehead, indicating benevolence and intellect; broad between the ears, showing courage; broad between the eyes, evincing quickness of perception, memory, and capacity to learn. He can be taught almost anything, can be trusted, and loves and trusts man; is not timid, will go anywhere, and stand without fastening; never kicks, bites, or runs away.

Fig. 14.

"Fig. 14 shows a marked contrast with fig. 13 in almost every respect; his narrow and contracted forehead shows a lack of intelligence, kindness, and tractability; is timid and shy in harness, vicious, unfriendly, disposed to kick, bite, balk, or run away, and is fit only for a mill or horse-boat. For all general uses he should be avoided, and by no means should such an organization be employed for breeding purposes."

IV.—COLOR.

W. C. Spooner, author of several veterinarian works, has the following remarks on color as a sign of other qualities in the horse:

"We have found both good and bad horses of every color, and the only rule we can admit as correct is, that certain colors denote deficient breeding, and therefore such animal is not likely to be so good as he looks, but is probably deficient in bottom or the powers of endurance. These colors are black, which prevails so much with cart-horses, and sorrel, dun, piebald, etc.; the possessors of which come from the North, and possess no Eastern blood. Black horses, unless evidently high bred, are very often soft and sluggish, with breeding insufficient for their work; the pedigree of the majority of them may be dated from the plow-tail, whatever admixtures there may have been since. White hair denotes a thin skin, which is objectionable when it prevails on the legs of horses, as such

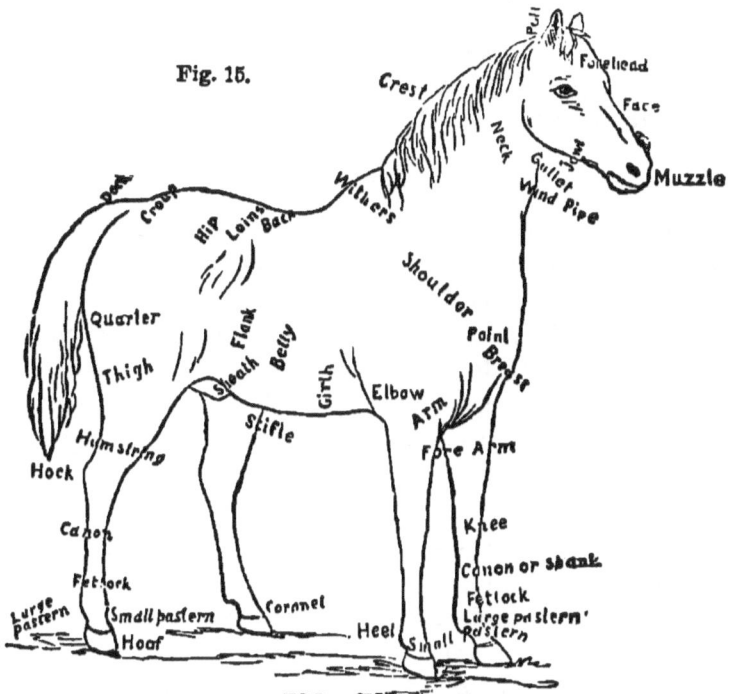

COMMON TERMS DENOTING THE PARTS OF A HORSE.

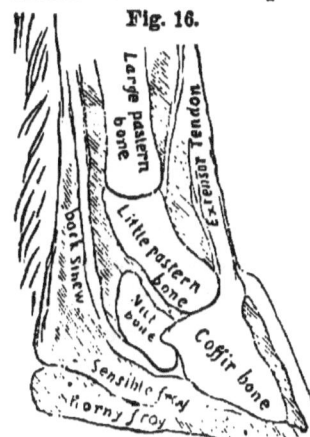

SECTION OF A HORSE'S FOOT.

animals are more disposed to swelled legs and cracked heels than others. Bay horses with black legs are greatly esteemed, yet we have known many determined slugs of this hue. Their constitution is, however, almost invariably good. Chestnut is the prevailing color with our race-horses, and consequently chestnut horses are generally pretty well bred, and possess the good and bad qualities which obtain most among thorough-breds. The Suffolk cart-horse is also distinguished by his light chestnut color; and it is no small recommendation to find that this **breed** has, for several years past, carried away the principal prizes at the annual shows of the Royal Agricultural Society of England. Gray is a very good color, and generally denotes a considerable admixture of Eastern blood."

V.—STABLES.

We condense from Stewart's admirable "Stable Book" the larger portion of the following useful hints and suggestions in reference to stables and their management.

1. *Stables as they Are.*—Stable architects have not much to boast of. When left to themselves they seem to think of little beyond shelter and confinement. If the weather be kept out and the horse be kept in, the stable is sufficient. If light and air be demanded, the doorway will admit them, and other apertures are superfluous.

The majority of stables have been built with little regard to the comfort and health of the horse. Most of them are too small, too dark, too close, or too open; and some are mere dungeons, destitute of every convenience.

2. *Situation of Stables.*—When any choice exists, a situation should be chosen which admits of draining, shelter from the coldest winds, and facility of access. Damp places are especially to be avoided. It is in damp stables that we expect to find horses with bad eyes, coughs, greasy heels, swelled legs, mange, and a long, dry, staring coat, which no grooming can cure. Take every precaution, then, against dampness in your stables.

3. *Size of Stables.*—They are seldom too large in proportion to the number of stalls; but are often made to hold too many horses. Horses require pure air as well as human beings; and the process of breathing has the same effect in their case as in ours—changing it to that poisonous substance, carbonic acid gas. With twenty or thirty horses in a single apartment no ordinary ventilation is sufficient to keep the air pure. Large stables, too, are liable to frequent and great alterations of temperature. When several horses are out, those which remain

are often rendered uncomfortably cold, and when the stable is full the whole are fevered or excited by excess of heat. Efficient ventilation—a very important object—is also much more difficult in a large than in a small stable.

In width the stable may vary from sixteen to eighteen feet; and in length it must have six feet for each stall. Large carthorses require a little more room both in length and breadth of stable. The number of stalls should not exceed sixteen, and it would be better if there were only eight.

Double-rowed stables, or those in which the stalls occupy both sides, require least space, and for horses kept at full work are sufficiently suitable, but for carriage horses single-rowed stables are better. If the double-rowed are used, the gangway should be wide, to prevent the horses from kicking at each other, as they are apt to do when they grow playful from half idleness.

4. *Windows.*—Windows are too much neglected in stables, and where they exist at all are generally too few, too small, and ill placed. Some think horses do not require light—that they thrive best in the dark; but many a horse has become blind for the want of light in his stable. When side windows can not be introduced, a portion of the hay loft must be sacrificed and light introduced from the roof. Side windows should be so arranged that the light will not fall directly upon the eyes of the horse.

5. *Floors.*—Stable floors may be of stone, brick, plank, or earth. One of the best kinds of stable floor, where the soil is dry, is made of a composition of lime, ashes, and clay, mixed up in equal parts into a mortar and spread from twelve to fifteen inches deep over the surface of the ground forming the bottom of the stable. It will dry in ten days and makes a very smooth, fine flooring, particularly safe, easy, and agreeable for horses to stand upon, and free from all the objections to stone, brick, and wood.[*]

---

[*] A. B. Allen.

6. *Draining.*—A gutter or other contrivance for carrying off the urine should always be made in a stable, otherwise it will be foul and damp. It should be conveyed into a tank and carefully saved as manure.

7. *Racks and Mangers.*—These should be so placed that the horse can eat from them with ease. The face of the rack next the horse should be perpendicular, or as nearly so as possible. Sometimes the face is so sloping and the rack so high that the horse has to turn his head almost upside down to get at his food.

The mangers or troughs from which the horse eats his grain are now sometimes made of cast iron, which we deem a great improvement over wood. The manger should be concave and not flat at the bottom. Mangers are generally placed too low. The bottom should be from three feet and a half to four feet from the ground, according to the height of the horse.

8. *Ventilation of Stables.*—Impure air, as we have already remarked, is hurtful to the horse as well as to the human being inducing disease and shortening life. To avoid it in our own case, we (sometimes!) ventilate our houses. If we would have our horses healthy we must do the same for the stable. Apertures, one for each stall, should be provided for carrying off the impure air. These should be so near the top of the building as practicable. It should be eight or ten inches square. Smaller apertures near the floor or not far from the horse's nostrils will serve to admit fresh air.*

9. *Warmth, etc.*—If you wish to have your horses thrive and continue healthy, you can not pay too much attention to their comfort. Their stables should be warm in winter and cool in summer. To secure these conditions, they should be properly constructed. [For plans, see "The House."] To keep stables sufficiently warm, no artificial means are required. It is enough that the outside air, except so much as is required for ventilation, be excluded during the coldest weather. Warm blankets should of course be used at the same time.

---

* See Chapter on Barns and Stables, in "The House."

VI.—FEEDING.

1. *The Best Food for Horses*.—Considerable care and system are necessary in feeding horses, so as to keep them in the best health and the highest working order.

"The best food for ordinary working-horses in America," A. B. Allen says, "is as much good hay or grass as they will eat, corn-stalks or blades, or for the want of these, straw, and a mixture of from sixteen to twenty-four quarts per day, of about half and half of oats and the better quality of wheat bran. When the horse is seven years old past, two to four quarts of corn or hominy or meal ground from the corn and cob is preferable to the pure grain. Two to four quarts of wheat, barley, rye, buckwheat, peas, or beans, either whole or ground, may be substituted for the corn. A pint of oil meal or a gill of flax-seed mixed with the other food is very good for a relish, especially in keeping up a healthy system and the bowels open, and in giving the hair a fine glossy appearance. Potatoes and other roots, unless cooked, do not seem to be of much benefit in this climate, especially in winter—they lie cold upon the stomach and subject the horse to scouring; besides, they are too watery for a hard-working animal. Corn is fed too much at the South and West. It makes horses fat, but can not give them that hard, muscular flesh which oats do; hence their softness and want of endurance in general work and on the road, in comparison with Northern and Eastern horses, reared and fed on oats and more nutritious grasses."

2. *Work and Digestion*.—Slow work aids digestion, empties the bowels, and sharpens the appetite. Hence it happens that on Sunday night and Monday morning there are more cases of colic and founder than during any other part of the week. Horses that never want an appetite ought not to have an unlimited allowance of hay on Sunday; they have time to eat a great deal more than they need, and the torpid state of the stomach and bowels, produced by a day of idleness, renders an additional quantity very dangerous. Farm and cart horses are fed immediately before commencing their labor, and the appetite with which they return shows that the stomach is not full.

During fast work digestion is suspended. In the general commotion excited by violent exertion, the stomach can hardly be in a favorable condition for performing its duty. The blood circulates too rapidly to permit the formation of gastric juice or its combination with the food; and the blood and the nervous influence are so exclusively concentrated and expended upon the muscular system, that none can be spared for carrying on the digestive process.

3. *Bulk Essential.*—Condensed food is necessary for fast-working horses. Their food must be in less compass than that of the farm or cart horse. But to this condensation there are some limits. Grain affords all, and more than all, the nutriment a horse is capable of consuming, even under the most extraordinary exertion. His stomach and bowels can hold more than they are able to digest. Something more than nutriment is wanted. The bowels must suffer a moderate degree of distension; more than a wholesome allowance of grain can produce.

When hay is very dear and grain cheap, it is customary in many stables to give less than the usual allowance of hay, and more grain. The alteration is sometimes carried too far, and is often made too suddenly. The horses may have as much grain as they will eat, yet it does not suffice without fodder. Having no hay, they will leave the grain to eat the litter. When the ordinary fodder, then, is very dear, its place must be supplied by some other which will produce a wholesome distension, though it may not yield so much nutriment. Straw or roots, either or both, may be used in such cases. The excessively tucked-up flank, and the horse's repeated efforts to eat his litter, show when his food is not of sufficient bulk, and this indication must not be disregarded.

4. *Quantity of Food.*—The quantity of food may be insufficient, or it may be in excess. The consumption is influenced by the work, the weather, the horse's condition, age, temper,

form, and health; these circumstances, especially the work, must regulate the allowance.

When the horse has to work as much and as often as he is able, his allowance of food should be unlimited.

When the work is such as to destroy the legs more than it exhausts the system, the food must be given with some restriction, unless the horse be a poor eater.

When the work is moderate, or less than moderate, a good feeder will eat too much.

When the weather is cold, horses that are much exposed to it require more food than when the weather is warm.

When the horse is in good working condition, he needs less food than while he is only getting into condition.

Young growing horses require a little more food than those of mature age; but, as they are not fit for full work, the difference is not great.

Old horses, those that have begun to decline in vigor, require more food than the young or the matured.

Hot-tempered, irritable horses seldom feed well; but those that have good appetites require more food to keep them in condition, than others of quiet and calm disposition.

Small-bellied, narrow-chested horses require more food than those of deep and round carcass; but few of them eat enough to maintain them in condition for full work.

Lame, greasy-heeled, and harness-galled horses require an extra allowance of food to keep them in working condition.

Sickness, fevers, inflammations, all diseases which influence health so much as to throw the horse off work, demand, with few exceptions, a spare diet, which, in general, consists of bran-mashes, grass, carrots, and hay.*

5. *Watering.*—This is a part of stable management little regarded by the farmer. He lets his horses loose morning and night, and they go to the nearest pond or brook and drink their fill, and no harm results, for they obtain that kind of water

---

* Stewart's Stable Book.

which nature designed them to have, in a manner prepared for them by some unknown influence of the atmosphere, as well as by the deposition of many saline admixtures.

The difference between *hard* and *soft* water is known to every one. There is nothing in which the different effect of hard and soft water is so evident as in the stomach and digestive organs of the horse. Hard water drawn fresh from the well will assuredly make the coat of a horse unaccustomed to it stare, and it will not unfrequently gripe and otherwise injure him. He is injured, however, not so much by the hardness of the well-water as by its coldness—particularly by its coldness in summer, and when it is in many degrees below the temperature of the atmosphere. The water in the brook and the pond being warmed by long exposure to the air, as well as having become soft, the horse drinks freely of it without danger.

If the horse were watered three times a day, and especially in summer, he would often be saved from the sad torture of thirst, and from many a disease. Whoever has observed the eagerness with which the over-worked horse, hot and tired, plunges his muzzle into the pail, and the difficulty of stopping him until he has drained the last drop, may form some idea of what he had previously suffered, and will not wonder at the violent spasms, and inflammation, and sudden death that often result. There is a prejudice in the minds of many persons against the horse being fully supplied with water. They think that it injures his wind, and disables him for quick and hard work. If he is galloped, as he too often is, immediately after drinking, his wind may be irreparably injured; but if he were oftener suffered to satiate his thirst at the intervals of rest he would be happier and better. It is a fact unsuspected by those who have not carefully observed the horse, that if he has frequent access to water he will not drink so much in the course of the day as another will do, who, to cool his parched mouth, swallows as fast as he can and knows not when to stop.

On a journey a horse should be liberally supplied with

water. When he is a little cooled, two or three quarts may be given to him, and after that his feed. Before he has finished his corn, two or three quarts more may be offered. He will take no harm if this is repeated three or four times during a long and hot day.*

VII.—GENERAL MANAGEMENT.

1. *Air.*—We have spoken of the necessity of ventilation. Hear what that great authority, Youatt, says:

"If the stable is close, the air will not only be hot but foul. The breathing of every animal contaminates it; and when in the course of the night, with every aperture stopped, it passes again and again through the lungs, the blood can not undergo its proper and healthy change; digestion will not be so perfectly performed, and all the functions of life are injured. Let the owner of a valuable horse think of his passing twenty or twenty-two out of the twenty-four hours in this debilitating atmosphere! Nature does wonders in enabling every animal to accommodate itself to the situation in which it is placed, and the horse that lives in the stable-oven suffers less from it than would scarcely be conceived possible: but he does not, and can not, possess the power and the hardihood which he would acquire under other circumstances.

"The air of the improperly close and heated stable is still further contaminated by the urine and dung, which rapidly ferment there, and give out stimulating and unwholesome vapors. When a person first enters an ill-managed stable, and especially early in the morning, he is annoyed not only by the heat of the confined air, but by a pungent smell, resembling hartshorn; and can he be surprised at the inflammation of the eyes, and the chronic cough, and the disease of the lungs, by which the animal, who has been all night shut up in this vitiated atmosphere, is often attacked; or if glanders and farcy should occasionally break out in such stables? It has been ascertained by chemical experiment that the urine of the horse

---

* Youatt.

contains in it an exceedingly large quantity of hartshorn; and not only so, but that, influenced by the heat of a crowded stable, and possibly by other decompositions that are going forward at the same time, this ammoniacal vapor begins to be rapidly given out almost immediately after the urine is voided."

2. *Litter.*—The facts just stated in reference to the plentiful escape of ammoniacal gas from the urine, show the necessity of frequently removing the litter which is soon saturated with it. It rapidly putrefies, emitting noisome odors and contaminating the air. Everything hastening decomposition should be carefully removed where life and health are to be preserved. Litter that has been much wetted and has begun to decay should be swept out every morning.

No heap of fermenting dung should be suffered to remain during the day in the corner or any part of the stable.

3. *Grooming.*—Of this little need be said to the farmer in reference to his working horses, since custom, and apparently without ill effect, has allotted to them so little of the comb and brush. "The animal that is worked all day and turned out at night," Youatt says, "requires little more to be done to him than to have the dirt brushed off his limbs. Regular grooming, by rendering his skin more sensible to the alteration of temperature and the inclemency of the weather, would be prejudicial. The horse that is altogether turned out, needs no grooming. The dandruff or scurf, which accumulates at the roots of the hair, is a provision of nature to defend him from the wind and the cold.

"It is to the stabled horse, highly fed and little or irregularly worked, that grooming is of so much consequence. Good rubbing with the brush or the curry-comb opens the pores of the skin, circulates the blood to the extremities of the body, produces free and healthy perspiration, and stands in the room of exercise. No horse will carry a fine coat without either unnatural heat or dressing. They both effect the same purpose; they both increase the insensible perspiration; but the first does it at the expense of health and strength, while the second, at the same time that it produces a glow on the skin and a determination of blood to it, rouses all the energies of the frame. It would be well for the proprietor of the horse if he were to insist—and to see that his orders are really obeyed—that the fine coat in which he and his groom so much delight is produced by honest rubbing, and not by a heated stable and thick clothing, and, most of all, not by stimulating or injurious spices. The horse should be regularly dressed every day, in addition to the grooming that is necessary after work.

"When the weather will permit the horse to be taken out, he should never be groomed in the stable, unless he is an animal of peculiar value, or placed for a time under peculiar circumstances. Without dwelling on the want of cleanliness, when the scurf and dust that are brushed from the horse lodge in his manger and mingle with his food, experience teaches, that if the cold is not too great, the animal is braced and invigorated to a degree that can not be attained in the stable, from being dressed in the open air. There is no necessity, however, for half the punishment which many a groom inflicts upon the horse in the act of dressing; and particularly on one whose skin is thin and sensible. The curry-comb should at all times be lightly applied. With many horses, its use may be almost dispensed with; and even the brush needs not to be so hard, nor the points of the bristles so irregular, as they often are. A soft brush, with a little more weight of the hand, will be equally effectual and a great deal more pleasant to the horse. A hair-cloth, while it will seldom irritate and tease, will be almost sufficient with horses that have a thin skin, and that have not been neglected. After all, it is no slight task to dress a horse as it ought to be done. It occupies no little time, and demands considerable patience as well as dexterity. It will be readily ascertained whether a horse has been well dressed, by rubbing him with one of the fingers. A greasy stain will detect the idleness of the groom. When, however, the horse is changing his coat, both the curry-comb and the brush should be used as lightly as possible.

"Whoever would be convinced of the benefit of friction to the horse's skin and to the horse generally, needs only to observe the effects produced by well hand-rubbing the legs of a tired horse. While every enlargement subsides, and the painful stiffness disappears, and the legs attain their natural warmth and become fine, the animal is evidently and rapidly reviving; he attacks his food with appetite, and then quietly lies down to rest."

4. *Exercise.*—Of this the farm horse generally has enough. His work is tolerably regular, not exhausting, and he generally maintains his health and has his life prolonged to an extent rare among horses of "leisure." But a gentleman's or a tradesman's horse suffers a great deal more from idleness than he does from work. A stable-fed horse should have two hours' exercise every day, if he is to be kept free from disease. Nothing of extraordinary, or even of ordinary, labor can be effected on the road or in the field without sufficient and regular exercise. It is this alone which can give energy to the system or develope the powers of any animal. The animal that, with the usual stable feeding, stands idle for three or four days, as is the case in many establishments, must suffer. He is predisposed to fever, or to grease, or, most of all, to diseases of the foot; and if, after three or four days of inactivity he is ridden far and fast he is almost sure to have inflammation of the lungs or of the feet.

VIII.—VICES AND BAD HABITS.

The vices and bad habits of the horse, like those of his master, are oftener than otherwise the consequence of a faulty education. We are convinced that innately vicious horses are comparatively few. We condense from Youatt the following hints on this subject.

1. *Restiveness.*—At the head of all the vices of the horse is restiveness, the most annoying and the most dangerous of all. It is the produce of bad temper and worse education; and, like all other habits founded on nature and stamped by education, it is inveterate. Whether it appears in the form of

kicking or rearing, plunging or bolting, or in any way that threatens danger to the rider or the horse, it rarely admits of cure. A determined rider may, to a certain extent, subjugate the animal; or the horse may have his favorites, or form his attachments, and with some particular person he may be comparatively or perfectly manageable; but others can not long depend upon him, and even his master is not always sure of him.

2. *Backing or Balking.*—Some horses have the habit of backing at first starting, and that more from playfulness than desire of mischief. A moderate application of the whip will usually be effectual. Others, even after starting, exhibit considerable obstinacy and viciousness. This is frequently the effect of bad breaking.

A large and heavy stone should be put behind the wheel before starting, when the horse, finding it more difficult to back than to go forward, will gradually forget this unpleasant trick. It will likewise be of advantage as often as it can be managed, so to start that the horse shall have to back up-hill. The difficulty of accomplishing this will soon make him readily go forward. A little coaxing or leading will assist in accomplishing the cure.

3. *Biting.*—This is perhaps sometimes the consequence of natural ferocity, but is more frequently acquired from the foolish teasing play of hostlers and stable-boys. At first his biting is half playful and half in earnest, but finally becomes habitual and degenerates into absolute viciousness. It is seldom that anything can be done in the way of cure. Kindness will aggravate the evil and no degree of severity will correct it. "I have seen," Professor Stuart says, "biters punished until they trembled in every joint and were ready to drop, but have never in any case known them cured by this treatment or by any other. The lash is forgotten in an hour, and the horse is as ready and determined to repeat the offense as before. He appears unable to resist the temptation, and in its worst form biting is a species of insanity."

But if biting can not be cured it may almost always be prevented, and every proprietor of horses, while he insists upon gentle and humane treatment of his animals, should strictly forbid this horse-play.

4. *Kicking.*—This, as *a vice*, is another consequence of the culpable habit of grooms and stable-boys of teasing the horse. That which is at first an indication of annoyance at the pinching and tickling of the groom, and without any design to injure, gradually becomes the expression of anger, and the effort to do mischief. The horse, likewise, too soon recognizes the least appearance of timidity, and takes advantage of the discovery. There is no cure for this vice after it has become a confirmed habit, and he can not be justified who keeps a kicking horse in his stable. Before the habit is inveterately established, a thorn-bush or a piece of furze fastened against the partition or post will sometimes effect a cure. When the horse finds that he is pretty severely pricked he will not long continue to punish himself.

5. *Rearing.*—This sometimes results from playfulness, carried, indeed, to an unpleasant and dangerous extent; but it is oftener a desperate and occasionally successful effort to unhorse the rider, and consequently a vice. The horse that has twice decidedly and dangerously reared should never be trusted again, unless, indeed, it was the fault of the rider, who had been using a deep curb and a sharp bit. Some of the best horses will contend against these, and then rearing may be immediately and permanently cured by using a snaffle bridle alone.

6. *Running Away.*—There is no certainty of cure for this vice. The only method which affords any probability of success is, to ride or drive such a horse with a strong curb and sharp bit; to have him always firmly in hand; and if he will run away and the place will admit of it, to give him (sparing neither curb nor whip) a great deal more running than he likes.

7. *Overreaching.*—This unpleasant noise, known also by the term "clicking," arises from the toe of the hind-foot knocking

against the shoe of the fore-foot. If the animal is young, the action of the horse may be materially improved; otherwise nothing can be done, except to keep the toe of the hind-foot as short and as round as it can safely be, and to bevel off and round the toe of the shoe, like that which has been worn off by a stumbling horse, and, perhaps, to lower the heel of the fore-foot a little.

8. *Rolling.*—Some horses have the habit of rolling in the stable, by which they are liable to get cast, bruised, and half strangled. The only remedy is to tie such a horse with just length of halter enough to lie down, but not allow of his resting his head on the ground. This is an unpleasant means of cure, and not always a safe one.

9. *Shying.*—This vice is often the result of cowardice, or playfulness, or want of work, but at other times it is the consequence of a defect of sight; and in its treatment it is of great importance to distinguish between these different causes. For the last, every allowance must be made, and care must be taken that the fear of correction is not associated with the imagined existence of some terrifying object. The severe use of the whip and the spur can not do good here, and are likely to aggravate the vice ten-fold. A word half encouraging and half scolding will tell the horse that there was nothing to fear, and will give him confidence in his rider on a future occasion.

The shying from skittishness or affectation is quite a different affair, and must be conquered: but how? Severity is altogether out of place. If he is forced into contact with the object by dint of correction, the dread of punishment will afterward be associated with that object, and on the next occasion his startings will be more frequent and more dangerous. The way to cure him is to go on, turning as little as possible out of the road, giving a harsh word or two and a gentle touch, and then taking no more notice of the matter. After a few times, whatever may have been the object which he chose to select as the pretended cause of affright, he will pass it almost without notice.

10. *Slipping the Halter.*—Many horses are so clever at this

trick that s arcely a night passes without their getting loose. It is a habit which may lead to dangerous results, and should be cured at once by some extra means of securing the halter in its place, or by a strap attached to it and buckled securely (but not tight enough to be a serious inconvenience), around the neck.

11. *Tripping.*—He must be a skillful practitioner or a mere pretender who promises to remedy this habit. If it arises from a heavy fore-hand and the fore-legs being too much under the horse, no one can alter the natural frame of the animal; if it proceeds from tenderness of the foot, grogginess, or old lameness, these ailments are seldom cured. Also, if it is to be traced to habitual carelessness and idleness, no whipping will rouse the drone. A known stumbler should never be ridden or driven by any one who values his safety or his life.

If the stumbler has the foot kept as short and the toe pared as close as safety will permit, and the shoe is rounded at the toe, or has that shape given to it which it naturally acquires in a fortnight from the peculiar action of such a horse, the animal may not stumble quite so much; or if the disease which produced the habit can be alleviated, some trifling good may be done, but in almost every case a stumbler should be got rid of, or put to slow and heavy work. If the latter alternative is adopted, he may trip as much as he pleases, for the weight of the load and the motion of the other horses will keep him upon his legs.

IX.—HINTS TO BUYERS.

1. *Warranty.*—A man should have a more perfect knowledge of horses than falls to the lot of most men, and a perfect knowledge of the seller also, who ventures to buy a horse without a warranty. This warranty is usually embodied in the receipt, which may be expressed as follows:

Received at Louisville, August 10th, 1858, from O. D., one hundred dollars for a gray horse warranted only five years old, sound, free from vice, and quiet to ride or drive. A. V.

"A receipt, including merely the word 'warranted,' extends only to soundness; 'warranted sound' goes no further; the age, freedom from vice, and quietness to ride and drive, should be especially named. This warranty comprises every cause of unsoundness that can be detected, or that lurks in the constitution at the time of sale, and to every vicious habit that the animal has hitherto shown. To establish a breach of warranty, and to be enabled to tender a return of the horse and recover the difference of price, the purchaser must prove that it was unsound or viciously disposed at the time of sale.

"No price will imply a warranty or be equivalent to one; there must be an express warranty. A fraud must be proved in the seller, in order that the buyer may be enabled to return the horse or maintain an action for the price. The warranty should be given at the time of sale. A warranty, or a promise to warrant the horse, given at any period antecedent to the sale, is invalid; for horse flesh is a very perishable commodity, and the constitution and usefulness of the animal may undergo a considerable change in the space of a few days. A warranty after the sale is invalid, for it is given without any legal consideration. In order to complete the purchase, there must be a transfer of the animal, or a memorandum of agreement, or the payment of the earnest-money. The least sum will suffice for earnest. No verbal promise to buy or to sell is binding without one of these. The moment either of these is effected, the legal transfer of property or delivery is made, and whatever may happen to the horse, the seller retains, or is entitled to, the money. If the purchaser exercises any act of ownership, by using the animal without leave of the vender, or by having any operation performed, or any medicine given to him, he makes him his own.

"If a person buys a horse warranted sound, and discovering no defect in him, and relying on the warranty, re-sells him, and the unsoundness is discovered by the second purchaser, and the horse returned to the first purchaser, or an action commenced against him, he has his claim on the first seller, and may demand of him not only the price of the horse, or the difference in value, but every expense that may have been incurred.

"Absolute exchanges of one horse for another, or a sum of money being paid in addition by one of the parties, stand on the same ground as simple sales. If there is a warranty on either side, and that is broken, an action may be maintained: if there be no warranty, deceit must be proved."

2. *What constitutes Unsoundness?*—"That horse is sound in whom there is no disease, and no alteration of structure that impairs or is likely to impair his natural usefulness. The horse is unsound that labors under disease, or has some alteration of structure which does interfere, or is likely to interfere, with his natural usefulness. The term '*natural usefulness*' must be borne in mind. One horse may possess great speed, but is soon knocked up; another will work all day, but can not be got beyond a snail's pace; a third with a heavy fore-hand is liable to stumble, and is continually putting to hazard the neck of his rider; another, with an irritable constitution and a loose, washy form, loses his appetite and begins to scour if a little extra work is exacted from him. The term unsoundness must not be applied to either of these; it would be opening far too widely a door to disputation and endless wrangling. The buyer can discern, or ought to know, whether the form of the horse is that which will render him likely to suit his purpose, and he should try him sufficiently to ascertain his natural strength, endurance, and manner of going. Unsoundness, we repeat, has reference only to disease, or to that alteration of structure which is connected with, or will produce, disease and lessen the usefulness of the animal."*

---

* Youatt.

II.

THE ASS AND THE MULE.

<small>O, that I had been writ down an ass!—*Dogberry.*</small>

I.—THE ASS.

BUFFON has well observed that the ass is despised and neglected only because we possess a more noble and powerful animal in the horse, and that if the horse were unknown, and the care and attention that we lavish upon him were transferred to his now neglected and despised rival, the latter would be increased in size and developed in mental qualities to an extent which it would be difficult to anticipate, but which Eastern travelers, who have observed both animals in their native climates, and among nations by whom they are equally valued, and the good qualities of each justly appreciated, assure us to be the fact.

The character and habits of the horse and the ass are in many respects directly opposed. The one is proud, fiery, impetuous, nice in his tastes, and delicate in his constitution; subject, like a pampered menial, to many diseases, and having many wants and habits unknown in a state of nature. The other, on the contrary, is humble, patient, quiet, and hardy.

For food the ass contents himself with the most harsh and disagreeable herbs, which other animals will scarcely touch; in the choice of water he is, however, very nice, drinking only that which is perfectly clear, and at brooks with which he is acquainted.

The qualities of the ass as a working animal are almost or quite unknown in this country, but in other lands he is found very serviceable to the poor who are not able to buy or to keep horses. He requires very little care, bears correction with firmness, sustains labor and hunger with patience, and is seldom or never sick.

The varieties of the ass, in countries favorable to their development, are great. In Guinea the asses are large, and in shape even excel the native horses. The asses of Arabia (Chardin says) are perhaps the handsomest animals in the world. Their coat is smooth and clean; they carry the head elevated; and have fine and well-formed legs, which they throw out gracefully in walking or galloping. In Persia also they are finely formed, some being even stately, and much used in draught and for carrying burdens, while others are more lightly proportioned, and used for the saddle by persons of quality; frequently fetching the large sum of 400 livres; and being taught a kind of ambling pace, are richly caparisoned and used by the rich and luxurious nobles.*

II.—THE MULE.

The principal objection to the ass, as a beast of burden, being his small size, the ingenuity of man early devised means to remedy this defect by crossing him with the horse; thus producing an intermediate animal with the size and strength of the latter, and the patience, hardiness, and sure-footedness of the former.

The mule is the offspring of the ass and the mare, or the female ass and the horse. In the latter case the produce is called a jennet, and is much less hardy, and therefore rarely bred.

Mules are much used in warm climates, where they are preferred to horses for many purposes. They are very numerous in our Southern States and not uncommon in the Middle and Western States.

Kentucky is the great mule-breeding State. Many thou-

---

* Blane's Encyclopedia of Rural Sports.

sands are annually raised there for the New York and Southern markets. A correspondent of the *American Veterinary Journal* says:

"The mule trade is one of the largest of Kentucky, and affords one of her chief sources of revenue. The mule is fed from weaning time (which is generally at the age of five or six months) to the full extent of its capacity to eat, and that, too, on oats and corn, together with hay and fodder. In lieu of the long food, soiling is usually adopted in the summer, as they are kept confined in a pound or paddock, containing an acre or two of ground, which is usually partially shaded, in herds of one hundred or one hundred and fifty. In this way they are kept until the fall after they are two years old, receiving a sort of forcing hot-house treatment. At this age they are taken to the Southern market, not always by the feeder, but more generally by the speculator or trader; there they are sold to the planter entirely unbroken. The planters are too cautious to buy a broken mule, lest it should prove to be an antiquated, broken-down beast, fattened up and sold for a young one—as it is more difficult to judge of his age than that of a horse. The external marks of time and service are not generally so apparent upon him. But it is a small job to break a mule. It is only necessary to have a steady horse to work him, with a second hand to drive him an hour or two to keep him up, after which he is considered ready for any service that the farmer may require of him. He may kick once or twice, but is unlike the spirited horse, who when he commences is apt to kick himself out of the harness before he stops.

"Persons who have tried them on the farm are pleased with them. They never get sick and rarely get lame, will do as much work as horses which will cost twice as much money, and at the same time will subsist on less and inferior food; for a mule will work very well on wheat straw and corn shucks, whereas the horse must have grain as well as a good allowance of long food. They are better for our servants to handle, as they can stand neglect and violent treatment better than the horse, and a blemish, such as the loss of an eye, does not impair their value so much as that of the horse."

To have large and handsome mules, the mare should be of a large breed and well proportioned, with rather small limbs, a moderate sized head, and a good forehead; and the ass should be of the large Spanish breed.

III.

CATTLE.

The noble, patient ox and gentle cow
Kind usage claim ; and he's a brute indeed,
Unworthy of companionship with them,
Who with neglect or cruelty repays
The debt he owes their race.—Knox.

I.—HISTORY

OF the ox tribe (*Bovidæ*) there are eight species —the ancient bison (*Bos urus*); the bison or American buffalo (*B. bison*); the musk ox (*B. moschatus*); the gayal (*B. frontalis*); the grunting ox (*B. grunniens*); the buffalo of Southern Africa (*B. caffer*); the common buffalo (*B. bubulus*); and the common domestic ox (*B. taurus*). It is with the last only that we have to do in the present work.

The ox has been domesticated and in the service of man from the remotest antiquity. The Bible informs us that cattle were kept by the early descendants of Adam (Gen. iv. 20). That their value has been duly appreciated in all ages and in all climates, is shown by authentic history. Both the Hindoos and the Egyptians placed the ox among their deities; and no quadruped certainly is more worthy to be thus exalted.

The parent race of the ox is supposed by some to have been much larger than any of the present varieties. The urus, in his wild state at least, was an enormous and fierce animal, and ancient legends have thrown around him an air of mystery. In almost every part of the continent of Europe and in England, skulls, evidently belonging to cattle, have been found far exceeding in size those of the present day; but these may have belonged to exceptional individuals.

Of the original race of British cattle no satisfactory description occurs in any ancient author; but it is believed that, with occasional exceptions, they possessed no great bulk or beauty. They were doubtless numerous, for Cæsar tells us, in his Commentaries, that the ancient Britons neglected tillage and lived on milk and flesh. It was that occupation and mode of life which suited their state of society. A few specimens of the pure ancient breed, descendants of cattle which escaped from their masters centuries since and became wild, may now be seen in the parks of gentlemen in England. They are very wild, and are said to be untamable.

The breeds of cattle in England are remarkable for their numerous varieties, caused by the almost endless crossings of one breed with another.

The breeds of cattle now found in America are all derived from Europe, and those of the United States mainly from England. The early importations were of inferior grades, as the grand improvements in British cattle, commenced by Bakewell, date back no farther than about the time of the Revolution. In New England the primitive stock is believed to have undergone considerable improvement, while in parts of the Middle and Southern States it has undoubtedly deteriorated.

II.—BREEDS.

A strict classification of the numerous breeds of cattle now existing in the United States would be difficult. Youatt arranges British cattle under three heads, according to the comparative size of their horns—the Long Horns, the Short Horns, and the Middle Horns. These classes are all represented here. The prevailing stock of the Eastern States is believed to be derived from the Middle Horns or North Devons, most of the excellent marks and qualities of which they possess. They have frequently been called the American Devons, and are highly esteemed. The most valuable working oxen are of this breed, which also contributes largely to the best displays of beef found in the markets of New York, Philadelphia, and Boston. The Long Horns or Craven cattle, although not numerous, are occasionally met with. The Short Horns are of more recent introduction, but this breed, with various crosses, is now perhaps the predominant one of the country.

It will be profitable to speak somewhat in detail, although briefly, of the several breeds—at least the more prominent ones—and we will begin with

Fig. 17.

A DEVON BULL.

1. *The Devon Breed.*—This is a handsome and valuable breed. The bull should have yellow horns; clear, bright, and prominent eyes; small, flat, indented forehead; a fine muzzle; small cheek; a clear yellow nose; a high and open nostril; a thick neck, with the hair about the head curled; a straight back; and be well set upon the legs. The head of the ox is smaller, otherwise he does not differ materially in shape from

52   DOMESTIC ANIMALS.

the bull. He is quicker in his motions than any other ox, and is generally docile, good tempered, and honest.

The cow is much smaller than the bull, but roomy for breeding, and distinguished for her clear, round eye and general beauty of features. With regard to the comparative value of the Devon cows for the dairy there is much difference of opinion, it being pretty generally asserted that their acknowledged grazing qualities render them unfit for the dairy, and that their milk is rich but deficient in quantity. Many superior judges,

Fig. 18.

A DEVON HEIFER.

however, prefer them even for the dairy. Both cows and oxen fatten faster and with less food than most others.* In color Devon cattle are generally red.

Our New England cattle, as we have said, are generally derived from this breed. Their horns are moderately long,

---

* Youatt.

smooth, and slender, and their prevailing color deep red; but sometimes they are dark brown, brindle, or nearly black. The oxen are remarkable for their docility, strength, and quickness. The cows are fair milkers. Both oxen and cows fatten readily.

2. *The Hereford Breed.*—Cattle of the Hereford breed are larger than those of the North Devon. They are broad across the hind-quarters; narrow at the sirloin; neck and head well

Fig. 19.

THE HEREFORD BULL, TROMP.

proportioned; horns of a medium size and turned up at the points; color a deep red, with the face, throat, and belly generally white. A spirited contest has been kept up for some time between the partisans of the Herefords and those of the Short Horns, both here and in England, each stoutly maintaining the superiority of their favorite breed. We are not disposed to take part in the controversy. The experience of persons not engaged in breeding either sort as a special business must finally settle it; in the mean time, candid people will acknowledge that both are excellent, each in its way.

Youatt says that the Herefords fatten to a much greater weight than the Devons, and that a Hereford cow will grow fat where a Devon would starve. They are very hardy, and will do well with only the same care required by our native breeds.

3. *The Sussex Breed.*—The Sussex ox holds an intermediate place between the Devon and the Hereford; with much of the activity of the first and the strength of the second, and the propensity to fatten, and the beautiful fine-grained flesh of both. Experience has shown that it combines as many of the good qualities of both as can be combined in one frame. The Sussex cow does not answer for the dairy, her milk, although of good quality, is so small in quantity that she is little regarded for making butter and cheese. The prevailing color of the Sussex cattle is a deep chestnut red.*

4. *Ayrshire Breed.*—The Ayrshire breed, which is considered the most valuable in Scotland, is of the small size and middle-horned race. In modern times it has been much improved. Mr. Aiton, in his Survey of Ayrshire, thus describes this fine breed:

"The most approved shapes in the dairy breed are, small head, rather long and narrow at the muzzle; eye small, but smart and lively; the horns small, clear, crooked, and their roots at considerable distance from each other; neck long and slender, tapering toward the head, with no loose skin below; shoulders thin; fore-quarters light; hind-quarters large; back straight, broad behind; the joints rather loose and open; carcass deep, and pelvis capacious and wide over the hips, with round, fleshy buttocks; tail long and small; legs small and short, with firm joints; udder capacious, broad, and square, stretching forward, and neither fleshy, low hung, nor loose; the milk-veins are large and prominent; teats short, all pointing outward, and at considerable distance from each other;

---

* Youatt.

skin thin and loose; hair soft and woolly; the head, bones, horns, and all parts of least value, small; and the general figure compact and well proportioned."

"The qualities of a cow," adds Mr. Aiton in another place, "are of great importance. Tameness and docility of temper greatly enhance the value of a milch cow. Some degree of hardiness, a sound constitution, health, and a moderate degree of spirits, are qualities to be wished for in a dairy cow, and what those of Ayrshire generally possess. The most valuable qualities which a dairy cow can possess are that she yields much milk, and that of an oily, butyraceous, and caseous nature; and that after she has yielded very large quantities of milk for several years, she shall be as valuable for beef as any other breed of cows known; her fat shall be much more mixed through the whole flesh, and she shall fatten faster than any other."

There have been several importations of Ayrshires into the United States, but they have, up to the present time, failed to establish themselves in general favor.

5. *Welsh Cattle.*—"The cattle of Wales are principally of the Middle Horns, and stunted in their growth from the poverty of their pastures. Of these there are several varieties. The Pembrokeshire are chiefly black, with white horns; are shorter legged than most other Welsh cattle; are larger than those of Montgomery, and have round and deep carcasses; have a lively look and good eyes; though short and rough, not thick; have not large bones, and possess, perhaps, as much as possible, the opposite qualities of being very fair milkers, with a propensity to fatten. The meat is equal to the Scotch. They will thrive, says Mr. Youatt, where others starve, and they rapidly outstrip most others when they have plenty of good pasture. The Pembroke cow has been called the poor man's cow. The Pembroke ox is a speedy and an honest worker, and when taken from hard work fattens speedily. Many are brought to London, and rarely disappoint the butcher."

6. *Irish Cattle.*—Of the Irish cattle there are two breeds—

the Middle Horns and the Long Horns. The Middle Horns are the original breed. "They are," Mr. Youatt says, "small light, active, and wild; the head commonly small; the horns short but fine, rather upright, and frequently, after projecting forward, turning backward; somewhat deficient in hind-quarters; high-boned, and wide over the hips, yet the bone not commonly heavy; the hair coarse and long, black or brindled, with white faces. Some are finer in the bone and in the neck, with a good eye and sharp muzzle, and great activity; are hardy, live upon very scanty fare, and fatten with great rapidity when removed to a better soil; they are good milkers. The Kerry cows are excellent in this respect. These last, however, are wild and remarkable leapers. They live, however, upon very little food, and have often been denominated, like those of Pembroke, the poor man's cow."

The other breed is of a larger size. It has much of the blood of the Lancashire or Craven breed, or true Long Horn. Their horns first turn outward, then curve and turn inward. Of each of these kinds, an immense number of both lean and fat stock are annually exported to England.

7. *The Long Horns.*—The Long Horns of England came originally from Craven, in Yorkshire, and derived their name from the length of their horns.

"The improved breed of Leicestershire is said to have been formed by Webster, of Cauley, near Coventry, in Warwickshire. Bakewell, of Dishley, in Leicestershire, afterward got the lead as a breeder, by selecting from the Cauley stock; and the stocks of several other eminent breeders have been traced to the same source.

"The Lancashire breed of long-horned cattle may be distinguished from other cattle by the thickness and firm texture of their hides, the length and closeness of their hair, the large size of their hoofs, and their coarse, leathery, thick necks. They are likewise deeper in their fore-quarters, and lighter in their hind-quarters than most other breeds; narrower in their shape, less in point of weight than the Short Horns, though better weighers in proportion to their size; and though they give considerably less milk, it is said to yield more cream in proportion to its quantity. They are more varied in color than any other breed; but whatever the color may be, they have in general a white streak along their back, which the breeders term *finched*, and mostly a white spot on the inside of the hough."*

8. *The Short Horn or Durham Breed.*—Durham and York-

Fig. 20.

THE SHORT-HORNED BULL, LORD ERYHOLM

shire, England, have for ages been celebrated for a breed of short-horned cattle possessing extraordinary value as milkers, "in which quality," the Rev. Henry Barry says, "taken as a breed, they have never been equaled. The cattle so distinguished were always, as now, very different from the improved race. They were generally of large size, thin skinned, sleek haired, bad handlers, rather delicate in constitution, coarse in

---

* Culley.

the offal, and strikingly defective in the substance of girth in the fore-quarters. As milkers they were most excellent, but when put to fatten, as the foregoing description will indicate, were found slow feeders, producing an inferior quality of meat, not marbled or mixed as to fat and lean; the latter sometimes of a very dark hue. Such, too, are the *unimproved* Short Horns of the present day."

The improved Short Horns are even more celebrated as feeders than as milkers, and in other respects differ widely from the original breed.

"The colors of the improved Short Horns," Mr. Youatt says, "are red or white, or a mixture of both;" "no *pure improved Short Horns*," he adds, "are found of any other color but those above named. That the matured Short Horns are an admirable grazier's breed of cattle is undoubted; they are not, however, to be disregarded as milkers; but they are inferior, from their fattening qualities, to many others as workers."

Mr. Dickson, an eminent cattle breeder, thus eloquently describes the Short Horn:

"The external appearance of the short-horned breed is irresistibly attractive. The exquisitely symmetrical form of the body in every position, bedecked with a skin of the richest hues of red, and the richest white approaching to cream, or both colors, so arranged or commixed as to form a beautiful fleck or delicate roan, and possessed of the mellowest touch; supported on clean, small limbs, showing, like those of the race-horse and the greyhound, the union of strength with fineness; and ornamented with a small, lengthy, tapering head, neatly set on a broad, firm, deep neck, and furnished with a small muzzle, wide nostrils, prominent, mildly-beaming eyes, thin, large, biney ears set near the crown of the head and protected in front with semicircularly bent, white, or brownish colored short (hence the name), smooth, pointed horns; all these parts combine to form a symmetrical harmony, which has never been surpassed in beauty and sweetness by any other species of the domesticated ox."

The graziers of Kentucky and other parts of the West have heretofore shown the greatest preference for the Short Horns, but, in their case, they are found to be subject to one serious objection. It is this: while they take on fat so readily when well fed and become so heavy, they are unable to retain it during the long journeys to the Eastern markets, where they generally arrive in too meager a condition to command the price of fat cattle. They require some breed which will be able to carry their fat along with them.*

9. *The Alderney or Jersey Breed.*—This breed of cattle is from Normandy and the Isle of Jersey, and, although small and awkwardly shaped, are much esteemed on account of the richness of their milk, of which, however, the quantity is small. English noblemen keep Alderney cows in their parks to furnish cream for their coffee.

When dried, the Alderney cow fattens with a rapidity that would hardly be thought possible from her gaunt appearance. In color, the Alderney breed is light red, dun, or fawn colored.

10. *The Galloway Breed.*—The Galloway breed of cattle is well known for various valuable qualities, and is easily distinguished by the want of horns. The Galloways are broad across the back, with a very slight curve between the head and the quarters, and broad at the loins, the whole body having a fine round appearance. The head is of moderate size, the ears large and rough, the chest deep, and the legs short. The prevailing color is black. This breed is highly esteemed, as there is no other kind which arrives at maturity so soon; and their flesh is of the finest quality. Their milk is very fine, but is not obtained in very large quantities. It is estimated that 30,000 of these cattle are annually sent out of Galloway.

Another valuable breed of polled (or hornless) cows is bred in Angus, which much resemble, in appearance, those of Galloway; they are, however, rather larger and longer in the leg, flatter sided, and with thinner shoulders.

---

* American Farmer's Encyclopedia.

In Norfolk and Suffolk a hornless breed of cows prevails, which are almost all descended from the Galloways, "whose general form," Mr. Youatt says, "they retain, with some of, but not all, their excellences; they have been enlarged, but not improved, by a better climate and soil. They are commonly of a red or black color, with a peculiar golden circle around the eye. They are taller than the Galloways, but thinner in the chine, flatter in the ribs, and longer in the legs; rather better milkers; of greater weight when fattened, though not fattening so kindly, and the meat is not quite equal in quality."

The Suffolk Dun cow, which is also of Galloway descent, is celebrated as a milker, and there is little doubt is not inferior to any other breed in the quantity of milk which she yields: this is from six to eight gallons per day. The butter produced, however, is not in proportion to the milk. It is calculated that a Suffolk cow produces annually about 1½ cwt. of butter.

The Suffolk Duns derive the last part of their name from their usual pale yellow color. Many, however, are red, or red and white. They are invariably without horns, and small in size, seldom weighing over 700 lbs. when fattened.*

11. *The Cream-Pot Breed.*—This is an American breed, and was originated by Colonel Jaques, of Ten Hills Farm, Somerville, Mass. It is a cross between the Short Horn and the native breed of New England. Mr. Jaques gives the following account of the origin of this famous breed:

"Hearing of cows that produce seventeen pounds of butter each per week, the inquiry arose, why not produce a breed of such cows that may be depended on? This I attempted, and have accomplished. I have made from one of my Cream-Pot cows nine pounds of butter in three days on grass feed only.

"The bull Cœlebs, an imported thorough-bred Durham, and Flora, a heifer of the same breed, and imported, and a native cow, whose pedigree is entirely unknown, comprise the elements of the Cream-Pot breed of cattle. The native cow was

---

* American Farmer's Encyclopedia.

bought in consequence of her superior quality as a milker, giving eighteen quarts a day, and averaging about fifteen. In the month of April the cream of two days' milk produced two and three-fourths pounds of butter, made of two and one-sixteenth quarts of cream, and required but two minutes' churning. Thus much for the mother of the Cream-Pots.

"I have bred my Cream-Pots with red or mahogany colored hair and teats, and gold-dust in the ears, yellow noses and skin, the latter silky and elastic to the touch, being like a fourteen-dollar cloth. My Cream-Pots are full in the body, chops deep in the flank, not quite as straight in the belly, nor as full in the twist, nor quite as thick in the thigh as the Durhams; but in other respects like them. They excel in affording a great quantity of rich cream, capable of being converted into butter in a short time, with little labor, and with a very small proportion of buttermilk, the cream producing more than eighty per cent. of butter. I have changed the cream to butter not unfrequently in one minute, and it has been done in forty seconds."

The late lamented Henry Colman, while Commissioner for the Agricultural Survey of Massachusetts, wrote as follows:

"Mr. Jaques is entitled to great credit for his care and judicious selection in continuing and improving his stock. I have repeatedly seen the cream from his cows, and its yellowness and consistency are remarkable, and in company with several gentlemen of the Legislature, I saw a portion of it converted to butter with a spoon in one minute. The color of Mr. Jaques' stock is a deep red, a favorite color in New England; they are well formed and thrifty on common feed; and if they continue to display the extraordinary properties by which they are now so distinguished, they promise to prove the most valuable race of animals ever known among us for dairy purposes, and equal to any of which we have any information."

III.—POINTS.

Were an ox of fine symmetry and high condition placed before a person not a judge of livestock, his opinion of its

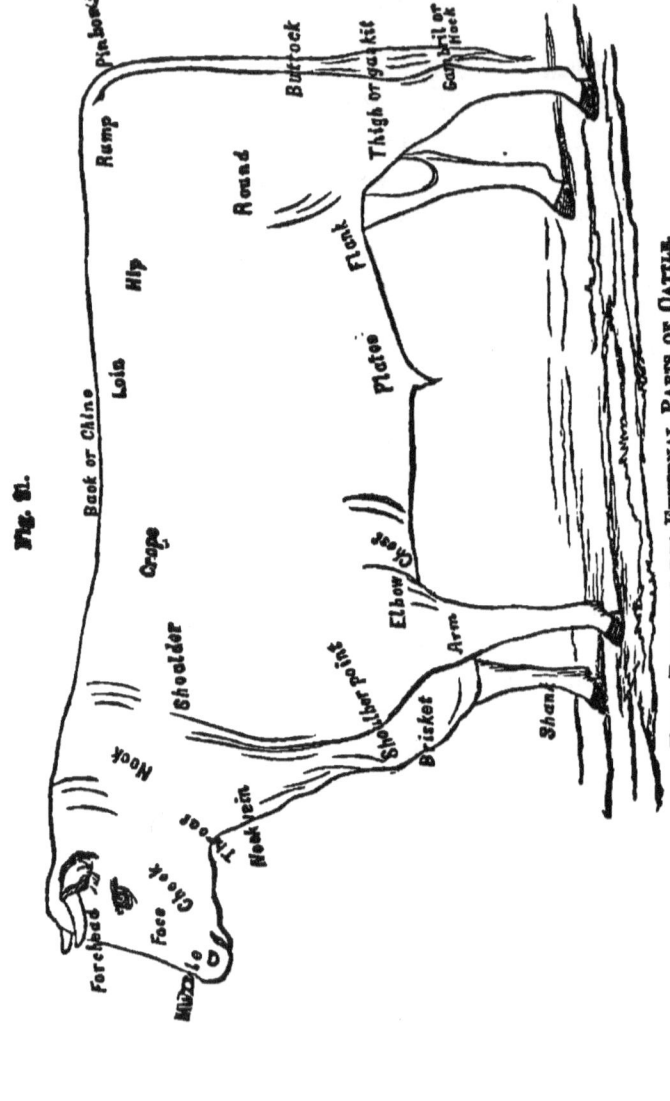

TERMS DENOTING THE EXTERNAL PARTS OF CATTLE.

excellences would be derived from a very limited view, and consequently from only a few of its qualities. He could not possibly discover, without tuition, those properties which had chiefly conduced to produce the high condition in which he saw the ox. He would hardly believe that a judge can ascertain merely by the eye, from its general aspect, whether the ox were in good or bad health; from the color of its skin whether it were of a pure or a cross breed; from the expression of its countenance whether it were a quiet feeder; and from the nature of its flesh whether it had arrived at maturity. The discoveries made by the hand of the judge might even stagger belief. He understands the "points" of cattle, and experience enables him to appreciate their individual and aggregate value.

The "points" by which cattle are characterized may profitably be described in detail:

1. The *nose* or *muzzle* in the Durhams or Short Horns should be of a rich cream color. In the Devon, Hereford, and Sussex it is preferred when a clear golden color. A brown or dark color indicates a cross.

2. The *forehead* should be neither narrow nor very broad. The *eye* should be prominent, and the *nostril* between the eye and the muzzle thin, particularly in the Devons.

3. The *horns* should be small, smooth, tapering, and sharp pointed, long or short, according to the breed, and of a white color throughout in some breeds, and tipped with black in others. The shape is less essential than the color.

4. The *neck* should be of medium length, full at the sides, not too deep in the throat, and should come out from the shoulders nearly on a level with the chine.

5. The top of the *plate bones* should not be too wide, but, rising on a level with the chine, should be well thrown back, so that there may be no hollowness behind.

6. The *shoulder point* should lay flat with the ribs, without any projection.

7. The *breast* should be wide and open, projecting forward.

8. The *chine* should lay straight and be well covered with flesh.

9. The *loin* should be flat and wide; almost as wide at the fore as the hinder part.

10. The *hip bones* should be wide apart, coming upon a level with the chine to the setting of the tail.

11. The *tip of the rump* should be tolerably wide, so that the tail may drop to a level between the two points; and the *tail* should come out broad.

12. The *thigh* should not be too full outside nor behind; but the inside or twist should be full.

13. The *back* should be flat and rather thin.

14. The *hind leg* should be flat and thin; the legs of medium length, and the hock rather turning out.

15. The *feet* should not be too broad.

16. The *flank* should be full and heavy when the animal is fat.

17. The *belly* should not drop below the breast, but on a line with it.

18. The *shoulder* should be rather flat, not projecting.

19. The *fore leg* should also be flat and upright, but not fleshy.

20. The *round* should not project, but be flat with the outside of the thigh.

21. The *jaws* should be rather wide.

22. The *ribs* should spring nearly horizontally from the chine and form a circle.

23. The *skin* should be loose, floating, as it were, on a layer of soft fat, and covered with thick, glossy, soft hair.

24. The *expression* of the *eye* and *face* should be calm and complacent.

A writer in the *Farmer's Magazine*, a number of years ago, described what are properly considered the good points of a cow, as exhibited in the Short Horn breed, in the following doggerel lines:

> She's long in her face, she's fine in her horn;
> She'll quickly get fat without cake or corn;
> She's clean in her jaws, and full in her chine;
> She's heavy in flank, and wide in her loin;
> She's broad in her ribs, and long in her rump;
> She's straight in her back, with never a hump;

> She's wide in her hip, and calm in her eyes;
> She's fine in her shoulders, and thin in her thighs
> She's light in her neck, and small in her tail;
> She's wide in her breast, and good at the pail;
> She's fine in her bone, and silky of skin;
> She's a grazier's without, and a butcher's within.

IV.—GENERAL MANAGEMENT.

1. *The Cow-house.*—The cow-house should be a capacious, well-lighted, and well-ventilated building, in which the cows or oxen can be kept dry, clean, and moderately warm. It is a mistaken idea that cattle suffer materially by *dry* cold. It is the wet and the damp walls, yard, and driving rains and fogs of winter, that are so injurious to them. In this respect the Dutch farmers are very particular. They have their cows regularly groomed, and the walks behind them sprinkled with sand.*

As a general thing, our farmers pay too little attention to the health and comfort of their cattle, and especially the cows. In many cases they are kept in a shamefully dirty condition. The floor of their stalls is allowed to be disgustingly filthy, the floors and walls full of vermin, and the hides of the animals covered with dust and dung. It is not only at the expense of their comfort that cattle suffer this neglect, but to the farmer's loss also. When you see a cow rubbing herself against a post, you may depend upon it that the animal is ill kept and requires a good scrubbing. Cattle, as well as horses, are greatly injured by want of proper attention to the cleanliness and ventilation of their habitation. They should stand on a slightly raised platform, which should be well littered with straw, refuse hay, leaves, sawdust, or some other dry material.

For tying up cattle, chains, leather straps, wooden bows, and stanchions are used. The stanchions are the most convenient for the person having charge of the cattle, but, we think, less comfortable for the cattle themselves than the other con-

---

* British Husbandry.

trivances mentioned. A good and cheap stanchion is constructed as follows:

"The sills of the stanchions are of oak joist, six by two inches; the top timbers are of hemlock, of the same dimensions; the stanchions of ash, one and a half by four inches; one of each set of stanchions is pinned between the sills and the corresponding top pieces. From the bottom of the sills to the top of the stanchions is five and a half feet. The slip stanchions are of the same size and material as the first named, but only pinned at the bottom, which allows of their sliding back at the top about sixteen inches, to admit the animal's head; it is then pushed to an upright position and fastened at the top by a drop-button or clapper, which is much more secure than when fastened by pins.

"For oxen and large cows, there is allowed a space for each of three and a half feet; for younger cattle about three feet to each. We have frequently seen the sill and top piece for stanchions made of solid timber, and mortices made for the stanchions. But there is much labor required in morticing, especially the top timber, so as to allow of the sliding back and forward of the slip stanchions. The kind we have attempted to describe can be readily and cheaply made by almost any farmer."*

2. *Feeding.*—While confined to the barn or cow-house and barn-yard, during the cold season, cattle should be fed with the utmost regularity; and a sufficient quantity of nutritious food supplied to keep them in good condition. In this country, hay is the principal common food of our oxen and cows. Roots are too seldom employed in ordinary feeding; and we have no doubt but that the health and, consequently, the condition and value of our cattle would be improved by giving them more turnips, beets, carrots, parsneps, etc., during the winter.

An English writer says: "Supposing a cow to calve early in April or May, there is no keeping to be compared with a sweet pasture for affording the best flavored milk and butter; therefore,

---

* Country Gentleman.

although on a principle of economy I have always recommended the house feeding of a cow (as one acre of good clover will support three cows during the summer, whereas an acre of pasture will but barely suffice for one during the same period, irrespectively of the manure saved by the former management), I make a decided exception where there is no necessity for minutely regarding economy at the expense of the discomfort of the cow, and the inferiority in flavor, if not in quantity, of cream and butter. Yet, even with liberty, and the animal's enjoyment of picking her food as she pleases, there will be necessity in summer for some artificially grown grasses, to supply any deficiency that may occur in the pasture, and provide for the house feeding, when the heat of the sun, the stinging of flies, or the bursting of a storm may render the shade and security of the cow-shed very grateful to your cows. In the early and cold spring, and before the grass has sufficiently sprung up, it is not any kindness to the cow, and it is a decided injury to the ground and vegetation to turn her out; at that season she requires the warmth which her stall affords, and the nourishment that nutritious hay and roots and bran impart."

The following hints from the pen of Henry Colman should be well heeded by every farmer. It is their own fault if American agriculturists do not profit by such truthful warnings.

"The farmers prejudice very greatly their own interest in suffering their milch cows to come out in the spring in low condition. During the time they are dry, they think it enough to give them the coarsest fodder, and that in limited quantities; this, too, at a time of pregnancy, when they require the kindest treatment and the most nourishing food. The calf itself under this treatment of the cow is small and feeble. He finds comparatively insufficient support from his exhausted dam; and the return which the cow makes in milk during the summer is much less than it would be if she came into the spring in good health and flesh. It requires the whole summer to recover what she has lost. The animal constitution can not be trifled with in this way.

"It is so with all livestock, and especially with young animals, at the period of their most rapid growth. They should not be prematurely forced; but, on the other hand, they should not be stinted or checked.

" In the feeding of cattle for market a great deal of practical skill is required, and constant observation of their condition, otherwise they may be surfeited and their appetite destroyed, or their digestive powers be overtasked, and the feed fail of its object.

"The articles usually employed in fattening cattle are hay and Indian meal, or corn and rye meal mixed, or pease and oats, or oats and corn ground together. Besides this, many farmers are in the practice of giving their stall-fed cattle occasionally certain quantities of potatoes. An excellent farmer, of fifty years' experience in the fatting of cattle, is of opinion that potatoes are good feed for fatting cattle in the fall and spring, when the weather is warm; but they do no good in cold weather unless they are cooked. I rely much upon his judgment and experience. The value of potatoes is differently estimated by different individuals; some considering five bushels, others rating four bushels, as equivalent to one bushel of corn."

An extensive cattle-dealer who has tried a variety of mixtures of feed, such as oats, brown-corn seed, etc., prefers Indian meal to every other feed. He disapproves of excessive feeding, and thinks it a great error to give too much. He deems four quarts, with hay, ordinarily enough; and ten quarts a day sufficient for any animal. He feeds twice a day with great regularity. His present cattle have never received over eight quarts per day each; and at first putting up, a much less quantity. He deems it best to reduce their feed of provender a few days before starting for market. He buys his cattle for feeding in the fall; and his present stock averaged in the cost seventy-five dollars per pair.*

---

* American Farmer's Encyclopedia.

"It is sometimes asked," Mr. Colman says, "whether oxen are injured in their growth from being worked. If their strength is prematurely and too severely taxed, or if they are subjected to severe usage, undoubtedly it must prove injurious; but, if otherwise, if reasonably worked and carefully and kindly attended, there is no doubt that their health and growth are promoted by it. It is often matter of inquiry, whether fatting cattle should be kept in close stalls, or be suffered to lie out-doors. The experience of all the farmers whom I have consulted, who have made any trial, is conclusive in this case, in favor of the superior thrift of animals kept constantly in the barn, or turned out only for watering and immediately put up again, over those which are kept in open sheds, or tied up for feeding only, and at other times allowed to lie in the yard. No exact experiments have been made in this country in relation to this subject; but experiments made abroad lead to the conclusion, that cattle thrive best in a high and equable temperature, so warm as to keep them constantly in a state of active perspiration, and that their thrift is much hindered by an exposure to severe alternations of heat and cold. It is certain, that in order to thrift, cattle can not be made too comfortable; their mangers should be kept clean; their stalls be well littered; and the cattle protected from currents of air blowing through crevices or holes in the floors or the sides of the stables, which prove often much more uncomfortable than an open exposure."

8. *Rearing Calves.*—Many different opinions prevail on the subject of rearing calves. The following plan, detailed by a Western breeder, we deem an excellent one:

"I have my cows so managed that they come in early in spring. I wean the calves after they have drawn the milk two or three times, while I milk at the same time, all clean, that which the calf may not be strong enough to draw. Then I allow the calves nearly all the milk the cows give, for four or six weeks, which gives them a good start; next, I teach them, when two or three weeks old, to eat some little of meal or threshed oats, and lick a little salt; at the same time I let them have access to some good hay; next, I reduce the quantity of new milk, and give them sweet milk minus the cream, and by degrees teach them to drink coppered milk, feeding ten or twelve together in a trough. This I consider better than milk which is just on a change from sweet to sour. As soon as practicable after there is a good bite of grass, I turn them into pasture, even with the cows, for they know not their dams. I still feed them with milk until about three months old, and all through the season if it can be had. In this wise calves are hearty, learn easy to eat anything which may be offered, and will winter better than calves which have drawn the milk from cows, and have received 'more knocks than nubbins.' They are also more gentle, easier turned to the yoke, or to milk, and are not afraid of their masters; but, on the contrary, learn to know the hands that feed them. By giving them a good chance the first winter, they generally make good thrifty cattle."

4. *Milking.*—In reference to milking, Martin Doyle says: "Cows in general are milked but twice a day, morning and evening; but some of the Durham cows, particularly when in full season and abundantly fed, will require to be milked at noon also. In this case nothing is really gained in the quantity of milk, and its quality is weakened, as twelve hours are required for the due chemical preparation of the milk. Therefore the tendency to this want of retention in a cow is not to be encouraged; the milk should only be drawn off at supernumerary times, if the udder be excessively distended, and the milk flows spontaneously. At each regular time of milking, the contents of the udder should be completely drawn off—the last drop is the richest: when there are two, three, or more cows, the dairy-maid, if she understands her business, will go with a separate vessel and milk the strippings into it until each udder is perfectly dry. This small portion of rich milk will give her more cream than a larger quantity, and she reserves it, if she be a prudent person, for her own tea.

"A cow should be handled with exceeding gentleness, other

wise milking may become an unpleasant or even a painful operation to her. If a cross-grained man or woman, with a vinegar face, handles the teats roughly, and bullies a cow of sensitiveness, she may refuse to let her milk flow, though she would yield to the first touch of a good-tempered person. If the udder be hard, it will require fomentation with lukewarm water and gentle rubbing. It sometimes happens that the teats become sore; in this case an application of sweet oil, after washing the affected part with soap and water, will probably cure it.

"A cow may be milked until within a month of calving, provided the milk does not curdle on being slightly warmed, or possess a salt taste; either would be an indication that no more milk should be taken."

V.—WEIGHT OF LIVE CATTLE.

Experienced drovers and butchers are in the habit, in buying cattle, to estimate their weight on foot. Long experience and much practice enables them to judge with considerable accuracy. They thus have the advantage of the less experienced farmer, who, for this reason, very often comes off "second best" in a bargain. We recommend to them the following rule, by means of which the weight of cattle may be ascertained with a very close approach to the accuracy of the scales.

Rule.—Take a string, put it around the breast, stand square just behind the shoulder-blade, measure on a rule the feet and inches the animal is in circumference; this is called the girth; then, with the string, measure from the bone of the tail which plumbs the line with the hinder part of the buttock; direct the line along the back to the forepart of the shoulder-blade; take the dimensions on the foot rule as before, which is the length; and work the figures in the following manner: Girth of the animal, say 6 feet 4 inches, length 5 feet 3 inches, which multiplied together, makes 31 square superficial feet, and that multiplied by 23, the number of pounds allowed to each superficial foot of cattle measuring less than 7 and more than 5 feet in girth, makes 713 pounds. When the animal measures less than 9 and more than 7 feet in girth, 31 is the number of pounds to each superficial foot. Again, suppose a pig or any small beast should measure 2 feet in girth and 2 along the back, which multiplied together makes 4 square feet, that multiplied by 11, the number of pounds allowed to each square foot of cattle measuring less than 3 feet in girth, makes 44 pounds. Again, suppose a calf, a sheep, etc., should measure 4 feet 6 inches in girth, and 3 feet 9 inches in length, which multiplied together make $15\frac{1}{4}$ square feet; that multiplied by 16, the number of pounds allowed to cattle measuring less than 5 feet and more than 3 in girth, makes 265 pounds. The dimensions of girth and length of horned cattle, sheep, calves, and hogs, may be exactly taken in this way, as it is all that is necessary for any computation, or any valuation of stock, and will answer exactly to the four quarters, sinking offal.*

This rule is so simple that any man with a bit of chalk can work it out, and its application will often save the farmer from losses which mere guess work is liable to occasion.

---

* **Valley Farmer.**

IV.

SHEEP.

Thy flocks the verdant hillside range—Anon.

I.—CHARACTERISTICS.

THE sheep (*Ovis aries*) is naturally a denizen of the hills. Its instincts, even in its domesticated state, attach it to the upland slopes; and when free to do so, it always seeks the highest grounds, where aromatic plants abound and the herbage is less succulent than in the valleys. The wild sheep, like the deer, is found to frequent all those places where saline exudations abound and to lick the salt earth. In its wild state it generally has horns, but these have nearly disappeared in most of the domestic breeds. The female goes with young twenty-one weeks, and usually produces only one at a birth. Twins, however, are not uncommon.

Immense flocks of sheep have been kept by man in all ages, but more generally for their wool and skins than for their flesh; for that is by no means generally relished. The Calmucks and Cossacks still prefer that of the horse and the camel, and the Spaniard, if he can procure other flesh, rarely eats that of the Merino. To a majority of Americans it is an object of dislike, although it is gaining in favor among us. Englishmen consume more mutton than any other people, but the taste for it is of modern origin with them.

The natural age of the sheep, according to Youatt, is about ten years, up to which age they will breed and thrive well; but there are instances of their breeding at the age of fifteen, and living twenty years.

II.—BREEDS.

Specimens of nearly or quite all the valuable breeds of sheep now known may, it is believed, be found in the United States. The principal of these are the Native (so called); the Spanish Merino; the Saxon Merino; the New Leicester or Bakewell; the South-Down; the Cotswold, the Cheviot, and the Lincoln. Between these breeds an almost infinite variety of crosses have taken place; so that, comparatively speaking, few flocks in the United States preserve entire the distinctive characteristics of any one breed, or that can lay claim to purity of blood.*

1. *The Native Breed.*—This name is applied to the common coarse-wooled sheep existing here previous to the importation of the improved breeds. They are, however, of foreign, and mostly of English origin, and probably are the result of the admixture of various breeds. This common stock of sheep, as a distinct family, has nearly disappeared, having been universally crossed, to a greater or less extent, with foreign breeds of later introduction; and especially with the Spanish and Saxon Merinos.

2. *The Spanish Merino Breed.*—Of this excellent breed there have been many importations from France and Spain. There are several varieties of the Merino, differing essentially in form, size, and quality of wool. American Merinos may be classed under three general heads, and are thus described:

"The *first* is a large, short-legged, strong, and exceedingly hardy sheep, carrying a heavy fleece, ranging from medium to fine, somewhat inclined to throatiness, bred to exhibit external concrete gum in some flocks, but not commonly so.

"The *second* general class of American Merinos are smaller than the preceding, less hardy; wool, as a general thing, finer, and covered with a black, pitchy gum on its extremities. The fleece is about one third lighter than in the first class.

"The *third* class, which have been bred mostly at the South, are still smaller and less hardy, and carry lighter and finer

---

* Randall's Sheep Husbandry.

fleeces, destitute of external gum. The sheep and the wool bear a close resemblace to the Saxon, and if not actually mixed with that blood, they have been formed into a similar variety by a similar course of breeding.

"Class *first* are larger and stronger sheep than those originally imported from Spain, and in well-selected flocks or individuals the fleece is of a decidedly better quality."*

The Merino, although a native of a warm climate, becomes readily inured to the greatest extremes of cold, flourishing even so far north as Sweden without degenerating in fleece or form.

Fig. 22.

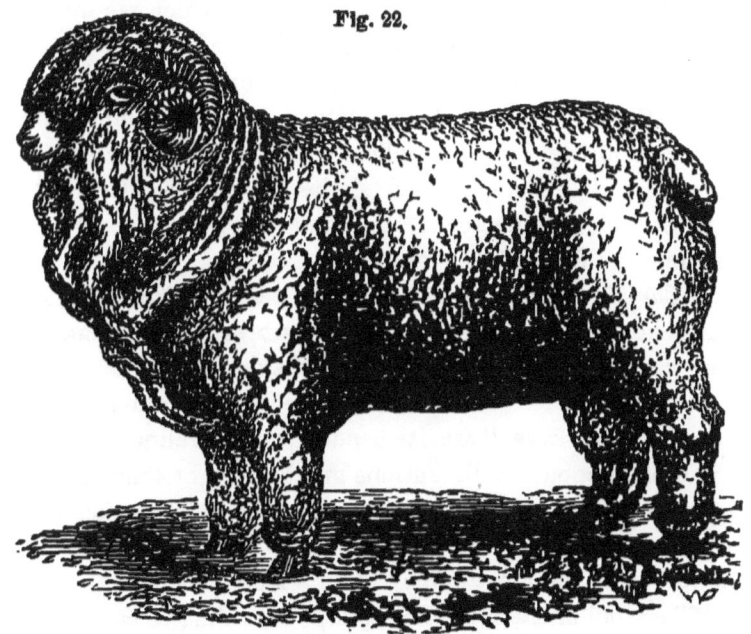

THE SPANISH MERINO.

It is patient, docile, hardy, and long lived. Its flesh, in spite of the prejudice which exists on the subject, is short-grained, and of a good flavor when killed at a proper age. It is longer in coming to maturity than most other breeds, and does not attain its full growth till it is about three years old.†

---

* Randall.   † Transactions of New York State Agricultural Society.

3. *The Saxon Merino Breed.*—The Saxon Merinos are descended from the Spanish, having been imported from Spain into Saxony in 1765. They have been considerably modified by their German breeding, the German shepherds having sacrificed hardiness, and indeed almost everything else, to fineness of staple.

There are very few flocks of pure Saxon sheep in the United States, the importations in several instances having been grade sheep, although sold as pure stock. Most flocks have again been crossed with Native or Spanish Merino sheep or with both; but the mixed breed thus produced, which we may call the American Saxons, have so long been bred toward the Saxons, that their wool equals that of the pure breed. They are hardier than the parent German stock, but still comparatively tender, requiring regular supplies of good food, protection from storms of all kinds, and good shelter in winter. In docility, patience under confinement, late maturity, and longevity, they resemble the Spanish Merinos.*

4. *The New Leicester Breed.*—This celebrated English breed comprehends the most excellent of the breed of Mr. Bakewell, their great improver, and of Mr. Culley's variety or improvement upon it. "The principal recommendations of this breed," Culley says, "are its beauty and its fullness of form; in the same apparent dimensions greater weight than any other sheep; an early maturity and a propensity to fatten equaled by no other breed; a diminution of the proportion of offal, and the return of the most money for the food consumed."

"The wool of the New Leicester," according to Randall, "is long, averaging, after the first shearing, about six inches, and the fleece of the American animal weighs about six pounds. It is of a coarse quality, and is little used in the manufacture of cloths. As a combing wool, however, it stands first, and is used in the manufacture of the finest worsteds, etc."

In England, the mutton of this breed is in great demand, and

Randall.

Fig. 21.

New Leicester Sheep.

brings good prices. It is not generally considered a profitable breed in this country, except, perhaps, on rich lowland farms in the vicinity of considerable markets.

5. *The South-Down Breed.* —The South-Down is an upland sheep of medium size, and its wool, in point of length, belongs to the medium class. There has been considerable controversy in reference to the value of the Downs in comparison with the other favorite breeds. Mr. Randall does not rate them very high for wool-bearing. But they are cultivated in England more particularly for their mutton, which in the English markets takes precedence of every other sort.

"The Down is turned off at two years old, and its weight at that age in England is from eighty to a hundred pounds. Notwithstanding its weight, the Down has a patience of occasional short keep, and an endurance of hard stocking equal to any other sheep. It is hardy, healthy, quiet, and docile. It withstands our American winters well. A sheep possessing such qualities must of course be valuable in upland districts in the vicinity of markets."*

Mr. J. C. Taylor, of Holmdel, N. J., in a communication published in the *Country Gentleman,* says:

"I contend that under a high state of management, the South-Downs are a very profitable sheep to keep, in proof of which (for I have the figures) I will cite my now yearling ram. Last July he was worth five dollars to sell for butchering, without anything more than good pasture; he served several ewes from the middle of September to the first of December, which was much against his growth. At seven cents per week, from July to December, say $1 50—cost of keep from December to May 2d, $5 41, making, with his worth in July, a total of $11 91. Had he been a wether I could have sold him on May 2d for $22 for butchering, leaving a clear gain of over $10 at from thirteen to fourteen months old! I ask the stock-raiser and feeder if this is not as profitable as long wools, or

---

* Randall.

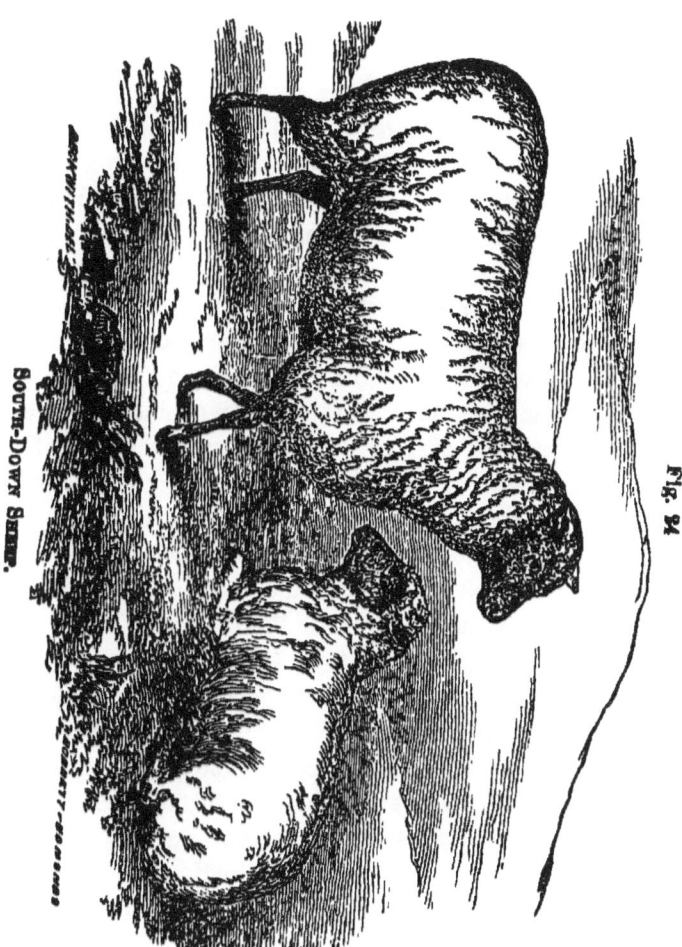

Fig. 24. SOUTH-DOWN SHEEP.

any other stock? Is it not more profitable? But the Downs are a superior sheep for crossing with common ewes to produce butcher's lambs, superior to *any long wools.*

"A few years ago a Mr. Beers went to Canada and procured a large lot of the Canada Leicester, and many of our farmers were induced by their large size (with their wool on) to buy them. I expected to be driven out of the market with my South-Downs; but at the first county fair (South-Downs having to show against long wool) I made a clean sweep of it, and there has never been one of them shown since. A certain farmer procured one of Mr. Beers' bucks, and also a South-Down; he divided his flock of ewes as nearly as possible between the two bucks; the result was, the half-blood Down lambs were all fat, and sold before any of the half-blood Leicesters were fit for market. This farmer finds the South-Downs *so profitable* that he keeps no other than a South-Down buck."

6. *The Cotswold Breed.*—"The Cotswold," Spooner says, "is a large breed of sheep, with a long and abundant fleece, and the ewes are very prolific and good nurses. They have been extensively crossed with the Leicester sheep, by which their size and fleece have been somewhat diminished, but their carcasses considerably improved, and their maturity rendered earlier. The wool is strong, mellow, and of good color, although rather coarse, from six to eight inches in length, and from seven to eight pounds per fleece. The quality of the mutton is considered superior to the Leicester."

We believe the Cotswolds have not been extensively bred in the United States, although there have been several importations. An improved variety of the Cotswolds, under the name of the New Oxfordshire sheep, have lately attracted considerable attention, and have frequently been successful candidates for prizes offered for the best long-wooled sheep at agricultural shows.

7. *The Cheviot Breed.*—The Cheviot sheep are a peculiar breed, which are kept on the extensive range of the Cheviot Hills. They are described as having "the face and legs gen-

erally white; the eye lively and prominent; the countenance open and pleasing; the ear large, and with a long space from the ear to the eye; the body long; and hence they are called 'long sheep,' in distinction from the black-faced breed. They are full behind the shoulder, have a long, straight back, are round in the rib, and well-proportioned in the quarters; the legs clean and small-boned, and the pelt thin, but thickly covered with fine, short wool; they possess very considerable fattening qualities, and can endure much hardship, both from starvation and cold."*

We have no acquaintance with this breed. There are probably but few of them in this country. Mr. Randall speaks very disparagingly of those which had fallen under his observation, but which may have not been fair specimens of their breed.

8. *The Lincoln Breed.*—Culley described the old breed of Lincolnshire sheep, half a century ago, as having "no horns, white faces, long, thin, and weak carcasses; the ewes weighing from 14 to 20 lbs. per quarter, the three-year old wethers from 20 to 30 lbs.; thick, rough, white leg, large bones, thick pelts, and long wool, from 10 to 18 inches, and weighing from 8 to 14 lbs. per fleece, and covering a slow-feeding, coarse-grained carcass of mutton." Culley, however, ran into the opposite extreme; if the Lincolnshire farmers bred only for the wool, he regarded only the mutton. A cross between the two produced a very profitable and much improved animal.

III.—CHOICE OF BREED.

"In selecting a breed for any given locality," Mr. Randall says, "we are to take into consideration, first, the feed and climate, or the surrounding natural circumstances; and second, the market facilities and demands. We should then make choice of that breed which, with the advantages posssessed, and under all the circumstances, will yield the greatest net value of marketable product.

---

* American Farmer's Encyclopedia.

"Rich lowland herbage, in a climate which allows it to remain green during a large portion of the year, is favorable to the production of large carcasses. If convenient to markets where mutton finds a ready sale at good prices, then all the conditions are realized which call for a mutton as contradistinguished from a wool-producing sheep. Under such circumstances, the choice should undoubtedly, in my judgment, rest between the improved English varieties—the South-Down, the New Leicester, and the improved Cotswold or New Oxfordshire. In deciding between these, minor and more specific circumstances are to be taken into account."

For wool-growing purposes he thinks the Merino "possesses a marked and decided superiority over the best breeds and families of coarse-wooled sheep;" and its inferiority as a mutton sheep, he thinks is not so great as is generally supposed.

IV.—GENERAL MANAGEMENT.

The following hints are all condensed from Randall's excellent work on Sheep Husbandry, to which the reader who may desire further details is referred.

1. *Barns, Sheds, etc.*—"Humanity and economy both dictate that sheep be provided with shelters to lie under nights, and to which they can resort *at will*. In our severe winter storms it is sometimes necessary, or at least by far the best, to feed under shelter for a day or two. It is not an uncommon circumstance, in New York and New England, for snow to fall to the depth of twenty or thirty inches, within twenty-four or forty-eight hours, and then to be succeeded by a strong and intensely cold west or northwest wind of two or three days' continuance,* which lifts the snow, blocking up the roads, and piling huge drifts to the leeward of fences, barns, etc. A flock without shelter will huddle closely together, turning their backs to the storm, constantly stepping and thus treading down the snow as it rises about them. Strong, close-coated sheep do not

---

* These terrible wind-storms are of much longer continuance in many parts of New England.

seem to suffer as much from the cold, for a period, as would be expected; but it is next to impossible to feed them enough or half enough, under such circumstances, without an immense waste of hay—entirely impossible, without racks. The hay is whirled away in an instant by the wind; and even if racks are used, the sheep leaving their huddle where they were kept warm and even moist by the melting of the snow in their wool, soon get chilled and are disposed to return to their huddle. Imperfectly filled with food, the supply of animal heat is lowered, and at the end of the second or third day the feeble ones have sunk down hopelessly, the yearlings and oldish ones have received a shock which nothing but careful nursing will recover them from, and even the strongest have suffered an injurious loss in condition.

"The simplest and cheapest kind of shed is formed by poles or rails, the upper ends resting on a strong horizontal pole supported by crotched posts set in the ground. It may be rendered rain-proof by pea-haulm, straw, or pine boughs.

"In a region where lumber is very cheap, planks or boards (of sufficient thickness not to spring downward, and thus open the roof), battened with slabs, may take the place of the poles and boughs; and they would make a tighter and more durable roof. If the lower ends of the boards or poles are raised a couple of feet from the ground, by placing a log under them the shed will shelter more sheep.

"These movable sheds may be connected with hay-barns, 'hay-barracks,' stacks, or they may surround an inclosed space with a stack in the middle. In the latter case, however, the yard should be *square*, instead of *round*, on account of the divergence in the lower ends of the boards or poles, which the round form would render necessary."

2. *Feeding-Racks.*—"When the ground is frozen, and especially when covered with snow, the sheep eats hay better on the ground than anywhere else. When the land is soft, muddy, or foul with manure, they will scarcely touch hay placed on it. It should then be fed in racks.

"These are of various forms. Fig. 25 gives the common box rack in the most general use in the North. It is ten feet long, two and a half wide, the lower boards a foot wide, the upper ones about ten inches, the two about nine inches apart,

Fig. 25.

BOX RACK.

and the corner posts three by three, or three and a half by two and a half inches. The boards are spiked on these posts by large flat-headed nails wrought for the purpose, and the lower edges of the upper boards and the upper edges of the lower ones are rounded so they shall not wear the wool off from the sheep's necks. The lower boards and the opening for the heads should be two or three inches narrower for lambs. If made of light wood, as they should be, a man standing in the inside and middle of one of these racks, can easily carry it about—an important desideratum. Unless over-fed, sheep waste very little hay in them."

An improvement upon the common box rack has holes eight inches wide, nine inches high, and about eighteen inches apart, instead of the continuous opening represented in the foregoing cut; but it is a little more expensive.

3. *Feeding.*—"In Germany great stress is laid on variety in the winter fodder, and elaborate systems of feeding are given. Variations of dry fodder are well enough, but hundreds and thousands of Northern flocks receive nothing but ordinary hay, consisting mainly of timothy (*Phleum pratense*), some red and white clover (*Trifolium pratense et repens*), and frequently a sprinkling of June or spear-grass (*Poa pratensis*), during the entire winter. Others receive an occasional fodder of cornstalks and straw, and some farmers give a daily feed of grain

through the winter. Where hay is the principal feed, it may be well, where it is convenient, to give corn-stalks (or 'blades') every fifth or sixth feed, or even once a day; or the daily feed, *not of hay*, might alternate between blades, pea-straw, straw of the cereal grains, etc. Should any other fodder besides hay be the principal one, as, for example, corn-blades or pea-haulm, each of the *other* fodders might be alternated in the same way. It is mainly, in my judgment, a question of convenience with the flock-master, provided a *proper supply of palatable nutriment within a proper compass* is given. Hay, clover, properly cured pea-haulm, and corn-blades are palatable to the sheep, and each contain the necessary supply of nutriment in the quantity which the sheep can readily take into its stomach. Consequently, from either of these, the sheep can derive its entire subsistence. Sheep should not run or be fed in yards with any other stock.

"The expediency of feeding grain to store sheep in the winter depends upon circumstances. Remote from markets, it is generally fed by the holders of large flocks. Oats are commonly preferred, and they are fed at the rate of a gill a head per day. Some feed half the same amount of (yellow) corn. Fewer sheep—particularly lambs, yearlings, and crones—get thin and perish, where they receive a daily feed of grain; they consume less hay, and their fleeces *are increased in weight.* On the whole, therefore, it is considered good economy. Where no grain is fed, three daily feeds of hay are given. It is a common and very good practice to feed greenish cut oats *in the bundle*, at noon, and give but two feeds of hay—one at morning and one at night. A few feed greenish cut peas in the same way. In warm, thawing weather, when sheep get to the ground, and refuse dry hay, a little grain assists materially in keeping up their strength and condition. This may furnish a useful hint for many parts of the South. When the feed is shortest in winter, in the South, there are many localities where sheep would get enough grass to take off their appetite for dry hay, but not *quite* enough to keep them in prime condition. A moderate daily feed of oats or peas, placed in the depository racks, would keep them strong, in good plight for the lambing season, and increase their weight of wool.

"Ruta-bagas, Irish potatoes, etc., make a good substitute for grain, as an extra feed for grown sheep. I prefer the ruta-baga to the potato in equivalents of nutriment. I do not consider either of them, or any other root, as good for lambs and yearlings as an equivalent in grain. Sheep may be *taught* to eat nearly all the cultivated roots; this is done by withholding salt from them, and then feeding the chopped root a few times rubbed with just sufficient salt to induce them to eat the root to obtain it, but not enough to satisfy their appetite for salt before they have acquired a taste for the roots.

" If there is one rule which may be considered more imperative than any other in sheep husbandry, it is that the utmost regularity be preserved in feeding. First, there should be regularity as to the *times* of feeding. However abundantly provided for, when a flock are foddered sometimes at one hour and sometimes at another—sometimes three times a day and sometimes twice—some days grain and some days none—*they can not be made to thrive.* . They will do far better on *inferior keep*, if fed with strict regularity. In a climate where they require hay three times a day, the best times for feeding are about sunrise in the morning, at noon, and an hour *before dark* at night. Unlike cattle and horses, sheep do not eat well *in the dark*, and therefore they should have time to consume their food before night sets in. Noon is the common time for feeding grain or roots, and is the best time if but two fodderings of hay be given. If the sheep receive hay three times, it is not a matter of much consequence with which feeding the grain is given, only that the practice be uniform.

"It is also highly essential that there be regularity preserved in the *amount* fed. The consumption of hay will, it is true, depend much upon the weather. The keener the cold, the more sheep will eat. In the South, much would also depend upon the amount of grass obtained. In many places a light, daily foddering would suffice—in others, a light foddering placed in the depository racks once in two days would answer the purpose. In the steady cold weather of the North, the shepherd readily learns to determine about how much hay will be consumed before the next foddering time; and this is the amount which should, as near as may be, be *regularly* fed. In feeding grain or roots there is no difficulty in preserving *entire regularity*, and it is vastly more important than in feeding hay. Of the latter a sheep will not over-eat and surfeit itself; of the former it will. And if not fed grain to the point of surfeiting, but still over-plenteously, it will expect a like amount at the next feeding, and failing to receive it will pine for it and manifest uneasiness. The effect of such irregularity on the stomach and system of *any* animal is bad, and the sheep suffers more from it than any other animal. I would much rather that my flock receive no grain at all than that they should receive it without regard to regularity in the amount. The shepherd should be required to *measure* out the grain to sheep in all instances—instead of *guessing* it out—and to measure it to each separate flock.

"In the North the grass often gets very short by the 10th or 15th of November, and it has lost much of its nutritiousness from repeated freezing and thawing. At this time, though no snow has yet fallen, it is best to give the sheep a light, daily foddering of bright hay, or a few oats in the bundle. Given thus for the ten or twelve days which precede the covering of the ground by snow, fodder pays for itself as well as at any other time during the year."

4. *Salt.*—"Salt, in my judgment, is indispensable to the health of sheep, particularly in the summer; and I know not a flockmaster among the hundreds, nay, thousands with whom I am acquainted, who differs with me in this opinion. It is common to give it once a week while the sheep are at grass.

"It is still better to give them free access to salt at all times by keeping it in a covered box, open on one side."

5. *Water.*—"Water is not indispensable in the summer pastures, the dews and the succulence of the feed answering as a

substitute. But my impression is decided that free access to water is advantageous to sheep, particularly to those having lambs; and I should consider it a matter of importance, on a sheep farm, to arrange the pastures, if practicable, so as to bring water into each of them."

6. *Shade.*—"No one who has observed with what eagerness sheep seek shade in hot weather, and how they pant and apparently suffer when a hot sun is pouring down on their nearly naked bodies, will doubt that, both as a matter of humanity and utility, they should be provided, during the hot summer months, with a better shelter than that afforded by a common rail fence. Forest trees are the most natural and best shades, and it is as contrary to utility as it is to good taste to strip them entirely from the sheep-walks. A strip of stone wall or close board fence on the south and west sides of the pasture will form a passable substitute for trees; but in the absence of all these, and of buildings of any kind, a shade can be cheaply constructed of poles and brush, in the same manner as the sheds of the same materials for winter shelter already described."

7. *Lambs.*—"Lambs are usually dropped in the North from the first to the fifteenth of May. In the South, they might safely come earlier. It is not expedient to have them dropped when the weather is cold and boisterous, as they require too much care; but the sooner the better after the weather has become mild, and the herbage has started sufficiently to give the ewes that green food which is required to produce a plentiful secretion of milk. It is customary in the North to have fields of clover, or the earliest of grasses, reserved for the early spring feed of the breeding ewes; and if these can be contiguous to their shelters, it is a great convenience—for the ewes should be confined in the latter, on cold and stormy nights, during the lambing season.

"If warm and pleasant, and the nights are warmish, I prefer to have the lambing take place in the pastures. I think sheep are more disposed to own and take kindly to their lambs thus, than in the confusion of a small inclosure. Unless particularly docile, sheep in a small inclosure crowd from one side to another when any one enters, running over young lambs, and pressing them severely, etc. Ewes get separated from their lambs, and then run violently round from one to another, jostling and knocking them about. Young and timid ewes get separated from their lambs, and frequently will neglect them for an hour or more before they will again approach them. If the weather is severely cold, the lamb, if it has never sucked, stands a chance to perish. Lambs, too, when just dropped, in a *dirty* inclosure, in their first efforts to rise, tumble about, and the membrane which adheres to them becomes smeared with dirt and dung—and the ewe refuses to lick them dry, which much increases the hazard of freezing.

"Lambs should be weaned at four months old. It is better for them and much better for their dams. The lambs when taken away should be put for several days in a field distant from the ewes, that they may not hear each other's bleatings. The lambs when in hearing of their dams continue restless much longer, and they make constant and frequently successful efforts to crawl through the fences which separate them. One or two tame old ewes are turned into the field with them, to teach them to come at the call, find salt when thrown to them, and eat grain, etc., out of troughs when winter approaches.

"The lambs when weaned should be put on the freshest and tenderest feed. I have usually reserved for mine the grass and clover sown, the preceding spring, on the grain fields which were seeded down.

"The dams, on the contrary, should be put for a fortnight on short, dry feed, to stop the flow of milk. They should be looked to once or twice, and should the bags of any be found much distended, the milk should be drawn and the bag washed for a little time in cold water. But on short feed they rarely give much trouble in this particular. When properly dried off they should be put on good feed to recruit, and get in condition for winter."

8. *Emasculation and Docking.*—" These should usually precede washing, as at that period the oldest lambs will be about a month old, and it is safer to perform the operations when they are a couple of weeks younger. Dry, pleasant weather should be selected. Castration is a simple and safe process. Let a man hold the lamb with its back pressed firmly against his breast and stomach, and all four legs gathered in front in his hands. Cut off the bottom of the pouch, free the testicle from the inclosing membrane, and then draw it steadily out, or clip the cord with a knife, if it does not snap off at a proper distance from the testicle. Some shepherds draw both testicles at once with their *teeth*. It is common to drop a little salt into the pouch. Where the weather is very warm, some touch the end of the pouch (and that of the tail, after that is cut off) with an ointment, consisting of tar, lard, and turpentine. In ninety-nine cases out of a hundred, however, they will do just as well, here, without any application.

" The tail should be cut off, say one and a half inches from the body, with a chisel on the head of a block, the skin being slid up toward the body with a finger and thumb, so that it will afterward cover the end of the stump. Severed with a knife, the end of the tail being grasped with one of the hands in the ordinary way, a naked stump is left which takes some time to heal.

" It may occur to some unused to keeping sheep, that it is unnecessary to cut off the tail. If left on, it is apt to collect filth, and if the sheep purges, it becomes an intolerable nuisance.

9. *Washing.*—" This is usually done here about the first of June. The climate of the Southern States would admit of its being done earlier. The rule should be to wait until the water has acquired sufficient warmth for bathing, and until cold rains and storms, and cold nights are no longer to be expected.

10. *Shearing.*—" It is difficult, if not impossible, to give intelligible practical instructions which would guide an entire novice in skillfully shearing a sheep. Practice is requisite. The

following directions from the American Shepherd* are correct, and are as plain, perhaps, as they can be made:

"'The shearer may place the sheep on that part of the floor assigned to him, resting on its rump, and himself in a posture with one (his right) knee on a cushion, and the back of the animal resting against his left thigh. He grasps the shears about halfway from the point to the bow, resting his thumb along the blade, which affords him better command of the points. He may then commence cutting the wool at the brisket, and proceeding downward, all upon the sides of the belly to the extremity of the ribs, the external sides of both thighs to the edges of the flanks; then back to the brisket, and thence upward, shearing the wool from the breast, front, and both sides of the neck—but not yet the back of it—and also the poll or fore-part, and top of the head. Now the "jacket is opened" of the sheep, and its position and that of the shearer is changed, by being turned flat upon its side, one knee of the shearer resting on the cushion, and the other gently pressing the fore-quarter of the animal, to prevent any struggling. He then resumes cutting upon the flank and rump, and thence onward to the head. Thus one side is complete. The sheep is then turned on to the other side, in doing which great care is requisite to prevent the fleece from being torn, and the shearer acts as upon the other, which finishes. He must then take his sheep near to the door through which it is to pass out, and neatly trim the legs, and leave not a solitary lock anywhere as a harbor for ticks. It is absolutely necessary for him to remove from his stand to trim, otherwise the useless stuff from the legs becomes intermingled with the fleece wool. In the use of the shears, let the blades be laid as flat to the skin as possible, not lower the points too much, nor cut more than from one to two inches at a clip, frequently not so much, depending on the part and compactness of the wool.'

"Cold storms sometimes destroy sheep, in this latitude, soon

---

* Pages 179, 180.

after shearing—particularly the delicate Saxons. I have known forty or fifty perish out of a single flock, from one night's exposure. The remedy, or rather the preventive, is to house them, or in default of the necessary fixtures to effect this, to drive them into dense forests. I presume, however, this would be a calamity of rare occurrence in the 'sunny South.' "*

V.—VALUE OF SHEEP TO THE FARMER.

The following suggestive remarks are from the *Country Gentleman*, and are worthy of every reader's attention:

"Sheep are profitable to the farmer, not only from the product of wool and mutton, but from the tendency which their keeping has to improve and enrich his land for all agricultural purposes. They do this:

"1. By the consumption of food refused by other animals in summer; turning waste vegetation to use, and giving rough and bushy pastures a smoother appearance, and in time eradicating wild plants so that good grasses and white clover may take their place. In this respect sheep are of especial value to pastures on soils too steep or stony for the plow. In winter, the coarser parts of the hay, refused by horses and cows, are readily eaten by sheep, while other stock will generally eat most of that left by these animals.

"For these reasons, among others, no grazing farm should be without at least a small flock of sheep, for it has been found that as large a number of cattle and horses can be kept with as without them, and without any injury to the farm for other purposes. A small flock, we said—perhaps half a dozen to each horse and cow would be the proper proportion. A va-

---

* Sheep Husbandry; with an Account of the Different Breeds and General Directions in regard to Summer and Winter Management, Breeding, and Treatment of Diseases. With Portraits and other Engravings. By Henry S. Randall. New York: A. O. Moore. This work is bound with "Youatt on the Sheep," under the general title of "The Shepherd's Own Book," and the volume should be in the hands of every one who would make sheep-breeding his principal business.

riety of circumstances would influence this point; such as the character of the pasturage, and the proportion of the same fitted and desirable for tillage.

"2. Sheep enrich land by the manufacture of considerable quantities of excellent manure. A farmer of long experience in sheep husbandry, thought there was no manure so fertilizing as that of sheep, and (of which there is no doubt) that none dropped by the animal upon the land suffered so little by waste from exposure. A German agricultural writer has calculated that the droppings from one thousand sheep during a single night would manure an acre sufficiently for any crop. By using a portable fence, and moving the same from time to time, a farmer might manure a distant field with sheep at less expense than that of carting and spreading barn manure.

"The value of sheep to the farmer is much enhanced by due attention to their wants. Large flocks kept together are seldom profitable, while small assorted flocks always pay well, if fed as they should be. To get good fleeces of wool, and large, healthy lambs from poor neglected sheep, is impossible. It is also true that the expense of keeping is often least with the flocks that are always kept in good condition. The eye and thought of the owner are far more necessary than large and irregular supplies of fodder. Division of the flock and shelter, with straw and a little grain, will bring them through to spring pastures in far better order than if kept together, with double rations of hay, one half of which is wasted by the stronger animals, while the weak of the flock pick up but a scanty living, and oftentimes fail to get that through the whole winter.

"We commend this subject to the consideration of our correspondents; it is one which needs greater attention on the part of the farming public."

VI.—AFFECTION OF THE EWE.

The Ettrick Shepherd tells the following story of the continued affection of the ewe for her dead lamb:

"One of the two years while I remained on the farm at Willenslee a severe blast of snow came on by night, about the latter end of April, which destroyed several scores of our lambs, and as we had not enow of twins and odd lambs for the mothers that had lost theirs, of course we selected the best ewes and put lambs to them. As we were making the distribution, I requested of my master to spare me a lamb for a ewe which he knew, and which was standing over a dead lamb in the end of the hope, about four miles from the house. He would not let me do it, but bid me let her stand over her lamb for a day or two, and perhaps a twin would be forthcoming. I did so, and faithfully she did stand to her charge. I visited her every morning and evening for the first eight days, and never found her above two or three yards from the lamb; and often as I went my rounds, she eyed me long ere I came near her, and kept stamping with her foot, and whistling through her nose, to frighten away the dog. He got a regular chase twice a day as I passed by; but however excited and fierce a ewe may be, she never offers any resistance to mankind, being perfectly and meekly passive to them.

"The weather grew fine and warm, and the dead lamb soon decayed; but still this affectionate and desolate creature kept hanging over the poor remains with an attachment that seemed to be nourished by hopelessness. It often drew tears from my eyes to see her hanging with such fondness over a few bones, mixed with a small portion of wool. For the first fortnight she never quitted the spot; and for another week she visited it every morning and evening, uttering a few kindly and heart-piercing bleats; till at length every remnant of her offspring vanished, mixing with the soil, or wafted away by the winds."

V.

SWINE.

*Where oft the swine, from ambush warm and dry,
Bolt out and scamper headlong to their sty.—Bloomfield.*

I.—NATURAL HISTORY.

THE hog (*Suidæ sus* of Linnæus), according to Cuvier, belongs to "the class *Mammalia*, order *Pachydermata*, genus *Suidæ* or *sus*."

Professor Low remarks, that "the hog is subject to remarkable changes of form and characters, according to the situation in which he is placed. When these characters assume a certain degree of permanence, a breed or variety is formed; and there is no one of the domestic animals which more easily receives the characters we desire to impress upon it. This arises from its rapid powers of increase, and the constancy with which the characters of the parents are reproduced in the progeny.

There is no kind of livestock that can be so easily improved by the breeder and so quickly rendered suited to the purposes required; and the same characters of external form indicate in the hog a disposition to arrive at early maturity of muscle and fat as in the ox and the sheep. The body is long in proportion to the limbs, or, in other words, the limbs are short in proportion to the body; the extremities are free from coarseness; the chest is broad and the trunk round. Possessing these characteristics, the hog never fails to arrive at early maturity, and with a smaller consumption of food than when he possesses a different conformation."

The wild boar, which was undoubtedly the progenitor of all the European varieties, and also of the Chinese breed, was formerly a native of the British Islands, and very common in the forests until the time of the civil wars in England.

The wild hog is now spread over the temperate and warmer parts of the old continent and its adjacent islands. His color varies with age and climate, but is generally a dusky brown with black spots and streaks. His skin is covered with coarse hairs or bristles, intersected with soft wool, and with coarser and longer bristles upon the neck and spine, which he erects when in anger. He is a very bold and powerful creature, and becomes more fierce and indocile with age. From the form of his teeth he is chiefly herbivorous in his habits, and delights in roots, which his acute sense of smell and touch enables him to discover beneath the surface. He also feeds upon animal substances, such as worms and larvæ which he grubs up from the ground, the eggs of birds, small reptiles, the young of animals, and occasionally carrion; he even attacks venomous snakes with impunity.

The female produces a litter but once a year, and in much smaller numbers than when domesticated. She usually carries her young for four months or sixteen weeks.

In a wild state the hog has been known to live more than thirty years; but when domesticated he is usually slaughtered for bacon before he is two years old, and boars killed for brawn seldom reach to the age of five. When the wild hog is tamed, it undergoes the following among other changes in its conformation. The ears become less movable, not being required to collect distant sounds. The formidable tusks of the male diminish, not being necessary for self-defense. The muscles of the neck become less developed, from not being so much exercised as in the natural state. The head becomes more inclined, the back and loins are lengthened, the body rendered more capacious, the limbs shorter and less muscular; and anatomy proves that the stomach and intestinal canals have also become proportionately extended along with the form of the body. The habits and instincts of the animal change; it becomes diurnal in its habits, not choosing the night for its search of food;

is more insatiate in its appetite, and the tendency to obesity increases.

The male forsaking its solitary habits, becomes gregarious, and the female produces her young more frequently, and in larger numbers. With its diminished strength and power of active motion, the animal also loses its desire for liberty. These changes of form, appetites, and habits, being communicated to its progeny, a new race of animals is produced, better suited to their altered condition. The wild hog, after it has been domesticated, does not appear to revert to its former state and habits; at least the swine of South America, carried thither by the Spaniards, which have escaped to the woods, retain their gregarious habits, and have not become wild boars.*

II.—OPINIONS RESPECTING THE HOG.

From the various allusions to the hog in the writings of the ancient Greeks and Romans, it is plain that its flesh was held in high esteem among those nations. The Romans even made the breeding, rearing, and fattening pigs a study, which they designated as *Porculatio*.

Varro states that the Gauls produced the largest and finest swine's flesh that was brought into Italy; and according to Strabo, in the reign of Augustus, they supplied Rome and nearly all Italy with gammons, hog-puddings, and sausages. This nation and the Spaniards appear to have kept immense droves of swine, but scarcely any other kind of livestock. . . . . In fact, the hog was held in very high esteem by all the early nations of Europe; and some of the ancients have even paid it divine honors.†

On the other hand, swine's flesh has been held in utter abhorrence by the Jews since the time of Moses, in whose laws they were forbidden to make use of it as food. The Egyptians also and the followers of Mohammed have religiously abstained from it. Paxton, in his "Illustrations of Scripture," says:

---

* American Farmer's Encyclopedia.   † Youatt.

"The hog was justly classed by the Jews among the vilest animals in the scale of animated nature; and it can not be doubted that his keeper shared in the contempt and abhorrence which he had excited. The prodigal son in the parable had spent his all in riotous living, and was ready to perish through want, before he submitted to the humiliating employment of feeding swine."

"Swine," Heroditus says, "are accounted such impure beasts by the Egyptians, that if a man touches one even by accident, he presently hastens to the river and, in all his clothes, plunges into the water. For this reason swine-herds alone of the Egyptians are not allowed to enter any of their temples; neither will any one give his daughter in marriage to one of that profession, nor take a wife born of such parents, so that they are necessitated to intermarry among themselves."

The Brahminical tribes of India share with the Jews, Mohammedans, and Egyptians this aversion to the hog. The modern Copts, descendants of the ancient Egyptians, rear no swine, and the Jews of the present day abstain from their flesh as of old.

It was Cuvier's opinion that "in hot climates the flesh of swine is not good;" and Mr. Sonnini remarks that "in Egypt, Syria, and even the southern parts of Greece, this meat, though very white and delicate, is so far from being firm, and is so overcharged with fat, that it disagrees with the strongest stomachs. It is therefore considered unwholesome, and this will account for its proscription by the legislators and priests of the East. Such abstinence was doubtless indispensable to health under the burning suns of Arabia and Egypt." How is it under the burning suns of Carolina and Georgia?

III.—BREEDS.

The various breeds which have been reared by crosses between those procured from different countries are so numerous, that to give anything like a detailed description of them would fill a large volume. We shall refer to only a few of the more important of them.

1. *The Land Pike.*—The old common breed of the country, sometimes called "land-pikes," may be described as "large, rough, long-nosed, big-boned, thin-backed, slab-sided, long-leg-

Fig. 26.

THE LAND PIKE HOG.

ged, ravenous, ugly animals." Speaking of this race, A. B. Allen says: "No reasonable fence can stop them, but, ever restive and uneasy, they rove about seeking for plunder; swilling grunting, rooting, pawing; always in mischief and always destroying. The more a man possesses of such stock the worse he is off." But this breed is rapidly disappearing. Crosses between the land-pike and the Chinese or the Berkshire producing a fine animal, the original breed is being very generally improved.

2. *The Chinese Breed.*—This breed was introduced into this country from China some forty years ago. The Chinese hog is small in limb, round in body, short in head, and very broad in cheek. When fattened, it looks quite out of proportion, the head appearing to be buried in the neck, so that only the tip of the nose is visible. It has an exceedingly thin skin and fine bristles.

The pure-blooded Chinese hog has been bred to only a limited extent in the United States, on account of the smallness of its size (it seldom attaining more than two hundred and fifty pounds), and its lack of hardiness in a cold climate. In this last respect, however, it is well adapted to the South. Crossed with the native hog it forms an excellent breed, which we may call the improved China breed. Hogs of this mixed breed are various in color—black, white, spotted, and gray and white; they are longer in body than the pure Chinese breed; small in the head and legs; broad in the back; round in the body; the hams well let down; skin thin; flesh delicate and finely flavored. They are easy keepers; small consumers; quiet in disposition; not disposed to roam; and when in condition may be kept so upon grass only.

3. *The Berkshire Breed.*—This was one of the earliest improved of the English breeds, and is deemed by many the most excellent of all the varieties at present known. It is certainly the most widely distributed and most generally approved. It is a breed which is distinguished by being, in general, of a tawny white, or rufous-brown color, spotted with black or brown; head well placed, large ears, generally standing forward, though sometimes hanging over the eyes; body thick, close, and well made; legs short, small in the bone; coat rough and curly, wearing the appearance of indicating both skin and flesh of a coarse quality. Such, however, is not the case, for they

Fig. 27.

THE BERKSHIRE HOG.

have a disposition to fatten quickly: nothing can be finer than the bacon, and the animals attain to a very great size.

The Berkshires, from which most of the present American stock has sprung, were imported in 1822. The breed has spread very rapidly over the country.

Fig. 28.

THE SUFFOLK HOG.

4. *The Suffolk Breed.*—The improved Suffolk breed originated in a cross between the original Suffolk hog and the Chinese. It is a very valuable breed, but much smaller in size than the Berkshire. The Suffolks are thick through the shoulders, very handsomely proportioned in body, and possessing beautiful hams. Their color is either white or light flesh color, when of the pure breed, and they are indeed an ornament to the farm.

It is said that they are less inclined to cutaneous diseases than numerous others, and do not, under any circumstances, produce that strong, musky flavored pork we sometimes find in market. They are not a gross, unwieldy animal, generally ranging from two hundred and fifty to three hundred pounds weight at twelve months of age, which latter weight they seldom exceed. They are clean feeders, and require much less than any other breed known.

For large hogs, a cross between these and the Berkshire is very desirable, and is preferred by Western breeders; but for a small breeder, or for family use, the pure Suffolks are preferable.*

5. *The Essex Breed.*—The Essex hogs are mostly black and white, the head and hinder parts being black and the back and belly white. The most esteemed Essex breeds, Youatt says, are entirely black, and are distinguished by having small teat-like appendages of the skin depending from the under part of the neck. They have smaller heads than the Berkshire hogs, and long, thin, upright ears; short bristles; a fine skin; good hind quarters, and a deep, round carcass. They are also small boned, and their flesh is delicately flavored. They produce large litters, but are reputed bad nurses.

Fig. 29.

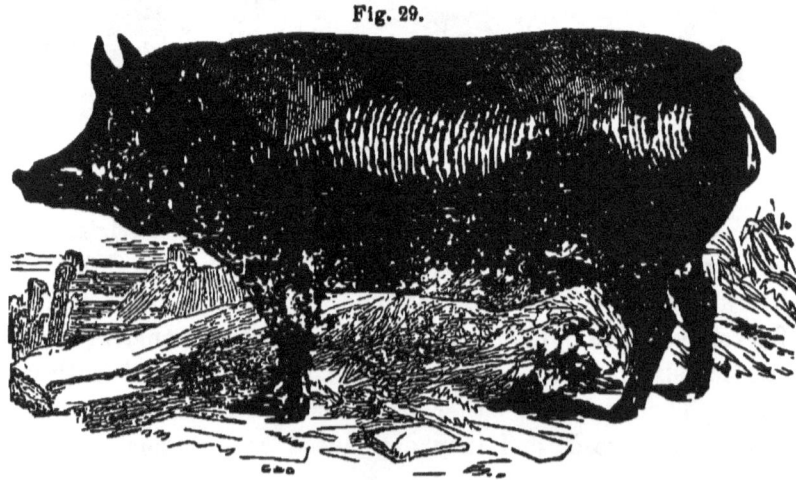

THE ESSEX HOG.

6. *The Chester Breed.*—This breed originated in Chester County, Pennsylvania, and is not so widely known as, according

---

* Country Gentleman.

to all intents, it deserves to be. A correspondent of the *Country Gentleman* gives the following account of the Chester hog:

"The Chester hog is the result of continued careful breeding and judicious crossing in this county during the last thirty-five or forty years. The first impulse to this improvement, it is said, was the importation of a pair of handsome hogs from China, some forty years since, by a sea-captain then residing in this vicinity. Of late years, however, many of our breeders have been laboring to bring the Chester hog up to an acknowledged standard of excellence—to define its points, and make it as distinctive in character, and as easily recognized, as a Berkshire or Suffolk. Their efforts, we think, have been successful.

"The genuine Chester is a pure white, long body and square built, with small, fine bone, and will produce a greater weight of pork, for the amount of food consumed, than any other breed yet tried among us. A very important characteristic of the breed is, that it will *readily fatten at any age.* Many hogs, it is well known, will not fatten while they are growing, or until they have reached their full size.

"The average weight of the Chester stock, at sixteen months old, is from 500 to 600 lbs., and when kept till two years old, they frequently run up to 700 and 800 lbs. Our spring pigs, when killed the following fall, weigh from 300 to 400 lbs., which is considered the most desirable weight for pork—producing hams of a more salable size and better quality. As a general rule, our farmers do not care to have their hogs weigh over 350 to 400 lbs. To reach this weight at nine months old, our hogs, of course, must be well fed. The Chester is not different from other stock in this respect—to thrive well, it must be well taken care of.

"Experiments have been made in crossing the Chester with other breeds—such as the Berkshire, Suffolk, etc., and the result has been an inferior stock to the pure Chester. It *does* improve the Berkshires to cross them with the Chester, but we have found no advantage in crossing the Chester with any other."

IV.—POINTS.

"There is evidently much diversity in swine in different circumstances and situations. Like other descriptions of stock, they should be selected with especial reference to the nature of the climate, the keep, and the circumstances of the management under which the farm is conducted. The chief points to be consulted in judging of the breeds of this animal are the form or shape of the ear, and the quality of the hair. The pendulous or lop ear, and coarse, harsh hair, are commonly asserted to indicate largeness of size and thickness of skin; while erect or prick ears show the size to be smaller, but the animals to be more quick in feeding.

"In the selection of swine, the best formed are considered to be those which are not too long, but full in the head and cheek; thick and rather short in the neck; fine in the bone; thick, plump, and compact in the carcass; full in the quarters, fine and thin in the hide; and of a good size according to the breed, with, above all, a kindly disposition to fatten well and expeditiously at an early age. Depth of carcass, lateral extension, breadth of the loin and breast, proportionate length, moderate shortness of the legs, and substance of the gammons and fore-arms, are therefore absolute essentials. These are qualities to produce a favorable balance in the account of keep, and a mass of weight which will pull the scale down. In proportion, too, as the animal is capacious in the loin and breast, will be generally the vigor of his constitution; his legs will be thence properly distended, and he will have a bold and firm footing on the ground."*

V.—FEEDING.

Have regular hours for feeding your hogs; nothing is more important. Irregularity irritates the digestive organs, and prevents the system from receiving the full benefit of the meal when it does come. Do not give them too much food at once,

---

* American Farmer's Encyclopedia.

as they are apt to gorge themselves; or, if any be left in the trough, to return to it frequently till it is all gone. In both cases their digestive organs, and consequently their ability to fatten, are impaired.

Swine will eat animal food, but it is not favorable to the flavor of their flesh, and should always be withheld while they are fattening.

Pigs always eat more when first put up to fatten than they do afterward, therefore the most nutritious food should be reserved till they are getting pretty fat.

In reference to fattening the hog, a writer in the *Boston Cultivator* remarks:

"If circumstances are favorable, he is inclined to lay up such a supply of fat during autumn as would render it unnecessary for him to undergo much exercise or exposure during inclement weather. With plenty of *lard oil* to keep his lamp burning, he would prefer dozing in a bed of leaves in the forest while the ground is covered with snow, rather than to *grub* daily for a living. He fattens most rapidly in such a state of the atmosphere as is most congenial to his comfort—neither too hot nor too cold; hence the months of September and October are best for making pork. The more agreeable the weather, the less is the amount of food required to supply the waste of life.

"Against fattening hogs so early in the season, it may be objected that Indian corn, the crop chiefly depended on for the purpose, is not matured. Taking everything into consideration, it may be better to begin to feed corn before it is ripe, or even at the stage of considerable greenness. After the plant has blossomed it possesses a considerable degree of sweetness; hogs will chew it, swallow the juice, and leave nothing but the dry fibrous matter, which they eject from their mouths when no more sweetness can be extracted. They thrive on this fodder, and will continue to eat it till the nutriment is concentrated in the ear, and then they will eat the cob and grain together till the cob gets hard and dry. Farmers who have practiced this mode of feeding consider it more advantageous than to leave the whole crop to ripen, unless they have a supply of old corn to feed with. Even in the latter case, it is questionable whether hogs will not do better on corn somewhat green than they would on hard corn, unground. True, it is not necessary that corn should be fed unground, but much is fed in this condition, no doubt at a loss.

"In many parts of the country, swine are fed considerably on articles which are not readily marketable, as imperfect fruits, vegetables, etc. Where such articles are used, cooking them is generally economical. A mixture of squashes (either summer or winter squashes), pumpkins—the nearer ripe the better—potatoes, beets, and apples, boiled or steamed, and a fourth or an eighth of their bulk of meal stirred in while the mass is hot, forms a dish on which hogs will fatten fast. If skimmed milk or whey can be had, the cooked food may be put with it into a suitable tub or vat, and a slight degree of fermentation allowed to take place before the whole is fed out. The animals will eat it with avidity, and probably derive more benefit from it than if it had not been fermented. Articles which are of a perishable nature should be used first in fattening swine, in order to prevent waste and turn all the products of the farm to the best account.

"Another quite important advantage of early feeding is the less trouble in regard to cooking the food and keeping it in proper condition to feed out. The cooking may be done out of doors, if convenience of feeding would be promoted by it, and there is no expense or trouble to guard the food against freezing."

The manner of fattening hogs, where Indian corn is used, as at the South and West, is to put them up in large, open pens on the ground, without litter and without shelter. Here they are left to burrow and sleep in mud and mire, exposed to all weathers, consuming, probably, before they get "ripe fat," one third if not half more than would be necessary were they sheltered in a warm pen, with clean litter, clean water, and rich food in abundance, free alike from exposure and excitement.

An ample supply of good drinking water should be kept within the reach of every animal.

VI.—THE PIGGERY.

In constructing a piggery, reference should be had to the comfort of the animals as well as to convenience in feeding them. It should be large, airy, and well-ventilated, and should have (at least in a large establishment) conveniences for cooking their food. It should by all means be comfortable and clean. It has been generally believed that the hog is naturally a filthy animal, delighting in mud and mire. This is certainly, in part at least, untrue. No animal more fully appreciates a clean, dry bed. To illustrate the value of cleanliness, a gentleman in Norfolk (England) put up six pigs of almost exactly the same weight, and all in equal health to fatten; treated them all, except in one particular, exactly alike, giving equal quantities of the same food to each for seven weeks. Three of these pigs were left to shift for themselves, so far as cleanliness is concerned, while the other three were carefully curried, brushed, and washed. The latter consumed, during the seven weeks, less food by five bushels than the former, and yet, when killed, weighed more by thirty-two pounds on an average. [For a plan for a piggery, see "The House."]

VI.

IMPROVEMENT OF BREEDS.

Like produces like.

I.—SELECTION.

WITH such examples before us as are furnished by the English Race Horse, the Durham Cow, and the South-Down sheep, where shall we place limits to the improvability of our various domestic animals? The ameliorations through which these improved breeds have been established were not accidental. They took place according to the fixed laws of animal life, brought to bear by the intelligence of man upon special points and for special objects. Other breeds even better than these may be produced by similar means. Bakewell, Culley, Seabright, Jaques, Knight, and other distinguished breeders and improvers of stock, have made use of no patented or secret process. What they have done, any intelligent farmer may do by the use of the same easily available means. To furnish a few hints in reference to these means is the purpose of this chapter.

In setting about originating a new breed of any particular species of animal, the first grand point is the selection of sire and dam. This must be made with reference to the particular qualities to which you desire to give prominence, as well as to the general excellence of constitution, form, and disposition which should distinguish the species. Thus Colonel Jaques, in originating the Cream-Pot breed of cows, already referred to, had the dairy and not the butcher in view, and took his measures accordingly. The results of a continued selection of breeders with reference to their qualities as milkers has been the establishment of a permanent breed distinguished probably above all others as dairy cows. So the sheep breeders of England, having the production of mutton as their principal object, have produced the New Leicester, the South-Down, and the New Oxfordshire breeds, distinguished for form, size, flavor, and fattening qualities; while the Spanish and German breeders of Merinos, caring only for the wool, have given their breeds pre-eminently excellent fleeces. Breeding carefully for a few generations with a distinct purpose in view, will not fail to produce astonishing and satisfactory results.

"The alteration," Sir John Seabright says, "which may be made in any breed of animals by selection can hardly be conceived by those that have not paid some attention to the subject."

To breed in the most successful manner, the male and female should be taken when they are in the highest state of health, and when all the powers and attributes which are wished for and which it is designed to propagate are in the most complete order and state of perfection.

II.—IN-AND-IN BREEDING.

It is a well-established fact in human physiology that the intermarriage of near relatives tends to both physical and mental degeneracy. Analogy would lead us to infer that the same results must follow close breeding among the lower animals; and facts, we think, prove conclusively that this is the case. Youatt, high authority on this subject, says:

"Breeding in-and-in has many advantages to a certain extent. It may be pursued until the excellent form and quality of the breed are developed and established. It was the source whence sprung the fine cattle and sheep of Bakewell, and the superior cattle of Colling; but disadvantages attend breeding 'in-and-in,' and to it must be traced the speedy degeneracy, the absolute disappearance, of the new Leicester cattle, and in the hands of many an agriculturist, the impairment of constitution and decreased value of the new Leicester sheep and the short-horned beasts. It has therefore become a kind of principle with the agriculturist to effect some change in his stock every second or third year; and that change is most conveniently effected by introducing a new bull or ram. These should be as nearly as possible of the same sort, coming from a similar pasturage and climate, but possessing no relationship, or at most a very distant one, to the stock to which he is introduced." These remarks apply to all descriptions of live-stock. In cattle, as well as in the human species, defects of organization and permanent derangements of function obtain, and are handed down when the relationship is close.

III.—CROSSING.

It is by judicious crossing of breeds that some of our best varieties of domestic animals have been obtained. A cross between a superior and an inferior breed results in a progeny superior to the latter, and, for a particular use, climate, or locality, often better than the former. Thus the cross between the English thorough-bred horse and the inferior mare of the common breed of New England gave us the Morgan breed, which for all the common purposes for which a horse is used is superior to the thorough-bred animal himself.

In breeding from stock with qualifications of different descriptions and in different degrees, the breeder will decide what are indispensable or desirable qualities, and will cross with animals with a view to establish them. His proceeding will be of the "give-and-take" kind. He will, if necessary, submit to the introduction of a trifling defect in order that he may profit by a great excellence; and between excellences perhaps somewhat incompatible he will decide which is the greatest, and give it the preference.

The following account of the way in which the new French breed of sheep, La Chamois, was originated, throws light upon an important principle in breeding; namely, that the influence of the male upon the offspring will be the stronger the purer and more ancient in the first place his own race may be; and in the next place, the less resistance is offered by the female through the possession of those qualities of purity and long descent which are so valuable in the sire.

The French writer says: "With a view to the experiment proposed, it was necessary to procure English rams of the purest and most ancient race, and unite with them French ewes of the modern breeds, or rather of mixed blood forming no distinct breed at all. It is easier than one might have supposed to combine these conditions. On the one hand, I selected some of the finest rams of the New-Kent breed, regenerated by Goord. On the other hand, we find in France many border countries lying between distinct breeds, in which districts it is easy to find flocks participating in the two neighboring races. Thus, on the borders of Berry and La Sologne one meets with flocks originally sprung from a mixture of the two distinct races that are established in those two provinces. Among these, then, I chose such animals as seemed least defective, approaching, in fact, the nearest to, or rather departing the least from, the form which I wished ultimately to produce. These I united with animals of another mixed breed, picking out the best I could find on the borders of La Beauce and Touraine, which blended the Tourangelle and native Merino blood of those other two districts. From this mixture was obtained an offspring combining the four races of Berry, Sologne, Touraine, and Merino, without decided character, without fixity, with little intrinsic merit certainly, but possessing the advantage of being used to our climate and management, and bringing to bear on the new breed to be formed, an influence almost annihilated by the multiplicity of its component elements.

"Now what happens when such mixed-blood ewes are put to a pure New-Kent ram? A lamb is obtained containing fifty hundredths of the purest and most ancient English blood, with twelve and a half hundredths of four different French races, which are individually lost in the preponderance of

English blood, and disappear almost entirely, leaving the improving type in the ascendant. The influence, in fact, of this type was so decided and so predominant, that all the lambs produced strikingly resembled each other, and even Englishmen took them for animals of their own country. But what was still more decisive, when these young ewes and rams were put together they produced lambs closely resembling themselves, without any marked return to the features of the old French races from which the grandmother ewes were derived. Some slight traces only might perhaps be detected here and there by an experienced eye. Even these, however, soon disappeared, such animals as showed them being carefully weeded out of the breeding flock. This may certainly be called '*fixing a breed*,' when it becomes every year more capable of reproducing itself with uniform and marked features."

IV.—ADDITIONAL HINTS.

Farmers, like men in other branches of business, have an eye on the profits of their industry; and the more intelligent of them are now fully convinced of the fact, that with proper care and protection the improved and finer breeds do give a greater product with the same amount of food than the inferior and coarser breeds. It costs but little if any more to keep a cow that will give a large quantity of rich milk than one that does not pay for her food; strong, active horses are far more profitable than poor, lazy ones; a bushel of corn will make twice as much pork when fed to a Berkshire or a Suffolk as to a Land-Pike or Racer, and the best sheep will yield double the wool and bring triple the price of the poorer kinds.

Now every farmer may, in a few years, make great improvement in his stock by selecting his best animals to breed from, with an occasional infusion of fresh blood from other flocks and herds (without reference to any of the celebrated improved breeds), combined with proper attention to their feeding and general management; but unless he has a particular taste for breeding animals, and unusual facilities for the business, he will find it more convenient and cheaper to make an infusion of the improved blood into his stock, choosing such as is best fitted for his purpose. A bull or a ram of one of the best breeds will soon, if judiciously managed, make a great change for the better in his stock.

Another important fact must be borne in mind. "Improved breeds owe their present degree of perfection, whatever it may be, only to the skill which has been exercised in their selection, breeding, and management for a number of generations and a long series of years. This attention, we learn from the extract above, *must be continued* if we wish to retain the valuable qualities that it has placed within our reach; and careful attention to the selection, the wants, the comfort, and the health of one's stock is thus shown to be not only the dictate of economy for the time being, but a matter of importance in the future, from the influence it exerts on the progeny as well as on the parent. Improvements may be *bred out* as fast or faster than it can be *bred in*. Until the average of care which our farm stock now receives becomes much greater, it may be inexpedient to advise the maintenance of a herd or flock of pure improved blood for ordinary farm purposes; but, by beginning with grades—employing the services of an improved male to engraft upon "native" stock—and by degrees acquiring the habit of paying closer attention to their necessities and comforts, not only will our cattle and sheep be gradually and fundamentally bettered, but the farmer will be preparing to avail himself of breeds already rendered capable of giving, with proper attention, the greatest product for a specified amount of food; and animals bred to this point will then come into his hands to be improved, not to be deteriorated."[*]

---

[*] Country Gentleman.

VII.

DISEASES AND THEIR CURE.

<small>Throw physic to the dogs.—*Shakspeare*.</small>

I.—HYGIENE.

"THROW physic to the dogs," if you will, but, be assured, they are quadrupeds of too much good sense to swallow it; and the other domestic animals will hardly take, except under compulsion, what their canine companions and protectors thus reject. You will find less difficulty in forcing it down the throats of their more frequently diseased and oftener doctored masters.

A large portion of almost every work on domestic animals is taken up with directions for the treatment of their diseases. Our limits do not permit us to dwell long on this point, nor do we deem it necessary.

In their wild state, animals are ordinarily subject to few if any diseases. They live according to the laws of their being—live naturally and healthfully, and, unless they meet a violent death at the hands of man or of some of their natural enemies, die a natural death. Our domestic animals, as they are generally managed, live under conditions less favorable to health, and sometimes, although with comparative infrequency, get sick. The fault is generally in the keeper or breeder, and not in the animal or in the conditions inseparable from its domestic state. With animals, as with men, disease arises from some infringement of the organic laws; but their masters, and not themselves, are responsible for the infringement. When they get sick, however, in consequence of the false conditions under which they are forced to live, man adds insult to injury by forcing his nauseous and poisonous drugs down their reluctant throats. If they recover in spite of both the disease and the remedy, drugs get the credit.

Well, let those use drugs who have faith in them, either in the treatment of themselves, their families, or their domestic animals; but the reader who looks in this little manual for directions for their use will be disappointed. We can not conscientiously give them.

Animals born of well developed and perfectly healthy parents (and none but perfectly healthy and well developed animals should ever be permitted to become breeders) may almost universally *be kept in perfect health*. With a sufficient quantity of wholesome food, pure water, protection against storms and cold in winter, complete ventilation and perfect cleanliness in their habitations, and general attention to their comfort and health, there will be little call for medical treatment of any kind; and in the rare cases which may occur, we would trust mainly to Nature, co-operating with her as we could by means of diet, air, exercise, and water, on the same principles precisely that are applied in the treatment of human beings without drugs.

The Water-Cure or Hydropathic system has not yet been extensively applied to animals; but so far as it has been adopted, it has produced the most satisfactory results; and for the benefit of such of our readers as may have lost their faith in drugs, and desire to make a trial of a more rational method, we lay before them the following essay, kindly furnished for this work by that distinguished physician and writer, R. T. Trall, M.D., Principal of the New York Hygeio-Therapeutic College.

II.—WATER-CURE FOR DOMESTIC ANIMALS.

BY R. T. TRALL, M.D.

The habits of domestic animals being, on the whole, less unphysiological than those of human beings, their diseases are, as a necessary consequence, less numerous and less complicated. They may all be grouped under the head of *fevers, inflam-*

mations, spasms or colics, fluxes, eruptions, and glandular affections. And for all of these disorders we are satisfied that proper attention to hygiene, as understood by the term Hydropathy or Water-Treatment, is as much superior to drug medication as it has proved to be in the case of human beings similarly affected.

Fever is easily known by the languor and lassitude which the animal manifests, with great indisposition to exercise, followed by chills or shivering, and this succeeded by preternatural heat on the surface, loss of appetite, furred tongue, frequent or hard or bounding pulse, etc. The animal should be placed in a clean, quiet, well-ventilated room, protected from currents of cold air in winter or the scorching rays of the sun in summer, and the temperature should be kept at a uniform and moderate degree continually.

When the skin becomes very hot, it should be washed or bathed all over, and a blanket or two immediately applied, so as to promote moderate perspiration. Or the wet sheet may be applied, taking care to cover it well with blankets, so as to arrest chilliness. When the sheet becomes quite warm, it should be removed, and the surface washed with cold water; and if the fever heat continues, it may be re-applied for an hour at a time, two or three times a day, until the morbid heat is entirely subdued.

The same general plan of treatment, with a slight modification, applies to all inflammatory complaints. With domestic animals as with human beings, the organs most liable to acute inflammation are the lungs and the bowels, and the only specialty of treatment in these affections, in addition to the general plan applicable to the constitutional disturbance we call fever, is the continual application of wet cloths well covered with dry ones to the chest or bowels, as either is the seat of the inflammation, and the employment of copious enemas of tepid water to free the bowels.

Spasmodic diseases of all kinds, and all the varieties of colic, are the results of local obstruction caused by over-exertion over-heating, or something improper or indigestible in the food. Grain, and especially Indian meal, fed to a horse while in a state of great heat or great fatigue from violent exertion, is frequently the immediate cause of colic and spasms. In these cases the animal should have his abdomen fomented with wet cloths applied as warm as can be borne; warm water should be given the animal to drink, or poured down his throat from a bottle, and copious enemas of warm water should be administered.

Fluxes—as *diarrhea, dysentery, cholera, influenza, catarrh,* etc.—are the indications of a general obstruction of the system or impurity of the fluids, with an effort at depuration in a particular direction. The usual practice of checking the discharge suddenly by pungents, stimulants, and astringents is always injurious and generally dangerous. On the contrary, the action of the surface should be restored by bathing, with friction or the dripping-sheet, and all irritating matters removed from the stomach and bowels by means of warm and tepid water, as in the case of colics. There will be no danger from the discharges if the cause is removed, and if it is not removed, the sudden suppression of the evacuations may terminate in a worse inflammation or speedy death.

Affections of the skin and glands are only to be cured by purifying the whole mass of blood. To repel an eruption from the surface, or rather a glandular tumor, is not curing the animal; indeed, it is only changing an external disease to an internal one. Thus attention to a pure diet, to fresh air, and to clean apartments, each and all are essential to recovery. Many of these *cachexies,* as they are called in medical books, originate from the effluvia of their own excretions, as in cases where the urine and feces are permitted to accumulate in the stalls, or under the floors of the stables.

VIII.

POULTRY.

Also fowls were prepared for me.—*Nehemiah* v. 18.

I.—THE DOMESTIC FOWL.

NOBODY knows when or by whom fowls were first domesticated. There are at most only two or three allusions to them in the Old Testament, and these are of doubtful import. In our motto, for instance, the word fowls may mean simply birds.

In the time of Aristotle, who wrote three hundred and fifty years before Christ, however, they were evidently common; for he speaks of them as familiarly as a naturalist of the present day. Everybody is familiar with the beautiful allusions to them in the New Testament.

The wild origin of our domestic fowl is entirely unknown. The race, like that of the Dodo, is probably extinct. The Wild Turkey will sooner or later share the same fate.

Crested or top-knotted fowls appear to have been unknown to the ancients. The earliest notice of them occurs in Aldrovandi, who speaks of a hen with "a crest like a lark."

Domestic fowls now abound in all warm and temperate climates, but disappear as we approach the poles. They were found in abundance on the islands of the Pacific Ocean by their earliest discoverers. How they got there nobody knows. Probably in the same way that their human inhabitants found their insular homes. Ellis, in his "Polynesian Researches," says: "The traditions of the people state that fowls have existed on the islands (Tahiti) as long as the people; that they came with the first colonists by whom the islands were peopled; or that they were made by Taarva at the same time that men were made."

The courage of the cock is emblematic, his gallantry admirable, his sense of discipline and subordination most exemplary. See how a good game-cock of two or three years' experience will, in five minutes, restore order into an uproarious poultry-yard! He does not use harsh means of coercion when mild will suit the purpose. A look, a gesture, a deep chuckling growl, gives the hint that turbulence is no longer to be permitted; and if these are not effectual, severer punishment is fearlessly administered. . . . . His politeness to females is as marked as were Lord Chesterfield's attentions to old ladies, and much more unaffected. Nor does he merely act the agreeable dangler; when occasion requires, he is also their brave defender, if he be good for anything.

"The hen is deservedly the acknowledged pattern of maternal love. When her passion of philoprogenitiveness is disappointed by the failure or subtraction of her brood, she will either go on sitting till her natural powers fail, or will violently kidnap the young of some other fowl and insist upon adopting them."*

The varieties of the domestic fowl are almost numberless, but only a few of them are worthy of more than a mere mention here. Among these we give the first place to—

1. *The Spanish Fowl.*—The thorough-bred Spanish fowl is entirely black, so far as feathers are concerned, with a greenish metallic luster. The combs of both the male and the female are very large and of a brilliant scarlet; that of the hen droops over on one side. Their most singular feature is a large white patch, or ear-lobe, on the cheek, which in some specimens extends over a large part of the face. It is a fleshy substance, similar to the wattle, and is small in the hens but large and conspicuous in the cocks, giving them a very striking appear-

---

* Rev. Edmund Saul Dixon.

Domestic Animals.

ance. There are few, if any, handsomer fowls than the genuine Spanish; although some that are called by that name, but are really nameless mongrels, are ugly enough for scarecrows.

The hens are great layers, being in this respect, we believe, superior to every other breed. Their eggs are very large, quite white, and of a peculiar shape, being quite thick at both ends, although tapering off a little at each. A correspondent of the *Country Gentleman*, relating his experience with them, says: "My last year's June pullets commenced to lay in December, and the first of February all of my Spanish hens laid more or less. I got, in the six months, from the first of March to the first of September, eighty-five dozen of eggs from seven pullets, and I now get from four to six eggs per day; and my honest

Fig. 30.

THE SPANISH FOWL.

conviction is, that the true Black Spanish hen will lay from 'five to ten per cent.' more weight of eggs than any other breed."

On the other hand, it must be confessed that these Spanish dames are not good mothers or nurses, even when they do sit, "which," as Dixon remarks, "they will not often condescend to do." This last trait of character will prove a recommendation rather than otherwise with those who care for eggs rather than chickens. When the latter are wanted, it is better to place the eggs under a hen of another and more motherly breed—a Dorking, for instance.

The Spanish fowls bear confinement very well; are not large eaters; grow rapidly; mature early; and are only excelled for the table by the Game fowl and the Dorking. The average weight of the mature birds is about six pounds for the male and five for the female.

It is important, but somewhat difficult at present, to procure the true, unmixed, white-faced Black Spanish breed.

There is another breed called the Gray or Speckled Spanish, but, however excellent they may be (and they are highly spoken of), they are probably a mixed breed.

2. *The Dorking Fowl.*—The Dorking takes its name from a town in Surrey County, England, where it is supposed to have originated.

The Dorkings are divided into the Colored and the White varieties; the former including the Gray, Speckled, Spangled, Japanned, etc. These are not *permanent* varieties, however, as they can not be bred true to color. The Gray and Spangled comprise the more common forms in which the Colored Dorking family is presented to us.

The White Dorking is a smaller-framed bird than the Gray, and should be perfectly white in plumage, bill, and legs. They should have rose-combs. They are less hardy than the colored variety, and not well adapted to a northern climate.

The Dorking is a fowl of rare beauty, large in size, symmetrical in form, and often gorgeous in plumage. Its flesh is white, firm, and of excellent flavor; and for the general purposes of the table it is inferior to none, although, as regards flavor alone, the Game fowl would perhaps take precedence.

As layers, the Dorking hens take high rank, but are, we think, inferior to the Spanish. They are persistent sitters, and make excellent mothers and nurses. The editor of the *American*

Fig. 31.

THE DORKING FOWL.

Agriculturist says: "A little knowledge in keeping them [the Dorkings] justified us in pronouncing them entitled to the same rank among barn-yard fowls that the Short Horns have taken among cattle; and years of experience in breeding them have confirmed us in this opinion."

John Giles, a well known poultry breeder of Woodstock, Conn., expresses the following opinion: "After forty-odd years' experience with the gallinaceous tribes, I say that, in my humble opinion, no breed of fowls will compare with the true Dorking as good mothers, sitters, and layers, giving eggs in abundance, chickens easily reared, and which come to perfection sooner than any other poultry. The flesh is of a delicate white, fine in the grain, and delicious flavor. The Black Spanish is only second to the true Dorking, in not raising their own young, seldom or ever wanting to sit; but what they lose in that point is more than made up by the abundance of eggs By some they are called the everlasting layers; eggs large; flesh and skin beautifully white and juicy; chickens grow rapidly."

A cross between the Dorking and the Game fowl is greatly esteemed, and is thought to be more profitable than the thorough-bred Dorking.

The possession of the fifth claw is generally considered as an essential characteristic of the Dorking, but it is not always present, and might and should be "bred out." The weight of the Dorking at maturity varies from five to eight pounds.

3. *The Polish Fowl.*—The origin of this family of fowls is entirely unknown. They do not exist in Poland at the present time, and there is no evidence that they were ever known there; but this is a matter of small moment. Their beauty

Fig. 32.

THE POLISH FOWL.

and excellence are undisputed. The large top-knot is one of the principal characteristics of the Polish fowl, and is conspicuous in all its varieties.

The varieties of the Polish or Poland fowl are numerous; but the principal ones are the White-Crested Black, the Golden Spangled, and the Silver Spangled.

In the White-Crested Black Poland cock the plumage, with the exception of the crest, should be uniformly black, with rich metallic tints of green. The shorter crest feathers at the base of the bill are black, the rest of the purest white. The beak and legs are generally black. The same colors are required in the hen. Their form and bearing are remarkably good. The cock should weigh from five to five and a half pounds, and the hen about four pounds.

The Golden Spangled and the Silver Spangled Polands are splendid birds. "The beautiful regularity of their markings, the vivid contrasts in their colors, together with their unique appearance generally, entitle them to the first rank among the more ornamental varieties."

The Polands, and especially the Black variety, are generally but not invariably great layers, commencing early in the spring, and seldom wanting to sit till late in the summer, if at all. They can not always be depended upon to hatch a *clutch* of chickens, even when they manifest a desire to sit, frequently deserting the nest after five or six days' occupation.* They are not quite so hardy as some other breeds, but with a fair degree of attention are easily reared. As a table fowl, the Polish is among the best.

4. *The Hamburg Fowl.*—Of the Hamburgs there are several varieties. The Silver Penciled, known also as the Bolton Gray, have the plumage white, with the exception of the wings and tail, which are furred with black. The average weight of the cock is about four and a half pounds. The hen usually weighs about a pound less. The Golden Penciled Hamburg

---

* Wingfield,

differs from the Silver Penciled chiefly in the ground color of its plumage, which is a yellowish buff or yellowish bay, and in being rather larger. The legs of both these varieties should be blue. The Silver Spangled and Golden Spangled differ from the Penciled sorts, in having black, circular, oval, or crescent-shaped spangles on the tail and wing, instead of bars. They are somewhat larger than the Penciled birds and have darker

Fig. 83.

THE SILVER SPANGLED HAMBURG FOWL.

legs. The Black Hamburg has a plumage of a uniformly rich, glossy-green black.

All the Hamburgs are beautiful fowls, rich in plumage and fine in form; great layers (the eggs, however, are small); seldom desire to sit; and are good for the table, falling but little below the best varieties in this respect, although not so large as some others.

They are impatient of confinement, and to do well must have

Fig. 34.

THE GOLDEN SPANGLED HAMBURG FOWL.

a wide range of grassy lawn or pasture. Of the different varieties we prefer the Golden Spangled, but others may choose differently.

5. *The Dominique Fowl.*—This is a very common breed in

Fig. 35.

THE DOMINIQUE COCK.

this country, but none the less valuable or beautiful on that account.

"The prevailing and true color of the Dominique fowl is a lightish ground, barred crosswise, and softly shaded with a slaty-blue, as indicated in the portrait of the cock figured on the previous page. The comb is variable, some being single, while others are double—most, however, are single. The iris, bright orange; feet, legs, and bill, bright yellow; and some light flesh color. We prefer the yellow legs and bill, and consider them well worthy of promotion in the poultry-yard.

"We seldom see bad hens of this variety; and take them 'all-in-all,' we do not hesitate in pronouncing them *one* of the *best* and most profitable fowls, being hardy, good layers, careful nurses, and affording excellent eggs, and the quality of their flesh highly esteemed. The hens are not large, but plump and full breasted. The eggs average about two ounces each, and are of porcelain whiteness."*

6. *The Leghorn Fowl.*—The Leghorns are believed to be cousins of the Spanish, whom they resemble in general form. They have been considerably experimented with in this country, and are highly extolled by some breeders; but the general verdict is that they are inferior to the Spanish.†

7. *The Shanghai Fowl.*—The Shanghai fowl was originally brought from the northern part of China, particularly about the city of Shanghai, from which it takes its name. It is the common domestic fowl of that part of the country.

The Shanghai cock is a large, bold, upright bird, strongly distinguished for the length, loudness, hoarseness, and awkwardness of his half guttural crow. Most of the sub-varieties

---

* Country Gentleman.

† A correspondent of one of the agricultural papers, however, gives the following testimony in their favor: "I have kept in different inclosures six of the most approved varieties of fowls, for four months (from the 1st of April to the present)—have registered the number of eggs laid by each variety every day, and the Leghorns have laid almost three eggs to any other bird's one not excepting the far famed Black Spanish."—R. W. PEARSALL, *Har'em*, N Y

128   DOMESTIC ANIMALS.

have large, single, serrated combs, the top running considerably beyond its point of attachment to the head. His neck is about nine inches long, and is somewhat arched; wings short, rounded outward, their shoulders concealed in the breast-feathers, and their tips covered by the body-feathers and the saddle-hackle. His breast is broad, but wanting in fullness; the thighs are wide apart, large, comparatively short, smooth in

Fig. 86.

THE SHANGHAI FOWL.

some, in others heavily feathered quite down to the knees; shanks should be short, and, with the booted, more or less feathered down the outer edge, quite to the end of the outer toe; the stern is densely covered with long downy feathers, technically called "fluff," well rounded out; the hackle, both of neck and saddle, is long and abundant; while the tail is short and sometimes covered by the long saddle-feathers. The weight of a full-grown bird is from ten to twelve pounds, while a few have weighed more. The hen agrees in general character with that of her liege lord, but is two or three pounds lighter.

The legs of both sexes should be yellow, though we have seen some very fine white birds with a greenish-blue leg, and superior black ones with dark legs.

The principal sub-varieties of the Shanghai family are the White, the Buff, the Cinnamon, the Partridge-colored, the Gray, or Brahmapootra of a few writers, the Dominique, and the Black.

About ten years ago there raged among our fowl fanciers a most alarming Shanghai fever. It had its "run," and its victims mostly survived. We presume they will never have a second attack.

We can not advise our readers to breed Shanghai fowls, and regret being obliged to mention them at all.

8. *The Cochin China Fowl, etc.*—A missionary in China says: "There is no difference at all between the Shanghais and Cochin Chinas. In reality they *all* are Shanghais. Cochin Chinese fowls are a *small, inferior* kind, not equal to the natives of the United States, and it is not believed that any have ever been taken to America;" and the editors of the "Poultry Book," lately published in London, quote from a letter they received from Mr. Robert Fortune, who has passed many years in various parts of China, as follows: "I firmly believe that what are called 'Cochin Chinas' and 'Shanghais' are one and the same."

Whether this testimony should be considered conclusive or not we leave the reader to judge, and believing none of the uncouth, awkward, and coarse-grained Asiatic fowls desirable, we herewith dismiss them.

9. *The Bantam Fowl.*—The Bantam is the smallest specimen of fowl, and may with propriety be called the Tom Thumb of the gallinaceous tribe, and stands comparatively, in size, to the Malay and Cochin fowl as that of the noble and stately Du-

ham to the diminutive Alderney cow. Though extremely small in size, the Bantam cock is elegantly formed, and remark-

Fig. 37.

WHITE BANTAM COCK AND HEN.

able for his grotesque figure, his courageous and passionate temper, his amusing pompousness of manner, his overweening assumption and arrogance; and his propensity to make fight, and force every rival to "turn tail," has caused him many difficulties.

The Bantam must be considered more as an object of curios-

Fig. 38.

BLACK BANTAM COCK AND HEN.

ity than utility, and of course must expect to be received with no peculiar favor, in this country, except as a "pet." They arrive at maturity early, are faithful sitters, good mothers, and will lay more eggs, though small, than any other variety. They are very domestic, often making their nests in the kitchen, depositing their eggs in the cradle or cupboard of the dwelling when permitted.*

The most beautiful of the Bantams is the Seabright, of which there are two sub-varieties—the Gold-laced and the Silver-laced.

The ground color of the Gold-laced should be a clear, golden, yellow-white; while in the Silver-laced it should be a pure silvery-white. The accompanying cut will give the reader a good idea of the form and bearing of these remarkable and beautiful fowls, as well as of the markings of their plumage.

The Seabright Bantam is emphatically the English gentleman's Bantam. Even lords and duchesses strive for the mastery in breeding this beautiful bird. This bird was first bred

Fig. 39.

THE SEABRIGHT BANTAM.

and introduced to the notice of English fanciers by the late Sir John Seabright, from whom they received their name.†

---

* Bement.   † Country Gentleman.

10. *The Game Fowl.*—The Game fowl is hardy, easily kept, and extra good for the table. The hens are fair layers, excellent sitters, exemplary mothers, and in every way well behaved

Fig. 40.

GAME COCK AND HEN.

fowls. The cocks have the reputation of being quarrelsome and tyrannical; but those who have studied their character most closely are of the opinion that, on this ground, they have been unjustly condemned. They are brave and powerful, but not pugnacious or vindictive. Bement says: "For those who do not wish to give much attention to fowls, there is, according to our opinion, no breed equal to the Game."

11. *Mongrel Fowls.*—The collections usually known under the name of Barn-door fowls or Dunghill fowls are merely rabbles of mongrels, in which the results of accidental or injudicious crosses have become apparent in all sorts of ways. There is a tendency among them to revert back to some one of the original breeds, and good fowls for all common uses are often found among them.

12. *Choice of Breed.*—We have mentioned the leading characteristics of the different kinds of fowls, in order to enable the reader to decide which is best adapted to his purpose. Were our advice asked in reference to the choice of a breed, we would recommend the Spanish where eggs are to be made the prin-

cipal object, and the Gray Dorking where chickens are wanted for the table or for market. In reference to merely ornamental poultry, let "fancy" rule.

13. *Accommodations.*—No one should attempt to keep fowls without providing for them the proper accommodations to insure their comfort and health. These need not be expensive. A very simple house with appropriate accessories in the form of a yard, nests, feeding troughs, water basins or fountains, roosts, etc., can all be very cheaply furnished; or they may be more extensive, elaborate, and costly, if the proprietor's wants require and his means permit. For plans and descriptions of these structures we must refer the reader to "The House," which forms another number of this series of manuals. We need only say here that they should be such as to secure warmth and efficient shelter from storms, without excluding light or air, both of which are essential to the well-being of fowls as well as human beings.

"Most farmers," Mr. Bement truly says, "pay little or no attention to their fowls, suffering them to roam and run about when and where they please; to lay and hatch where it suits them best, and to roost on trees, under sheds, on the wagon, cart, hay-rigging, etc.—soiling by their droppings plows, harrows, or whatever may chance to be within reach. This treatment is no less unprofitable than inhuman. No wonder such farmers get no eggs during the winter, and generally come to the conclusion that poultry keeping does not 'pay.'"

Whatever may be the form or size of your poultry-house, it should be so constructed as to secure as equable a temperature as possible. This end is best attained by having the walls and roof lined, leaving an open space of from four to six inches between the outer and inner walls, which may be filled in with chaff, saw-dust, or dry tan. This will make it warm in winter and cool in summer. In addition to the inclosed portion, the house should have a broad piazza or shed attached, to which the fowls may retire for shelter in stormy weather.

Hens always seek to avoid observation when laying, and it is well to gratify this natural feeling in the construction of their nests. A screen of lattice-work in front of the boxes, or a few evergreen boughs properly placed, will secure the required seclusion without preventing the circulating of the air.

In reference to the poultry-yard Mr. Bement says:

"Where it is intended to keep a large number of fowls, let the yard be of ample dimensions, which of course must be regulated by the number intended to be kept. Those contracted seven-by-nine pens which meet our eyes throughout the country are not calculated to answer the purpose for which they were intended. Half an acre, at least, for every hundred fowls (and more than that number should never be kept in one flock), is little space enough for them to roam in; and in order to unite all the advantages desirable in a poultry-yard, it is indispensable that it neither be too cold during winter nor too hot during summer; and it must be rendered so attractive to the hens as to prevent their laying in any chance place away from it. To shield them from the chilling blasts of winter and the scorching rays of the sun in summer, we would recommend planting evergreens on the borders of the yard, and shade trees in the center. This, with a good covering of grass, would leave little to be desired on that part. And if the fowls can have access to a grass field occasionally, and the soil *dry*, then, so far as the ground and situation are concerned, nothing to be wished for remains.

"A picket fence, from six to seven feet high, will be sufficient to prevent the fowls from flying over."

14. *Feeding.*—The fowl is as omnivorous as a pig or a man, and perhaps a little more so; nevertheless grain is their staple. Of this they ought to have a variety, as they do not thrive so well when fed constantly with one kind. Corn, wheat, barley, oats, and buckwheat make good feed for them. It is better to have all kinds of grain, intended for feeding fowls, and especially corn, coarsely ground or cracked. It will be found that they require a smaller quantity in this state. It should be scalded, or at least mixed to the consistency of a stiff batter

with water, before feeding it to them. Vegetables, such as potatoes, carrots, parsneps, beets, etc., boiled and mashed, are acceptable and wholesome. Lettuce, cabbage, Scotch kale, etc., chopped up fine, are excellent for all kinds of poultry in the winter. A few chopped onions may occasionally be added; and also a little flesh-meat, either raw or cooked, cut into small pieces.

The editor of the *Country Gentleman* thinks that it is better to feed poultry in winter from three to four times daily, than twice, which is the ordinary custom. By frequent feeding, the birds eat but a little at a time, and never injure themselves; but when fed but once or twice daily, there is danger of their overeating, which frequently produces fatal results. Our rule is, to so regulate the quantity given at each time, that each fowl shall have all it wishes, and have nothing left. Our experience confirms what many have said, that regular and frequent feeding is better for the health of the fowl, at any season of the year, than it is to fill a vessel with grain and allow them access to it at all times. We also think that poultry will eat less with frequent feeding than by twice feeding daily.

Lime is necessary for the formation of egg-shells, and should always be accessible. The best form is that of calcined oyster shells, pounded in small fragments. A box of sand and gravel, and another of ashes, should be added.

Pure water is another essential that can not be too strenuously insisted upon, impure water being a grand source of the diseases of poultry.

Cleanliness must be strictly attended to in all your arrangements for fowls; and the inside of the poultry-house should be whitewashed twice, at least, during the year, as a preventive against vermin.

15. *Incubation, and Rearing Chickens.*—For sitting, choose good-sized hens. Those with short legs, broad body, and large wings are best adapted to the duty. It is also generally remarked that the worst layers are the best sitters. All the eggs for a brood, which should not exceed thirteen, should be

so nearly as possible of the same age. None of them should be more than ten days old; and the reason why they should be of about the same date is, that they may be hatched simultaneously. Select eggs of average size and ordinary shape. Give the hen a quiet place to sit, and take care that she be not disturbed. In twenty-one days (sometimes a day or two earlier in warm weather) a good sitter will bring out the chicks. The first day after hatching they do not want food and should be left in the nest. The next day they may be put into a good coop in a dry, sheltered situation, and fed with coarse cornmeal mixed up with water, hard-boiled eggs chopped fine, or fresh curd. Feed a little at a time and often, and beware of overfeeding. When a little older, cracked corn, millet, wheat, barley, etc., may be fed to them. Have plenty of pure water in a shallow dish (so that they may drink without getting into it and wetting their feathers) always before them. After five or six days they may be allowed to range at will outside of the coop, but should not be allowed to come out while the dew is on the ground. When two or three weeks old, or, indeed, with the hardier breeds much earlier, the hen may be permitted to lead them out. The most important caution now is to guard them well against sudden unfavorable changes of temperature, and especially against cold rain-storms.

16. *The Poultry Pentalogue.*—Somebody in England has written a little work which he calls the "Poultry Pentalogue," in which the whole art of fowl-breeding is summed up in five grand rules:

1. Pure breed;
2. A constant infusion of fresh blood, and the careful avoidance of in-and-in breeding;
3. A varied diet;
4. Equable temperature; and—
5. Strict cleanliness.

Good rules and easily remembered. We commend them to our readers, who may profitably apply them to other stock besides fowls.

II.—THE GUINEA FOWL.

"There is no doubt," Wingfield says, "from the description given by Columella and Varro, that the Guinea fowl was reared on the farms of the Romans, and that it was first made known to them during their wars in Africa." They have hardly found the favor among poultry keepers that their merits would warrant. They are prolific layers of excellent eggs, and as table birds are by no means to be despised. They are shy, and love to make their nests in dark, obscure places, far

Fig. 41.

THE GUINEA FOWL.

from home; for which reason their eggs are generally placed under a common hen to be hatched and fostered. They give no notice of laying or sitting.

A brood of Guinea fowls is an excellent guard. They love roosting in the trees; and at night, if any footstep disturb them, their loud cries are sure to give notice to the farmer that a trespass is committing.

The Guinea fowl is delicate eating, and is in fine season about

Lent. The young chickens must be treated in the same manner and with the same food as young turkeys, and they must be kept warm and dry. In fatting, they should be shut up in a house for a fortnight, and fed four or five times a day with sweet barley-meal, moistened with milk and good lard. They pine if confined any length of time.

The great drawbacks to the rearing of Guinea fowls are the vigilance required to watch for their nest, and the harsh screaming of their cry.

III.—THE DOMESTIC TURKEY.

The domestic turkey is not so far removed from the wild state as the domestic fowl. There is no dispute about his origin, the wild turkey not being yet extinct, and not differing so widely from the tenants of our barn-yards as to give room for doubt on that point. In fact, as it is stated in the "American Poulterer's Companion," if kept in the neighborhood of large forests they will often stroll thither, without any design to return, such is the natural wildness of their species.

We have three varieties of the domestic turkey in this country—the Black, the Buff-colored, and the White. The Black is generally preferred, it being the most hardy. The Buff-colored is placed next in the order of merit. The White variety is very beautiful, but is smaller and less hardy.

Turkeys are generally considered very difficult to rear; and it is undoubtedly true that considerable care, patience, and skill are required to insure uniform success. Mr. Bement says: "If attempts to rear turkeys have not been crowned with success, it is entirely owing to the unskillfulness and inexperience of those to whom they have been intrusted; and so long as one persists in thwarting the females when sitting; in opening the shells of the eggs in order to help the passage of the tardy chicks; in pressing them, so soon as they are born, to eat against their will; and in leaving them exposed to intense heat, or to cold and dampness, so long will their death, in the course of a month, be the undoubted consequence. It is less trouble to say the breed is difficult to rear, than to acknowledge at once that negligence, unskillfulness, and barbarity are the causes."

The principal requisites for the successful rearing of turkeys, according to the experienced author of the "Poulterer's Companion," are:

1. Good stock to breed from, both male and female. Both should be large and fully grown. They ought to be at least two years old.

2. Fresh blood, secured by changing the cock every year.

3. Good keeping through the winter.

4. No unnecessary interference with the process of incubation, which lasts four weeks.

5. Shelter, protection, and careful feeding of the chicks for a few weeks, after which the mother may be liberated from the coop to lead them out.

Curd chopped fine, crumbs of bread softened in water or milk, are good for their first food; but they will soon eat anything that is fit for the parent turkey, except unbroken grain.

Early in the fall they should be fed night and morning with dry corn; and when the weather becomes colder they may profitably be supplied at frequent intervals with boiled potatoes, mashed with corn meal and skimmed milk, given to them warm. On this diet they will grow and fatten rapidly.

The turkey is an out-door bird and requires, at most, only an open shed for shelter during severe storms, and even this will seldom be occupied if a good tree be at hand. They have not yet acquired all the effeminate artificial habits of the domestic fowl.

The critical periods with the turkey are about the third day after they are hatched, and when they have thrown out the "red head," as it is called, which they do when about six weeks old. To carry them safely through the first, avoid overfeeding, and secure them against unfavorable changes of temperature. In the latter case, give them a plenty of food, and render it as nutritious as possible by adding boiled eggs, wheaten grits, bruised hemp seed, or bruised beans.

140   DOMESTIC ANIMALS.

Cobbett says: "As to fattening turkeys, the best way is to never let them get poor. Barley meal mixed with skimmed milk and given them fresh will make them fat in a short time. Boiled potatoes mixed with corn meal will furnish a change of sweet food which they relish much, and of which they may eat as much as they can."

IV.—THE DOMESTIC GOOSE.

The domestic goose has acknowledged the sway of man for ages—perhaps since the days of Noah. Homer mentions them, where Penelope, relating her dream, says: "I have twenty geese at home, that eat wheat out of water, and I am delighted to look at them." Their cackling, it will be remembered, saved

Fig 42.

EMBDEN OR BREMEN GEESE.

Rome from the Gauls, B.C. 388. Their wild original is unknown, the wild geese of the present day being of a different species.

Of the common domestic goose there is really but one variety divided into several sub-varieties, marked by more or less permanent distinctive characteristics—of these the Toulouse goose and the Bremen goose are probably the best. The former is gray and the latter white. The White China goose probably belongs to a distinct species. It is a beautiful bird, but comes properly under the head of ornamental poultry, of which we have little to say. It can be kept with advantage only in a warm climate.

Where there are facilities for keeping them, geese are considered the most profitable of all our domestic birds. The chief requisites for goose keeping are a pond or pool of water and a pasture for grazing.

The domestic gander is polygamous, but should not, Mormon-like, be allowed an unlimited number of wives. Three is sufficient, and some recommend to allow only two geese to each gander. Comfortable and well-ventilated apartments should be provided for geese, so constructed as to secure them against rats, weasels, skunks, etc. A separate room for the sitting goose is desirable. Her period of incubation is about thirty days. Thirteen eggs are the usual number given to the goose. She always covers them when absent from the nest.

"On the first day after the goslings are hatched," Mr. Bement says, "they may be let out, if the weather be warm, care being taken not to let them be exposed to the unshaded heat of the sun, which might kill them. The food given them is prepared with some barley or Indian meal coarsely ground, bran, and raspings of bread, which are still better if soaked and boiled in milk, or lettuce leaves and crusts of bread boiled in milk. On the second day a fresh-cut turf is placed before them, and its fine blades of grass or clover are the first objects which seem to tempt their appetites. A little boiled hominy and rice, with bread crumbs, form their food for the first few days, fresh water in a shallow vessel, which they can dabble in and out without difficulty, being duly provided. Afterward advantage must be taken of a fine warm sun to turn them out on grass for a few hours; but if cold and damp, they should remain in their house, in which every attention should be paid to cleanliness by a constant supply of clean straw. After two weeks we cease these special precautions against exposure to the weather, and find them perfectly able to shift for themselves, in company with their mothers and the others of their race. For some weeks, however, extra supplies of food, such as bran or corn meal mixed with boiled or steamed vegetables, may be given them twice a day, morning and evening, continuing to give them this food till the wings begin to cross on the back, and after this, green food, which may be mixed with it, such as lettuce, cabbage, beet leaves, and such like. The pond is strictly forbidden them under all circumstances for the first two weeks, and in severer weather for a longer period. Exposure to heavy rain out of doors, and a damp floor in the house where they are placed at night, are the main hazards to be avoided."

One of the greatest sources of profit in goose keeping is the sale of the feathers; but plucking them from the living geese is a practice so full of cruelty that we can not conscientiously give any directions for the process. A writer in one of the magazines recommends *shearing* instead of plucking. He says: "Feathers are but of a year's growth, and in the moulting season they spontaneously fall off, and are supplied by a fresh fleece. When, therefore, the geese are in full feather, let the plumage be removed, very close to the skin, by sharp scissors, clipping them off as sheep are shorn; they will be renewed at moulting in the usual course of nature. The produce would not be much reduced in quantity, while the quality would be greatly improved, and an indemnification be experienced in the consciousness of not having tortured the poor bird, and in the uninjured health of the fowl, and the benefit obtained in the succeeding crop. After this operation shall have been performed, the down from the breast may be removed by the same means."

V.—THE DOMESTIC DUCK.

The origin of the tame duck is not a well settled point. Dixon supposes it to have been imported from India and China in or about the year 1493.

Of the numerous varieties known to the poulterer, Mr. Giles, of Woodstock, Conn., whom we have already had occasion to quote, recommends, for those who desire to keep ducks for use and not for ornament merely, the Rouen, the Java, and the Aylesbury.

The Rouen duck, originally from Rouen, France, is of a dark-brown plumage; legs and feet a dark dusky red; bill at the base black, tapering down toward the point a dark green, sometimes streaked with yellow; long in the body, with a small neck. The drakes are invariably the color of the wild Mallard drake, having a white ring around the neck; legs and feet a bright red; bill a bright yellow; flesh darker and higher flavored than the common duck. Very prolific, hardy, and easy to raise; will weigh at full maturity from eighteen to twenty pounds a pair.

The Java duck, originally from Java. Plumage a glossy black; neck long; round body; legs and feet black, and black bill. Drakes are black, head and neck bordering on a dark green; yellow bill; with bright red legs and feet. The Java ducks will attain to nearly the same weight as the Rouens—flesh similar.

The Aylesbury duck, originally from the town of Aylesbury, England. Plumage a beautiful white, with white bill; legs and feet a bright pink, ornamental in appearance; easy to propagate; producing white downy feathers, white skin, and delicate, savory flesh; will weigh from fifteen to eighteen pounds the pair. Sit the eggs under hens, and have them hatch out early. With care you can have large ducks.

The Wild Mallard duck is often domesticated. It is a very beautiful bird and becomes quite tame, rearing broods like the common duck; but no permanent tame race has yet been derived from them.

The Musk or Brazilian duck is from the tropical regions of South America. It is a singular bird in appearance and in habits, but we see little to recommend it, either for use or ornament.

The Wood duck, the most beautiful of its genus, so common in all parts of the North American continent, is also easily domesticated. It also will breed in its domesticated state.

Ducks are easily kept where there is access to a pond, pool, stream, or swamp. They will eat almost anything, animal or vegetable. The refuse of the kitchen garden is always acceptable to them, and where grass is not attainable, something of this kind must be regularly supplied.

"The duck-house," Bement says, "should, if possible, be of brick, and paved with the same material, with considerable inclination, so that the wet, when the floor is sluiced down, may at once pass off. Wood is seldom secure against rats, and does not so well suit the cleaning process of water and the lime-brush, and few places require their application more frequently. Do not crowd your birds, and always arrange for good ventilation. When the flock is large, separate the young ones, that they may thus have the advantage of better food, and that no risk may be incurred of finding the eggs of the older ones trodden under foot and broken at your morning visit. On this account the laying ducks should always have plenty of room, and be kept by themselves. Ducks, for these reasons, as well as for the sake of cleanliness, should never share the habitation of fowls, and from geese they are liable to persecution. Yet, where fowls are kept, a little contrivance will suffice to make their berth, even in a fowl-house, tolerably comfortable. In winter, a thin bedding of straw or rushes should be placed on the floor, and frequently changed."

The duck is a prolific layer, and her eggs are very rich and highly flavored, and are much relished by some persons. One duck's egg is considered of equal culinary value to two fowl's eggs.

According to Mr. Parmentier, one drake is sufficient for

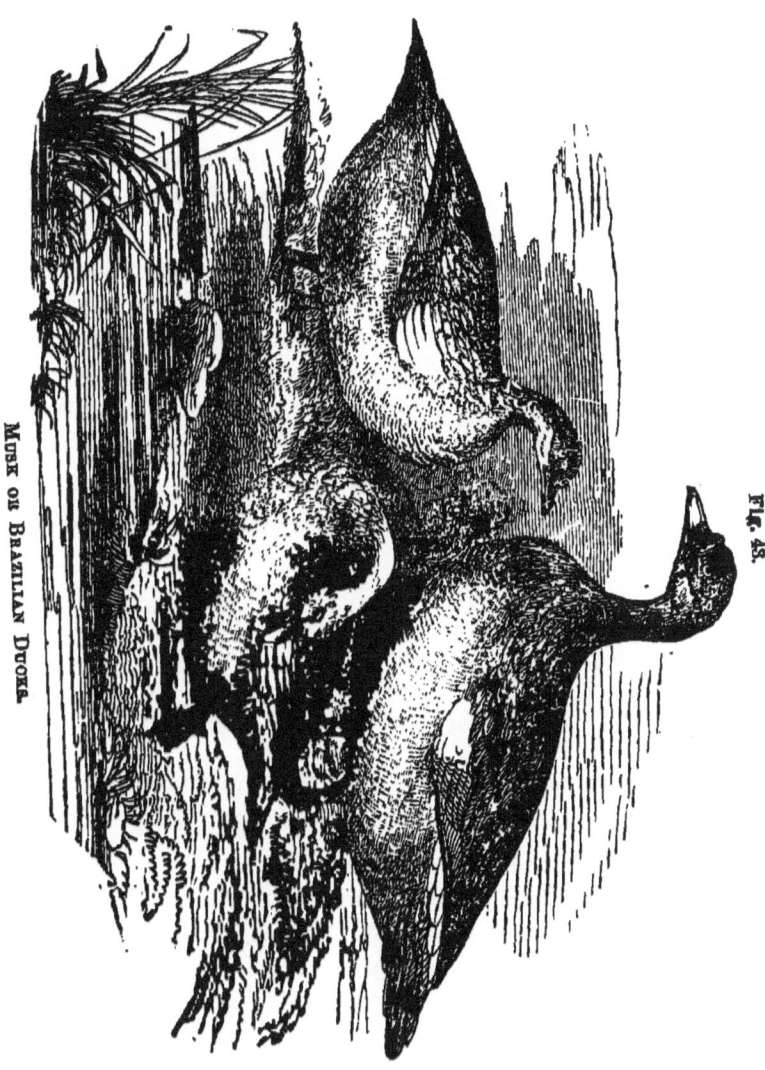

Fig. 43.—Musk or Brazilian Ducks.

eight or ten ducks, but others limit the number to from four to six.

Ducks are not so easily persuaded to lay in nests prepared for them, but prefer to choose a place out-of-doors to deposit their eggs. If the nest selected be tolerably secure, it is better to allow them to sit there than to attempt their removal. Thirteen eggs are a full allowance for a duck, and these should be as fresh as possible. The period of incubation varies considerably, but twenty-eight days is perhaps about the average time. The treatment of the young brood should be similar to that recommended for goslings. Boiled potatoes and hominy, or coarse corn meal, make excellent food for them. It is better to give them no uncooked food for several weeks after they are hatched.

To fatten ducks you must give them a plenty of good grain (corn and oats are to be preferred), and not allow them access to too much garbage. All fish and flesh, and especially putrid animal matter, of which they are fond, must be excluded from their diet, or the flavor of their flesh will be destroyed.

VI.—PREPARATION OF POULTRY FOR MARKET.

Messrs. Drew & French, extensive dealers in farm and market-garden produce, fruits, eggs, poultry, etc., 85 Barclay Street, New York, in answer to various inquiries addressed to them, carefully prepared and published, some time ago, the following directions, which should be as carefully followed by all who send poultry to the city markets and wish to get the highest price for it:

"*First*—Give no food for twenty-four hours previous to killing. Food in the crop is liable to sour, and always injures the sale. Purchasers object to paying for undigested food.

"*Second*—'Sticking' in the neck with a penknife is the best mode of killing. If the head is cut off, the skin recedes, and the neck bone looks repulsive.

"*Third*—Most of the poultry coming to this market is badly scalded' or 'wet picked.' 'Dry picked' is preferred, and sells a little higher, other things being equal. Great care should be taken in picking to remove all the pin-feathers, and to avoid tearing the skin, particularly upon the legs, where it is most likely to be broken. If properly scalded, it looks best.

"*Fourth*—The intestines should not be drawn. After picking, the head may be taken off, and the skin drawn over the neck bone and tied. This is best, though much comes with heads on.

"*Fifth*—Next in order, it should be 'plumped,' by being dipped about two seconds into water nearly or quite boiling hot, and then at once into cold water about the same length of time. Some think the hot plunge sufficient without the cold. It should be entirely cold but not frozen, before being packed. If it reaches market sound without freezing, it will sell all the better.

"*Sixth*—For packing, if practicable, use clean hand-threshed rye straw. If this can not be had, wheat or oat straw will answer, if clean and free from dust. Place a layer of straw at the bottom of the box, then alternate layers of poultry and straw—taking care to stow snugly, backs upward, filling vacancies with straw, and filling the package so that the cover will draw down snugly upon the contents. Boxes holding not over 300 lbs. are the best packages.

"*Seventh*—Number the packages; mark the contents of each on the cover; place the invoice of the lot in one package, marked 'bill,' sending duplicate by mail; direct plainly to the consignee, placing the name of the consigner in one corner."

IX.

BEE-KEEPING.

> Oh, Nature kind! Oh, laborer wise!
>   That roam'st along the summer ray,
> Glean'st ev'ry bliss thy life supplies,
>   And meet'st prepar'd thy wintry day:
> Go—envied, go—with crowded gates,
> The hive thy rich return awaits;
> Bear home thy store in triumph gay,
> And shame each idler on thy way.—*Anon.*

I.—THE WONDERS OF THE BEE-HIVE.

THE accounts given, by naturalists and writers on bee-keeping, of the instincts and habits of the bee seem truly fabulous; and yet they are all founded on observation, and there seems to be no reason for calling them in question.

A hive of bees, we are told, consists of three kinds—females, males, and workers. The females are called queens, and only

Fig. 44.

THE QUEEN BEE.

Fig. 45.

THE DRONE.

one is permitted to live in the same hive; but one is essential to its establishment and maintenance. The males are called drones, and may exist in hundreds, or even thousands, in a hive. The workers, or neuters, are the most numerous, and perform all the labor, collecting the honey, secreting the wax, and building the cells. The females and workers have stings at the end of the abdomen, but the drones have none. The queen lives in the interior of the hive, and seldom leaves it except to lead forth a swarm. If she be removed from the hive, the whole swarm will follow her. The queen is not only the governor, but also the mother of the community, she being the only breeder out of 20,000 or 30,000 bees, on which account she is loved, respected, and obeyed with all the external marks of devotion which human beings could give to a beloved monarch.

Fig. 46.

THE WORKER.

The queen deposits her eggs in cells previously prepared by the workers to receive them. The eggs producing workers are deposited in six-sided horizontal cells; the cells of the drones are somewhat irregular; those of the queens are larger than the others, circular, and hang perpendicularly. The eggs producing workers are laid first, the queen laying about two hundred eggs daily. The eggs of the drones afterward laid are less numerous than those of the workers, in the proportion of about one to thirty. Eggs for queens are deposited in their proper cells,

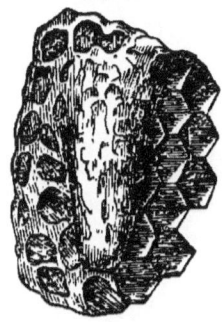

Fig. 47.

A ROYAL CELL.

one in each, at intervals of one or two days. The eggs and larvæ of the royal family do not differ in appearance from those of the workers, but the young are more carefully nursed, and fed with a more stimulating kind of food called "royal jelly," which causes them to grow so rapidly that in five days the larva is prepared to spin its web, and on the sixteenth day becomes a perfect queen. But as only one queen can reign in the hive, the young ones are kept close prisoners; and carefully guarded against the attacks of the queen mother so long as there is any prospect of her leading out a swarm. When the old queen departs with a swarm, a young one is liberated, who immediately seeks the destruction of her sisters, but is prevented by the guards. If she lead forth another swarm, a second queen is liberated, and so on until further swarming is considered impossible, when the reigning queen is permitted to destroy her sisters. In cases where no new swarm is to be sent off, the queen mother is permitted to assume the office of destroyer. If at any time two queens happen to come out simultaneously, it is said that a mortal combat takes place at once, and the victor is acknowledged to be the rightful sovereign. On the loss of a queen, the whole swarm is thrown into the greatest confusion, and if there be no worker eggs or brood out of which a queen can be made by the peculiar process of feeding already mentioned, all labor ceases and the bees soon die.

There are three substances for which the bees forage the fields. First, a resin, or gum, which is on trees; next, the pollen, or fine dust, of flowers; and lastly, the saccharine matter that is in the flowers. When the cells are to be built, they bring home the resin, and stop all the cracks or crevices in the hive, so that neither the rain nor any insect can get in to trouble them. Then they set forth to bring materials for wax, to construct their cells. The wax is made from pollen. The bees swallow it, and then hang themselves in festoons in the hive. In the course of twenty-four hours small rings make their appearance on the body. Then the bee detaches itself from the rest of the group, and, descend-

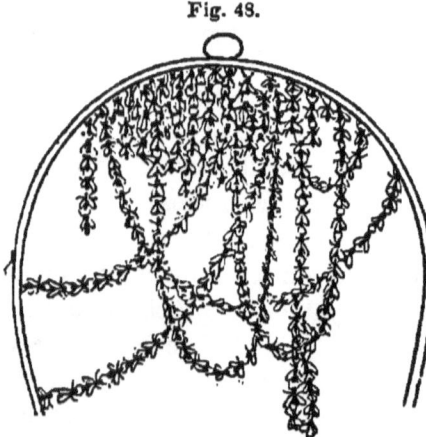

Fig. 48.

FESTOONS OF BEES SECRETING WAX.

BEE-KEEPING.

ing to the bottom of the hive, removes the substance which has now become wax. Each bee follows in its turn, and deposits its contribution, which is directly made use of by the architects in building the cells.

A WAX-WORKER.

The honey-cells are all six-sided, and of the most perfect regularity. Were they squares, or triangles, or circles, they would not fit as closely together, consequently there would be a waste of room.

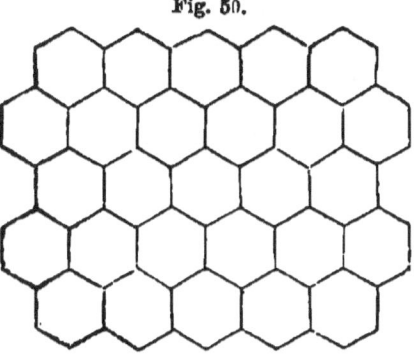

CELLS.

"There is a substance called bee bread, which is necessary to the life of the bee. It is made from pollen, but is entirely unlike wax. In securing it, the bee darts into a flower, and covers its body with the yellow dust. Now it must contrive some way to get rid of it, and God has made the last joint but one of each leg like a brush. These brushes are passed all over the body, and the pollen is collected in two little heaps. The thighs of the last pair of the bees' legs are furnished with two cavities, and these make nice little baskets to carry home their treasure. The dust collected from a thousand flowers is now kneaded into little balls, and when these have increased to the size of a grain of pepper, the bee flies home, and enters the cell head foremost. The balls are then taken from the baskets, and, being moistened with a little honey, become bee bread."*

BEE'S LEG MAGNIFIED.

---

* Student and Schoolmate.

One of the greatest wonders of the bee-hive is the mode in which it is ventilated. Fresh air is no less necessary to bees than to human beings, and as no provision is made for its supply in the construction of their dwelling, they secure it in this way: "They arrange themselves in files along the bottom of the hive. Those outside place their heads toward the entrance, and those within in an opposite direction. When thus stationed, they flap their wings so rapidly that we can not see that they have any wings at all. This rapid motion drives a current of air into the hive, to keep the honey and comb cool."

Fig. 52.

GLASS HIVE, SHOWING THE ARRANGEMENT OF COMB.

II.—THE APIARY AND HIVES.

The situation selected for an apiary or bee-house should be well sheltered from strong winds, and should not be near any large sheet of water. The hives should face the south, the east, or the southeast. They should be placed in a right line; and it is better to place them on shelves, one above another, than in rows upon the ground. The distance between the hives should be not less than two feet, and their height from the ground about the same. Near the apiary should be some small trees and shrubbery, on which swarms may alight; but large trees are objectionable. The grass should be frequently mowed around the bee-house, to prevent dampness and destroy the lurking-places of noxious vermin.

Much difference of opinion exists in reference to the best form and construction for a bee-hive, and many ingenious plans have been offered by the inventive genius of our country for their improvement. Some of these have peculiar excellences and are worthy of a careful trial, but few if any of them are without some serious objections; so that practical bee-keepers generally prefer hives of the simplest construction. One of the best hives is made of pine boards an inch or an inch and a quarter thick. The best size is twelve inches square inside and fourteen inches deep. The top should be made of boards fifteen inches square. The boards should be joined carefully, and it is well to apply a coat of paint to the edges before putting them together. Small notches should be made at the bottom for the passage of the bees; and cross sticks put in for the support of the comb. If the inside of the hive be planed and covered with a thin coating of melted beeswax, it will save the bees much labor. Boxes for caps or covers may be fitted to these hives. These may be about seven inches deep and twelve square. They must fit closely the tops of the hives, and may be furnished with glass jars or other vessels for the reception of the honey. Several holes should be made in the top of the hive for the passage of the bees.

In Poland, where finer honey is produced and bees more successfully cultivated than anywhere else, the excavated trunks of trees are used for hives. Logs a foot or more in diameter and nine feet long are scooped or bored for the length of six feet from one end, the bore being from six to eight inches in diameter. A longitudinal slit is made in this hollow cylinder nearly the whole length and four inches wide. Into this slit is fitted a slip of wood with notches on the edges large enough to admit a single bee. This slip is hung on hinges and forms a door, by the opening of which the condition of the swarm can be seen and the honey be taken out. The top being covered, the trunk is set upright, with the opening toward the south. Sections of hollow trees are often used in this country for hives.

It is often desirable to carry honey to market without removing it from the hive in which it was made, and as few persons will purchase the contents of a large hive, one constructed in sections has a great advantage in that particular at least.

According to the views of Mr. Harasti, a skillful bee-cultivator, as quoted in the "Farmer's Encyclopedia," a good bee-hive ought to possess the following properties: First, it should be capable of enlargement or contraction according to the size of the swarm. Secondly, it should admit of being opened without disturbing the bees, either for the purpose of cleaning it from insects, increasing or dividing the swarm, etc. Thirdly, it should be so constructed that the produce may be removed without injury to the bees. Fourthly, it should be internally clean, smooth, and free from cracks or flaws. All these properties seem best united in the section-hive, which is constituted of two, three, four, or more square boxes of similar size as to width, placed over each other. Such hives are cheap, and so simple that almost any one can construct them.

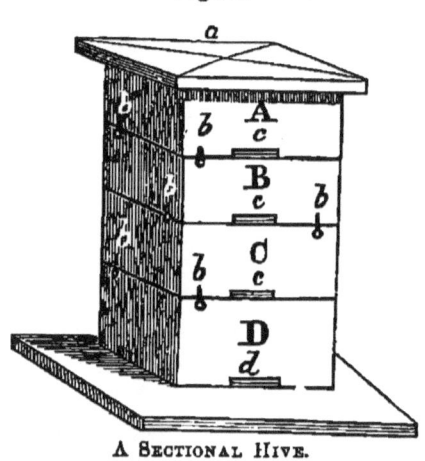

Fig. 53.

A SECTIONAL HIVE.

The boxes A, B, C, D may be made from ten to fourteen inches square and about five inches in depth, inside measure. Every bee-keeper should have his boxes made of the same size, so as to fit on to each other. Every hive must have a common top-board, a, which should project over the sides of the hive. The top-board of each section should have about sixteen holes bored through at equal distances from each other, and not larger than three fourths or smaller than four fifths of an inch. Or, instead of such holes, chinks of proper size may be cut through to allow the bees to pass up and down. At the lower part of each box or section, in front, there must be an aperture or little door, c, c, c, d, just high enough to let the bees pass, and about an inch and a half wide. The lowermost aperture, d, is to be left open at first, and when the hive is filled the upper ones may be successively opened. By placing over the holes in the top of the upper section, glass globes, jars, tumblers, or boxes, the bees will rise into and fill them with honey. These may be removed at any time after being filled. The holes in the tops of the hive which do not open into the glasses or boxes should of course be plugged up. These glass jars, etc., must be covered over with a box, so as to keep them in the dark. Every box or section, on the side opposite the little door, should have a narrow piece of glass inserted, with a sliding shutter, by drawing out which the condition of the hive can always be inspected. To make the bees place their combs in parallel lines, five or six sticks or bars may be placed at the top of every section, running from front to rear. The bees will attach their combs to these bars, and the intermediate space will afford sufficient light to see them work. The slides covering the glasses should never be left open longer than is just necessary for purposes of inspection.

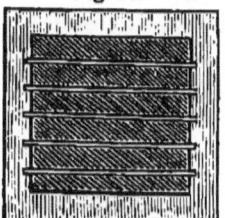

Fig. 54.

When one section is removed from the top, a wire or long thin knife must be previously run between this and the one immediately below, so as to destroy the attachments. Then remove the upper section, placing the top upon the one below, which is now the highest division of the hive. Another section is to be placed beneath, lifting up the whole hive for the purpose. Sometimes a second section has to be put under during a good season. If the swarm is not very large, three or even two boxes will be sufficient for its accommodation. The boxes or sections may be secured upon each other by buttons, *b, b*, or rabbets, and the joints closed with cement.

The plan of Mr. Luda, of Connecticut, by which the bees are made to build their cells and deposit their honey in the chamber of a dwelling-house appropriated for the purpose, in neat little drawers, from which it may be taken fresh by the owner, without killing the bees, has obtained deserved celebrity. The hive has the appearance of, and is, in part, a mahogany bureau or sideboard, with drawers above and a closet below, with glass doors. This case or bureau is designed to be placed in the chamber of a house, or any other suitable building, and connected with the open air or outside of the house by a tube passing through the wall. The bees work and deposit their honey in drawers. When these or any of them are full, or it is desired to obtain honey, one or more of them may be taken out, the bees allowed to escape into the other parts of the hive, and the honey taken away. The glass doors allow the working of the bees to be observed; and it is said that the spaciousness, cleanliness, and even the more regular temperature of such habitations, render them the more industrious and successful.

III.—GENERAL DIRECTIONS.

1. *Swarming.*—Huish, in his "Treatise on Bees," says: "*The swarming of bees* generally commences in June; in some seasons earlier, and in cold climates or seasons later. The first swarming is so long preceded by the appearance of drones and hanging out of working bees, that if the time of their leaving the hive is not observed it must be owing to want of care. The signs of the second are, however, more equivocal, the most certain being that of the queen, a day or two before swarming, at intervals of a few minutes, giving out a sound a good deal resembling that of a cricket. It frequently happens that the swarm will leave the old hive and return again several times, which is always owing to the queen not having accompanied them, or from having dropped on the ground, being too young to fly to a distance. Gooseberry, currant, or other low bushes, should be planted at a short distance from the hives, for the bees to swarm upon, otherwise they are apt to fly away."

When they collect where they can not be shaken off and the hive can not be placed near them, they may be brushed off into a gauze sack, or any vessel in which they can be kept and carried to the hive, which should be set upon a table a little raised on one side to allow their passage. If seen before they alight, they may often be secured by drawing a large woolen stocking upon the end of a pole and holding it up among them, as they are apt to consider it a favorable object on which to collect.

"When a hive yields more than two swarms, these should uniformly be joined to others that are weak, as, from the lateness of the season and deficiency in number, they will otherwise perish. This junction is easily formed, by inverting at night the hive in which they are, and placing over it the one you intend them to enter. They soon ascend, and apparently with no opposition from the former possessors. Should the weather for some days after swarming be unfavorable for the bees going out, they must be fed with care until it clears up, otherwise the young swarm will run great risk of dying."

Some recommend drawing off swarms without waiting for them to set forth of their own accord. We find the process thus described in the *Southern Homestead:*

"Those who are using a common hive when desiring to draw off a swarm, should let the hive be turned bottom upward, and the new hive set upon it; strike lightly upon the lower hive, and many of the bees will ascend into the upper hive; when a sufficient number has collected in the new hive for a swarm, take it off and set it upon the bench, and return the old one to its former position. In doing this, to insure success, it is necessary that one of the queens should accompany the new swarm, which may be known in the course of a day or two, for if they have no queen, they will not stay in the new hive, but will return to the old one; but if they have a queen, they soon manifest a disposition to commence work, and in the course of twenty-four hours some of the bees may be seen standing near the entrance of the hive, amusing themselves by raising their bodies to the full length of their legs, and giving their wings a rapid motion, making a steady buzzing noise. This may be considered as an indication of their satisfaction and the success of the operation. Some consider mid-day the most favorable time for doing this; others again prefer the evening—but either will answer, and the trouble attending is not greater than that of hiving them when the swarms are allowed to come out in the common manner, and the danger of having them go off is avoided. Another very great advantage of this method is, the young swarms commence working early, by which they are more likely to lay up sufficient food for the winter."

2. *Robbing the Hives.*—The old practice, still followed by many, is to kill the bees by suffocation, whenever the most favorable time has arrived for taking the honey. To suffocate the bees, the hive is inverted over an empty hive or a hole in the ground in which some rags smeared with sulphur are burning. The bees drop down and are buried to prevent resuscitation. This is believed by some shrewd and experienced beekeepers to be the most profitable if not the most humane plan.

Polish apiarists cut out the comb annually to lessen the tendency to swarming, and thus obtain the largest amount of honey. In sectional hives it is readily taken out without killing the bees; and where these improved hives, as they are called, are not used, the comb may be cut out by merely stupefying the bees with sulphur or tobacco smoke. The time for taking up hives depends somewhat upon the season and pasturage; but the quantity of honey does not generally increase after the first of September.

3. *Wintering.*—To winter safely a swarm of bees, thirty pounds of honey are considered requisite. Only strong swarms are profitable to winter; therefore those that are found in the fall to be weak in numbers and with little honey had better be taken up. In the northern portions of the United States means are generally used to protect the swarms in winter, by removal to some cool and dry out-house or cellar; but many apiarists contend that this practice is not only useless but hurtful, and that hives should not be removed from their usual situations.

4. *Feeding.*—Bees are sometimes fed, when not able to supply their own wants, with a syrup made by dissolving brown

sugar in water and then boiling it to evaporate the water. Honey is the best food, but is generally (unless "Southern" or West India honey be used) too expensive; and, in fact, as a matter of profit, feeding should never be attempted.

5. *Killing the Drones.*—Knowing that the drones consume an immense amount of honey without producing any, and believing that a few of them will answer all the purposes required, Mr. P. J. Mahan, of Philadelphia, recommends getting rid of them, and thus saving the honey that they would consume. His plan for accomplishing this is to cut out the comb containing the cells in which they are to hatch. This, he says, is difficult in the common or box-hive and quite impossible in nearly all patent hives; but quite easy in Rev. L. L. Langstroth's Movable Comb Hive, in which the combs are built in a frame, similar to a slate or a picture in a frame, which being suspended on a narrow rabbet do not touch or come in contact with the hive at the top, bottom, or sides. Old combs can be put into the frames and be given to the bees to fill for their own use or for breeding combs.

"By cutting out the combs referred to," Mr. Mahan continues, "the bee-keeper makes a saving of all the honey fed to them before they are matured; the time occupied by the bees in feeding and nursing them; and last, though not least, assuming one foot as the average, which is capable of producing over 4,000 drones, by destroying this there is space sufficient to build combs in which 7,200 cells for hatching the workers will be erected; which, as we have done away with the drones, is fully equal to an accession of 14,400 working bees."[*]

This matter is certainly worthy of the attention of bee-keepers, and should be fully investigated.[†]

---

[*] Southern Planter.

[†] A large portion of the matter in this chapter, not credited to other sources, has been condensed from the excellent articles on "Bees and Bee-Keeping," in the "New American Encyclopedia."

APPENDIX.

HORSE-TAMING—RAREY'S SYSTEM.

1. The Theory.

The one principle which you must establish firmly in your mind, and which is so essential in horse-taming that it is almost the corner-stone of the theory is the law of kindness. Next to kindness you must have patience, and next to patience indomitable perseverance. With these qualities in us, and not possessing fear or anger, we undertake to tame horses, with perfect assurance of success, if we use the proper means. The horse receives instruction in, and by the use of, four of his senses—namely, seeing, hearing, smelling, and feeling. You must remember that the horse is a dumb brute, has not the faculty of reasoning on experiments that you make on him, but is governed by instinct. In a natural state he is afraid of man, and never, until you teach him that you do not intend to hurt him, will that fear cease—we mean that wild, natural fear—for you must have him fear you as well as love you, before you can absorb his attention as much as is necessary to break him to your liking. It is a principle in the nature of a horse not to offer resistance to our wishes, if made known in a way that he understands, and in accordance with the laws of his nature.

In subjugating the horse, we must make a powerful appeal to his intelligence. This can only be done by a physical operation. It is an undisputed fact that the battles of all animals (except such as are garnished with horns) are fought by seizing each other by the throat. A dog that has been thus held by his antagonist for a few minutes, on being released, is often so thoroughly cowed that no human artifice can induce him to again resume the unequal contest. This is the principle upon which horse-taming is founded.

2. Practical Rules.

1. *Choking—First Method.*—Choking a horse is the first process in taming, and is but the beginning of his education. By its operation a horse becomes docile, and will thereafter receive any instruction which he can be made to understand. Teaching the animal to lie down at our bidding, tends to keep him permanently cured, as it is a perpetual reminder of his subdued condition.

It requires a good deal of practice to tame a horse successfully; also a nice judgment to know when he is choked sufficiently, as there is a bare possibility that he might get more than would be good for him. We advise persons not perfectly familiar with a horse to resort rather to the strapping and throwing-down process (unless he is very vicious) described below; this, in ordinary cases, will prove successful. It is the fault of most people who have owned a horse to imagine that they are expert in his management; while, on the contrary, many professional horsemen are the very worst parties to attempt a subjugation. Unless a man have a good disposition, he need not attempt horse-taming.

In practicing the method exhibited in fig. 55, retire with the animal to be operated upon into a close stable, with plenty of litter upon the floor (tan-bark or sawdust is preferable). In the first place fasten up the left fore-leg with the arm strap, in such a manner that it will be permanently secured. Then take a broad strap and buckle and pass it around the neck just back of the jaw-bone. Draw the strap as tight as possible, so tight as to almost arrest the horse's breathing. The strap must not be buckled, but held in this position to prevent slipping back. The animal will struggle for a few minutes, when he will become perfectly quiet, overpowered by a sense of suffocation; the veins in his head will swell; his eyes lose their fire; his knees totter and become weak; a slight vertigo will ensue, and growing gradually exhausted, by backing him around the stable, he will come down on his knees, in which position it is an easy matter to push him on his side, when his throat should be released. Now pat and rub him gently for about twenty minutes, when, in most instances, he will be subdued. It is only in extreme cases necessary to repeat the operation of choking. The next lesson is to teach him to lie down which is described in the account of the fourth method of taming. No horse can effectually resist the terrible effects of being choked.

Fig. 55.

It must be constantly borne in mind, that the operator must not be boisterous or violent, and that the greatest possible degree of kindness is absolutely essential. When the horse is prostrate, he should be soothed until his eyes show that he has become perfectly tranquil.

2. *Second Method.*—The plan described in fig. 56 is very simple, though not as expeditious as the previous one. Buckle or draw a strap tight around the neck, lift a fore-leg, and fasten around it the opposite end of the strap, the shorter the better. In the engraving, for the sake of clearness, the strap is

represented too long. It will be seen that in this plan the horse is made the instrument by which the punishment is inflicted. When he attempts to put

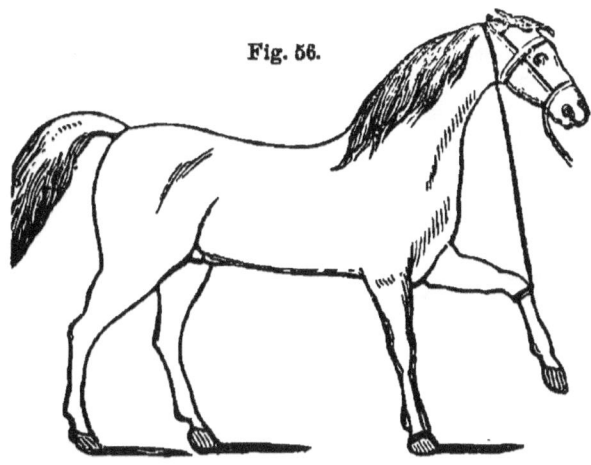

Fig. 56.

his foot down, his head goes with it, and he thus chokes himself. Care should be taken that he does not pitch on his head, and thus endanger his neck.

3. *Third Method.*—Secure the horse with a stout halter to the manger. If extremely unruly, muzzle him. Sooth him with the hands for a few minutes, until he becomes somewhat pacified. Then seize him by the throat (as in fig. 57), close to the jawbone, with the right hand, and by the mane with the left. Now forcibly compress his windpipe until he becomes so exhausted that, by lightly kicking him on the fore legs, he will lie down, after which he should be treated as previously described.

Fig. 57.

This process requires courage in the operator, and also great muscular strength.

4. *Fourth Method.*—The horse to be operated upon should be led into a close stable. The operator should be previously provided with a stout leather halter; a looped strap to slip over the animal's knee; a strong surcingle, and a long and short strap—the first to fasten round the fore-foot which is at liberty.

164   APPENDIX.

and the second to permanently secure the leg which is looped up. The application of the straps will be better understood by reference to fig. 58.

In the first place, if the horse be a biter, muzzle him; then lift and bend his left fore-leg, and slip a loop over it. The leg which is looped up must be secured by applying the short strap, buckling it around the pastern joint and forearm; next put on the surcingle, and fasten the long strap around the right forefoot, and pass the end through a loop attached to the surcingle; after which fasten on a couple of thick leather knee-pads—these can be put on in the first place if convenient. The pads are necessary, as some horses in their struggles come violently on their knees, abrading them badly. Now take a short hold of the long strap with your right hand; stand on the left side of the horse, grasp the bit in your left hand; while in this position back him gently about the stable, until he becomes so exhausted as to exhibit a desire to lie down, which desire should be gratified with as little violence as possible; bear your

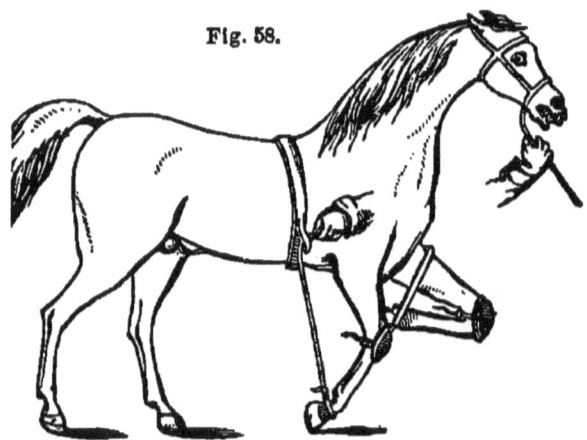

Fig. 58.

weight firmly against the shoulder of the horse, and pull steadily on the strap with your right hand; this will force him to raise his foot, which should be immediately pulled from under him. This is the critical moment; cling to the horse, and after a few struggles he will lie down. In bearing against the animal do not desist from pulling and pushing until you have him on his side. Prevent him from attempting to rise by pulling his head toward his shoulder. As soon as he is done struggling, caress his face and neck; also, handle every part of his body, and render yourself as familiar as possible. After he has lain quietly for twenty minutes let him rise, and immediately repeat the operation, removing the straps as soon as he is down; and if his head is pulled toward his shoulder it is impossible for him to get up. After throwing him from two to five times the animal will become as submissive and abject as a well-trained dog, and you need not be afraid to indulge in any liberties with him. A young horse is subdued much quicker than an old one, as his habits are not confirmed. An incorrigible horse should have two lessons a day; about the fourth lesson he will be permanently conquered. If the operation is repeated several times, he can be made to lie down by simply lifting up his fore-leg and repeating the words, "Lie down, sir," which he must be previously made familiar with.

5. *Additional Hints.*—The following rules will serve as a guide to the amateur operator, and should be strictly observed:

First. The horse must not be forced down by violence, but must be tired out till he has a strong desire to lie down.

Second. He must be kept quiet on the ground until the expression of the eye shows that he is tranquillized, which invariably takes place by patiently waiting and gently patting the horse.

Third. Care must be taken not to throw the horse upon his neck when bent, as it may easily be broken.

Fourth. In backing him, no violence must be used, or he may be forced on his haunches, and his back broken.

Fifth. The halter and off-rein are held in the left hand, so as to keep the head away from the latter; while, if the horse attempts to plunge, the halter is drawn tight, when, the off-leg being raised, the animal is brought on his knees, and rendered powerless for offensive purposes.—*New York Tribune.*

P.

	PAGE
Piggery	107
Poultry	118
" Pentalogue	136
" Preparation of for Market	246

S.

	PAGE
Sheep, Breeds of	73
" Native	74
" Spanish Merino	74
" Saxon do.	76
" New Leicester	76
" South-Down	78
" Cheviot	80
" Lincoln	81
" Choice of Breed	81
" General Management of	82
" Value of to the Farmer	92
Swine, Natural History of	95

	PAGE
Swine, Opinions respecting	97
" Breeds	98
" The Land Pike	99
" Chinese	99
" Berkshire	100
" Suffolk	101
" Essex	102
" Chester	102
" Points of	104
" Feeding	104
Stables	29
Swarming	156

T.

	PAGE
Turkey	138
Taming Horses	161

W.

	PAGE
Water-Cure for Animals	115

NEW AND STANDARD BOOKS ON
Architecture, Agriculture, Field Sports, & The Horse,

Alphabets, Ornamental & Fancy. Geo. E. Woodward. 4to.	$6 00
Artistic Drawing Studies. Geo. E. Woodward. Quarto....	6 00
Breechloader, The. By "Gloan." Illustrated............	1 25
Copley's Alphabets, Plain and Ornamental...............	3 00
Crack Shot (The Rifle). By E. C. Barber. Illustrated....	1 25
Cupper's Universal Stair-Builder.......................	2 50
Dead Shot (The Gun). By "Marksman." Illustrated.....	1 25
Dog, The. By Dinks, Mayhew and Hutchinson...........	3 00
Elliott's Lawn and Shade Trees. Illustrated.............	1 00
Eveleth's School-House Architecture. Quarto	4 00
Flax Culture. Paper...................................	10
Frank Forester's American Game. Illustrated...........	1 50
Frank Forester's Field Sports. 2 vols. Illustrated.......	4 00
Frank Forester's Fish and Fishing. 100 Illustrations	2 50
Frank Forester's Horse of America. 2 vols., 8vo.........	5 00
Frank Frester's Young Sportsman's Manual. Illustrated,	2 00
Fuller's Forest Tree Culturist. Fully Illustrated.........	1 00
Gun, Rod, and Saddle. Illustrated.....................	1 00
Harney's Barns, Outbuildings, and Fences	4 00
Horse Portraiture—Breeding and Training Trotters, etc..	2 00
How to Get a Farm and Where to Find One..............	1 00
Husmann's Grapes and Wine. Illustrated	1 00
Hussey's National Cottage Architecture. Quarto	4 00
Jacques' Garden, Farm, and Barn-yard....................	1 50
Jacques' Manual of the House. (126 Designs)..........	1 00
Lewis' Practical Poultry Book. 100 Illustrations.........	1 50
Miner's Domestic Poultry Book. Illustrated	1 00
Monckton's National Carpenter and Joiner. Quarto......	5 00
Monckton's National Stair Builder. Quarto	5 00
Our Farm of Four Acres. 12mo........................	60
Phin's Open-Air Grape Culture. New edition............	1 00
Randall's Practical Shepherd. New edition. Illustrated..	2 00
Rural Church Architecture. (20 Designs)...............	4 00
Ten Acres Enough. New edition. Illustrated...........	1 00
Thomery System of Grape Culture. Flexible cloth.......	30
Todd's Young Farmer's Manual. 3 vols..........Per set,	4 50
Vol. 1. The Farm and Workshop.........	1 50
Vol. 2. How to Make Farming Pay...............	1 50
Vol. 3. Wheat Culture.......................	1 50
Trout Culture. By J. H. Slack, M. D.....................	1 00
Wallace's American Stud Book. 1,000 pages, 8vo......	10 00
Wallace's American Trotting Register. 8vo..............	10 00
Wheeler's Homes for the People. Fully Illustrated.......	2 00
Wheeler's Rural Homes. Fully Illustrated................	1 50
Willard's Practical Butter Book. Illustrated	1 00
Willard's Practical Dairy Husbandry. Ills...............	3 00
Woodward's Cottages and Farm-Houses. 188 Designs and Plans	1 00
Woodward's Country Homes. 150 Designs and Plans......	1 00
Woodward's Designs for the Fret Saw....................	50
Woodward's Graperies and Horticultural Buildings.......	1 00
Woodward's National Architect. Vol. 1. (1,00 Designs)..	7 50
Woodward's National Architect. Vol. 2. (100 Quarto Plates)	7 50
Woodward's Suburban and Country Houses. 70 Designs and Plans................	1 00

FOR SALE AT ALL BOOKSTORES.

THE
EXCELSIOR EDITION

OF

Standard Juvenile Fiction,

COMPRISING

ROBINSON CRUSOE,	6 Illustrations,	$1.00
ARABIAN NIGHTS,	6 "	1.00
GULLIVER'S TRAVELS,	6 "	1.00
SWISS FAMILY ROBINSON,	6 "	1.00
PILGRIM'S PROGRESS,	6 "	1.00
DON QUIXOTE,	62 "	1.00

All published uniform with this Volume.

THE AMERICAN NEWS COMPANY,

NEW YORK.

www.ingramcontent.com/pod-product-compliance
Lightning Source LLC
Chambersburg PA
CBHW051234300426
44114CB00011B/736